THE ORIGINS OF CHRISTIANITY

HOWARD CLARK KEE

Professor of the History of Religion
Bryn Mawr College

PRENTICE-HALL, INC. *Englewood Cliffs, New Jersey*

THE ORIGINS
OF CHRISTIANITY

Sources and Documents

Library of Congress Cataloging in Publication Data

KEE, HOWARD CLARK, comp.
   Origins of Christianity.

   Includes bibliographical references.
   1. Bible. N. T.—History of contemporary events—
Sources.   2. Hebrew literature (Selections: Extracts,
etc.)   3. Apocryphal books.   I. Title.
BR129.K44   225.9'5   73-4830
ISBN   0-13-642553-4

THE ORIGINS OF CHRISTIANITY:
, SOURCES AND DOCUMENTS
Howard Clark Kee

10   9   8   7   6   5   4   3   2   1

PRENTICE-HALL INTERNATIONAL, INC., *London*
PRENTICE-HALL OF AUSTRALIA, PTY. LTD., *Sydney*
PRENTICE-HALL OF CANADA, LTD., *Toronto*
PRENTICE-HALL OF INDIA PRIVATE LIMITED, *New Delhi*
PRENTICE-HALL OF JAPAN, INC., *Tokyo*

ACKNOWLEDGMENTS

pp. 253–57, *The Acts of Thomas*, trans. by A. J. F. Klijn, Leiden, E. J. Brill,
pp. 120–25. Reprinted by permission of the publisher.

pp. 11–20, 117–25, *Apocrypha*, from the Revised Standard Version of the *Apocrypha*, copyright © 1957, by the Division of Christian Education, National Council of the Churches of Christ in the U.S.A. Used by permission.

pp. 67–74, 102–9, 111–13, 173–96, *The Apocrypha and Pseudepigrapha of the Old Testament*, ed. R. H. Charles, Oxford: The Clarendon Press, 1913, Vol. II. Reprinted by permission of the publisher.

pp. 78–83, *Apuleius*, from *The Loeb Classical Library*, trans. by W. Adlington, Cambridge, Mass.: Harvard University Press. Reprinted by permission of The Loeb Classical Library and the publisher.

pp. 147–49, Nahman Avigad and Yigael Yadin, *A Genesis Apocryphon*, Jerusalem, The Magnes Press of the Hebrew University, and Heikhal Ha-Sefer, 1956, pp. 43–44. Reprinted by permission of the publisher.

pp. 128–36, 151–55, J. Bowker, *The Targums and Rabbinic Literature*, Cambridge University Press, 1969. Reprinted by permission of the publisher.

pp. 198–210, Millar Burrows, *The Dead Sea Scrolls*, New York: The Viking Press, 1955. Copyright © 1955 by Millar Burrows. Reprinted by permission of the publisher.

pp. 85–89, E. M. Butler, *Ritual Magic*, New York: Cambridge University Press. Reprinted by permission of the publisher.

pp. 55–57, 167–71, Herbert Danby, *The Mishnah*, Oxford: The Clarendon Press, 1933. Reprinted by permission of the publisher.

pp. 259–60, Adolf Deissmann, *Bible Studies*, Edinburgh, Scotland: T. & T. Clark. Reprinted by permission of the publisher.

pp. 83–84, 262–65, Adolf Deissmann, *Light from the Ancient East*, trans. by L. M. R. Strachan, Baker Book House. Reprinted by permission of the publisher.

pp. 212–16, 231–36, *Diogenes Laertius*, I, II, from *The Loeb Classical Library*, trans. by R. D. Hicks, Cambridge, Mass.: Harvard University Press. Reprinted by permission of The Loeb Classical Library and the publisher.

pp. 249–52, Jean Doresse, *The Secret Books of the Egyptian Gnostics*, New York, Viking Press, 1960. Copyright © 1960 by Hollis and Carter Ltd., London. Reprinted by permission of the publisher. Translated by Philip Mairet.

pp. 236–38, *Epictetus*, I, II, from *The Loeb Classical Library*, trans. by W. A. Oldfather, Cambridge, Mass.: Harvard University Press. Reprinted by permission of The Loeb Classical Library and the publisher.

pp. 90–99, *Eusebius* I, from *The Loeb Classical Library*, trans. by Kirsopp Lake, Cambridge, Mass.: Harvard University Press. Reprinted by permission of The Loeb Classical Library and the publisher.

pp. 216–19, 228–30, *The Fathers According to Rabbi Nathan*, trans. by Judah Goldin, New Haven, Conn.: Yale University Press. Copyright © 1955 by Yale University Press. Reprinted by permission of the publisher.

pp. 22–44, 62–67, *Josephus*, III, VII, VIII, from *The Loeb Classical Library*, trans. by H. St. J. Thackeray, Ralph Marcus, and A. Wikgren, Cambridge, Mass.: Harvard University Press. Reprinted by permission of The Loeb Classical Library and the publisher.

pp. 221–24, *Lucian* IV, from *The Loeb Classical Library*, trans. by A. M. Harmon,

Cambridge, Mass.: Harvard University Press. Reprinted by permission of The Loeb Classical Library and the publisher.

pp. 142–44, *Mekilta de-Rabbi Ishmael*, trans. by Jacob Z. Lauterbach, Philadelphia: The Jewish Publication Society of America, 1933, Vol. II. Reprinted by permission of the publisher.

pp. 244–47, *The Odes and Psalms of Solomon*, ed. by Rendel Harris and Alphonse Mingana, Manchester: The John Rylands Library, 1920, Vol. II. Reprinted by permission of the publisher.

pp. 44–51, *Philo Alexandrinus, Legatio ad Gaium*, trans. by E. Mary Smallwood, Leiden, E. J. Brill. Reprinted by permission of the publisher.

pp. 109–11, 145–46, *Philo*, II, VIII, from *The Loeb Classical Library*, trans. by F. H. Colson, Cambridge, Mass.: Harvard University Press. Reprinted by permission of The Loeb Classical Library and the publisher.

pp. 219–21, 229, *Philostratus*, I, II, from *The Loeb Classical Library*, trans. by F. C. Conybeare, Cambridge, Mass.: Harvard University Press. Reprinted by permission of The Loeb Classical Library and the publisher.

pp. 51–53, *Pliny*, II, from *The Loeb Classical Library*, trans. by William Melmouth, Cambridge, Mass.: Harvard University Press. Reprinted by permission of The Loeb Classical Library and the publisher.

pp. 156–63, *The Talmudic Anthology*, ed. by Louis I. Newman, New York: Behrman House, Inc., Publishers, 1945. Reprinted by permission of the publishers.

pp. 113–14, *Virgil*, I, from *The Loeb Classical Library*, trans. by H. R. Fairclough, Cambridge, Mass.: Harvard University Press. Reprinted by permission of The Loeb Classical Library and the publisher.

Preface

This collection of ancient sources and documents in translation has been developed out of a sense of the importance of placing in the hands of students of Christian origins those materials that will help provide them with a sense in some depth of the cultural, religious, and historical situation in which Christianity arose. Of particular significance are the documents of rabbinic and sectarian Judaism, most of which are accessible only in expensive and unwieldy volumes. Every professor's selection of materials to be included will be different from those of his colleagues, and I have no illusions that my choice will match the sense of "what is important" to all or even most of my colleagues. But I hope that what has been included will be of service in the form in which it is presented: arranged partly by form and partly topically, with a maximum of text and a minimum of introduction and comment. The illustrations range from familiar monuments to simple everyday objects, and were chosen in the hope that they would give the student a feel for what it meant to live in the eastern provinces in the early Roman Empire.

I am indebted to my colleague, Professor Samuel Tobias Lachs for his suggestions concerning the rabbinic material, and to my assistant, Miss Lenore Kline, for her aid in preparing the materials for the press.

HOWARD CLARK KEE
Thomas Library
Bryn Mawr College

Contents

ix

THE ORIGINS OF CHRISTIANITY

Introduction

Obviously, the writings we call the New Testament remain the primary sources for knowledge of the origins of Christianity. But sometimes overlooked is the fact that the study of early Christian history and literature would be seriously limited if the only sources utilized were those in the New Testament. This is true for several reasons: (1) The New Testament writers, with the exception of Luke, were not conscious of setting down historical records that might be read and studied outside the circle of believers for whom the writings were produced. Accordingly, they felt no need to correlate the events of the life of Jesus or the apostles with what was going on in the wider Roman world, so that—except for Luke in his gospel and the Acts—nearly the whole of the narrative is presented without reference to time or contemporary events. The result is that at times the reader of the New Testament has the sense that what is described there took place in a kind of vacuum in time and space. It is essential, therefore, that careful study of the origins of Christianity be informed by knowledge of the religious, political, and cultural conditions of the world in which Christianity arose.

(2) Closely related to this dimension of the study of Christian origins is the linguistic problem: the New Testament never defines its terms, but

rather employs the language of the Roman world and of its own religious traditions as though the connotations of this language were self-evident. Crucial terms, such as "kingdom of God," are never explained, but are used in a way that assumes understanding on the part of the reader. Only by exploring the complex of possible meanings behind such important words and phrases can the reader of the New Testament have some assurance of comprehending the intention of the writers.

(3) The aim of the New Testament writers was to convert rather than merely to inform the reader. As a result, it is a great advantage to the modern reader to be informed about the religious aspirations and potential competition that might have been operative in the minds of the early readers of these documents. Otherwise, to read the New Testament is to be aware of only one side of a debate. Although the other side can rarely be reconstructed with certainty, there is a great advantage in being able to understand how moral and religious ideas were expressed, in both content and method of communication.

(4) In their present form, the writings of the New Testament for the most part represent the end result of editorial processes. A few may have come virtually unchanged from the hand of their authors, although in every case the scribes who copied the manuscripts of these books made slight changes which have resulted in thousands of variants in the ancient Greek copies of the New Testament. But in the case of the gospels, and possibly Acts as well, there is evidence that the sayings and narratives were for a considerable period of time transmitted orally before being fixed in their present literary form. By seeing examples of this oral transmission of popular tales and moral concepts from the Jewish and Graeco-Roman cultures, we can increase our understanding of the processes by which the New Testament writings assumed their present form. In the letters of Paul are incorporated fragments of credal formulae and ancient hymns, both of which reflect the language and literary conventions of the world of his time. The same phenomena are evident in other New Testament writings as well, for example, in the hymns in the Lukan birth stories (Lk. 1–2), which resemble the poems in which Jews of the first century before and after the birth of Jesus expressed their hopes for the coming of God's rule on earth.

It would be a mistake, however, to assume that everything about Christianity had its antecedents in the thought-worlds of Judaism and Hellenistic-Roman culture. Christianity was distinctive, but it is idle to speak of distinctiveness without knowing what the points of similarity are and at what points Christianity diverged from the patterns of thought and expression that were otherwise characteristic of its time.

The study of the origins of Christianity would be difficult enough if the background of the investigation could be limited to first-century Judaism alone. Jesus lived and died a Palestinian Jew, and his original followers were all Palestinian Jews by birth and conceptual background. But Palestinian Judaism of this period is imperfectly known; until very recently our knowledge of it was limited largely to one branch of Jewish religious literature, the Pharisaic. Apart from paraphrases in Aramaic (the Semitic language that from Persian times on replaced Hebrew as the common language spoken among Jews), the religious traditions of the rabbis seem to have been preserved only orally until the second century A.D. It was their interpretation of the Law of Moses and of the later traditions of Israel that survived the catastrophe of the destruction of the temple in A.D. 70 and of the city of Jerusalem in A.D. 135. The priestly function died out with the loss of the temple, and the priestly viewpoint seems to have vanished with it. The rabbis were careful to preserve those traditions favorable to their own point of view, with the result that even the limited reconstruction of the history of Judaism that can be accomplished for the period before the destruction of the temple is one-sidedly pro-Pharisaic.

Although our knowledge of the religious developments within Judaism has been largely limited to Pharisaic-oriented sources, there are extensive sources for historical information, especially in the political sphere. I Maccabees gives detailed information of the rise of the independent Jewish state in the second century B.C. and its collapse under the combined weight of corruption from within and Roman pressure from without. Josephus, the great Jewish historian, provides a full account of the political arrangements between the Romans and the Herods, and of the insurrectionist movements that led to the suppression of revolt by the Romans in A.D. 66–70. Inscriptions and non-Palestinian sources help to fill out the picture of the place of Jews in the Roman empire of this period, and enable us to infer the situation that the early Christians confronted in seeking to promote Christianity throughout the civilized world.

Mention was made earlier of the limitation on knowledge of Judaism that prevailed until recently. That restriction was lifted by the discovery two decades ago of a library of religious writings left behind in caves overlooking the Dead Sea by the members of a sect of Judaism who fled from their desert center at the advent of Roman rule in the years just before the fall of Jerusalem (that is, about 70 A.D.). The community is almost certainly identical with the Essenes, known from the writings of Josephus, Philo of Alexandria, and Pliny the Elder, whose historical geography, called *Natural History*, included a detailed account of this group and its monastic existence. Included among the writings found in the ruins of the community settlement, known as Qumran by the Arabs who live in the vicinity, are original Essene documents describing the origins and regulations of the community, copies of the scriptures and of commentaries on scripture, writings that are modeled after scripture but that claim to give esoteric information to the community about its future according to God's plan for bringing in the New Age.

Now that this new information is available we are in a better position to make some judgments about the extent to which early Christianity resembled or differed from the kind of Pharisaic Judaism documented in the rabbinic sources, as well as to trace its possible relationships to another flourishing Jewish movement in Palestine: that of the Essenes.

By no means were all the Jews of the first century living in Palestine, however. There were large numbers in Syria and Mesopotamia, as well as in colonies throughout the Mediterranean world. Of the Jews in Babylon, we have only the information preserved in the rabbinic traditions, which preserved a Babylonian as well as a Jerusalem Talmud (see pp. 54–62). But in Alexandria, an entire quarter of the city was occupied by Jews, although there were Jews living in other sections of the city as well. Under the influence of the philosophical traditions there, which were eclectic and speculative, the Jewish concept of wisdom was greatly developed. In common with the wisdom motif of the ancient Near East, Judaism had created a literature which offered practical wisdom for the man concerned to live at peace in the present world. Documentation for this theme in Jewish literature is provided by the Book of Proverbs and by some of the psalms. But in Alexandria, wisdom came to be regarded as a kind of instrument—almost a personification—by which God had created the world and through which he disclosed his truth about the creation and the future to those who were willing to meditate and be instructed. It was presumably in Alexandria that this speculative type of wisdom produced such documents as the Wisdom of Solomon, in which the creative role of wisdom is depicted. The Wisdom of Ben Sira was translated into Greek there, and the scriptures were interpreted in allegorical fashion there as well. Just as the later Stoics interpreted the activities of the Olympian gods as allegories of the operation of eternal principles and potencies rather than as literal narratives about divinities, so Philo of Alexandria regarded the outward form of scripture as of little significance, and turned his attention and skills instead to unfolding the underlying meaning of the Law of Moses and the biblical narratives. He regarded them as hidden accounts of the mystical ascent of the soul to behold God.

The Alexandrine Jews, by translating or writing their religious literature in Greek, were doing more than making this material available to non–Semitic-speaking people; they were opening the door to an accommodation of Jewish tradition to Gentile culture. For example, once the ineffable name of the God of Israel, YHWH, came to be rendered by the common hellenistic designation for deity, *kurios* (lord), the way was clear for synthesizing Jewish and pagan terminology and concepts. Philo was at pains to show that truth was one, and that the moral and philosophical truth he had discovered in the thought of Plato or of the Stoics was wholly compatible with the truth contained in scripture. And yet this eagerness to discover religious unity behind the cultural diversity was not peculiar to Alexandrine Jews; it is evident among pagan religious writers as well, and the fact that it was so widespread had important consequences for the growth of Christianity as a universal religion.

The very fact that the early Christians soon began to use the common language of the eastern Roman empire—Greek—gave them an enormous boost in propagating the faith throughout the Gentile world, but it also paved the way for converting the basically Jewish orientation of the new religion into forms that would be far more inclusive in their appeal. Thus, although Christianity very early learned Greek, both linguistically and conceptually, it also learned to employ for its purposes the literary and popular modes of communication that were essential to the spread of its message and to the development of its community structures. Accordingly, we are in a better position to interpret the New Testament writings when we see how the literary and rhetorical methods of the pagan world have been adapted by the Christians for their purposes. Paul, for example, writes letters that are in many respects like the letters that were being sent in his day, copies of which have been preserved on papyrus and published by scholars in the present century; but there are some distinctive features of his letters that can be most clearly seen only when contrasted with the prevailing styles. The same useful similarities and contrasts may be discerned when Paul's method of argumentation is examined against the background of the methods employed by his contemporaries.

In seeking to make a universal appeal, the early Christian propagandists could not restrict themselves to the traditions and heroes of ancient Israel, with whom Gentiles might have difficulty in identifying. Instead, it was essential that the Christian message be restated in terms that would strike fire with the religious aspirations of the Gentile world. To see how the New Testament writers went about achieving this, we must look at the documents in which the religious quests of the early empire find expression. With some of these forms of religion we have a problem similar to that involved in reconstructing first-century Judaism: the documents that have survived are from a later period, and we can only extrapolate backwards from the information we possess to try to establish what existed earlier. This is particularly problematical in relation to the move-men known as Gnosticism, which in its developed form viewed man as a creature whose origins were in the spirit world, but whose enslavement in the material body could be remedied only through the Heavenly Revealer, who pointed the way to heaven, the realm of the spirit, to the elect. From the middle of the second century A.D. on, the blending of this mythological view of reality with Christian ideas can be fully docu-mented. But two questions lack definitive answers: When was this myth-ology tied in with Christian tradition? And did the mythology exist prior to its incorporation into Christianity, or did it originate as a perver-sion of Christianity? The discovery in the 1940s of a library of Gnostic writings in Upper Egypt provides extensive new resources for detailed knowledge of Gnosticism and furnishes a basis for reconstructing its de-velopment from simpler to more complex forms. But unfortunately, the new documents do not provide answers to either of the two questions posed above. All the documents show some kinship with Christianity, so that the issue of a non-Christian Gnostic mythology cannot be proved, although of course it cannot be denied. The apparently earliest forms of the new Gnostic literature are dated by scholars to the middle of the sec-ond century A.D., and these show the closest links with the canonical New Testament material. Specifically, the Gospel of Thomas closely resembles the sayings material of the synoptic gospels, even though Thomas has altered the sayings at many points in the direction of Gnostic interpreta-tion of reality. It seems plausible to assume that there was some kind of mythological picture of a Heavenly Revealer that existed in the first cen-tury A.D. and that was utilized by some Christians who sought redemp-tion through Jesus, not in the future age (as in Jewish and early Chris-tian eschatology), but in the transcendent realm beyond time and space. The Wisdom tradition of Judaism and the Greek mythological concept of Hermes as the mediator of messages from the gods to man were both readily adaptable to the Gnostic redeemer concept, so that all three of these phenomena influenced the development of Christian thought in the second century or perhaps even in the first century.

The only attempt within the New Testament itself to trace the devel-opment of Christianity is in the book of Acts, and it ends at an inconclu-sive moment with Paul about to go on trial for his life. Quite apart from the question of the historical reliability of Acts, this state of affairs leaves us with no choice but to try to infer from the New Testament and later writings how the church did in fact develop beyond the first generation of the followers of Jesus. Even the fate of his disciples is no more than hinted at in the New Testament material. Eusebius of Caesarea, court advisor and historian in the palace of Constantine, the first emperor to

Observes Ptolemy VIII, whose reign was interrupted by usurpers, but who remained as King of Egypt from 146 to 117 B.C., although at times he shared the throne with others. In Jewish tradition he is reported to have ordered that the Jews of Alexandria be chained and thrown in front of elephants as punishment for their support of his rival. A miracle occurred, and the elephants turned on the friends of the king, and the Jews were delivered (Josephus: Contra Apion 2:4–5). Reverse: Ptolemy the King, with an eagle.

embrace Christianity (early fourth century), had an extensive library that included ancient sources and archives of the early church. He quoted from these extensively in his *Ecclesiastical History,* and it is on these excerpts that we are almost entirely dependent for what information we have about the end of the apostolic age. For what it may be worth as genuine historical evidence, sections of Eusebius' material is included. Another potential source—the so-called Apostolic Fathers—has not been included in the present work, because the collection of writings is readily available, and because these writings are more of the substance of early Christian thought than of the milieu and circumstances in which it developed.

Finally, the sources quoted here provide primary evidence for the view of the empire that the Roman emperors promoted or at least allowed to develop, with their modification of the hellenistic notion of the divinity of the king. The inevitable conflicts that arose, first between Jews and the idolatrous claims of the emperors and later between the Christians and the imperial cult, are documented in evidence from first-hand observers.

The collecting of sources to illumine the first-century Roman world, with its love of miracle, its use of magic, its yearning for peace of mind or otherworldly redemption, and its concern for morality, could be extended almost indefinitely. But it is to be hoped that a sufficient range has been included here to convey something of the sense of depth of religious feeling and aspiration operative in the world as the first generations of Christians began the move, not merely from Palestine to the wider world, but from the relatively unified world of Judaism to the culturally diverse world of the Gentiles among whom Christianity as an institution and a way of life was to take root and flourish.

HISTORICAL SOURCES

Political History

JUDAISM

I Maccabees

The book known as I Maccabees was probably begun during the reign of Simon the Maccabee (142–135 B.C.), but was completed after his death, approximately 125 B.C. Composed in Hebrew, it has survived and has been known since ancient times solely in its Greek translation. Based largely on eyewitness accounts and on the author's own detailed knowledge of the land and the events, it is a remarkably accurate and precise documentary account, although the author's knowledge of Roman institutions is understandably but regrettably faulty. Some of the letters purporting to have been written by or to foreign rulers, such as the letters to and from the Spartans, are almost certainly later interpolations, made in the interests of attaching international importance to the events of Jewish history. What basis this correspondence has in fact is almost impossible to determine. But taking into consideration the unqualified admiration the writer has for the Maccabees, he has produced a first-rate historical narrative of the period.

The importance of this work for the study of Christian origins lies in the fact that it describes in concrete and vivid detail the religious problem created within Judaism by the resistance of Jews in Palestine to hellenization under the Seleucid rulers of Syria and the initially successful attempt to create once again an independent Jewish state. Even as the Maccabean state was taking form there were some Jews who believed that it was up to God alone to establish his Rule in the earth, although they differed among themselves as to how He would accomplish this. Some (later known as the Essenes) withdrew from the main stream of life to await the New Age of God's Kingdom. Some saw as their main task to fulfill the Law in their own lives and within the common life of the religious community: these became known as the Pharisees. But until the destruction of Jerusalem in A.D. 135, the hope burned as it did in the time of the Maccabees for the establishment of a political state, as in the great days of David and Solomon. It is to this political ideal that I Maccabees bears eloquent witness. And it was in the midst of such conflicting claims and aspirations that the early Christians launched their announcement about the coming Kingdom of God.

I MACCABEES 1:20–2:28

(20)* And after Antiochus had attacked Egypt, he returned in the one hundred and forty-third year,[1] and went up against Israel and

---

*Numbers in superscript refer to line numbers.

[1]The Seleucid era began on October 1, 312 B.C., when Seleucus I, one of the generals of Alexander the Great and heir to Syria in terms of Alexander's will, ascended to the throne. Antiochus' attack on Palestine took place, therefore, in 169 B.C.

Antiochus Epiphanes on a coin of his reign. It was he whose idolatrous claims and demands led to the Maccabean revolt. The king represents himself as Zeus, seated on a throne, holding in his left hand a royal staff and in his right the figure of the goddess of victory, Nike. In her hand is the victor's wreath. The inscription read, Of Antiochus the King, God Manifest, Bearer of Victory. (Source: American Numismatic Society)

Jerusalem with a great army. (21) He entered arrogantly into the sanctuary and took away the golden altar and the lampstand and all its accessories (22) and the table of the Bread of the Presence and the pouring vessels, and the bowls, and the golden censers, and the veil, and the crowns, and all the golden ornaments that were on the facade of the temple he pulled off. (23) He also took the silver and the gold, and the precious vessels, as well as the hidden treasures, which he found. (24) And when he had carried off the whole of this, he returned to his own land, having caused a great massacre and spoken with great arrogance.

(25) As a consequence, there was great mourning in Israel, in every place where they were.[2] (26) The princes and the elders mourned, the virgins and the young men became weak, and the beauty of women was changed. (27) Every bridegroom took up lamentation, and even the bride sitting in the marriage chamber was in mourning. (28) The land was moved by the fate of its inhabitants, and all the house of Jacob was covered with humiliation.

(29) After two years the king sent his chief collector of tribute to the cities of Judah. He came to Jerusalem with a great host (30) and spoke peaceful words to the people, but the whole thing was deceitful, for when the people took him at his word, he fell suddenly on the city, struck it a severe blow, and destroyed many of the people of Israel. (31) And when he had taken spoils from the city, he set it on fire, and razed its houses and walls on every side. (32) The women and children were taken captive and the cattle were seized. (33) Then the enemy built the Citadel of David with a great and strong wall, and with mighty towers, and made it a stronghold for themselves. (34) In it they placed a sinful people, wicked men, who fortified themselves within it. (35) They stored it also with arms and provisions. When they had gathered together the spoils of Jerusalem, they stored them there as well. In this way they became a severe menace, (36) for it provided them a place to lie in wait opposite the sanctuary, an evil adversary for Israel in every way. (37) By this means they shed innocent blood on every side of the sanctuary and defiled it. (38) Because of them, the inhabitants of Jerusalem fled, with the result that the city became a dwelling place for foreigners, and was instead strange to those who were born within her, since her own offspring had left her. (39) Her sanctuary became barren like a desert. Her feasts were turned into mourning, her sabbaths into dishonor, her honor into contempt. (40) As one she had been glorious, so now she was filled with dishonor; she who formerly had been exalted was now turned to lamentation.

(41) Furthermore, King Antiochus wrote to all his kingdom that all

---

[2]That is, the Jews. Many of the cities of Palestine had few or no Jewish inhabitants. This was true of both coastal and inland cities that were dominated by hellenistic culture, and considered by pious Jews to be unfit places to live. The old Philistine cities—Ashdod, Ashkelon, Gaza, Ekron, and Gath—were not conquered by the invading Hebrews, and were dominated by hellenistic culture, as the recent excavations at Ashdod have clearly shown.

people should be one,[3] (42) and that every one should abandon his own laws. All the heathen agreed to the king's commandment, (43) and even many of the Israelites were pleased to accept his religion, sacrificing to idols and profaning the sabbath. (44) For the king had sent letters by messengers to Jerusalem and the cities of Judah requiring them to practice regulations that were alien to their land: (45) the messengers were under instruction that they should prohibit burnt offerings and sacrifices and drink offerings in the temple; that they should profane the sabbaths and the feast days. (46) Further, they were to pollute the sanctuary and the holy people, (47) to set up altars and groves and shrines of idols, to sacrifice the flesh of swine and unclean animals. (48) The people of Judah were ordered to leave their sons uncircumcised and to make themselves ceremonially polluted with all manner of uncleanness and profanation (49) with the aim in view that they might forget their Law and change all its ordinances. (50) If anyone would not conform to the king's decree, he was to die.

(51) In the same manner he wrote to his whole kingdom, and appointed overseers over all the people who commanded the cities of Judah to offer sacrifice, city by city. (52) Then many of the people went along with this; in so doing they forsook the Law and committed evils in the land. (53) As a result, the Israelites were driven into hiding places wherever they could flee for refuge. (54) Now on the fifteenth day of the month Kislev, in the one hundred forty-fifth year,[4] they set up the desolating sacrilege on the altar and built idol altars throughout the whole of the cities of Judah. (55) They burned incense at the doors of their houses and in the streets, (56) and when they had torn in pieces the books of the Law which they found, they burned them with fire. (57) And wherever anyone was found with the book of the covenant or if anyone conformed to the Law, the king's decree was that they should put him to death. (58) Thus they kept performing acts of violence against Israel month by month, against whomever they found in the cities.

(59) On the twenty-fifth day of the month they offered sacrifices on the idol altar, which was placed upon the altar of God. (60) In keeping with the decree, they put to death the women who had caused their children to be circumcized; (61) they hanged their infants about their necks, and slaughtered households and those that had circumcized their children. (62) Many in Israel, however, were resolute and were determined in themselves not to eat any unclean thing. (63) They chose rather to die in order that they might not be defiled by unclean food or that they might not profane the holy covenant; and

---

[3]The unity of all mankind was a major dogma and ideal of the hellenistic rulers from Alexander on. Jews could not accept this view and still continue to regard themselves as the elect covenant community; to accept such a distinction-free view of man would have forced them to abandon the laws of separateness that were essential elements in the Mosaic Law.

[4]The year corresponds to 168 B.C., and the month, Kislev, is roughly the equivalent of our December.

they did indeed die. (64) And there was very great wrath against Israel.

(2:1) In those days Mattathias, the son of John, the son of Simeon, a priest of the sons of Joarib, moved from Jerusalem and lived in Modin.[5] (2) And he had five sons: John, called Caddi; (3) Simon, called Thassi; (4) Judah, who was called Maccabeus; (5) Eleazar, called Avaran; and Jonathan, whose surname was Apphus.

(6) When he saw the blasphemies that were being committed in Judah and Jerusalem, (7) he said, "Woe is me! Why was I born to see this misery of my people, and of the holy city, and to dwell there when it was delivered into the hand of the enemy, and the sanctuary was given over to strangers? (8) Her temple is become like a man without glory. (9) Her vessels are carried away into captivity, her infants are slain in the streets, and her young men are killed by the sword of the enemy. (10) What nation has not had a part in her kingdom and obtained some of her spoils? (11) All her adornments are taken away; instead of a free woman she has become a bondslave. (12) And behold, our sanctuary, which is our beauty and our glory, has been made desolate, and the Gentiles have profaned it. (13) Why then shall we live any longer?"

(14) Then Mattathias and his sons tore their clothes and put on sackcloth and mourned bitterly.

(15) At that time the king's officers, who were assigned to compel the people to commit apostasy, came into the city of Modin in order that they might coerce its inhabitants to offer sacrifice. (16) Many of Israel came to the officers, as did Mattathias and his sons as well. (17) Then the king's officers said to Mattathias: "You are a leader, an honorable and great man in this city, supported by your sons and brothers; now become the first to fulfill the king's commandment, just as all the other nations have done, as well as men of Judah and those who have stayed in Jerusalem. (18) In this way you and your sons will be included among the king's friends, and you and your sons will be honored with silver and gold and many rewards."

(19) Then Mattathias replied, speaking in a loud voice; "Though all the nations that are under the king's dominion obey him, and though every one of them departs from the religion of his fathers and gives in to the king's commands, (20) yet will I and my sons and my brothers walk in the covenant of our fathers. (21) God forbid that we should forsake the Law and the ordinances. (22) We will not obey the king's word, to depart from our religion either to the right or the left."

(23) Now when he had finished speaking these words, according to the king's commandment, there came one of the Jews in the sight of all to sacrifice on the altar which was in Modin. (24) When Mattathias saw this, he was inflamed with zeal and his heart quivered. Driven by righteous indignation, he ran and killed the man as he was sacri-

---

[5]Modin is a small town located on what was in antiquity the main route leading down through the hills of Judea from Jerusalem on the crest of the ridge to Lydda and Jaffa on the seacoast.

ficing at the altar. (25) And at the same time he also killed the officer sent by the king to enforce his commandment by compelling the people to sacrifice, and he knocked down the altar. (26) Thus he acted zealously for the law of God, as Phineas[6] had done to Zambri, the son of Salom. (27) And Mattathias went throughout the city calling out with a loud voice, "Whoever is zealous for the Law and maintains the covenant, let him follow me." (28) So he and his sons fled into the mountains and left all that they had in the city.

3:1–9

(3:1) Then[7] his son Judas, called Maccabeus, assumed command in his stead, (2) and all his brothers helped him, and so did all those who had sided with his father, and they fought with joy the battle of Israel. (3) So he increased the great glory of his people and put on a breastplate as a giant, and girded his armor of war about him, and fought battles, protecting his troops with the sword. (4) In his deeds he was like a lion, and like a lion's whelp roaring for his prey. (5) For he pursued the wicked and sought them out and consumed with fire those that harassed his people. (6) The lawless drew back for fear of him, and all the doers of evil were put to confusion because salvation prospered in his hand. (7) He brought grief to many kings, but through his deeds he made Jacob glad, and his memory is blessed forever. (8) Moreover he went through the cities of Judah, destroying the irreligious persons in them and thus turning away wrath from Israel. (9) Accordingly, he was renowned to the ends of the earth, and he gathered to himself such men as were prepared to fight to the death.

4:6–61

(6) But as soon as it was day, Judas appeared in the plain[8] with three thousand men, who had neither the arms nor the swords that they might have wished. (7) They saw the camp of the Gentiles, which was strong and well-fortified, surrounded with cavalry, and with soldiers expert in war. (8) Then Judas said to the men who were with him, "Do not fear their numbers nor be afraid of their attack. (9) Remember how our fathers were delivered at the Red Sea, when Pharaoh pursued them with an army. (10) So now let us call out to heaven, if perhaps the Lord will have mercy on us, and remember the covenant of our fathers, and destroy this army before us this day. (11) Thus all the Gentiles may know that there is one who delivers and saves Israel."

---

[6]Phineas, according to Numbers 25, on finding an Israelite having intercourse with a Midianite woman, ran them both through with a spear.

[7]That is, after the death of Mattathias in 166 B.C. His dying admonitions to his sons are recorded in I Macc. 2:49–68, and the date of his death as well as his place of burial—at Modin—are given in 2:69–70.

[8]After the Maccabean forces had bested the Syrians in a series of guerilla engagements and battles, Antiochus sent a huge army to crush the revolt (3:10–4:5). The troops of Antiochus were encamped near Emmaus, at a point where the Jerusalem-Jaffa road descends from the hills to the coastal plain.

(12) When the foreigners looked up and saw them coming against them, (13) they went out from the camp to battle. Those that were with Judas sounded the trumpets. (14) So the battle was joined, and the Gentiles were overwhelmed and fled into the plain. (15) Those in the rear ranks, however, were slain with the sword. They pursued them as far as Gezer[9] and to the plains of Idumea,[10] and Ashdod,[11] and Jamnia,[12] so that three thousand of the enemy were slain on a single day. (16) With this accomplished, Judas and his army returned from pursuing them.

(17) Then Judas said to the people, "Do not be greedy for loot, since there is a battle before us. (18) Gorgias and his army are near us in the mountains, but stand up now against our enemies and defeat them; after that you may take the plunder."

(19) Just as Judas was finishing his address, a contingent of the enemy appeared coming down out of the mountains. (20) When they perceived that the Jews had put their forces to flight and were burning their encampment—for the smoke that was visible disclosed what had occurred—(21) they were terrified. And when they saw the troops of Judas in the plain ready for battle, (22) they all of them fled into the land of the foreigners.[13]

(23) Then Judas returned to plunder the enemy camp, where they obtained much gold, silver, and blue silk, and sea purple,[14] and other great riches. When they returned home, they sang songs of thanksgiving and praised the Lord of heaven, because he is good, because his mercy endures forever. (25) Thus Israel had a great deliverance that day.

(26) Now all the foreigners that had escaped came and told Lysias what had happened. (27) When he heard this, he was puzzled and disheartened, because neither had the things occurred that he had intended for Israel nor did such things as the king had commanded take place. (28) So the next year Lysias gathered together sixty thousand choice infantrymen and five thousand horsemen, in order to sub-

---

[9]Gezer was a stronghold guarding the coastal plain from Bronze Age to hellenistic times.

[10]Idumea was the southern part of the Judean hills (around Hebron) where the Edomites (Idumeans) were forced to migrate by the Nabatean Arabs, who occupied the area southeast of the Dead Sea in the sixth century B.C.

[11]Azotus (or more accurately, Ashdod), a leading city and a major port, is mentioned in the Bible and in ancient literature as a leading city of the Philistines from Iron Age times (ca. 1000 B.C.) on. It provided an important cultural link between the Palestinian coast and the Greek world.

[12]Jamnia (Jabneh) is a small city about midway between Ashdod and Jaffa. Later it became a center of rabbinic learning, after the Jews were driven out of Jerusalem as a result of the revolts that ended in A.D. 70. Jamnia was located in what was traditionally Philistine territory.

[13]That is, of the Philistines. The cluster of cities along the southern Palestinian coast had never been under Israelite control, nor were they later for any extended period of time under Jewish control.

[14]A costly dye made from murex shells. An installation for producing this dye, together with thousands of the shells, has recently been excavated at the site of one of the ports of ancient Ashdod, now known by archaelogists as Tell Mor.

due them. (29) They came into Idumea and pitched their tents at Beth-Zur,[15] and Judas met them with ten thousand men. (30) When he saw that mighty encampment, he prayed and said: "Blessed art Thou, O savior of Israel, who didst thwart the attack of that mighty man[16] by the hand of thy servant David, and didst give the army of foreigners into the hand of Jonathan the son of Saul and his armor-bearer: (31) Surround this army by the hand of thy people Israel, and let their troops and horsemen be a humiliation to them. (32) Make them be cowardly, and cause the boldness of their strength to dwindle. May they tremble at their own destruction. (33) Hurl them down by the sword of those that love thee, and let all those that know thy name praise thee with songs."

(34) So they joined in battle, and about five thousand men of the army of Lysias were killed; directly in front of the eyes of the rest of the enemy force were they slain.[17] (35) When Lysias saw his army put to flight and observed the courage of Judas' soldiers—how they were ready to live or die valiantly—he withdrew to Antioch. There he gathered together an even larger army of mercenaries with the aim of marching once again into Judea.

(36) Then Judas and his brothers said, "Behold our enemies are overwhelmed; let us go up to purify and rededicate the sanctuary." (37) At this proposal all the troops assembled themselves together and went up to Mount Zion. (38) And when they saw the sanctuary desolate and the altar profaned and the gates burned up and brush growing in the courts as in a forest or on one of the mountains, and the priests's chambers in ruins, (39) they tore their clothes, made great lamentations and threw ashes on themselves. (40) They fell down with their faces to the ground and blew a signal with the trumpets and cried to heaven.

(41) Then Judas appointed certain men to fight against the garrison that was still in the stronghold[18] until he could cleanse the sanctuary. (42) So he chose priests whose manner of life was blameless, who delighted in the Law. (43) These cleansed the sanctuary and carried out to an unclean place the defiled stones. (44) After they had discussed what to do with the altar of burnt offerings that had been profaned, (45) they thought best to pull it down, so that it would not be a reproach against them because the heathen had defiled it. So they pulled it down (46) and stored the stones in the temple mountain in a convenient place, until there should come a prophet to show what should be done with them. (47) Then they took rough-hewn stones according

---

[15]Beth-Zur, an important hellenistic stronghold guarding one of the main access routes to the southern Judean hills.

[16]Goliath, the Philistine giant killed by David while he was still a shepherd boy (I Samuel 17:1–58).

[17]The Greek text is elliptical here, but it seems to say that the main body of the Syrian troops was in a position to see 5000 of their comrades fall but not able to come to their aid.

[18]Apparently the reference is to a massive tower that overlooked the temple area and that continued to be occupied by Syrian soldiers even after the rest of the city had been taken over by the Maccabean forces.

to the Law and built a new altar resembling the former one. (48) They reconstructed the sanctuary and the interior parts of the temple and consecrated its courts. (49) They also made new sacred vessels, and brought into the temple the lampstand, the altars of burnt offerings and of incense and the table. (50) They burned incense on the altar and they lit the lamps that were on the lampstand to give light in the temple. (51) Then they set the loaves on the table, hung up the curtains and finished all the work they had set out to do.

(52) Now on the twenty-fifth day of the ninth month, which is called the month Kislev, in the one hundred forty-eighth year,[19] they rose up early in the morning (53) and offered sacrifice according to the Law on the new altar of burnt offerings that they had made. (54) At the very time and on precisely the day that the heathen had profaned it, it was dedicated with songs and harps and lutes and cymbals. (55) Then all the people fell on their faces, worshipping and praising the God of heaven, who had given them good success. (56) So they performed the dedication of the altar for eight days offering burnt offerings with gladness and sacrificing the sacrifices of deliverance and praise. (57) They also decorated the facade of the temple with crowns of gold and with shields; they restored the gates and chambers, supplying them with doors. (58) Thus there was very great gladness among the people in that the reproach by the Gentiles had been taken away.

(59) Then Judas and his brothers, with the whole congregation of Israel, established that the days of the dedication of the altar should be kept at the appropriate season from year to year for a period of eight days, beginning with the twenty-fifth day of the month Kislev, with joy and gladness. (60) Also at that time they built up Mount Zion, surrounding it with high walls and strong towers, so that the Gentiles should not come and defile it as they had done before. (61) And they placed there a garrison to guard it. And further, they fortified Beth-Zur, to maintain it as a defense for the people against Idumea.

I MACCABEES 8:1–32

(8:1) Now Judas had heard of the fame of the Romans, that they were strong and powerful men who regard with great favor all who would make a treaty of friendship with them and who gave assurances of amity to all that came to them. (2) Further, he heard that the Romans were men of great valor, and he was told of the wars and noble deeds they had accomplished among the Galatians, how they had conquered them and brought them under tribute; (3) and what they had done in the region of Spain, for gaining control of the silver and gold mines that are there, (4) and that by their strategy and persistence they had conquered the whole territory even though it was very far from them; and that they had vanquished also the kings that came against them from the ends of the earth, to such an extent that

---

[19]This would be 164 B.C.

they had overwhelmed them and given them a disastrous defeat with the result that the rest of the kings paid tribute to them year by year.

(5) Besides this he heard how the Romans had defeated Philip[20] in battle and Perseus,[21] king of the Macedonians, and had overcome others who lifted themselves up against them. (6) They heard also how Antiochus,[22] the great king of Asia, who came against the Romans in battle accompanied by a hundred and twenty elephants, with cavalry, chariots and a very great army, was overwhelmed by them; (7) and how they took him alive and decreed that he and those who reigned after him should pay a heavy tribute, that they should give hostages, and that they should turn over to the Romans such choice lands as were agreed upon. (8) The regions of India,[23] Media,[24] and Lydia,[25] they took from him and gave to King Eumenes.[26] (9) The Greeks had planned to come and destroy them, (10) but since the Romans had advance knowledge of it, they sent against them a certain general who fought with them and killed many of them and carried away as captives their wives and children, and took plunder from them and took over their lands and pulled down their fortifications and made slaves of them down to this day. (11). It was told him further how they destroyed and brought under dominion all other kingdoms and islands that ever offered resistance to them, but with their friends and allies they maintained amity; (12) that they conquered kingdoms near and far, with the result that all who heard of their name was afraid of them; (13) and also they establish as kings those whom they want to help gain the rule, but those whom they do not want to rule they displace.

Finally, he was told that they were a people of supreme power; (14) yet for all this none of them wore a crown or was clothed in the purple of royalty, lest anyone become inflated with pride thereby; (15) and how they made for themselves a senate house in which three hundred and twenty men sat daily, always deliberating in behalf of the people the better to insure public order; (16) and that they committed their government to one man every year,[27] who ruled over all

---

[20]Philip V of Macedon, who ruled from 220–179 B.C., but who was defeated by the Romans in Thessaly in 197 B.C.

[21]Perseus, an illegitimate son of Philip V, succeeded him as king, but was defeated by the Romans in 168 B.C.

[22]Antiochus III, king of Syria from 223–187 B.C.

[23]This is historically impossible, since the Seleucids never controlled India and were therefore in no position to turn it over to the Romans.

[24]The Seleucids were forced by the Romans to turn over to them territory northwest of the Taurus Range.

[25]A rich territory in SW Asia Minor that became a client state subject to Rome.

[26]Eumenes II, king of the rich city-state Pergamos from 197–158 B.C.; his assistance to the Romans against the Seleucids was rewarded by the grant of these rich territories.

[27]Several of the details of the information given here about Rome are inaccurate: the senate sat at stated times, but not daily; there were two consuls, not one; there was considerable rivalry for leadership. But there is no reason to doubt the intention of the writer to give an accurate account or to question the general historicity of this picture of the dealings between the Maccabees and the Romans.

their land, and that all were obedient to him, and that there was neither envy nor jealousy among them.

(17) In consideration of these things, Judas chose Eupolemus, the son of John, the son of Accos, and Jason, the son of Eleazar, and sent them to Rome to make an alliance of friendship and mutual assistance with them, (18) and to urge the Romans to take the yoke from them; for they saw that the kingdom of the Greeks was oppressing Israel with slavery. (19) So they went to Rome, which was a very great journey, and came into the senate house, where they spoke as follows:

(20) "Judas, who is also known as Maccabeus, with his brothers and the people of the Jews, have sent us to you to make an alliance and a treaty of peace with you, so that we might be registered as your allies and friends."

(21) This report pleased the Romans well. (22) And this is the copy of the epistle that the senate wrote back again on tablets of brass and sent to Jerusalem, in order for the Jews to have their a memorial of peace and mutual assistance:

(23) "May things go well for the Romans and for the nation of the Jews, at sea and on land for ever and ever; and may both sword and enemy be far from them. (24) If there should come first any war against Rome or any of her allies throughout all their dominion, (25) the people of the Jews shall help them with all their heart, as the time shall be appointed; (26) neither shall the Jews provide anything for those who make war on the Romans, or aid them with food, weapons, money, or ships, as it has seemed good to the Romans; but they shall keep their agreements without taking anything in exchange. (27) In the same way, if war should come first upon the nation of the Jews, the Romans will help them with all their heart, according as occasion may dictate to them. (28) Neither shall food be given to those who side against the Jews, nor weapons, nor money, as it has seemed good to the Romans, but they shall keep their obligations and do so without deceit. (29) According to these articles the Romans make a covenant with the nation of the Jews, (30) but if hereafter the one party or the other shall think it fitting to add or delete anything, they may do it at their pleasures, and whatever they shall add or take away shall be ratified. (31) And on the matter of the evils that Demetrius[28] is perpetrating against the Jews, we have written him saying, 'Why have you made heavy the yoke upon our friends and allies the Jews?' If they have further complaints against you, we will meet our just obligations to them, and fight against you by sea and land.' "

Josephus, Antiquities of the Jews

Born in the year Gaius Caligula became emperor (A.D. 37), Joseph(us) ben Matthias was descended from priests on his father's side and from the royal Hasmonean (Maccabean) family on his mother's. He was given every advantage as a child, including a thorough education in scriptural

---

[28]Demetrius I, who reigned from 162–150 B.C. as Seleucid King of Syria.

and rabbinic learning. In addition to his exposure to the teachings of the Pharisees and the Sadducees, he spent three years in the ascetic community of the Essenes in the Jordan Valley. His own religious position was Pharisaic, which enabled him to combine devotion to the Law of Moses with an attitude of passive accommodation toward Rome.

A visit to Rome in the year 64 impressed him with the wisdom of the attitude of acceptance toward Rome, with its unbeatable power, so when he returned to his native Palestine and found the Jewish nationalists fomenting revolt, he devoted all his energies and powers of persuasion to deterring the insurrectionists. His efforts were unavailing, however. When the fighting started, he was given some kind of special assignment in Galilee which seems to have included achieving a peaceful settlement between the nationalists and the Romans. He was apparently regarded by the insurrectionists as a traitor and by the Romans as a spy. Whatever his connections and motives, he was captured by Vespasian, whose rise to imperial power he had earlier and accurately predicted; attached as a kind of prisoner-advisor to the Roman forces, he accompanied Vespasian to Alexandria and then returned for the siege of Jerusalem, where he functioned as mediator and interpreter between the Romans and his fellow Jews.

After the fall of Jerusalem (A.D. 70), Vespasian having been proclaimed emperor by the army in 69, Josephus was assured of a place in imperial favor, and even of living accommodations in the imperial household. It was in Rome that most of his writing was done, although he seems to have written a first edition of his *Wars* in Aramaic, his native tongue, and addressed it to Jews living in the eastern parts of Syria and Mesopotamia, where large numbers of his coreligionists remained from the time of Babylonian exile (6th century B.C.). The second edition was composed before A.D. 79 with the help of Greek-speaking literary aides, as he acknowledges in the introduction to the Greek version, which alone has survived. His *Antiquities of the Jews* appeared late in the reign of Domitian (probably between 93 and 94 A.D.). In it Josephus shows dependence on other historical sources, such as I Maccabees and records kept in the court of Herod the Great. It was impossible, of course, for him to have been a first-hand observer of so long a span of history.

From the second century on, Christians were disappointed that Josephus paid so little attention to Christianity, mentioning it only twice and then only in passing (*Antiquities* XVIII:63; XX:200). In order to remedy what they regarded as an oversight, some of his Christian readers expanded the references, thereby transforming Josephus into a witness in behalf of Jesus as Messiah. (See discussion of this in H. C. Kee, *Jesus in History*, New York: Harcourt Brace Jovanovich, 1970, pp. 31–34.)

Obverse: Antiochus VII Sidetes (138–129 B.C.). A Seleucid ruler who invaded the Jewish state, then under the rule of John Hyrcanus of the Hasmonean family, predecessor of Alexander Jannaeus. Under Hyrcanus the Maccabean kingdom reached its height, but Sidetes beseiged Hyrcanus in Jerusalem until he paid a huge indemnity. Reverse: Pallas, the thunder-goddess, with the inscription, King Antiochus Euergetes (Performer of Good Deeds).

In spite of the absence from his account of information we might wish he had included, and in spite of his pro-Roman prejudices and his attempts at self-vindication, he remains one of our most important ancient sources, not only for the history of Judaism in the first centuries before and after the birth of Jesus, but for detailed knowledge of palace politics both in Jerusalem and in Rome, as well as for information in depth about imperial policy in dealing with an eastern province.

In Book XIII of his *Antiquities* Josephus describes the reign of one of the most notorious of the descendants of the Maccabees—the family was known as the Hasmoneans—in the person of Alexander Jannaeus. His reputation rested on the cruelty with which he treated his fellow Jews.

ANTIQUITIES: XIII:379–383

(379) Alexander[1] thereupon fled to the mountains, where out of pity for him at this reverse[2] six thousand Jews gathered to his side. And at this Demetrius withdrew in alarm. But later on the Jews fought

---

[1]The reign of Alexander Jannaeus as king of the Jews lasted from 103–76 B.C. His cruel and ruthless tyranny, his excesses in suppressing dissent, both from within his own family and from his subjects, included crucifying his political foes and earned him a place as a model of inhumanity. The internal strife within the Jewish state was aggravated by his harsh methods and the way was thus prepared for intervention by the Romans.

[2]The defeat mentioned was the outcome of a battle in which the Seleucid king, Demetrius III, was joined by Jewish troops fighting against their own despotic ruler, Alexander. But the setback for Alexander was only temporary, and he retaliated ruthlessly against the Jews who continued to oppose his rule.

(380) against Alexander and were defeated, many of them dying in battle. The most powerful of them, however, he brought back to Jerusalem; and there he did a thing that was as cruel as could be: while he feasted with his concubines in a conspicuous place, he ordered some eight hundred of the Jews to be crucified, and slaughtered their children and wives before the eyes of the still living wretches. This was the revenge he (381) took for the injuries he had suffered; but the penalty he exacted was inhuman for all that, even though he had, as was natural, gone through very great hardships in the wars he had fought against them, and had finally found himself in danger of losing both his life and his throne, for they were not satisfied to carry on the struggle by themselves but (382) brought foreigners as well, and at last reduced him to the necessity of surrendering to the king of the Arabs[1] the territory which he had conquered in Moab and Galaaditis and the strongholds therein, in order that he might not aid the Jews in the war against him; and they (383) committed countless other insulting and abusive acts against him. But still he seems to have done this thing unnecessarily, and as a result of his excessive cruelty he was nicknamed Thrakidas (the "Cossack") by the Jews. Then his opponents, numbering in all about eight thousand, fled by night and remained in exile so long as Alexander lived. And he, being rid of the trouble they had caused him, reigned thereafter in complete tranquility.

In Book XIV of the *Antiquities* Josephus describes one of the dark moments in Jewish history: the seizure of Jerusalem and its temple by the Romans under Pompey. Except for brief periods of revolt (A.D. 66–70 and 132–135), the Jews were not again in control of Jerusalem until modern times.

ANTIQUITIES: XIV:57–67; 69–73

(57) And Pompey,[2] being seized with anger at this,[3] placed Aristobulus[4] under arrest, and himself went to the city,[5] which was

---

[1] From the sixth century B.C. down into Roman times the Nabatean Arabs controlled the area bordering the Arabian Desert from Damascus south to the Gulf of Aqaba. Their capital was the spectacular rock-hewn city, Petra. Moab is the mountainous area to the east of the Dead Sea; Galaaditis is geologically similar territory north of Moab and east of the Jordan Valley.

[2] Member of the famous Roman triumvirate, along with Julius Caesar and Crassus, Pompey invaded Syria and then Palestine on the pretext of pacifying the local warring populace, but the result was to establish Roman hegemony in the area for the next seven centuries.

[3] The immediate occasion for Pompey's wrath was Aristobulus' refusal to follow through on his earlier promise of three hundred talents to be given to Pompey. When Gabinius, Pompey's general, arrived at Jerusalem to pick up the bribe, Aristobulus refused to admit him to the city.

[4] Arstobulus, son of Alexander Jannaeus and Alexandra, succeeded his mother as king at her death in 69 B.C. by persuading his brother, Hyrcanus, to abdicate in his favor.

[5] That is, Jerusalem.

strongly fortified on all sides except on the north, where it was weak. For it is surrounded by a broad and deep ravine which takes in the temple, and this is very strongly protected by an encircling wall of stone.

(58) But among the men within the city there was dissension, for they were not of one mind concerning their situation; to some it seemed best to deliver the city to Pompey, while those who sympathized with Aristobulus urged that they shut Pompey out and make war on him because he held Aristobulus prisoner. It was this party that made the first move and occupied the temple, and cutting the bridge[6] that stretches (59) from it to the city, prepared themselves for a siege. But those of the other faction admitted Pompey's army and handed over to him the city and the palace. Pompey thereupon sent his legate Piso with an army to guard the city and the palace, and fortified the houses adjoining the (60) temple and the places round the temple outside. His first step was to offer conciliatory terms to those within, but as they would not listen to his proposals, he fortified the surrounding places with walls, with Hyrcanus willingly assisting him in all ways. And at dawn Pompey pitched his camp on the north side of the temple, where it was open to (61) attack. But even here stood great towers, and a trench had been dug, and the temple was surrounded by a deep ravine; for there was a steep slope on the side toward the city after the bridge was destroyed, and at this spot Pompey by great labour day by day had caused earthworks to be raised, for which the Romans cut down the timber round about. (62) And when these were high enough, though the trench was filled up with difficulty because of its immense depth, he moved up and set in place the siege engines and instruments of war that had been brought from Tyre, and began to batter the temple with his catapults. But if it (63) were not our national custom to rest on the Sabbath day, the earthworks would not have been finished, because the Jews would have prevented this; for the Law permits us to defend ourselves against those who begin a battle and strike us, but it does not allow us to fight against an enemy that does anything else.

(64) Of this fact the Romans were well aware, and on those days which we call the Sabbath, they did not shoot at the Jews or meet them in hand to hand combat, but instead they raised earthworks and towers, and brought up their siege-engines in order that these might be put (65) to work the following day. And one may get an idea of the extreme piety which we show toward God and of our strict observance of the laws from the fact that during the siege the priests were not hindered from performing any of the sacred ceremonies through fear, but twice a day, in the morning and at the ninth hour, they performed the sacred ceremonies at the altar, and did not omit

---

[6]The temple hill was separated from the wealthy suburbs on the western hill of Jerusalem by a valley that was much deeper then than it is now. A viaduct made it possible to cross to the temple without descending into the valley. The recently discovered piers of what is probably a similar viaduct crossing this valley are associated with Herod's vastly enlarged version of the temple complex, work on which did not begin until a half century after Pompey's invasion.

any of the sacrifices even when some (66) difficulty arose because of the attacks. And indeed when the city was taken, in the third month, on the Fast Day, in the hundred and seventy-ninth Olympiad,[7] in the consulship of Gaius Antonius and Marcus Tullius Cicero, and the enemy rushed in and were slaughtering the (67) Jews in the temple, those who were busied with the sacrifices none the less continued to perform the sacred ceremonies; nor were they compelled, either by fear for their lives or by the great number of those already slain, to run away, but thought it better to endure whatever they might have to suffer there beside the altars than to neglect any of the ordinances.

(69) Now when the siege-engine was brought up, the largest of the towers was shaken and fell, making a breach through which the enemy poured in; first among them was Cornelius Faustus, the son of Sulla, who with his soldiers mounted the wall, and after him the centurion Furius, with those who followed him, on the other side, and between them Fabius, another centurion, with a strong and compact body of men. And there was slaughter everywhere. For some of the Jews were slain (70) by the Romans, and others by their fellows; and there were some who hurled themselves down the precipices, and setting fire to their houses, burned themselves within them, for they could not bear to accept their fate. And so of the Jews there fell some twelve thousand, but of the (71) Romans only a very few. One of those taken captive was Absalom, the uncle and at the same time father-in-law of Aristobulus. And not light was the sin committed against the sanctuary, which before that time had never been entered or seen. For Pompey and not a few of his men went (72) into it and saw what it was unlawful for any but the high priests to see. But though the golden table was there and the sacred lampstand and the libation vessels and a great quantity of spices, and beside these, in the treasury, the sacred moneys amounting to two thousand talents, he touched none of these because of piety, and in this respect also he acted in a manner worthy of his virtuous character. And on (73) the morrow he instructed the temple servants to cleanse the temple and to offer the customary sacrifice to God, and he restored the high priesthood to Hyrcanus[8] because in various ways he had been useful to him and particularly because he had prevented the Jews throughout the country from fighting on Aristobulus' side; and those responsible for the war he executed by beheading.

III

Antipater, an Idumean adventurer and father of Herod the Great, had served variously as an intermediary between Jewish leaders and the Nabatean Arabs of East Jordan, and between the Jews and the Roman invaders. His knack of shifting to the winning side was evident when he

---

[7] That is, 63 B.C.

[8] Hyrcanus, son of Alexandra, had been dethroned in the dynastic struggle for control of the high priesthood sketched in Note 3.

abandoned Pompey and helped Julius Caesar gain control of Egypt. Brave and politically adroit, Antipater's son Herod inherited these characteristics, with the result that he was appointed by the Romans as governor of Samaria and northern Palestine. Then in 40 B.C. the Roman senate confirmed him as king of the Jews, with Caesar and Mark Antony jointly sponsoring him. In this capacity he ruled over all of Palestine, as well as over territories to the north and east of the Jordan Valley. He sought to lend legitimacy to his kingship by taking as his wife Mariamne, a woman of the Hasmonean royal line. His love for her was turned to distrust, fed by the rumors perpetrated by those who sought to destroy her, until finally Herod had her put to death. His subsequent remorse and grief brought on what we would call a depression and fostered a neurotic suspicion of everyone, from which he never recovered. His efficiency as an administrator and ruler remained, but his insensitive, even ruthless attitude toward his subjects engendered their hatred of him. The final paragraph of the section of Josephus' *Antiquities* here excerpted reports Herod's will, in which he distributed his realm among his surviving sons and daughter.

Not only do Herod and his sons figure directly in the New Testament as the rulers who dominated the land from the time of his birth until his crucifixion, but the fact that they ruled through collaboration with the Romans was a major factor in the political tensions of the period that made any such talk as that of Jesus and his followers about "the Kingdom of God" take on revolutionary overtones. On the other hand, construction of the Jerusalem temple, begun under Herod the Great and completed much later, was a chief source of Jewish pride, the major factor in the economy of Jerusalem, and the House of God.

ANTIQUITIES: XV:267–276

For this reason[1] Herod went still farther (267) in departing from the native customs, and through foreign practices he gradually corrupted the ancient way of life, which had hitherto been inviolable. As a result of this we suffered considerable harm at a later time as well, because those things were neglected which had formerly induced piety in the masses. For in the first place he established athletic (268) contests every fifth year in honour of Caesar, and he built a theatre in Jerusalem, and after that a very large amphitheatre in the plain, both being spectacularly lavish but foreign to Jewish custom, for the use of such buildings and the exhibition of such spectacles have not been traditional [with the Jews]. Herod, however, celebrated the (269) quinquennial festival in the most splendid way sending no-

---

[1]The reason was that no members of the Hasmonean line survived to challenge Herod's power or to remind him of his obligation to Jewish traditions.

tices of it to the neighbouring peoples and inviting participants from the whole nation. Athletes and other classes of contestants were invited from every land, being attracted by the hope of winning the prizes offered and by the glory of victory. And the leading men in various fields were assembled, for Herod offered (270) very great prizes not only to the winners in gymnastic games but also to those who engaged in music and those who are called thymelikoi.[2] And an effort was made to have all the most famous persons come to the contest. He also offered considerable gifts to drivers of four-horse and two-horse chariots and to (271) those mounted on race-horses. And whatever costly or magnificent efforts had been made by others, all these did Herod imitate in his ambition to see his spectacle become famous. (272) All round the theatre were inscriptions concerning Caesar and trophies of the nations which he had won in war, all of them made for Herod of pure gold and silver. As for serviceable ob-

---

[2]Probably refers to performers, such as actors or musicians.

A large scale model of Jerusalem in the first century
A.D. *In the foreground is the Tyropean Valley which separated the Temple Hill from the newer quarter of the city on the western hill. To the left is one of the viaducts that enabled pedestrians to cross the valley from the Temple area more easily. The large enclosure at the top of the picture is the Temple area, with the Porch of Solomon on the right and the central shrine in the center. In the shadow is the massive Tower of Antonia, built by Herod to guard the Temple; it probably served as headquarters for the Roman garrison and is the traditional site for the imprisonment and trial of Jesus.* (Source: H. C. Kee)

jects, there was no valuable garment or vessel of precious stones which was not also on (273) exhibition along with the contests. There was also a supply of wild beasts, a great many lions and other animals having been brought together for him, such as were of extraordinary strength or of very rare kinds. When the practice began of involving them in combat with one another or setting condemned men to fight against them, foreigners were astonished (274) at the expense and at the same time entertained by the dangerous spectacle, but to the natives it meant an open break with the customs held in honour by them. For it seemed glaring impiety to throw men to wild beasts for the pleasure of other men as spectators, and it seemed a further impiety to change (275) their established ways for foreign practices. But more than all else it was the trophies that irked them, for in the belief that these were images surrounded by weapons, (276) which it was against their national custom to worship, they were exceedingly angry.

xv:380–402

It was at this time, in the eighteenth year of his reign,[3] (380) after the events mentioned above, that Herod undertook an extraordinary work, (namely) the reconstructing of the temple of God at his own expense, enlarging its precincts and raising it to a more imposing height. For he believed that the accomplishment of this task would be the most notable of all the things achieved by him, as indeed it was, and would be great enough to assure his eternal remembrance. (381) But since he knew that the populace was not prepared for or easy to enlist in so great an undertaking, he thought it best to predispose them to set to work on the whole project (382) by making a speech to them first, and so he called them together and spoke as follows: "So far as the other things achieved during my reign are concerned, my countrymen, I consider it unnecessary to speak of them, although they were of such a kind that the prestige which comes from them to me is (383) less than the security which they have brought to you. For in the most difficult situations I have not been unmindful of the things that might benefit you in your need, nor have I in my building been more intent upon my own invulnerability than upon that of all of you, and I think I have, by the will of God, brought the Jewish nation to such a state of prosperity as it has never known before. (384) Now as for the various buildings which we have erected in our country and in the cities of our land and in those of acquired territories, with which, as the most beautiful adornment, we have embellished our nation, it seems to me quite needless to speak of them to you, knowing them as you do. But that enterprise which I now propose to undertake is the most pious and beautiful one of our time as I will now make clear. (385) For this was the temple which our fathers built to the Most Great God after their return from Babylon, but it lacks sixty cubits[4] in height, the amount by which the first

---

[3]In the year 20–19 B.C.
[4]Sixty cubits equals approximately 90 feet.

temple, built by Solomon, exceeded it. And yet no one should condemn our fathers for neglecting their pious duty, for it was not their fault that this temple is smaller. (386) Rather it was Cyrus and Darius, the son of Hystaspes, who prescribed these dimensions for building, and since our fathers were subject to them and their descendants and after them to the Macedonians,[5] they had no opportunity to restore this first archetype of piety to its former size. But since, by the will of God, I am now ruler and there continues to be a long period of peace and an abundance (387) of wealth and great revenues, and—what is of most importance—the Romans, who are, so to speak, the masters of the world, are (my) loyal friends, I will try to remedy the oversight caused by the necessity and subjection of that earlier time, and by this act of piety make full return to God for the gift of this kingdom."

These were Herod's words, and most of the people were (388) astonished by his speech, for it fell upon their ears as something quite unexpected. And while the unlikelihood of his realizing his hope did not disturb them, they were dismayed by the thought that he might tear down the whole edifice and not have sufficient means to bring his project [of rebuilding it] to completion. And this danger appeared to them to be very great, (389) and the vast size of the undertaking seemed to make it difficult to carry out. Since they felt this way, the king spoke encouragingly to them, saying that he would not pull down the temple before having ready all the materials needed for its completion. (390) And these assurances he did not belie. For he prepared a thousand wagons to carry the stones, selected ten thousand of the most skilled workmen, purchased priestly robes for a thousand priests and trained some as masons, others as carpenters, and began the construction only after all these preparations had diligently been made by him.

After removing the old foundations, he laid down others (391) and upon these he erected the temple, which was a hundred cubits in length ... and twenty more in height, but in the course of time this dropped as the foundations subsided. And this part we decided to raise again in the time of Nero. (392) The temple was built of hard, white stones, each of which was about twenty-five cubits in length, eight in height and twelve in width. And in the whole of it, as also in the royal portico, either side was the lowest, while the middle portion was the (393) highest, so that this was visible at a distance of many stades[6] to those who inhabited the country, especially those who lived opposite or happened to approach it. The entrance-doors, which with their lintels were equal [in height] to the temple itself, he adorned with multi-coloured hangings, with purple colours and with inwoven designs of (394) pillars. Above these, under the cornice, spread a golden vine with grape-clusters hanging from it, a marvel of size and artistry to all (395) who saw with what costliness of material it had been constructed. And he surrounded the temple with very large proticoes, all of which he made in proportion [to the temple],

---

[5]That is, the Seleucids who dominated Palestine from their capital at Antioch in Syria.

[6]A stade is approximately 600 feet or 180 meters.

and he surpassed his predecessors in spending money, so that it was thought that no one else had adorned the temple so spendidly. Both [porticoes] were [supported] by (396) a great wall, and the wall itself was the greatest ever heard of by man. The hill was a rocky ascent that sloped gently up toward the eastern (397) part of the city to the topmost peak. This hill our first king, (398) Solomon, with God-given wisdom surrounded with great works above at the top. And below, beginning at the foot, where a deep ravine runs round it, he surrounded it with enormous stones bound together with lead. He cut off more and more of the area within as [the wall] became greater in depth, so that the size and height of the structure, which was square, were immense, and the great size of the stones was seen along (399) the front surface, while iron clamps on the inside assured that the joints would remain permanently united. When this work reached the top of the hill, he levelled off the summit, and filled in the hollow spaces near the walls, and made the upper surface smooth and even (400) throughout. Such was the whole enclosure, having a circumference of four stades, each side taking up the length of a stade. Within this (401) wall and on the very summit there ran another wall of stone, which had on the eastern ridge a double portico of the same length as the wall, and it faced the doors of the temple, for this lay within it. This portico many of the earlier kings adorned. Round about the entire (402) temple were fixed the spoils taken from the barbarians, and all these King Herod dedicated, adding those which he took from the Arabs.

XV:410–423

In the western part of the court [of the temple] there were (410) four gates. The first led to the palace by a passage over the intervening ravine, two others led to the suburb, and the last led to the other part of the city, from which it was separated by many steps going down to the ravine and from here up again to the hill. For the City lay opposite the temple, being in the form of a theatre and being bordered by a deep ravine along its whole southern side. The fourth front (411) of this [court], facing south, also had gates in the middle, and had over it the Royal Portico, which had three aisles, extending in length from the eastern to the western ravine. It was not possible for it to extend farther. And it was a structure more noteworthy than any under the sun. For while the depth of the ravine was great, and no (412) one who bent over to look into it from above could bear to look down to the bottom, the height of the portico standing over it was so very great that if anyone looked down from its rooftop, combining the two elevations, he would become dizzy and his vision would be unable to reach the end of so measureless a depth. Now the columns [of the portico] (413) stood in four rows, one opposite the other all along—the fourth row was attached to a wall built of stone—and the thickness of each column was such that it would take three men with outstretched arms touching one another to envelop it; its height was twenty-seven feet, and there was a double moulding running round its base. The number of all the columns was a hundred and sixty-two, and their capitals were (414) ornamented in the Corinthian style of carving, which caused amazement by the magnificence of its whole effect. Since there were four rows, (415) they made three aisles among them, under the porticoes. Of these the two side ones corresponded and were made in the same way, each being thirty feet in width, a stade in length, and over fifty feet in height. But the middle aisle was one and a half times as wide and twice as high, and thus it greatly towered over those on either side. The ceilings [of the porticos] were ornamented with deeply cut wood-carvings (416) representing all sorts of different figures. The ceiling of the middle aisle was raised to a greater height, and the front wall was cut at either end into architraves with columns built into it, and all of it was polished, so that these structures seemed incredible to those who had not seen them, and were beheld with amazement by those who set (417) eyes on them. Such, then, was the first court. Within it and not far distant was a second one, accessible by a few steps and surrounded by a stone balustrade with an inscription prohibiting the entrance of a foreigner under threat of the penalty of death.[7] On its southern and (418) northern sides the inner court had three-chambered gateways, equally distant from one another, and on the side where the sun rises it had one great gateway, through which those of us who were ritually clean (419) used to pass with our wives. Within this court was the sacred

---

[7]The translation of this inscription is given on pp. 259 below.

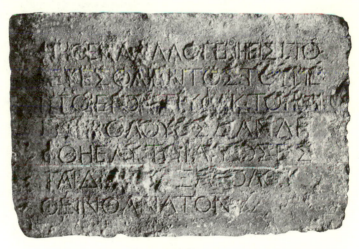

Inscription from the balustrade of the Temple in Jerusalem built by Herod the Great, marking the point beyond which Gentiles were not permitted to pass. (Source: Quarterly of the Dept. of Antiquities of Palestine 6/1938)

(court) which women were forbidden to enter, and still farther within was a third court into which only priests were permitted to go. In this [priests court] was the temple, and before it was an altar, on which we used to sacrifice whole burnt-offerings to God. Into none of these (420) courts did King Herod enter since he was not a priest and was therefore prevented from so doing. But with the construction of the porticoes and the outer courts he did busy himself, and these he finished building in eight years.

The temple itself was built by the priests in a year and six (421) months, and all the people were filled with joy and offered thanks to God, first of all for the speed [of the work] and next for the king's zeal, and as they celebrated they acclaimed the restoration. Then the king sacrificed three hundred oxen to God, and others did similarly, (422) each according to his means. The number of these [sacrifices] it would be impossible to give, for it would exceed our power to give a true estimate. And it so happened that the day on which the work of (423) the temple was completed coincided with that of the king's accession, which they were accustomed to celebrate, and because of the double occasion the festival was a very glorious one indeed.

XVII: 188–192

Then because of the change of mind he had undergone, he (188) once more altered his will and designated Antipas, to whom he had left his throne, to be tetrarch of Galilee and Peraea, while he bestowed the kingdom on Archelaus. Gaulonitis, Trachonitis, Batanaea[8] and (189) Paneas[9] were to be given as a tetrarchy to his son Philip, who was a full brother of Archelaus, while Jamneia, Azotus and Phasaelis were given over to his sister Salome along with five hundred thousand pieces of coined silver. He also provided for all his other relatives and left them wealthy through gifts of money and the assignment of revenues. (190) To Caesar he left ten million pieces of coined silver besides vessels of gold and of silver and some very valuable garments, while to Caesar's wife Julia and some others he left five million pieces (of silver). Having done this he died, on the fifth day after having his son Antipater killed. He had reigned for thirty-four years from the time when he had put Antigonus to death, and for thirty-seven years from the time when (191) he had been appointed king by the Romans.[10] He was a man who was cruel to all alike and one who easily gave in to anger and was contemptuous of justice. And yet he was as greatly favoured by fortune as any man has ever been in that from being a commoner he was made king, and (192) though encompassed by innumerable perils, he managed to escape them all and lived on to a very old age. As for the affairs of his household and his relation to his sons, he had, in his own opinion at least, enjoyed

---

[8]Territories north and east of the Sea of Galilee.

[9]A city located near the main sources of the Jordan. A shrine there to the pagan god, Pan, gave the name to the place, Panias (or in Latin form, Paneus).

[10]Equivalent to 4 B.C.

very good fortune since he had not failed to get the better of those whom he considered his enemies, but in my opinion he was very unfortunate indeed.

Josephus, Jewish Wars

Our final excerpts from Josephus are all drawn from his *Jewish Wars* and describe the insurrectionist movement and its suppression by the Romans in 66–73 A.D. Josephus was an eyewitness of much that he reports, and although he was ambivalent about the revolt—he fought at first with his fellow Jews and then joined the Romans in defeating them—he was by no means a nonpartisan.

IV:147–161

(147) In the end,[1] to such abject prostration and terror were the people reduced and to such heights of madness rose these brigands, that they actually took upon themselves the election to the high priesthood. (148) Abrogating the claims of those families from which in turn the high priests had always been drawn, they appointed to that office ignoble (149) and low born individuals, in order to gain accomplices in their impious crimes; for persons who had undeservedly attained to the highest (150) dignity were bound to obey those who had conferred it. Moreover, by various devices and libellous statements, they brought the official authorities into collision with each other, finding

---

[1]The events here depicted occurred as the Roman invasion of Palestine approached its climax: the attack on Jerusalem. The city was swollen with refugees, who further taxed its already limited supplies of food and water. Torn by warring factions and terrorized by brigands, there was little order to the life of the city and no proper preparations were made for its defense.

A Jewish coin minted in Jerusalem during the revolt of A.D. 66–70. The three pomegranates seem to have no symbolic significance; the letters in archaic Hebrew read, "Jerusalem the Holy."

their own opportunity in the bickerings of those who should have kept them in check; until, glutted with the wrongs which they had done to men, they transferred their insolence to the Deity and with polluted feet invaded the sanctuary.

(151) An insurrection of the populace was at length pending, instigated by Ananus, the senior of the chief priests, a man of profound sanity, who might possibly have saved the city, had he escaped the conspirators' hands. At this threat these wretches converted the temple of God into their fortress and refuge from any outbreak of (152) popular violence, and made the Holy Place the headquarters of their (153) tyranny. To these horrors was added a spice of mockery more galling than their actions. For, to test the abject submission of the populace and make trial of their own strength, they essayed to appoint the high (154) priests by lot, although, as we have stated, the succession was hereditary. As pretext for this scheme they adduced ancient custom, asserting that in old days the high priesthood had been determined by lot; but in reality their action was the abrogation of established practice and a trick to make themselves supreme by getting these appointments into their own hands.

(155) They accordingly summoned one of the highpriestly clans, called Eniachin, and cast lots for a high priest. By chance the lot fell to one who proved a signal illustration of their depravity; he was an individual named Phanni, son of Samuel, of the village of Aphthia, a man who not only was not descended from high priests, but was such a clown that he scarcely knew what the high priesthood meant. (156) At any rate they dragged their reluctant victim out of the country and, dressing him up for his assumed part, as on the stage, put the sacred vestments upon him and instructed him how to act in keeping with (157) the occasion. To them this monstrous impiety was a subject for jesting and sport, but the other priests, beholding from a distance this mockery of their law, could not restrain their tears and bemoaned the degradation of the sacred honours.

(158) This latest outrage was more than the people could stand, and as if for the overthrow of a despotism one and all were now roused. (159) For their leaders of outstanding reputation, such as Gorion, son of Joseph, and Symeon, son of Gamaliel, by public addresses to the whole assembly and by private visits to individuals, urged them to delay no longer to punish these wreckers of liberty and purge the sanctuary of its bloodstained polluters. Their efforts were supported by the most (160) eminent of the high priests, Jesus,[2] son of Gamalas, and Ananus, son of Ananus, who at their meetings vehemently upbraided the people for (161) their apathy and incited them against the Zealots; for so these miscreants called themselves, as though they were zealous in the cause of virtue and not for vice in its basest and most extravagant form.

---

[2]Jesus is a rough transliteration of the Greek, Iēsous, which is in turn a transliteration of the Hebrew *Yeshua*, or *Yehoshua*, which means "Yahweh will save." The name was very common among Jews, although it is best known today obviously because of Jesus of Nazareth.

VI: 193–200

(193) Meanwhile,[3] the victims perishing of famine throughout the city were dropping in countless numbers and enduring suffering (194) indescribable. In every house, the appearance anywhere of but a shadow of food was a signal for war, and the dearest of relatives fell to blows, snatching from each other the pitiful supports of life. The (195) very dying were not credited as in want; nay, even those expiring were searched by the brigands, lest any should be concealing food beneath a fold of his garment and feigning death. Gaping with hunger, (196) like mad dogs, these ruffians went staggering and reeling along, battering upon the doors in the manner of drunken men, and in their perplexity bursting into the same house twice or thrice within a single (197) hour. Necessity drove the victims to gnaw anything, and objects which even the filthiest of brute beasts would reject they condescended to collect and eat: thus in the end they abstained not from belts and shoes and stripped off and chewed the very leather of their bucklers. (198) Others devoured tufts of withered grass: indeed some collectors of stalks sold a trifling quantity for four Attic drachmas. But why tell (199) of the shameless resort to inanimate articles of food induced by the famine, seeing that I am here about to describe an act unparalleled in the history whether of Greeks or barbarians, and as horrible to relate (200) as it is incredible to hear? For my part, for fear that posterity might suspect me of monstrous fabrication, I would gladly have omitted this tragedy, had I not innumerable witnesses among my contemporaries. Moreover, it would be a poor compliment that I should pay my country in suppressing the narrative of the woes which she actually endured.

JEWISH WARS: VI: 271–280

(271) While the temple blazed,[4] the victors plundered everything that fell in their way and slaughtered wholesale all who were caught. No pity was shown for age, no reverence for rank; children and greybeards, laity and priests alike were massacred; every class was pursued and encompassed in the grasp of war, whether suppliants for mercy or offering (272) resistance. The roar of the flames streaming far and wide mingled with the groans of the falling victims; and, owing to the height of the hill and the mass of the burning pile, one

---

[3]By A.D. 70 the Romans under Titus had surrounded Jerusalem with armies and were in process of constructing a circumvallation or encompassing wall to prevent the besieged Jews in the city from escaping. In spite of great acts of bravery on the part of the besieged, who sapped the Roman earthworks and attacked the Roman camps during the night, their plight was hopeless, as Josephus told them in lengthy harangues shouted up to the Jews gathered at the top of the city's fortified walls.

[4]Finally in late August of A.D. 70 the walls were breached and the temple complex itself set afire. Josephus claims that this was done by the Jewish defenders, but his view likely reflects his pro-Roman apologetic rather than the facts.

would have thought that the whole city was ablaze. And then the din —nothing more deafening or appalling could be conceived than that. There were the war-cries of (273) the Roman legions sweeping onward in mass, the howls of the rebels encircled by fire and sword, the rush of the people who, cut off above, fled panic-stricken only to fall into the arms of the foe, and their shrieks as they met their fate. With the cries on the hill were blended (274) those of the multitude in the city below; and now many who were emaciated and tongue-tied from starvation, when they beheld the sanctuary on fire, gathered strength once more for lamentations and wailing. Peraea and the surrounding mountains contributed their echoes, deepening (275) the din. But yet more awful than the uproar were the sufferings. You would indeed have thought that the temple-hill was boiling over from its base, being everywhere one mass of flame, but yet the stream of blood was more copious than the flames and the slain more numerous than (276) the slayers. For the ground was nowhere visible through the corpses; but the soldiers had to clamber over heaps of bodies in pursuit of the (277) fugitives. The brigand crowd succeeded in pushing through the Romans and with difficulty forcing their way into the outer court of the temple, and thence to the city; while what was left of the populace took refuge on the outer portico. Of the priests some, at the first, tore up the (278) spikes from the sanctuary, with their leaden sockets, and hurled them at the Romans, but afterwards, finding their efforts unavailing (279) and the flames breaking out against them, they retired to the wall, which was eight cubits broad, and there remained. Two persons of (280) distinction, however, having the choice of saving their lives by going over to the Romans or of holding out and sharing the fortune of the rest, plunged into the fire and were consumed with the temple, namely Meirus, son of Belgas, and Josephus, son of Dalaeus.

JEWISH WARS: VI:288–300

(288) (3) Thus it was that the wretched people were deluded at that time by charlatans and pretended messengers of the deity; while they neither heeded nor believed in the manifest portents that foretold the coming desolation, but, as if thunderstruck and bereft of eyes and mind, disregarded the plain warnings of God. So it was when a star, (289) resembling a sword, stood over the city, and a comet which continued for a year. So again when, before the revolt and the commotion that (290) led to war, at the time when the people were assembling for the feast of unleavened bread, on the eighth of the month Xanthicus,[5] at the ninth hour of the night, so brilliant a light shone round the altar and the sanctuary that it seemed to be broad daylight; and this continued for (291) half an hour. By the inexperienced this was regarded as a good omen, (292) but by the sacred scribes it was at once interpreted in accordance with after-events. At that same feast a cow that had been brought by (293) someone for sacrifice gave birth to a lamb in the midst of the court of the temple; moreover, the east-

---

[5] Probably April.

ern gate of the inner court—it was of brass and very massive, and, when closed towards evening, could scarcely be moved by twenty men; fastened with iron-bound bars, it had bolts which (294) were sunk to a great depth into a threshold consisting of a solid block of stone—this gate was observed at the sixth hour of the night to have opened of its own accord. The watchmen of the temple ran and (295) reported the matter to the captain, and he came up and with difficulty succeeded in shutting it. This again to the uninitiated seemed the best of omens, as they supposed that God had opened to them the gate of blessings; but the learned understood that the security of the temple (296) was dissolving of its own accord and that the opening of the gate meant a present to the enemy, interpreting the portent in their own minds as indicative of coming desolation. Again, not many days after (297) the festival, on the twenty-first of the month Artemisium, there appeared a miraculous phenomenon, passing belief. Indeed, what I am (298) about to relate would, I imagine, have been deemed a fable, were it not for the narratives of eyewitnesses and for the subsequent calamities (299) which deserved to be so signalized. For before sunset throughout all parts of the country chariots were seen in the air and armed battalions hurtling through the clouds and en-compassing the cities. Moreover, at the feast which is called Pentecost, the priests on entering the inner (300) court of the temple by night, as their custom was in the discharge of their ministrations, reported that they were conscious, first of a commotion and a din, and after that of a voice as of a host, "We are departing hence."

But a further portent was even more alarming. Four years before the war, when the city was enjoying profound peace and prosperity, there came to the feast at which it is the custom of all Jews to erect tabernacles to God, one Jesus, son of Ananias, a rude peasant, who, standing in the temple, suddenly began to cry out, "A voice from the east, a voice from the west, a voice from the four winds; a voice against Jerusalem and the sanctuary, a voice against the bridegroom and the bride, a voice against all the people."

JEWISH WARS: VI:403–419

(403) The Romans, now[6] masters of the walls, planted their stand-ards on the towers, and with clapping of hands and jubilation raised a paean in honour of their victory. They had found the end of the war a much lighter task than the beginning; indeed, they could hardly believe that they had surmounted the last wall without bloodshed, and, seeing none to oppose them, were truly perplexed. Pouring into the alleys, swords (404) in hand, they massacred indiscriminately all whom they met, and burnt the houses with all who had taken refuge within. Often in the course (405) of their raids, on entering the houses

---

[6]By late September the upper part of the city was in Roman hands and Jerusalem was entirely subdued. The remaining rebels fled, and with their leaders took refuge in the Herodian fortresses of Machaerus east of the Dead Sea and at Masada near the southwestern shore. Josephus gives details of the fall of these last strongholds of the insurrectionists in Book VII of the *Jewish Wars*.

they would find whole families dead and the rooms filled with the victims of the famine, and then shuddering at the sight, retire empty-handed. Yet, while they (406) pitied those who had thus perished, they had no similar feelings for the living, but, running everyone through who fell in their way, they choked the alleys with corpses and deluged the whole city with blood, insomuch that many of the fires were extinguished by the gory stream. (407) Towards evening they ceased slaughtering, but when night fell the fire gained the mastery, and the dawn of the eighth day of the month Gorpiaeus[7] broke upon Jerusalem in flames—a city which had suffered such calamities (408) during the siege, that, had she from her foundation enjoyed an equal share of blessings, she would have been thought unquestionably enviable; a city undeserving, moreover, of these great misfortunes on any other ground, save that she produced a generation such as that which caused her overthrow.

(409) (ix.1) Titus, on entering the town, was amazed at its strength,

---

[7]September 26, A.D. 70.

Stones fallen from the foundation of the temple in Jerusalem lying on the street south of the temple. Still in position on the right are the enormous dressed stones from the lower walls of the temple. The largest of these, visible in the second course from the bottom, measures more than thirty feet in length, three feet in height, and six feet in breadth. These are the "wonderful stones" mentioned in Mark 13:1.

but chiefly at the towers, which the tyrants, in their infatuation, had (410) abandoned. Indeed, when he beheld their solid lofty mass, the magnitude of each block and the accuracy of the joinings, and marked how great was (411) their breadth, how vast their height, "God indeed," he exclaimed, "has been with us in the war. God it was who brought down the Jews (412) from these strongholds; for what power have human hands or engines against these towers?" He made many similar observations to his friends at that time, when he also liberated all prisoners of the tyrants who were found in the forts. And when, at a later period, he demolished (413) the rest of the city and razed the walls he left these towers as a memorial of his attendant fortune, to whose co-operation he owed his conquest of defences which defied assault.

(414) Since the soldiers were now growing weary of slaughter, though numerous survivors still came to light, Caesar issued orders to kill only those who were found in arms and offered resistance, and to (415) make prisoners of the rest. The troops, in addition to those specified in their instructions, slew the old and feeble; while those in the prime of life and serviceable they drove together into the temple and shut them up in the court of the women. Caesar appointed one of his freedmen (416) as their guard, and his friend Fronto to adjudicate upon the lot (417) appropriate to each. Fronto put to death all the seditious and brigands, information being given by them against each other; he selected (418) the tallest and most handsome of the youth and reserved them for the triumph; of the rest, those over seventeen years of age he sent in chains to the works in Egypt, while multitudes were presented by Titus to the various provinces, to be destroyed in the theatres by the sword (419) or by wild beasts; those under seventeen were sold. During the days spent by Fronto over this scrutiny, eleven thousand of the prisoners perished from starvation, partly owing to their jailers' hatred, who denied them food, partly their own refusal of it when offered; moreover, for so vast a multitude even corn failed.

Josephus took up residence in Rome as an army pensioner, as we learn from his autobiography. It is likely that he was a witness of the triumph accorded Titus on his return from the suppression of the Jewish revolt. Titus, who had remained in Palestine to complete the subjugation of the rebellious Jews when his father had returned to Rome to be acclaimed as emperor, had now gone back for the triumphal procession offered him by the grateful Senate and Roman people, as was the custom for receiving victors returning from major conflicts. The sacred objects from the temple that were carried in the triumph are depicted on the reliefs still preserved (though mutilated) on the inner faces of Titus' triumphal arch in the Roman forum.

As may be inferred from the gospels, especially Mark 13 and parallels in MT 24–25 and LK 21, the early Christians regarded the destruction of

Jerusalem as a sign of God's judgment on the Jews for the rejection of Jesus. It is likely that some Christians thought that the fall of the city was the final sign that the New Age was about to arrive.

JEWISH WARS: VII:132–152

(132) It is impossible adequately to describe the multitude of those spectacles and their magnificence under every conceivable aspect, whether in works of art or diversity of riches or natural rarities; for (133) almost all the objects which men who have ever been blessed by fortune have acquired one by one—the wonderful and precious productions of various nations—by their collective exhibition on that day displayed (134) the majesty of the Roman empire. Silver and gold and ivory in masses, wrought into all manner of forms, might be seen, not as if carried in procession, but flowing, so to speak, like a river; here were tapestries borne along, some of the rarest purple, others embroidered by Babylonian art with perfect portraiture; transparent gems, some set in golden (135) crowns, some in other fashions, swept by in such profusion as to correct our erroneous supposition that any of them was rare. Then, too, there were carried images of their gods, of marvellous size and no mean (136) craftsmanship, and of these not one but was of some rich material. Beasts of many species were led along all caparisoned with appropriate trappings. The numerous attendants conducting each group of animals (137) were decked in garments of true purple dye, interwoven with gold; while those selected to take part in the pageant itself had about them choice ornaments of amazing richness. Moreover, even among the mob of (138) captives, none was to be seen unadorned, the variety and beauty of their dresses concealing from view any unsightliness arising from bodily disfigurement.

(139) But nothing in the procession excited so much astonishment as the structure of the moving stages; indeed, their massiveness afforded (140) ground for alarm and misgiving as to their stability, many of them being three or four stories high, while the magnificence of the fabric was a source at once of delight and amazement. For many were (141) enveloped in tapestries interwoven with gold, and all had a framework of gold and wrought ivory. The war was shown by numerous (142) representations, in separate sections, affording a very vivid picture (143) of its episodes. Here was to be seen a prosperous country devastated, there whole battalions of the enemy slaughtered; here a party in flight, there others led into captivity; walls of surpassing compass demolished by engines, strong fortresses overpowered, cities with well-manned (144) defences completely mastered and an army pouring within the ramparts, an area all deluged with blood, the hands of those incapable of resistance raised in supplication, temples set on fire, houses pulled down over (145) their owners' heads, and, after general desolation and woe, rivers flowing, not over a cultivated land, nor supplying drink to man and beast, but across a country still on every side in flames. For to such sufferings were the Jews destined when they plunged into the war; and (146) the art and magnificent workmanship of these structures now portrayed the inci-

This relief from the inner face of the Arch of Titus in Rome was placed there to mark his triumphal return from suppression of the Jewish Revolt of A.D. 66–70, and shows the sacred temple vessels from Jerusalem being carried in procession; the seven-branched lamp-stand, the sacred trumpets, and the table for the sacred bread. (Source: Art Reference Bureau)

dents to those who had not witnessed them, as though they were (147) happening before their eyes. On each of the stages was stationed the general of one of the captured cities in the attitude in which he was taken. A number of ships also followed.

(148) The spoils in general were borne in promiscuous heaps; but conspicuous above all stood out those captured in the temple at Jerusalem. These consisted of a golden table, many talents in weight, and a lampstand, likewise made of gold, but constructed on a different pattern from (149) those which we use in ordinary life. Affixed to a pedestal was a central shaft, from which there extended slender branches, arranged trident-fashion, a wrought lamp being attached to the extremity of each branch; of these there were seven, indicating the honour paid to that (150) number among the Jews. After these, and last of all the spoils, (151) was carried a copy of the Jewish Law. Then followed a large party carrying images of victory, all made of ivory and gold. Behind them (152) drove Vespasian, followed by Titus; while Domitian rode beside them, in magnificent apparel and mounted on a steed that was itself a sight.

ROMAN POLICY IN THE EASTERN PROVINCES

The sources brought together here are of four different types and from four different times. But they have in common the exercise of Roman power in the eastern empire. The first consists of excerpts from Josephus' *Antiquities*, in which we learn how Antipater, the Idumean, secured his place as king over the Jews, even though he was not a Jew, and how Caligula decreed special tax regulations for the Jews in order to enable them to meet their obligations to Rome while at the same time to obey their own laws and to maintain their cultic system. The second group of excerpts is from Philo of Alexandria, from a treatise describing his experiences as head of a delegation that visited Rome to plead with the emperor Gaius Caligula (ruled A.D. 37–41) not to pursue policies that were in direct conflict with the laws and sensibilities of his Jewish subjects in Alexandria and Palestine.

The excerpts in the third section, also from Philo's treatise, deal with a decree according to which a provincial legislative body in Asia Minor passed a decree honoring the emperor Augustus (ruled 30 B.C.–14 A.D.) as a divine savior. When Caligula claimed later that he was a god, the growing incompatiblity of both the Jewish and Christian religions with this idea eventually led to hostility between the young Christian church and the empire, as is reflected in the fourth section of excerpts, the letter of Pliny the Younger, Roman governor in the Black Sea provinces of Bithynia and Pontus, to his emperor Trajan (ruled A.D. 98–117) and Trajan's reply.

Josephus, Antiquities

ANTIQUITIES: XIV: 156–162

(156) Now when Caesar[1] had settled the affairs of Syria, he sailed away. And Antipater,[2] after escorting Caesar out of Syria, returned to Judea and at once raised again the wall which had been demolished by Pompey, and going about the country suppressed disorders therein by both (157) threatening and advising the people to remain quiet. For, he said, those who were on the side of Hyrcanus[3] would be left in peace and could live undisturbed in the enjoyment of their own possessions, but if they clung to the hope of achieving something by revolution and were counting on any gains therefrom, they would have

---

[1] This was Julius Caesar, who was then (47 B.C.) in the process of conquering the eastern Mediterranean and arranging for his clients to control the territories his troops had conquered.

[2] Antipater was an Idumean opportunist whose skills in diplomacy, political dealings, warfare, and administration were superb. All these capacities were inherited in a heightened degree by his more famous son, Herod.

[3] Hyrcanus, last of the priests of the Hasmonean family. Through cooperation and marriage with the descendants of the Hasmoneans, Antipas and Herod, who were Idumeans (Semitic but not Jewish) sought to give legitimacy to their own non-Jewish family claims to royal leadership in Palestine.

in him a master in place of a king, and in the Romans and Caesar bitter enemies in place of rulers. For they would not allow any man to be removed from office whom they themselves had placed therein. Through such words he restored order throughout the country by his own efforts.

(158) But as he saw that Hyrcanus was dull and sluggish, he appointed his eldest son Phasael governor of Jerusalem and the surrounding region, and entrusted Galilee to his second son Herod, who was still quite young; (159) he was, in fact, only fifteen years old. But his youth in no way hindered him, and being a young man of high spirit, he quickly found an opportunity for showing his prowess. For on learning that Ezekias, a bandit leader, was overrunning the borders of Syria with a large troop, he caught and killed him and many of the bandits with him. This (160) achievement of his was greatly admired by the Syrians, for he had cleared their country of a gang of bandits of whom they longed to be rid. And so they sang his praises for this deed throughout their villages and cities, saying that he had given them peace and the secure enjoyment of their possessions. And through this action he became known to Sextus Caesar, a kinsman of the great Caesar and governor of (161) Syria. Thereupon the desire to emulate Herod's achievements seized His brother Phasael, and being moved by the thought of the reputation Herod had won, he was ambitious not to be behind him in achieving like fame; and so he made the inhabitants of Jerusalem feel very friendly toward him, and though he kept the city under his own rule, he did not show any lack of discretion in governing it or abuse his authority. (162) This situation made it possible for Antipater to receive from the nation the respect shown a king and such honour as might be enjoyed by one who is an absolute master. With all this glory, however, he did not, as so often seems to happen, in any way alter his friendship and loyalty to Hyrcanus.

ANTIQUITIES: XIV: 202–204

(202) Gaius Caesar,[4] Imperator for the second time, has ruled that they shall pay a tax for the city of Jerusalem, Joppa excluded, every year except in the seventh year, which they call the sabbatical year, because in this time they neither take fruit from the trees nor do they (203) sow. And that in the second year they shall pay the tribute at Sidon, consisting of one-fourth of the produce sown, and in addition, they shall also pay tithes to Hyrcanus and his sons, just as they paid to their forefathers. And that no one, whether magistrate or promagistrate, praetor or legate, shall raise auxiliary troops in the (204) territories of the Jews, nor shall soldiers be allowed to exact money from them, whether for winter quarters or on any other pretext, but they shall be free from all molestation. And whatever they may here-

---

[4]Gaius Caesar, better known by his nickname, Caligula (Little Boot), was emperor briefly from 37–41 A.D. Spoiled as a child by the army, his rule was arbitrary and ended in his madness. This decree in behalf of the Jews, however, was eminently sane, and shows how eager Rome was to make special concessions to the Jews.

after acquire or buy or possess or have assigned to them, all these they shall keep.

ANTIQUITIES: XIV:265–267

(265) Now there are many other such decrees, passed by the Senate and the Imperators of the Romans, relating to Hyrcanus and our nation, as well as resolutions of cities and rescripts of provincial governors in reply to letters on the subject of our rights, all of which those who will read our work without malice will find it possible to take on faith from the documents we have cited. For since we have furnished (266) clear and visible proofs of our friendship with the Romans, indicating those decrees engraved on bronze pillars and tablets which remain to this day and will continue to remain in the Capitol, I have refrained from citing them all as being both superfluous and disagreeable; for I cannot suppose that anyone is so stupid that he will actually refuse (267) to believe the statements about the friendliness of the Romans towards us, when they have demonstrated this in a good many decrees relating to us, or will not admit that we are making truthful statements on the basis of the examples we have given. And herein we have set forth our friendship and alliance with the Romans in those times.

PHILO OF ALEXANDRIA, Ad Gaium:

Pleas to Caligula

PP. 76–80

People say that at the beginning of the mental derangement [Gaius] used the following argument: "The keepers of the animals, oxherds, goatherds, and shepherds, are not themselves oxen or goats or sheep, but human beings, who have been given a higher destiny and condition; in the same way one must suppose that I, who am the herdsman of the noblest herd, the human race, am a superior being, above the human plane and endowed with a higher and more divine destiny." Having impressed this idea on his mind, the fool began to carry a fantasy about with him, believing it to be an absolute truth. Then, when once his courage had risen and he had risked introduction of this blasphemous deification of himself to the masses, he tried to act in an appropriate and consistent way and advanced little by little to the top as if up a ladder. He began to equate himself with the first so-called demi-gods, Dionysus, Heracles, and the Dioscuri, making a mockery of Trophonius, Amphiareus, Amphilochus, and the rest, oracles, rites, and all, when he compared their powers with his own. Then, as in a theatre, he put on first one costume and then another, sometimes a lion-skin and club, both gilded, when he was arrayed as Heracles, and sometimes a cap on his head, when he dressed up as the Dioscuri; at other times he dressed up as Dionysus with ivy, thyrsus, and fawn-skins. He resolved to differ from the demi-gods in that, whereas each of them had his own honors and did not lay claim to those which the others shared, his jealous greed appropriated the honors of all of them alike, or rather, appropriated the demi-gods themselves.

PP. 93–97

Gaius' madness, his wild and frenzied insanity, reached such a pitch that he went beyond the demi-gods and began to climb higher and to go in for the worship paid to the greater gods,[1] Hermes, Apollo, and Ares, who are supposed to be of divine parentage on both sides. It was the worship due to Hermes first. He dressed up with herald's staff, sandals, and cloak, displaying order amid disorder, consistency amid confusion, and reason amid mental derangement. Then, when he saw fit, he discarded these attributes and changed his appearance and dress, to those of Apollo. He wore a radiate crown, grasped a bow and arrows in his left hand, and held out the Graces in his right hand, as if it were correct to have good things ready at hand to proffer and to let them hold the superior position, on the right, while subordinating punishments and assigning the inferior position, on the left, to them. Well-trained choirs at once took up their positions, singing paeans to him—choirs which had shortly before been calling him Bacchus, Evaeus, and Lyaeus, and chanting hymns in his honor, when he assumed the costume of Dionysus. Often he would put on a breastplate and march forth sword in hand with helmet and shield, and be hailed as Ares.[2] On either side of him marched the attendants of this new Ares, a rabble of murderers and executions, who would undertake despicable services for him when he was in a murderous frame of mind and thirsted for human blood.

PP. 115–116

It was only of the Jews that Gaius was suspicious, on the grounds that they were the only people who deliberately opposed him and had been taught from their very cradles, as it were, by their parents, tutors, and teachers and—more than that—by their holy Laws and even by their unwritten customs, to believe that the Father and Creator of the universe is one God. All other men, women, cities, nations, countries, and regions of the world—I can say almost the whole inhabited earth—although they deplored what was happening, flattered Gaius none the less, glorifying him more than was reasonable, and increasing his vanity. Some people even introduced into Italy the barbaric custom of *proskunesis* [that is, prostrating oneself before a ruler], and thus debased the nobility of Roman freedom.

---

[1]The Romans, like the Greeks, distinguished between deified men—usually actual heroes, but including also legendary figures—and the great gods. The former were venerated, but worship was offered to the latter. Gaius was at first content to have himself venerated as one of the deified heroes, but later aspired to be included among the Olympian deities.

[2]Ares, or Mars, the god of war.

PP. 118–127

... The change being effected was not a small one but an absolutely fundamental one, namely, the apparent transformation of the created, destructible nature of man into the uncreated, indestructible nature of God, which the Jewish nation judged to be the most horrible of blasphemies; for God would change into man sooner than man into God. This was quite apart from the acceptance of the other evils of unbelief in, and ingratitude towards, the Benefactor of the whole world, Who by His own might gives good things in lavish abundance to all parts of his universe.

Accordingly, total and truceless war was waged against the Jewish nation. What heavier burden could a slave have than a hostile owner? Subjects are the slaves of an emperor, and even if this was not the case with Gaius' predecessors, because they rule reasonably and legally, yet it was the case under Gaius, who had cut all humanity out of his heart and made a cult of illegality; for he regarded himself as the law, and broke the laws of the lawgivers of every country, as if they were empty words. So we were enrolled not simply as slaves but as the lowest of slaves, when the Emperor turned into a tyrant.

When the promiscuous and unruly Alexandrian mob discovered this, it supposed that a most opportune moment had come its way and attacked us. It unmasked the hatred which had long been smoldering and threw everything into chaos and confusion. As if we had been surrendered by the Emperor to sufferings admitted to be of the severest kind or had been defeated in war, they attacked us with insane and bestial fury. They invaded our homes and drove out the householders, wives and children and all, so as to leave the houses unoccupied. They no longer waited for the darkness of night in fear of arrest, like burglars, to steal our furniture and treasures, but they carried them off openly in broad daylight, and displayed them to those they met, as people who have inherited things or bought them from their owners. If several people agreed to join forces in plunder, they divided out their loot in the middle of the marketplace, often before the eyes of its real owners, jeering and laughing as they did so. This was terrible in itself, of course. Wealthy men became paupers and well-to-do people penniless, suddenly deprived of hearth and home although they were innocent of any crime, and driven out of their houses as exiles, to live in the open air day and night and die either of sunstroke or of exposure by night. Yet this is easier reading than what follows. For the Greeks joined in driving many thousands of men, women, and children out of the whole city into a very small part of it, like sheep or cattle into a pen. They supposed that within a few days they would find piles of bodies of Jews, who had died either of starvation through lack of the necessities of life, since they had no forewarning of this sudden calamity to enable them to make suitable provision against it, or of overcrowding or suffocation. Their quarters were extremely cramped, and moreover the surrounding air became foul and surrendered its life-giving qualities to the respirations, or rather, the gasps of the dying. So, no longer able to stand the lack of space, the Jews overflowed on to the desert, the shores, the cemeteries, longing to breathe pure, healthy air. Any who had already been caught in other parts of the city, or who visited it from the country in ignorance of the calamities which had descended upon us, experienced sufferings of every kind. They were stoned, or wounded with tiles, or battered to death with branches of ilex or oak on the most vulnerable parts of their bodies, especially their heads.

PP. 132–134

The prefect of the country, who could have put an end to this mob-rule single-handed in an hour had he chosen to, pretended not to see and hear what he did see and hear, but allowed the Greeks to make war without restraint and so shattered the peace of the city. They consequently became still more excited and rushed headlong into outrageous plots of even greater audacity. Assembling enormous hordes together, they attacked the synagogues, of which there are many in each section of the city. Some they smashed, some they rased to the ground, and others they set on fire and burned, giving no thought even to the adjacent houses in their madness and frenzied insanity. For nothing is swifter than fire when it gets plenty of fuel. I say nothing about the simultaneous destruction and burning of the objects set up in honor of the emperor—gilded shields and crowns, monuments, and inscriptions—which should have made the Greeks keep their hands off everything else also. But they derived confidence from the fact that they had no punishment to fear from Gaius, who, as they well knew, felt an indescribable hatred for the Jews. . . .

Philo of Alexandria, Ad Gaium:

Augustus as Divine Savior

PP. 143–151

What about the nature of the Emperor whose every virtue outshone human nature, who through the greatness of his imperial rule and of his valor alike became the first to bear the title "Augustus," who did not receive the title by inheritance from his family as a part of a legacy, but was himself the source of the reverence paid to his successors also? What about the man who pitted himself against the general confusion and chaos as soon as he took charge of public affairs? For islands were struggling for supremacy against continents and continents against islands, with the Romans of the greatest distinction in public life as their generals and leaders. Again, large parts of the world were battling for mastery of the empire, Asia against Europe and Europe against Asia; European nations and Asian nations from the ends of the earth had risen up and were engaged in grim warfare, fighting with armies and fleets on every land and sea, so that almost the whole human race would have been destroyed in internecine conflict and disappeared completely, had it not been for one man, one *princeps*, Augustus, who deserves the title of "Averter of Evil." This is the Caesar who lulled the storms which were crashing everywhere, who healed the sicknesses common to Greeks and barbarians alike, which descended from the South and East and swept across to the West and North, sowing misery in the lands and seas in between. This is he who not merely loosened but broke the fetters which had confined and oppressed the world. This is he who both ended the wars which were before everyone's eyes and those which were going on out of sight as a result of the attacks of pirates. This is he who cleared the sea of pirate-ships and filled it with merchant-ships. This is he who set every city again at liberty, who reduced disorder to order, who civilized all the unfriendly, savage tribes and brought them into harmony with each other, who enlarged Greece with many other Greek lands, and who hellenized the most important parts of the barbarian world. This is he who safeguarded peace, gave each man his due, distributed his favors widely without stint, and never in his whole life kept any blessing or advantage back.

During the forty years of this wonderful benefactor's rule over Egypt, the Alexandrians neglected him and did not make a single dedication on his behalf in the synagogues—neither a statue nor a wooden image nor a painting. Yet if new and exceptional honors had been voted to anyone, it should have been appropriate in his case. This was not merely because he founded and originated the Augustan dynasty, nor because he was the first and greatest universal benefactor, who ended the rule of many by handing the ship of state over to a single helmsman, namely himself with his remarkable grasp of the science of government, to steer. . . . It was because the whole world voted him honors equal to those of the Olympians. Temples, gateways, vestibules, and colonnades bear witness to this, so that the imposing buildings erected in any city, new or old, are surpassed by the beauty and size of the temples of Caesar, especially in our own Alexandria. There is no other precinct like our so-called "Augusteum," the temple of Caesar, the protector of sailors. . . . The extensive precinct is furnished with colonnades, libraries, banqueting-halls, groves, gateways, open spaces, unroofed enclosures, and everything that makes for lavish decoration. It gives hope of safety to sailors when they set out to sea and when they return.

PP. 155–158

(Augustus) knew that the large district of Rome beyond the Tiber was owned and inhabited by Jews. The majority of them were Roman freedmen. They had been brought to Italy as prisoners of war and manumitted by their owners, and had not been able to alter any of their national customs. Augustus therefore knew that they had synagogues and met in them, especially on the Sabbath, when they receive public instruction in their national philosophy. He also knew that they collected sacred money from their "first-fruits" and sent it up to Jerusalem by the hand of envoys who would offer the sacrifices. But despite this he did not expel them from Rome or deprive them of their Roman citizenship because they remembered their Jewish nationality

also. He introduced no changes into their synagogues, he did not prevent them from meeting for the exposition of the Law, and he raised
no objections to their offering of the "first-fruits." On the contrary, he
showed such reverence for our traditions that he and almost all his
family enriched our Temple with expensive dedications. He gave orders for regular sacrifices of holocausts to be made daily in perpetuity
at his own expense, as an offering to the Most High God. These sacrifices continue to this day, and will continue always as a proof of his
truly imperial character. Moreover, at the monthly distributions in
Rome, when all the people in turn received money or food, he never
deprived the Jews of this bounty, but if the distributions happened
to be made on a Sabbath, when it is forbidden to receive or give anything or to do any of the ordinary things of life in general, especially
commercial life, he instructed the distributors to reserve the Jews'
share of the universal largesse until the next day.

PP. 186–189

While we were considering our case, expecting at any moment to
be summoned into (Gaius') presence, a man came up to us completely
out of breath, his eyes bloodshot and troubled. He drew us aside a
little from the others—there were a few people standing near—and
said, "Have you heard the news?" Then before he could tell us he
broke off in floods of tears. He began again, but broke off a second
and a third time. When we saw this, we were alarmed and begged
him to tell us the business on which he said he had come. "For," we
said, "you surely have not come just to let us witness your weeping.
If your news is worthy of tears, do not indulge in grief on your own.
We are used to disasters by this time." With difficulty and still sob-
bing he managed to say in a choked voice, "Our Temple is gone!
Gaius has given orders for a colossal statue to be set up right inside
the shrine, named after Zeus himself." We were amazed at what he
said and stood rooted to the ground in horror, unable to move. We
stood dumb and helpless on the point of collapse, our whole bodies
unnerved.

PP. 263–268

... When Gaius noticed that (Agrippa[3]) was worried and per-
plexed—he was clever at divining a man's hidden wishes and feelings
from his visible expression—he said, "Are you perplexed, Agrippa? I
will put an end to your perplexity.... Your fine noble countrymen,
the only people in the whole world who do not acknowledge Gaius
as a god, are now apparently courting death by disobedience. When
I gave orders for a statue of Zeus to be set up in the Temple, they

---

[3]This Agrippa (not to be confused with Augustus' aide and son-in-law, who died
in 12 B.C.) was Herod Agrippa I, grandson of Herod the Great. It is he who imprisoned Peter and executed James, the son of Zebedee, according to Acts 12. His own
gruesome death by an avenging angel is reported in Acts 12:20–23. From other
sources we know that he died in A.D. 44.

all collected in a body and trooped out of Jerusalem and the whole country, allegedly in order to make a petition, but in actual fact in order to oppose my commands." Before Gaius had time to add more, Agrippa's anguish of mind made him change color in every possible way; in one moment he became flushed, pale, and livid. He was already shivering from head to foot. Trembling and shuddering convulsed every limb and part of his body. His sinews became limp and slack, and he staggered and finally collapsed and would have fallen, had not some of the bystanders caught him. They carried him home as they were instructed. He was in a coma and conscious of none of the mass of troubles.... As a result, Gaius was even more exasperated, and intensified his hatred for Jews. He said, "If my closest and dearest friend, Agrippa, who is under great obligation to me, is such a slave of his national customs that he cannot bear to hear a word spoken against them but faints and almost dies, what must one expect of the other Jews, who have no powerful incentive for acting otherwise?"

In the course of describing Jewish resistance to offering divine honors to the emperor and to any idolotrous practice performed by the Roman state as it influenced Jews, Philo mentions the actions of the Roman ruler who figures most prominently in the narrative of the gospels: Pontius Pilate, who was procurator of Judea from A.D. 26 to 36. It was, of course, his ruthlessness in suppressing the beginning of a revolt, or even any action by Jews which might have led to a revolt that brought about the execution of Jesus.

PP. 299–305

... Pilate[4] was an official who had been appointed procurator of Judea. With the intention of annoying the Jews rather than of honoring Tiberius, he set up gilded shields in Herod's palace in the Holy City. They bore no figure and nothing else that was forbidden, but only the briefest possible inscription, which stated two things—the name of the dedicator and that of the person in whose honor the dedication was made. But when the Jews at large learnt of his action, which was indeed already widely known, they chose as their spokesman the king's four sons, who enjoyed rank and prestige equal to that of kings, his other descendants, and their own officials, and besought Pilate to undo his innovation in the shape of the shields, and not to violate their native customs, which had hitherto been invariably preserved inviolate by kings and emperors alike. When Pilate, who was a man of inflexible, stubborn, and cruel disposition, obstinately re-

---

[4]Pontius Pilate was appointed procurator of Judea in A.D. 26 and held office until 36. As procurator, he was directly responsible to the emperor himself, rather than to the legate or governor of Syria, the larger province of which Judea was geographically a part. By both Philo and Josephus, Pilate is portrayed as arbitrary and ruthless in suppressing what he thought to be incipient revolts on the part of the Jews.

fused, they shouted, "Do not cause a revolt! Do not cause a not break the peace! Disrespect done to our ancient laws brings no honor to the emperor. Do not make Tiberius an excuse for insulting our nation. He does not want any of our traditions done away with. If you say that he does, show us some decree or letter or something of the sort, so that we may cease troubling you and appeal to our master by means of an embassy." This last remark exasperated Pilate most of all, for he was afraid that if they really sent an embassy, they would bring accusations against the rest of his administration as well, specifying in detail his venality, his violence, his thefts, his assaults, his abusive behavior, his frequent executions of untried prisoners, and his endless savage ferocity. . . . When the Jewish officials . . . realized that Pilate was regretting what he had done, although he did not wish to show it, they wrote a letter to Tiberius, pleading their cause as forcibly as they could. What words, what threats Tiberius uttered against Pilate when he read it! It would be superfluous to describe his anger, since his reaction speaks for itself. For immediately, without even waiting until the next day, he wrote to Pilate, reproaching and rebuking him a thousand times for his new-fangled audacity and telling him to remove the shields at once and have them taken from the capital to the coastal city of Caesarea . . . to be dedicated in the Temple of Augustus. In this way both the honor of the Emperor and the traditional policy regarding Jerusalem were alike preserved.

Pliny's Letter to the Emperor Trajan;[1]

Trajan's Reply

XCVI

It is a rule, Sir, which I inviolably observe, to refer myself to you in all my doubts; for who is more capable of guiding my uncertainty or informing my ignorance? Having never been present at any trials of the Christians, I am unacquainted with the method and limits to be observed either in examining or punishing them. Whether any difference is to be made on account of age, or no distinction allowed between the youngest and the adult; whether repentance admits to a pardon, or if a man has been once a Christian it avails him nothing to recant; whether the mere profession of Christianity, albeit without crimes, or only the crimes associated therewith are punishable—in all these points I am greatly doubtful.

In the meanwhile, the method I have observed towards those who have been denounced to me as Christians is this: I interrogated them whether they were Christians; if they confessed it I repeated the question twice again, adding the threat of capital punishment; if they still

---

[1]Trajan was emperor from 98 to 117, during which time there were revolts among the Jews in Egypt and Cyrene, and the threat of invasion from the east by the Parthians was very real. Any suspicion of secret societies, especially with political overtones, would invite swift reprisals at the hand of the Roman authorities.

persevered, I ordered them to be executed. For whatever the nature of their creed might be, I could at least feel no doubt that contumacy and inflexible obstinacy deserved chastisement. There were others also possessed with the same infatuation, but being citizens of Rome, I directed them to be carried thither.

These accusations spread (as is usually the case) from the mere fact of the matter being investigated and several forms of the mischief came to light. A placard was put up, without any signature, accusing a large number of persons by name. Those who denied they were, or had ever been, Christians, who repeated after me an invocation to the Gods, and offered adoration, with wine and frankincense, to your image, which I had ordered to be brought for that purpose, together with those of the Gods, and who finally cursed Christ—none of which acts, it is said, those who are really Christians can be forced into performing—these I thought it proper to discharge. Others who were named by that informer at first confessed themselves Christians, and then denied it; true, they had been of that persuasion but they had quitted it, some three years, others many years, and a few as much as twenty-five years ago. They all worshipped your statue and the images of the Gods, and cursed Christ.

They affirmed, however, that the whole of their guilt, or their error, was, that they were in the habit of meeting on a certain fixed day before it was light, when they sang in alternate verses a hymn to Christ, as to a god, and bound themselves by a solemn oath, not to do any wicked deeds, but never to commit any fraud, theft or adultery, never to falsify their word, nor deny a trust when they should be called upon to deliver it up; after which it was their custom to separate, and then reassemble to partake of food—but food of an ordinary and innocent kind. Even this practice, however, they had abandoned after the publication of my edict, by which, according to your orders, I had forbidden political associations. I judged it so much the more necessary to extract the real truth, with the assistance of torture, from two female slaves, who were styled *deaconesses*: but I could discover nothing more than depraved and excessive superstition.

I therefore adjourned the proceedings, and betook myself at once to your counsel. For the matter seemed to me well worth referring to you—especially considering the numbers endangered. Persons of all ranks and ages, and of both sexes are, and will be, involved in the prosecution. For this contagious superstition is not confined to the cities only, but has spread through the villages and rural districts; it seems possible, however, to check and cure it. 'Tis certain at least that the temples, which had been almost deserted, begin now to be frequented; and the sacred festivals, after a long general demand for sacrificial animals, which for some time past have met with but few purchasers. From hence it is easy to imagine what multitudes may be reclaimed from this error, if a door be left open to repentance.

xcvii Trajan's Response to Pliny

The method you have pursued, my dear Pliny, in sifting the cases of those denounced to you as Christians is extremely proper. It is not

[Handwritten marginal annotations:]

anon man

If they behaved to normal Roman custom they were released.

What to said they did

This implies Pliny knew the stories about incest and cannibalism

Christianity

Interesting — like w/ Inquisition and Pogroms

possible to lay down any general rule which can be applied as the fixed standard in all cases of this nature.[2] No search should be made for these people; when they are denounced and found guilty they must be punished; with the restriction, however, that when the party denies himself to be a Christian, and shall give proof that he is not (that is, by adoring our Gods) he shall be pardoned on the ground of repentance, even though he may have formerly incurred suspicion. Informations without the accuser's name subscribed must not be admitted in evidence against anyone, as it is introducing a very dangerous precedent, and by no means agreeable to the spirit of the age.

just adore the Gods

no anonymous accusation

---

[2]It is not clear from Trajan's response that the issue had actually arisen before; here he seems reluctant to appeal to precedent. But interpreters of Revelation have linked the words of the hymn in Rev. 4:11, "our Lord and God," with the reported insistence of Domitian (emperor from 81–96) that he be addressed a *dominus et deus* (lord and god), so that it is possible that the issue of divine honors to the emperor had arisen among the churches of Asia Minor decades earlier than the time of Pliny's governorship there.

Religious History

JEWISH RELIGIOUS INSTITUTIONS AND PRACTICES

The two major sources for our knowledge of Jewish institutions in Palestine in the early Christian centuries are Josephus and the Talmud. The Talmud consists of (1) the traditional law of Judaism known as the Mishnah as it developed down to the end of the second century A.D., and (2) the discussions of the law that were attached to Mishnah down to the sixth century. Actually there were two Talmuds, the Palestinian (completed ca. 350, abbreviated T.J.) and the Babylonian (completed ca. 500 A.D., abbreviated T.B.) Of the six main divisions of the Mishnah, the second is called Mo'ed (Festivals). Mo'ed is in turn divided into twelve tractates, of which we are here concerned with two: Pesahim, concerned with Passover offerings, and Megilla, the Scroll of Esther, concerned in part with the institutions of the synagogue. For the description of the temple, we are dependent on Josephus, whose detailed portrait of the temple appears in connection with his narrative of the destruction of Jerusalem by the Romans in A.D. 67–70. The final excerpts, from the letters of Aristeas, describe the legendary origins of the Greek translation of the Hebrew Bible by which it was made available for both Jews and

Gentiles in the lands of the Dispersion at a time when Greek was the universal language.

Passover:

The Pesahim Tractate

It is impossible to determine how many of the regulations set down in the Mishnah were in effect in the first century, or more specifically, in the time of Jesus. The fact that the views of Hillel and Shammai are mentioned, however, suggests that we are dealing with early (late first century B.C.) practices, at least in part.

It may be important that at one of the few places in the New Testament where passover is explicitly mentioned in the narrative—the accounts of the Last Supper in Matthew, Mark, and Luke—neither unleavened bread nor bitter herbs are mentioned. A likely explanaton for this seeming omission is that the final meal of Jesus with his followers was not a passover celebration, but was eaten the night before the passover occurred in the year of Jesus' death. This is implied by some of the gospel tradition (e.g., Luke 22:15–16 in RSV: "I have earnestly desired to eat this passover with you before I suffer; for I tell you I shall not eat it until it is fulfilled in the kingdom of God"), and it is explicitly stated in John 13:1 ("Now before the feast of the Passover . . .").* In any case, the death of Jesus, and hence the meal by which his death was recalled, came to be interpreted in the early church against the background of the Jewish passover tradition, as Paul declares in I Cor. 5:7: "Christ our paschal lamb has been sacrificed for us."

10:1–9

(1) On the eve of Passover, from about the time of the Evening Offering, a man must eat naught until nightfall. Even the poorest in Israel must not eat unless he sits down to table, and they must not give them less than four cups of wine to drink, even if it is from the [Paupers'] Dish.   *MK. 14: 12, 17*

(2) After they have mixed him his first cup, the School of Shammai say: He says the Benediction first over the day and then the Benediction over the wine. And the School of Hillel say: He says the Benediction first over the wine and then the Benediction over the day.   *MK. 14: 22*

(3) When [food] is brought before him he eats it seasoned with lettuce, until he is come to the breaking of bread; they bring before him unleavened bread and lettuce and the *haroseth*, although *haroseth*

---

*For an attempt to explain away the difficulties and to establish that the Last Supper was a passover meal, see Joachim Jeremias, *The Eucharistic Words of Jesus*. rev. ed., New York, Scribner, 1961.

is not a religious obligation. R. Eliezer b. R. Zadok says: It is a religious obligation. And in the Holy City they used to bring before him the body of the Passover-offering.

(4) They then mix him the second cup. And here the son asks his father [and if the son has not enough understanding his father instructs him how to ask], "Why is this night different from other nights? For on other nights we eat seasoned food once, but this night twice; on other nights we eat leavened or unleavened bread, but this night all is unleavened; on other nights we eat flesh roast, stewed, or cooked, but this night all is roast." And according to the understanding of the son his father instructs him. He begins with the disgrace and ends with the glory; and he expounds from *A wandering Aramean was my father* . . . until he finishes the whole section [Deut 26:5 ff].

MK. 14:1

(5) Rabban Gamaliel used to say: Whosoever has not said [the verses concerning] these three things at Passover has not fulfilled his obligation. And these are they: Passover, unleavened bread, and bitter herbs: "Passover"—because God passed over the houses of our fathers in Egypt; "unleavened bread"—because our fathers were redeemed from Egypt; "bitter herbs"—because the Egyptians embittered the lives of our fathers in Egypt. In every generation a man must so regard himself as if he came forth himself out of Egypt, for it is written, *And thou shalt tell thy son in that day saying, It is because of that which the Lord did for me when I came forth out of Egypt.* Therefore are we bound to give thanks to praise, to glorify, to honour, to exalt, to extol, and to bless him who wrought all these wonders for our fathers and for us. He brought us out from bondage to freedom, from sorrow to gladness, and from mourning to a Festival-day, and from darkness to great light, and from servitude to redemption; so let us say before him the Halleluyah.

(6) How far do they recite [the *Hallel*]? The School of Shammai say: To *A joyful mother of children*. And the School of Hillel say: To *A flintstone into a springing well*. And this is concluded with the *Ge'ullah*. R. Tarfon says: "He that redeemed us and redeemed our fathers from Egypt and brought us to this night to eat therein unleavened bread and bitter herbs." But there is no concluding Benediction. R. Akiba adds: "Therefore, O Lord our God and the God of our fathers, bring us in peace to the other set feasts and festivals which are coming to meet us, while we rejoice in the building-up of thy city and are joyful in thy worship; and may we eat there of the sacrifices and of the Passover-offerings whose blood has reached with acceptance the wall of thy Altar, and let us praise thee for our redemption and for the ransoming of our soul. Blessed art thou, O Lord, who hast redeemed Israel!"

MK. 14: 26

(7) After they have mixed for him the third cup he says the Benediction over his meal. [Over] a fourth [cup] he completes the *Hallel* and says after it the Benediction over the song. If he is minded to drink [more] between these cups he may drink; only between the third and the fourth cups he may not drink.

MK. 14: 37, 40

(8) After the Passover meal they should not disperse to join in revelry. If some fell asleep [during the meal] they may eat [again];

but if all fell asleep they may not eat [again]. R. Jose says: If they but dozed they may eat [again]; but if they fell into deep sleep they may not eat [again].

(9) After midnight the Passover-offering renders the hands unclean. The Refuse and Remnant make the hands unclean. If a man has said the Benediction over the Passover-offering it renders needless a Benediction over the Passover-offering. So R. Ishmael. R. Akiba says: "Neither of them renders the other needless."

Hanukah:

Megillat Taanith

Because the festival of Hanukah commemorated an event from Maccabean times—the rededication of the temple, following its desecration by the Seleucids of Syria—it was not described in those writings generally recognized as scripture in Palestine and Babylonia, and therefore had no place in the Mishnah, which was fundamentally an exposition of scripture. The account in full of the rededication itself was preserved in I Maccabees, but the legends are reported in Megillat Taanith, a scroll of fasts which originated in the period before the fall of Jerusalem, but which received its present form in the time of Hadrian (reigned 117–135 A.D.).

> Rabbi Hanina said: The Tabernacle was finished on the twenty-fifth day of Kislev[1] but it was not put together until the first of Nisan, so that this might occur in the month of Exodus. And did that day on this account lose its importance? Nay, for the Hasmoneans instituted on it the Dedication of the restored Holy Temple.
>
> PESIKTA RABBATI, PISKA, 6

> Seven Hanukot are inaugurated with lights: the Creation with moonlight (the first moon after Creation appeared on Friday); the Tabernacle and the Two Temples[2] with the Lightning of the Menorah; the festival of the Hasmoneans with the kindling of the Lamps in their temporary receptacles; the Wall of Jerusalem with the Procession of the Lights; and the Millennium, with the Seven-Fold Light of the Sun.
>
> PESIKTA RABBATI, PISKA, 2, AND
> COMMENTARY OF DAVID LURIA

---

[1]The reference is to the Temple of Solomon, built in the tenth century B.C., and to the rebuilt structure following the return of the Jews from Babylonian exile in the time of Zerubbabel (ca. 525 B.C.). But the temple that the Romans destroyed was the vastly enlarged structure in hellenistic style begun and brought nearly to completion by Herod the Great (37–4 B.C.).

[2]*Kislev* is approximately the equivalent of our month of December.

On the twenty-fifth of Kislev the eight days of Hanukah begin, and on them no funeral orations may be held. Why is this prohibition? Because a miracle occurred when the Hasmoneans came to kindle the Temple lights, and one day's supply of ritually pure oil lasted for eight days. But since the season is named Hanukah, Dedication, and the miracle lasted only seven days, why do we not imitate Moses and Solomon who celebrated the festival of Dedication only seven days? Because the Hasmoneans[3] were occupied with the work of restoration for eight days. Why, then, must we observe the second memorial of Hanukah lights, when other miracles were commemorated only by the prohibition against funeral orations? Because the first act of the Restoration was the kindling of the Temple lights. Though the Menorah was not yet restored, seven spears, coated with tin, were used to fashion a temporary Menorah. And why the third Memorial, the chanting of the Hallel? Because the Israelites had a great deliverance from a mighty enemy.

MEGILLAT TAANIT, 9

The Synagogue:

The Megilla Tractate

The time and circumstances of the origin of the synagogue are not known, but a commonly held view is that the institution originated during the exile of the Jews in Babylon, during which time the practice developed of meeting regularly for the reading and study of the Law of Moses. Out of this gradually, it is supposed, the meeting place became a center for worship and instruction and then a place of prayer. The service seems to have centered around the reading and exposition of the law —a practice that is presupposed in the narrative about Jesus in the synagogue at Nazareth in Luke 4:16 ff. With the destruction of the Temple in Jerusalem, however, the synagogue was the sole surviving institution capable of meeting the worship needs of Jews in Palestine, who now became as totally dependent on the synagogue as were the Jews living in the lands of the dispersion with vast distances separating them from Jerusalem and its temple. Because the Pharisees were nonpriestly in origin and because their main role had been as interpreters of the Law, it was inevitable that they should move into positions of leadership in the synagogues, and that their interpretations of the Law should become the dominant ones in synagogue worship and exposition. The synagogues

---

[3]*Hasmonean* is the family name of Mattathias, whose sons were the leaders of the guerrilla warfare that freed the Jews from Seleucid control. The eldest son of Mattathias, Judah, was given the nickname *Maccabee*, probably meaning "hammer." But the brothers of Judah, who successively assumed the leadership over the Jews in the second century B.C., were also known as the Maccabees.

thus became the central focus of Jewish religious life, and the Pharisees utilized this institution as their chief base of power to dominate Jewish life from this time on. Pharisaism became the normative voice of Judaism. In the selections from Megilla given below we can see the emerging procedures for handling synagogue property and for setting up the yearly patterns of reading and exposition.

3:1–6

(1) If the people of a town sell their open space they must buy a synagogue with the price thereof; if they sell a synagogue they must buy an Ark [with the price thereof]; if an Ark, they must buy [Scroll] wrappings; if wrappings, they must buy Books [of the Scriptures]; if Books, they must buy [a copy of] the Law. But if they sold [a copy of] the Law they may not buy Books [of the Scriptures]; or if Books [of the Scriptures], they may not buy wrappings; or if wrappings, they may not buy an Ark; or if an Ark, they may not buy a synagogue; or if a synagogue, they may not buy an open space. So, too, with the residue [of the price of any of these]. They may not sell to a private person what was a public possession, for thereby they lower its sanctity. So R. Judah. They said to him: If so, [they may] not [sell] aught from a larger town to a smaller.

(2) They may not sell a synagogue except it is on the condition that when they will they may take it back again. So R. Meir. But the Sages say: They may sell it for all time except for (use as) four things: a bath-house, a tannery, an immersion-pool, or a urinal. R. Judah says: They may sell it for a courtyard and the buyer may do with it what he will.

(3) Moreover R. Judah said: [Even] if a synagogue was in ruins lamentation for the dead may not be made therein, nor may they twist ropes therein or stretch out nets therein, or spread out produce [to dry] on its roof, or make of it a short by-path; for it is written, *And I will bring your sanctuaries into desolation*—their sanctity [endures] although they lie desolate. If herbs spring up therein they may not be plucked up because of grief of soul. MK. 11: 16

(4) If the first day of the month Adar falls on the Sabbath, they read the section [in the Law] "Shekels"; if it falls in the middle of the week they read it earlier on the Sabbath that goes before, and on the next Sabbath they break off [from the reading of the four portions prescribed for the month of Adar]. On the second [Sabbath of the month they read the section] *Remember what Amalek did*; on the third, the section of "The Red Heifer"; on the fourth, the section *This month shall be unto you*. . . . On the fifth they revert to the set order. At all these times they break off [from the set order in the reading of the Law]: on the first days of the months, at the [Feast of the] Dedication, at Purim, on days of fasting, and at *Maamads* and on the Day of Atonement.

(5) At passover they read the section "The Set Feasts" in the Law of the priests; at Pentecost, [the section] "Seven weeks"; at the New Year, *In the seventh month in the first day of the month.* . . . ," on the

Day of Atonement, *After the death...* ; on the first Festival-day of the Feast [of Tabernacles] they read the section "The Set Feasts" in the Law of the Priests, and, on all the other days of the Feast, about the offerings at the Feast.

(6) At the [Feast of the] Dedication [they read the section] "The princes"; at Purim, *Then came Amalek...*; on the first days of the months, *And on the first days of your months...*; at the *Maamads*, from the story of Creation; on the days of fasting, "The Blessings and the Cursings." They make no break in the reading of the curses, but the one [reader] reads them all. On Mondays and Thursdays and on

LK. 4: 16, 17

Sabbaths at the Afternoon Prayer they read according to the set order; and these are not taken into account. For it is written, *And Moses declared unto the children of Israel the set feasts of the Lord*—the law prescribed for them is that they should be read each one in its time.

4:1–10

LK. 4:20

(1) He that reads the Scroll may stand or sit. If one reads it, or if two read it, they have fulfilled their obligation. Where the custom is to say a Benediction [after it] they say it; where it is not the custom, they do not say it. On a Monday and a Thursday and on the afternoon of a Sabbath the Law is read by three: they may not take from them or add to them, and they do not close with a reading from the Prophets. He that begins the reading from the Law and he that completes it say a Benediction the one at the beginning and the other at the end.

(2) And in the beginnings of the months and during mid-festival the Law is read by four; they may not take from them or add to them, and they do not close with a reading from the Prophets. He that begins the reading from the Law and he that completes it say a Benediction the one at the beginning and the other at the end. This is the general rule: when the Additional Prayer is appointed and it is not a Festival-day, the Law is read by four. On a Festival-day it is read by five, on the Day of Atonement by six, and on the Sabbath by seven. They may not take from them but they may add to them, and they

LK. 4:17

close with a reading from the Prophets. He that begins the reading from the Law and he that completes it say a Benediction the one at the beginning and the other at the end.

(3) If there are less than ten present they may not recite the *Shema*[1] with its Benedictions, nor may one go before the Ark,[2] nor may they lift up their hands, nor may they read the [prescribed por-

---

[1]*Shema* is the first word of and the usual designation for Israel's ancient confessional formula, found in Deut. 6:4 ff.

[2]During the period when the Temple stood, the "ark" referred to the sacred box, kept in the Holy of Holies, in which were believed to be preserved the tables of the Law given to Moses (Ex. 25:10–22; 37:1–9), and other memorable objects from Israel's past. But the term was transferred to the box or cabinet in which were kept the scrolls on which the scriptures were written. These included not only the Law of Moses, but the prophets and the other sacred writings as well. The link in terminology is obvious, however: both the tablets and the scrolls were thought of as the record of God's self-disclosure to his chosen people.

tion of] the Law or the reading from the Prophets, nor may they observe the Stations [when burying the dead] or say the Benediction of the Mourners or the mourners' consolation, or the Benediction over the newly wed, nor may they make mention of the name of God in the Common Grace. Also [the redemption value of dedicated] immovable property [is assessed by] nine and a priest; and similarly [for the Valuation-vow of] men.

(4) He that reads in the Law may not read less than three verses; he may not read to the interpreter more than one verse, or, in [a reading from] the Prophets, three verses; but if these three are three separate paragraphs, he must read them out singly. They may leave out verses in the Prophets, but not in the Law. How much may they leave out? Only so much that he leaves no time for the interpreter to make a pause.

LK. 3:18

(5) He that gives the concluding reading from the Prophets recites also the *Shemaʿ* with its Benedictions; and he goes before the Ark, and he lifts up his hands [in the Benediction of the Priests]. If he is a minor, his father or his teacher goes before the Ark on his behalf.

(6) A minor may read in the Law and interpret, but he may not recite the *Shemaʿ* with its Benedictions or go before the Ark or raise his hands [in the Benediction of the Priests]. He whose clothes are ragged may recite the *Shemaʿ* with its Benedictions and interpret, but he may not read in the Law or go before the Ark or lift up his hands. He that is blind may recite the *Shemaʿ* with its Benedictions and interpret. R. Judah says: He that has never seen the light may not recite the *Shemaʿ* with its Benedictions.

(7) If a priest has blemishes in his hands, he may not raise his hands [in the Benediction of the Priests]. R. Judah says "Moreover if a man's hands are dyed with woad or madder he may not lift up his hands, because the people would gaze on him."

(8) If a man said, "I will not go before the Ark in coloured raiment," he may not even go before it in white raiment. [If he said], "I will not go before it in sandals," he may not even go before it barefoot. If a man made his Phylacteries[3] round, it is a danger and is no fulfilling of the commandment. If he put them on his forehead or on the palm of his hand, this is the way of heresy. If he overlaid them with gold or put them over his sleeve, this is the way of the sectaries.

MT. 23:5

(9) If a man said [in his prayer], "Good men shall bless thee!" this is the way of heresy; [if he said,] "Even to a bird's nest do thy mercies extend," or "May thy name be remembered for the good [which thou hast wrought]!" or "We give thanks, we give thanks!" they put him to silence. If a man does not read literally the laws about the forbidden degrees, they put him to silence. If a man says *And thou shalt not give any of thy seed to make them pass through (the fire) to Molech* [means] "and thou shalt not give of thy seed to make it pass to heathendom," they put him to silence with a rebuke.

(10) The story of Reuben is read out but not interpreted; the story

---

[3]Phylacteries are small containers on which miniature copies of portions of scripture were kept. They were fastened to the forehead and to the back of the hand by pious Jews, in literal fulfillment of the injunction in Deut. 6:8.

of Tamar is read out and interpreted. The first story of the calf is read out and interpreted, and the second is read out but not interpreted. The Blessing of the Priests and the story of David and of Amnon are read out but not interpreted.[1] They may not use the chapter of the Chariot as a reading from the Prophets; but R. Judah permits it. R. Eliezer says "They do not use the chapter *Cause Jerusalem to know* as a reading from the Prophets."

The Temple:

Josephus, Jewish Wars

The excerpt given below begins at the point where Titus is about to lay siege to Jerusalem. Josephus interrupts the narrative of the war, however, in order to give his reader a detailed picture of the city and its architectural and cultural prize: the temple on Zion.

V:47–53

(47) As Titus[2] advanced into enemy territory, his vanguard consisted of the contingents of the kings with the whole body of auxiliaries. Next to these were the pioneers and camp-measures, then the officers' baggage-train; behind the troops protecting these came the commander-in-chief, escorted by the lancers and other picked troops, (48) and followed by the legionary cavalry. These were succeeded by the engines, and these by the tribunes and prefects of cohorts with a picked escort; after them and surrounding the eagle came the ensigns preceded by their trumpeters, and behind them the solid column, six (49) abreast. The servants attached to each legion followed in a body, preceded by the baggage-train. Last of all came the mercenaries with a (50) rearguard to keep watch on them. Leading his army forward in this orderly array, according to Roman usage, Titus advanced through Samaria to Gophna,[3] previously captured by his father and now garrisoned. After resting here one night he set forward at dawn, and at the end of a full (51) day's march encamped in the valley which is called by the Jews in their native tongue "Valley of Thorns,"

---

[1]The sordid story of David's disposing of faithful Uriah in order to marry Bathsheba, and the account of Amnon, David's son who raped his half-sister, were part of scripture and therefore to be read, but their moral level was so low and their implications for an evaluation of moral standards of the House of David so embarrassing that exposition of the stories was forbidden (I Samuel 12 and 13).

[2]Titus was placed in command of the Roman troops attacking Jerusalem by his father, Vespasian, who had been called back to Rome in order to become emperor in A.D. 69. Marching by stages up the Palestinian coast as far as Caesarea, the Roman seat of power, Titus turned inland to Samaria, and from there marched south along the ridge of Judean hills toward Jerusalem.

[3]A small city, now the Christian Arab village of Jiphna, some twenty miles north of Jerusalem.

close to a village named Gabath Saul,[4] which means "Saul's hill," at a distance of about thirty furlongs from Jerusalem. From here, with some six hundred picked (52) horsemen, he rode forward to reconnoitre the city's strength and to test the mettle of the Jews, whether, on seeing him, they would be terrified into surrender before any actual conflict; for he had learnt, (53) as indeed was the fact, that the people were longing for peace, but were overawed by the insurgents and brigands and remained quiet merely from inability to resist.

V:136–141

(136) The city was fortified by three walls, except where it was enclosed by impassable ravines, a single rampart there sufficing.[5] (137) It was built, in portions facing each other, on two hills separated by a central valley, in which the tiers of houses ended.

Of these hills, that on the upper city was far higher and had a straighter ridge than the other; consequently, owing to its strength it was called by King David—the father of Solomon the first builder of the temple—the Stronghold, but we called it the upper agora.[6] The second hill, which bore the name of Acra[7] and supported the lower city, (138) was a hog's back. Opposite this was a third hill, by nature lower than Acra, and once divided from it by another broad ravine. Afterwards, (139) however, the Hasmonaeans, during the period of their reign, both filled up the ravine, with the object of uniting the city to the temple, and also reduced the elevation of Acra by leveling its summit, in order that it might not block the view of the temple. The Valley of the (140) Cheesemakers,[8] as the ravine was called, which, as we said, was lower, extends down to Siloam; for so we called that fountain of sweet and abundant water. On the exterior the two hills on which the city stood (141) were encompassed by deep

---

[4]The site is clearly visible a few miles north of Jersusalem on the east side of the present main highway. The fortress built there by Saul, Israel's first king, has been excavated in recent years.

[5]The problem of fortifying the city was most difficult on the north side of the temple hill, since there alone the ground does not drop off precipitously. Heavy walls and a massive fortress-tower were erected there in an effort to prevent breaching the walls from that side.

[6]Excavations have shown that the oldest structures on the upper, western hill, including the citadel, go back only to Maccabean times. David's city was on the southern slope of the lower eastern hill. But local tradition very early transferred the name "Zion" to the higher western ridge and called the hellenistic fortress there "The Tower of David."

[7]Overlooking the temple enclosure from the north is the massive tower of Antonia, the present remains of which go back to Herod the Great.

[8]The *Tyropeon Valley* separating the eastern and western hills of Jersusalem has filled in considerably since the time that Josephus wrote, but it is still clearly visible as a long depression that begins southeast of the present Damascus Gate (actually built first by Hadrian), and slopes away to the south and east, running along below the Western Wall of the temple platform.

ravines, and the precipitous cliffs on either side rendered the town nowhere accessible.

V:148–162

(148) This wall was built by Agrippa[9] to enclose the later additions to the city, which were quite unprotected; for the town, overflowing with inhabitants, had gradually crept beyond the ramparts. Indeed, the (149) population, uniting to the hill the district north of the temple, encroached so far that even a fourth hill was surrounded with houses. This hill, which is called Bezetha, lay opposite Antonia, but was cut off from it by a deep fosse, dug on purpose to sever the foundations of (150) Antonia from the hill and so to render them at once less easy of access and more elevated, the depth of the trench materially increasing (151) the height of the towers. The recently built quarter was called in the vernacular Bezetha, which might be translated into Greek as "New Town." Seeing then the residents of this district in need of defence, (152) Agrippa, the father and namesake of the present king, began the above-mentioned wall; but, fearing that Claudius Caesar might suspect from the vast scale of the structure that he had designs of revolution and revolt, he desisted after merely laying the foundations. Indeed (153) the city would have been impregnable, had the wall been continued as it began; for it was constructed of stones twenty cubits long and ten broad, so closely joined that they could scarcely have been undermined with tools of iron or shaken by engines.[10] The wall itself was ten (154) cubits broad, and it would doubtless have attained a greater height than it did, had not the ambition of its founder been frustrated. (155) Subsequently, although hurriedly erected by the Jews, it rose to a height of twenty cubits, besides having battlements of two cubits and bulwarks of three cubits high, bringing the total altitude up to twenty-five cubits.[11]

(156) Above the wall, however, rose towers, twenty cubits broad and twenty high, square and solid as the wall itself, and in the joining and beauty of the stones in no wise inferior to a temple. Over this solid masonry, twenty cubits in altitude, were magnificent apartments, (157) and above these, upper chambers and cisterns to receive the rain-water, each tower having broad spiral staircases. Of such towers the third (158) wall had ninety, disposed at intervals of two hundred cubits; the line of the middle wall was sixty. The whole circumference of the city was thirty-three furlongs.[12] But wonderful as was the third wall throughout, (159) still more so was the tower Psephinus, which rose at its northwest angle and opposite to which Titus encamped.

---

[9]That is, Herod Agrippa, grandson of Herod the Great. Appointed king of an area north and east of the Sea of Galilee by the Emperor Caligula (37–41), he effectively interceded before the Roman Senate in behalf of Claudius' claim to be recognized as emperor. Claudius rewarded Agrippa by designating him as king over all the territories formerly ruled by his grandfather, though Agrippa's reign was brief (41–44 A.D.).

[10]Judging by the enormous stones still to be seen in the lower courses of the masonry platform on which Herod built the temple and its courts, these dimensions (approximately 67 by 7 by 9 feet) may not be exaggerated.

[11]The height would be about 10 yards.

[12]More than four miles.

For, being seventy (160) cubits high,[13] it afforded from sunrise a prospect embracing both Arabia and the utmost limits of Hebrew territory as far as the sea; (161) it was of octagonal form.

Over against this was the tower Hippicus, and close to it two others, all built by King Herod into the old wall, and for magnitude, beauty and strength without their equal in the world. For, apart from (162) his innate magnanimity and his pride in the city, the king sought, in the super-excellence of these works, to gratify his private feelings; dedicating them to the memory of three persons to whom he was most fondly attached, and after whom he named these towers —brother, friend, and wife. The last, as we have previously related, he had for love's sake actually slain; the others he had lost in war, after valiant fight.

V:176–194

(176) Adjoining and on the inner side of these towers, which lay to the north of it, was the king's palace, baffling all description: (177) indeed, in extravagance and equipment no building surpassed it. It was completely enclosed within a wall thirty cubits high,[14] broken at equal distances by ornamental towers, and contained immense banqueting-halls and bed-chambers for a hundred guests. The interior fittings (178) are indescribable—the variety of the stones (for species rare in every other country were here collected in abundance), ceilings wonderful (179) both for the length of the beams and the splendour of their surface decoration, the host of apartments with their infinite varieties of (180) design, all amply furnished, while most of the objects in each of them were of silver or gold. All around were many circular cloisters, (181) leading one into another, the columns in each being different, and their open courts all of greensward; there were groves of various trees intersected by long walks, which were bordered by deep canals, and ponds everywhere studded with bronze figures, through which the water was (182) discharged, and around the streams were numerous cotes for tame pigeons. However, it is impossible adequately to delineate the palace, and the memory of it is harrowing, recalling as it does the ravages of (183) the brigands' fire. For it was not the Romans who burnt it to the ground, but this was done, as we have said already, by conspirators within the walls at the opening of the revolt. The conflagration beginning at Antonia passed to the palace, and spread to the roofs of the three towers.

(184) Though the temple, as I said, was seated on a strong hill, the level area on its summit originally barely sufficed for shrine and altar, the ground around it being precipitous and steep. But king (185) Solomon, the actual founder of the temple, having walled up the eastern side, a single portico was reared on this made ground;[15] on its other

---

[13]More than 100 feet high.

[14]About 45 feet.

[15]The portico on the southwest corner of the Herodian temple enclosure was named for Solomon, as is confirmed by the Gospel of John (10:23), but the entire structure, including the portico, dates from about 900 years after the time of Solomon. However costly Solomon's temple may have been, Herod's was far larger, far more complex, and probably much more costly.

sides the sanctuary remained exposed. In course of ages, however, through the constant additions of the people to the embankment, the hilltop by this process of levelling up was widened. They further broke (186) down the north wall and thus took in an area as large as the whole temple enclosure subsequently occupied. Then, after having enclosed (187) the hill from its base with a wall on three sides, and accomplished a task greater than they could ever have hoped to achieve—a task upon which long ages were spent by them as well as all their sacred treasures, though replenished by the tributes offered to God from every quarter (188) of the world—they built around the original block the upper courts and the lower temple enclosure. The latter, where its foundations were lowest, they built up from a depth of three hundred cubits; at some spots this figure was exceeded.[16] The whole depth of the foundations was, (189) however, not apparent; for they filled up a considerable part of the ravines, wishing to level the narrow alleys of the town. Blocks of stone were used in the building measuring forty cubits; for lavish funds and popular enthusiasm led to incredible enterprises, and a task seemingly interminable was through perseverance and in time actually achieved.

(190) Nor was the superstructure unworthy of such foundations. The porticos, all in double rows, were supported by columns five and twenty (191) cubits high—each a single block of the purest white marble—and ceiled with panels of cedar. The natural magnificence of these columns, (192) their excellent polish and fine adjustment, presented a striking spectacle, without any adventitious embellishment of painting or sculpture. The porticos were thirty cubits broad, and the complete circuit of them, embracing the tower of Antonia, measured six furlongs. The open court was from end to end variegated with paving of all manner of stones.

(193) Proceeding across this towards the second court of the temple, one found it surrounded by a stone balustrade, three cubits high and of (194) exquisite workmanship; in this at regular intervals stood slabs giving warning, some in Greek, others in Latin characters, of the law of purification, to wit that no foreigner was permitted to enter the holy place,[17] for so the second enclosure of the temple was called.

V:206–219

(206) Fifteen steps led up from the women's compartment to the greater gate, these steps being shallower than the five at each of the other gates.

(207) The sacred edifice itself, the holy temple, in the central position, was approached by a flight of twelve steps. The facade was of equal height and breadth, each being a hundred cubits;[18] but the

---

[16]The retaining walls were explored to their foundations in the nineteenth century, and have been further excavated in recent years. Josephus does indulge in exaggeration as to the height of the walls, which are more like 150 feet than the 150 yards he describes.

[17]Several of the original examples of this inscription have been found. A translation of the inscription is given on pg. 259.

[18]A cubit is usually considered to be about 18 inches.

building behind was narrower by forty cubits, for in front it had as it were shoulders extending twenty cubits on either side. The first gate was seventy cubits high and twenty-five broad and had no doors, displaying (208) unexcluded the void expanse of heaven; the entire face was covered with gold, and through it the first edifice was visible to a spectator without in all its grandeur and the surroundings of the inner gate (209) all gleaming with gold fell beneath his eye. But, whereas the sanctuary within consisted of two separate chambers, the first building alone stood exposed to view, from top to bottom, towering to a height of ninety cubits, its length being fifty and its breadth twenty. The gate (210) opening into the building was, as I said, completely overlaid with gold, as was the whole wall around it. It had, moreover, above it (211) those golden vines, from which depended grape clusters as tall as a man; and it had golden doors fifty-five cubits high and sixteen broad. Before these hung a veil of equal length, of Babylonian tapestry, with (212) embroidery of blue and fine linen, of scarlet also and purple, wrought with marvellous skill. Nor was this mixture of materials without its mystic meaning: it typified the universe. For the scarlet (213) seemed emblematical of fire, the fine linen of the earth, the blue of the air, and the purple of the sea; the comparison in the two cases being suggested by their colour, and in that of the fine linen and purple by their origin, as the one is produced by the earth and the other by (214) the sea. On this tapestry was portrayed a panorama of the heavens, the signs of the Zodiac excepted.[19]

(215) Passing within one found oneself in the ground-floor of the sanctuary. This was sixty cubits in height, the same in length, and twenty cubits in breadth. But the sixty cubits of its length were (216) divided. The first portion, partitioned off at forty cubits, contained within it three most wonderful works of art, universally renowned: a (217) lampstand, a table, an an altar of incense. The seven lamps (such being the number of the branches from the lampstand) represented the planets; the loaves on the table, twelve in number, the circle of the Zodiac and the year; while the altar of incense, by the thirteen (218) fragrant spices from sea and from land, both desert and inhabited, with which it was replenished, signified that all things are of God and for God.

(219) The innermost recess measured twenty cubits, and was screened in like manner from the outer portion by a veil. In this stood nothing whatever: unapproachable, inviolable, invisible to all, it was called the Holy of Holy.

Scriptures for the Diaspora:

Letter of Aristeas

A novelistic and apologetic account of the circumstances and process by which the Hebrew Bible was translated into Greek, the Letters of

---

[19]Josephus may be correct here, but the signs of the zodiac were the most popular decorative motif in Palestinian synagogues from the third century until at least 500 A.D., judging by excavated remains of mosaic pavements from ancient synagogues.

Aristeas purport to have been written by an Egyptian courtier, Aristeas, during the reign of Ptolemy Philadelphus (285–247 B.C.). But the historical anachronisms, including references to the Hebrew writings as scripture—a term that did not come into use until centuries afterward—betray the letters as pseudonymous and as coming from centuries after the time of Philadelphus. Their aim is to foster social respect and political freedom for Jews living in the lands of the Dispersion, and to invite intellectual respect for the Jewish sacred books. Of great interest to the modern reader is the attempt of the author to provide rational explanations for the dietary and other laws that Jews must have had difficulty in justifying to their Gentile associates. The letters incorporate older material, but probably gained their present form in the early part of the first century A.D.

The first excerpt is an account given to Aristeas' brother, Philocrates, of the journey to Jerusalem undertaken to secure permission from the High Priest, Eleazar, for the translation project. The second demonstrates Aristeas' piety and his shrewdness in persuading the king to free the Jewish slaves while he is favorably disposed toward Judaism during the negotiations about the translation of the Law. It is the third excerpt that offers rational explanations for the dietary laws. The fourth, regarding a favorite setting of ancient writers—a royal banquet—provides the translators an opportunity to show their wisdom, and the final excerpt serves as a testimony to the divine nature of the Jewish Law and as a warning to those who might want to tamper with it.

SECTIONS 3–11

(3) It was my devotion to the pursuit of religious knowledge that led me to undertake the embassy to the man[1] I have mentioned, who was held in the highest esteem by his own citizens and by others both for his virtue and his majesty and who had in his possession *documents of* the highest value to the Jews in his own country and in foreign lands for the interpretation of the divine law, for their (4) laws are written on leather parchments in Jewish characters. This *embassy* then I undertook with enthusiasm, having first of all found an opportunity *of pleading* with the king[2] on behalf of the Jewish captives who had been transported from Judea to Egypt by the king's father, when he first obtained possession of this city and conquered (5) the land of Egypt. It is worthwhile that I should tell you this story, too, since I am convinced that you, with your disposition towards holiness and your sympathy with men who are living in accordance with the holy law, will all the more readily listen to the account which I propose to set forth, since you yourself have lately come to us from the

---

[1]Eleazar, the High Priest in Jerusalem.
[2]Ptolemy II Philadelphus.

island and are anxious to hear everything that (6) tends to build up the soul. On a former occasion, too, I sent you a record of the facts which I thought worth relating about the Jewish race—the record which I had obtained from the most learned high (7) priests of the most learned land of Egypt. As you are so eager to acquire the knowledge of those things which can benefit the mind, I feel it incumbent upon me to impart to you *all the information in my power. I should feel the same duty* towards all who possessed the same disposition but I feel it especially towards you since you have aspirations which are so noble, and since you are not only my brother in character no less than in blood but are one with me as (8) well in the pursuit of goodness. For neither the pleasure derived from gold nor any other of the possessions which are prized by shallow minds confers the same benefit as the pursuit of culture and the study which we expend in securing it. But that I may not weary you by a too lengthy introduction, I will proceed at once to the substance of my narrative. (9) Demetrius of Phalerum,[3] the president of the king's library, received vast sums of money, for the purpose of collecting together, as far as he possibly could, all the books in the world. By means of purchase and transcription, he carried out, to the best of his ability, the purpose of the king. On one occasion when I was present he was asked, "How many thousand books are there *in the library?*" (10) and he replied, "More than two hundred thousand, O king, and I shall make endeavour in the immediate future *to gather together* the remainder also, so that the total of five hundred thousand may be reached. I am told that the laws of the Jews are worth transcribing and deserve (11) a place in your library." "What is to prevent you from doing this?" replied the king. "Everything that is necessary has been placed at your disposal." "They need to be translated," answered Demetrius, "for in the country of the Jews they use a peculiar alphabet (just as the Egyptians, too, have a special form of letters) and speak a peculiar dialect. They are supposed to use the Syriac tongue, but this is not the case; their language is quite different." And the king when he understood all the facts of the case ordered a letter to be written to the Jewish High Priest that his purpose (which has already been described) might be accomplished.

SECTIONS 14–20

(14) . . . Having, as has already been stated, obtained an opportunity for securing their emancipation, I addressed the king with the following arguments. "Let us not be so unreasonable as to allow our (15) deeds to give the lie to our words. Since the law which we wish not only to transcribe but also to translate belongs to the whole Jewish race, what justification shall we be able to find for our embassy while such vast numbers of them remain in a state of slavery in your king-

---

[3] An Athenian politician and philosopher of the peripatetic School, who fled to Egypt when he and his clique were driven out of power in Athens. He is credited with having supplied the ruler of Egypt, Ptolemy Lagus, with the idea of the great library of Alexandria.

dom? In the perfection and wealth of your clemency release those who are held in such miserable bondage, since as I have been at pains to discover, the God who gave them their law is the God who maintains your kingdom. They worship the same God—the Lord and Creator of the Universe, as all other men, as we ourselves, O king, though we call him by different names, such as Zeus or Dis. (16) This name was very appropriately bestowed upon him by our first ancestors, in order to signify that He through whom all things are endowed with life and come into being, is necessarily the ruler and lord of the universe. Set all mankind an example of magnanimity by releasing those who are held in bondage."

(17) After a brief interval, while I was offering up an earnest prayer to God that He would so dispose the mind of the king that all the captives might be set at liberty—(for the human race, being the creation of God, is swayed and influenced by Him. Therefore with many divers prayers I called upon Him who ruleth the heart that *the king* might be constrained to grant my request. For I had great hopes with regard to the salvation of the men since I was assured that God would grant a fulfilment of my prayer. For when men from pure motives plan some action in the interest of righteousness and the performance of noble deeds, Almighty God brings their efforts and purposes to a successful issue—*the king* raised his head and looking up at me with a cheerful countenance asked, "How many thousands do you think they will number?" Andreas, who was standing (19) near, replied, "A little more than a hundred thousand." "It is a small boon indeed," said the king, "that Aristeas asks of us!" Then Sosibius and some others who were present said, "Yes, but it will be a fit tribute to your magnanimity for you to offer the enfranchisement of these men as an act of devotion to the supreme God. You have been greatly honoured by Almighty God and exalted above all your forefathers in glory and it is only fitting that you should render to Him the greatest thankoffering in your power." Extremely (20) pleased *with these arguments* he gave orders that an addition should be made to the wages *of the soldiers by the amount of the redemption money,* that twenty drachmae should be paid *to the owners* for every slave, that a public order should be issued and that registers of the captives should be attached to it. He showed the greatest enthusiasm in the business, for it was God who had brought our purpose to fulfilment in its entirety and constrained him to redeem not only those who had come into Egypt with the army of his father but any who had come before that time or had been subsequently brought into the kingdom. It was pointed out to him that the ransom money would exceed four hundred talents.

SECTIONS 139–151

(139) Now our Lawgiver[4] being a wise man and specially endowed by God to understand all things, took a comprehensive view of each

---

[4]Moses, to whom was attributed the whole of the Pentateuch (the first five books of the Jewish Bible), including even the account of his own death.

particular detail, and fenced us round with impregnable ramparts and walls of iron, that we might not mingle at all with any of the other nations, but remain pure in body and soul, free from all vain imaginations, worshipping the one Almighty God above the whole creation. (140) Hence the leading Egyptian priests having looked carefully into many such matters, and being cognizant with [our] affairs, call us "men of God." This is a title which does not belong to the rest of mankind but only to those who worship the true God. The rest are *not of God* but of meats and drink and clothing. For their whole (141) disposition leads them to find solace in these things. Among our people such things are reckoned of no account, but throughout their (142) whole life their main consideration is the sovereignty of God. Therefore lest we should be corrupted by any abomination, or our lives be perverted by evil communications, he hedged us round on all sides by rules of purity, affecting alike what we eat, or drink, or touch, (143) or hear, or see. For though, speaking generally, all things are alike in their natural constitution, since they are all governed by one and the same power, yet there is a deep reason in each individual case why we abstain from the use of certain things and enjoy the common use of others. For the sake of illustration I will run over (144) one or two points and explain them to you. For you must not fall into the degrading idea that it was out of regard to mice and weasels and other such things that Moses drew up his laws with such exceeding care. All these ordinances were made for the sake of righteousness (145) to aid the quest for virtue and the perfecting of character. For all the birds that we use are tame and distinguished by their cleanliness, feeding on various kinds of grain and pulse, such as for instance pigeons, turtle-doves, locusts, partridges, geese also, (146) and all other birds of this class. But the birds which are forbidden you will find to be wild and carnivorous, tyrannising over the others by the strength which they possess, and cruelly obtaining food by (147) preying on the tame birds enumerated above. And not only so, but they seize lambs and kids, and injure human beings too, whether dead or alive, and so by naming them unclean, he gave a sign by means of them that those, for whom the legislation was ordained, must practise righteousness in their hearts and not tyrannise over any one in reliance upon their own strength nor rob them of anything, but steer their course of life in accordance with justice, just as the tame birds, already mentioned, consume the different kinds of pulse that grow upon the earth and do not tyrannise to the destruction of their (148) own kindred. Our legislator taught us therefore that it is by such methods as these that indications are given to the wise, that they must be just and effect nothing by violence, and refrain from tyrannising (149) over others in reliance upon their own strength. For since it is *considered* unseemly even to touch such *unclean* animals, as have been mentioned, on account of their particular habits, ought we not to take every precaution lest our own characters should be (150) destroyed to the same extent? Wherefore all the rules which he has laid down with regard to what is permitted in the case of these *birds* and other animals, he has enacted with the object of teaching us a moral lesson. For the division of the hoof and the separation of the claws are intended to teach us that we must discriminate between our individual actions with a view to the practice of (151) virtue. For the strength of our whole body and its activity depend upon our shoulders and limbs. Therefore he compels us to recognise that we must perform all our actions with discrimination according to the standard of righteousness—more especially because we have been distinctly separated from the rest of mankind.

SECTIONS 277–292

(277) The king loudly applauded the answer and asked another, "Why is it that the majority of men never become virtuous?" "Because," he replied, "all men are by nature intemperate and inclined to pleasure.

(278) Hence, injustice springs up and a flood of avarice. The habit of virtue is a hindrance to those who are devoted to a life of pleasure because it enjoins upon them the preference of temperance and righteousness. For it is God who is the master of these things."

(279) The king said that he had answered well, and asked, "What ought kings to obey?" And he said, "The laws, in order that by righteous enactments they may restore the lives of men. Even as you by such conduct in obedience to the Divine command have laid up in store for yourself a perpetual memorial."

(280) The king said that this man, too, had spoken well, and asked the next, "Whom ought we to appoint as governors?" And he replied, "All who hate wickedness, and imitating your own conduct act righteously that they may maintain a good reputation constantly. For this is what you do, O mighty King," he said, "and it is God who has bestowed upon you the crown of righteousness."

(281) The king loudly acclaimed the answer and then looking at the next man said, "Whom ought we to appoint as officers over the forces?" And he explained. "Those who excel in courage and righteousness and those who are more anxious about the safety of their men than to gain a victory by risking their lives through rashness. For as God acts well towards all men, so too you in imitation of Him are the benefactor of all your subjects."

(282) The king said that he had given a good answer and asked another, "What man is worthy of admiration?" And he replied, "The man who is furnished with reputation and wealth and power and possesses a soul equal to it all. You yourself show by your actions that you are most worthy of admiration through the help of God who makes you care for these things."

(283) The king expressed his approval and said to another "To what affairs ought kings to devote most time?" And he replied, "To reading and the study of the records of official journeys, which are written in reference to the *various* kingdoms, with a view to the reformation and preservation of the subjects. And it is by such activity that you have attained to a glory which has never been approached by others, through the help of God who fulfils all your desires."

(284) The king spoke enthusiastically to the man and asked another, "How ought a man to occupy himself during his hours of relaxation and recreation?" And he replied, "To watch those plays which

can be acted with propriety and to set before one's eyes scenes taken from life and enacted with dignity and decency is profitable and
(285) appropriate. For there is some edification to be found even in these amusements, for often some desirable lesson is taught by the most insignificant affairs of life. But by practising the utmost propriety in all your actions, you have shown that you are a philosopher and you are honoured by God on account of your virtue."

(286) The king, pleased with the words which had just been spoken, said to the ninth man, "How ought a man to conduct himself at banquets? And he replied, "You should summon to your side men of learning and those who are able to give you useful hints with regard to the affairs of your kingdom and the lives of your subjects (for you could not find any theme more suitable or more educative than this) (287) since such men are dear to God because they have trained their minds to contemplate the noblest themes—as you indeed are doing yourself, since all your actions are directed by God."

(288) Delighted with the reply, the king inquired of the next man, "What is best for the people? That a private citizen should be made king over them or a member of the royal family?" And he replied, (289) "He who is best by nature. For kings who come of royal lineage are often harsh and severe towards their subjects. And still more is this the case with some of those who have risen from the ranks of private citizens, who after having experienced evil and borne their share of poverty, when they rule over multitudes turn out to be
(290) more cruel than the godless tyrants. But, as I have said, a good nature which has been properly trained is capable of ruling, and you are a great king, not so much because you excel in the glory of your rule and your wealth but rather because you have surpassed all men in clemency and philanthropy, thanks to God who has endowed you with these qualities."

(291) The king spent some time in praising this man and then asked the last of all, "What is the greatest achievement in ruling an empire?" And he replied, "That the subjects should continually dwell in a state of peace, and that justice should be speedily administered
(292) in cases of dispute. These results are achieved through the influence of the ruler, when he is a man who hates evil and loves the good and devotes his energies to saving the lives of men, just as you consider injustice the worst form of evil and by your just administration have fashioned for yourself an undying reputation, since God bestows upon you a mind which is pure and untainted by any evil."

SECTIONS 312–319

(312) When the matter was reported to the king, he rejoiced greatly, for he felt that the design which he had formed had been safely carried out. The whole book was read over to him and he was greatly astonished at the spirit of the lawgiver. And he said to Demetrius, "How is it that none of the historians or the poets have ever thought it worth their while to allude to such a wonderful achievement"
(313) And he replied, "Because the law is sacred and of divine origin. And some of those who formed the intention of *dealing with it* have

been smitten by God and therefore desisted from their purpose." (314)
He said that he had heard from Theopompus that he had been driven
out of his mind for more than thirty days because he intended to
insert in his history some of the incidents from the earlier and somewhat unreliable translations of the law. When he had recovered a
little, he besought God to make it clear to him why the misfortune
(315) had befallen him. And it was revealed to him in a dream, that
from idle curiosity he was wishing to communicate sacred truths to
common men, and that if he desisted he would recover his health. I
have heard, too from the lips of Theodektes, one of the tragic poets,
that when he was about to adapt some of the incidents recorded in
the book for one of his plays, he was affected with cataract in both
his eyes. And when he perceived the reason why the misfortune had
befallen him, he prayed to God for many days and was afterwards
restored.

(317) And after the king, as I have already said, had received the
explanation of Demetrius on this point, he did homage and ordered
that great care should be taken of the books, and that they should
(318) be sacredly guarded. And he urged the translators to visit him
frequently after their return to Judea, for it was only right, he said,
that he should now send them home. But when they came back, he
ordered preparations to be made for them to return home, and
(319) treated them most munificently. He presented each one of them
with three robes of the finest sort, two talents of gold, a sideboard
weighing one talent, all the furniture for three couches.

THE IMPERIAL CULT IN THE EAST

From earliest times the monarchs of the East had been regarded by
their subjects as sons of the deity, either in the literal sense, as among the
Pharaohs of Egypt, whose act of begetting a son was the means of ongo-
ing rebirth of the son of the god, or in a more figurative sense, as among
the rulers of Mesopotamia, where the king was annually enthroned as the
divine agent and thereby son of the god. When Alexander came to Egypt
and the Middle East, he was acclaimed as divine son by priests and populace. This convenient device for gaining popular support was carefully
fostered by the successors of Alexander, especially the Seleucids of Egypt
and the Ptolemies of Egypt.

With the coming of the struggle for power among the Roman leaders,
it was quickly recognized by the contenders that it would be to their advantage if they could be identified in the popular mind with one or another of the gods. Thus Antony associated himself with Hercules and
Dionysius, while Octavian (Augustus) identified himself with Aeneas (the
hero who had founded Rome, according to a legend developed by Virgil)
and with Apollo, the god of the sun. Romans were reluctant to give
divine honors to living persons, but that was not the case in the East. The

inscription translated below, dating from about 9 B.C., is wholly in keeping with the ancient traditions of seeing in the earthly monarch the embodiment of divinity.

A bas-relief of the mystery of Mithra, the Persian solar deity, who is here slaying the bull in the central act of the mithraic mythology. Beside him are the torch-bearers, who symbolized heat and cold, life and death, the rise and setting of the sun. Above them are the signs of the zodiac, and below them are the sacred snake, cup and lion. Other actions and persons in the elaborate mystical cult of Mithra are depicted in the panels above and on the sides. The relief formed the central features of the Mithraic chapels, which were usually located underground. The relief was illuminated in such a way as to inspire awe in those being inducted into the successive stages of Mithraism, which were the Raven, the Secret One, the Soldier, the Lion, the Persian, the Runner of the Sun, and the Father. Broad in its appeal, especially to the military, the shrines of Mithra have been found from the Balkans to northern Britain. In the fourth century attempts were made to have it become the major religion of the empire instead of Christianity. (Source: From a relief now in the Vatican Museum.)

Decree of the Synod of the Province of Asia

... whether the natal day of the most divine Caesar [Augustus] is to be observed most for the joy of it or for the profit of it—a day which one might justly regard as equivalent to the beginning of all things, equivalent, I say, if not in reality, at any rate in the benefits it has brought, seeing that there was nothing ruinous or that had fallen into a miserable appearance that he has not restored. He has given another aspect to the universe, which was only too ready to perish, had not Caesar—a blessing to the whole of mankind—been born. For which reason each individual may justly look upon this day as the beginnings of his own life and physical being, because there can be no more of the feeling that life is a burden, now that he has been born...

Resolved by the Greeks of the province of Asia, on the proposal of the High-priest Apollonius, the son of Menophilus, of Azani: Whereas the Providence which orders the whole of human life has shown a special concern and zeal and conferred upon life its most perfect ornament by bestowing Augustus, whom it fitted for his beneficent work among mankind by filling him with virtue, sending him as a Savior, for us and for those who come after us, one who should cause wars to cease, who should set all things in fair order, and whereas Caesar, when he appeared, made the hopes of those who forecast a better future [look poor compared with the reality], in that he not only surpassed all previous benefactors, but left no chance for future ones to go beyond him, and the glad tidings [Greek, *euangelia*] which by his means went forth into the world took its rise in the birthday of the God; and whereas, after that Asia had passed a resolution Smyrna [under] Lucius Volcacius Tullus, Papias of . . . being clerk . . . , conferring a wreath upon the man who should invent the greatest honors to be shown the god, Paullus Fabius Maximus, Proconsul of the province . . . devised what had hitherto been unknown among the Greeks in honor of Augustus, to wit, that from his birth time should be reckoned in human affairs; Resolved, with Good Fortune and Well-being, by the Greeks of the province of Asia: The first day of the month for all the cities shall be the ninth day before the Kalends of October [23 September] which is the natal day of Augustus . . .

(FRAGMENT OF A LETTER OF THE PROCONSUL TO THE CITIES OF ASIA.)
TEXT IN DITTENBERGER, O.G.I., NO. 458.

POPULAR RELIGION IN THE EARLY EMPIRE:

[INITIATION INTO THE MYSTERIES AND SYNCRETISTIC SAVIOR CULTS]

The mystery religions of the ancient world exercised an enormous appeal, cutting across all cultures and levels of society. The humblest subject might well walk in the same procession as his monarch in their common devotion to the gods—or more frequently goddesses—whose worship promised access to the knowledge of sacred truth and through possession of that knowledge to eternal life. Some of the cults were localized, such as the mysteries of Demeter, the earth mother, at Eleusis, a short distance west of Athens, and the Mysteries of the Great Gods on the island of Samothrace in the northern Aegean. Others seem to have been carried out at various places, as is the case with the mystery of Isis, the fertility goddess of the Nile who became a universal redemptrix in the early centuries of our era.

Under Ptolemy I, the hellenistic ruler of Egypt from 305 to 285 B.C., a new cult was established in honor of Serapis, a composite deity whose attributes included features of Osiris (the God of the Nile), Aesclepius (the god of healing), Jupiter (the supreme Olympian god, Zeus, adapted for Roman use), and Pluto the god of the underworld). In their efforts to create a one-world culture, the hellenistic rulers found a cult as inclu-

Dionysus, god of wine and mystic savior, accompanied in a procession by satyrs and maenads. Wine, together with the music of lyre and flute, was used to induce ecstasy in the devotees of Dionysus. From an Athenian vase of the 6th/5th cent. B.C. *(Source:* Metropolitan Museum of Art)

sive as that of Serapis enormously useful, because people of diverse backgrounds could unite in honoring this divinity. The two brief excerpts that conclude this section are respectively a dedicatory inscription honoring several deities, but chiefly Isis, and a letter extolling the virtues of Serapis. From both it is evident that the values of devotion to these mystical saviors was not limited to a narrow "religious" sphere, but permeated and transformed the whole of life for the devotees.

Apuleius (Lucius Apuleius Africans): Metamorphoses

Born in North Africa about 123 A.D., educated in Carthage and in Athens, Apuleius perfected his Latin in Rome. On his mother's side, he was related to Plutarch (A.D. 46–120) and considered himself a Platonist, although his extant writings are not philosophical but religious and mystical. Under the guise of telling a string of popular tales, Apuleius reveals the story of his own personal and religious pilgrimage. He depicts the experiences of a man who was bewitched and changed into an ass, and was then restored to pure human form through the grace of the goddess, Isis. Only through her intervention and the transformation she effected in him was he able to achieve his true humanity. The *Metamorphoses* is the best ancient witness we possess to the religious appeal of initiation into the mysteries and to the inner sense of fulfillment that the experience provided.

> About the first watch of the night, when as I had slept my first sleep, I awaked with sudden fear, and saw the moon shining bright as when she is at the full, and seeming as though she leaped out of the sea. Then I thought with myself that this was the most secret time, when that goddess had most puissance and force, considering that all human things be governed by her providence; and that not only all beasts private and tame, wild and savage, be made strong by the governance of her light and godhead, but also things inanimate and without life; and I considered that all bodies in the heavens, the earth, and the seas be by her increasing motions increased, and by her diminishing motions diminished: then as weary of all my cruel fortune and calamity, I found good hope and sovereign remedy, though it were very late, to be delivered of all my misery, by invocation and prayer to the excellent beauty of this powerful goddess. Wherefore shaking off my drowsy sleep I arose with a joyful face, and moved by a great affection to purify myself, I plunged by head seven times into the water of the sea; which number of seven is convenable and agreeable to holy and divine things, as the worthy and sage philosopher Pythagoras hath declared. Then very lively and joyfully, though with a weeping countenance, I made this oration to the puissant goddess:

"O blessed queen of heaven, whether Thou be the Dame Ceres which art the original and motherly nurse of all fruitful things in the earth, who, after the finding of Thy daughter Proserpine, through the great joy which Thou didst presently conceive, didst utterly take away and abolish the food of them of old time, the acorn, and madest the barren and unfruitful ground of Eleusis to be ploughed and sown, and now givest men a more better and milder food; or whether Thou be the celestial Venus, who, in the beginning of the world, didst couple together male and female with an engendered love, and didst so make an eternal propagation of human kind, being now worshipped within the temples of the Isle Paphos; or whether Thou be the sister of the god Phoebus, who hast saved so many people by lightening and lessening with they medicines and pangs of travail and art now adored at the sacred places of Ephesus; or whether Thou be called terrible Proserpine, by reason of the deadly howlings which Thou yieldest, that hast power with triple face to stop and put away the invasion of hags and ghosts which appear unto men, and to keep them down in the closures of the Earth, which dost wander in sundry groves and art worshipped in divers manners; Thou, which dost luminate all the cities of the earth by Thy feminine light; Thou, which nourishest all the seeds of the world by Thy damp heat, giving Thy changing light according to the wanderings, near or far, of the sun: by whatsoever name or fashion or shape it is lawful to call upon Thee, I pray Thee to end my great travail and misery and raise up my fallen hopes, and deliver me from the wretched fortune which so long time pursued me. Grant peace and rest, if it please Thee, to my adversities, for I have endured enough labour and peril. Remove from me the hateful shape of mine ass, and render me to my kindred and to mine own self Lucius: and if I have offended in any point Thy divine majesty, let me rather die if I may not live."

When I had ended this oration, discovering my plaints to the goddess, I fortuned to fall again asleep upon that same bed; and by and by (for mine eyes were but newly closed) appeared to me from the midst of the sea a divine and venerable face, worshipped even of the gods themselves. Then, by little and little, I seemed to see the whole figure of her body, bright and mounting out of the sea and standing before me: wherefore I propose to describe her divine semblance, if the poverty of my human speech will suffer me, or her divine power give me a power of eloquence rich enough to express it. First she had a great abundance of hair, flowing and curling, dispersed and scattered about her divine neck; on the crown of her head she bare many garlands interlaced with flowers, and in the middle of her forehead was a plain circlet in fashion of a mirror, or rather resembling the moon by the light that it gave forth; and this was borne up on either side by serpents that seemed to rise from the furrows of the earth, and above it were blades of corn set out. Her vestment was of finest linen yielding divers colours, somewhere white and shining, somewhere yellow like the crocus flower, somewhere rosy red, somewhere flaming; and (which troubled my sight and spirit sore) her cloak was utterly dark and obscure covered with shining black, and being wrapped round her from under her left arm to her right shoulder in manner of a shield, part of it fell down, pleated in most subtle fashion, to the skirts of her garment so that the welts appeared comely. Here and there upon the edge thereof and throughout its surface the stars glimpsed, and in the middle of them was placed the moon in mid-month, which shone like a flame of fire; and round about the whole length of the border of that goodly robe was a crown or garland wreathing unbroken, made with all flowers and all fruits. Things quite diverse did she bear: for in her right hand she had a timbrel of brass, a flat piece of metal curved in manner of a girdle, wherein passed not many rods through the periphery of it; and when with her arm she moved these triple chords, they gave forth a shrill and clear sound. In her left hand she bare a cup of gold like unto a boat, upon the handle whereof, in the upper part which is best seen, an asp lifted up his head with a wide-swelling throat. Her odoriferous feet were covered with shoes interlaced and wrought with victorious palm. Thus the divine shape, breathing out the pleasant spice of fertile Arabia, disdained not with her holy voice to utter these words unto me:

"Behold, Lucius, I am come; thy weeping and prayer hath moved me to succour thee. I am she that is the natural mother of all things, mistress and governess of all the elements, the initial progeny of worlds, chief of the powers divine, queen of all that are in hell, the principal of them that dwell in heaven, manifested alone and under one form of all the gods and goddesses. At my will the planets of the sky, the wholesome winds of the seas, and the lamentable silences of hell be disposed; my name, my divinity is adored throughout all the world, in divers manners, in variable customs, and by many names. For the Phrygians that are the first of all men call me the Mother of the gods at Pessinus; the Athenians, which are sprung from their own soil, Cecropian Minerva; the Cyprians, which are girt about the sea, Paphian Venus; the Cretans which bear arrows, Dictynnian Diana; the Sicilians, which speak three tongues, infernal Proserpine; the Eleusians their ancient goddess Ceres; some Juno, other Bellona, other Hecate, other Rhamnusia, and principally both sort of the Ethiopians which dwell in the Orient and are enlightened by the morning rays of the sun, and the Egyptians, which are excellent in all kind of ancient doctrine, and by their proper ceremonies accustom to worship me, do call me by my true name, Queen Isis. Behold I am come to take pity of thy fortune and tribulation; behold I am present to favour and aid thee; leave off thy weeping and lamentation, put away all thy sorrow, for behold the healthful day which is ordained by my providence. Therefore be ready and attentive to my commandment; the day which shall come after this night is dedicate to my service by an eternal religion; my priests and ministers do accustom, after the wintry and stormy tempests of the sea be ceased and the billows of his waves are still, to offer in my name a new ship, as a first-fruit of their navigation; and for this must thou wait, and not profane or despise the sacrifice in any wise. For the great priest shall carry this day following in procession, by my exhortation, a garland of roses next to the timbrel of his right hand; delay not, but, trusting to my will, follow that my procession passing amongst the crowd of the people, and when thou comest to the priest, make as though thou wouldst kiss his hand, but snatch at the roses and thereby put away the skin and shape of an ass, which kind of beast I have long time abhorred and despised. But above all things beware thou doubt not nor fear of any of those things as hard and difficult to be brought to pass; for in this same hour that I am come to thee, I am present there also, and I command the priest by a vision what he shall do, as here followeth: and all the people by my commandment shall be compelled to give thee place and say nothing. Moreover, think not that amongst so fair and joyful ceremonies, and in so good company, that any person shall abhor thy ill-favoured and deformed figure, or that any man shall be so hard as to blame and reprove thy sudden restoration to human shape, whereby they should gather or conceive any sinister opinion of thee; and know thou this of certainty, that the residue of thy life until the hour of death shall be bound and subject to me; and think it not an injury to be always serviceable towards me whilst thou shalt live, since as by my mean and benefit thou shalt return again to be a man. Thou shalt live blessed in this world, thou shalt live glorious by my guide and protection, and when after thine allotted space of life thou descendest to hell, there thou shalt see me in that subterranean firmament shining (as thou seest me now) in the darkness of Acheron, and reigning in the deep profundity of Styx, and thou shalt worship me as one that hath been favourable to thee. And if I perceive that thou art obedient to my commandment and addict to my religion, meriting by thy constant chastity my divine grace, know thou that I alone may prolong thy days above the time that the fates have appointed and ordained."

... Then the priest, being admonished the night before, as I might well perceive, and marvelling that now the event came opportunely to fulfil that warning, suddenly stood still, and holding out his hands thrust out the garland of roses to my mouth: which garland I (trembling and my heart beating greatly) devoured with a great affection. As soon as I had eaten them, I was not deceived of the promise made unto me: for my deform and assy face abated, and first the rugged hair of my body fell off, my thick skin waxed soft and tender, my fat belly became thin, the hoofs of my feet changed into toes, my hands were no more feet but returned again to the work of a man that walks upright, my neck grew short, my head and mouth became round, my long ears were made little, my great and stony teeth waxed less, like the teeth of men, and my tail, which before cumbered me most, appeared nowhere. Then the people began to marvel, and the religious honoured the goddess for so evident a miracle, which was foreshadowed by the visions which they saw in the night, and the facility of my reformation, whereby they lifted their hands to heaven and with one voice rendered testimony of so great a benefit which I received of the goddess.

When I saw myself in such estate, I was utterly astonished and stood still a good space and said nothing; for my mind could not contain so sudden and so great joy, and I could not tell what to say, nor what word I should first speak with my voice newly found, nor what thanks I should render to the goddess. But the great priest, understanding all my fortune and misery by divine advertisement, although he also was amazed at this notable marvel, by gestures commanded that one should give me a linen garment to cover me; for as soon as I was transformed from the vile skin of an ass to my human shape, I hid the privities of my body with my hands as far as a naked man might do. Then one of the company put off his upper robe, and put it on my back; which done, the priest, looking upon me with a sweet and benign countenance, began to say in this sort: "O my friend Lucius, after the endurance of so many labours and the escape of so many tempests of fortune, thou art now at length come to the port and haven of rest and mercy. Neither did thy noble lineage, thy dignity, neither thy excellent doctrine anything avail thee; but because thou didst turn to servile pleasures, by a little folly of thy youthfulness, thou hast had a sinister reward of thy unprosperous curiosity. But howsoever the blindness of fortune tormented thee in divers dangers, so it is that now by her unthoughtful malice thou art come to this present felicity of religion. Let fortune go and fume with fury in another place; let her find some other matter to execute her cruelty; for fortune hath no puissance against them which have devoted their lives to serve and honour the majesty of our goddess. For what availed the thieves? The beasts savage? Thy great servitude? The ill, toilsome, and dangerous ways? The fear of death every day? What availed all those, I say, to cruel fortune? Know thou that now thou art safe, and under the protection of that fortune that is not blind but can see, who by her clear light doth lighten the other gods: wherefore rejoice, and take a convenable countenance to thy white habit, and follow with joyful steps the pomp of this devout and honourable procession; let such, which be not devout to the goddess, see and acknowledge their error: 'Behold, here is Lucius that is delivered from his former so great miseries by the providence of the goddess Isis, and rejoiceth therefore and triumpheth of victory over his fortune.' And to the end thou mayest live more safe and sure, make thyself one of this holy order, to which thou wast but a short time since pledged by oath, dedicate thy mind to the obeying of our religion, and take upon thee a voluntary yoke of ministry: for when thou beginnest to serve and honour the goddess, then shalt thou feel the more the fruit of thy liberty."

When morning came and that the solemnities were finished, I came forth sanctified with twelve stoles and in a religious habit, whereof I am not forbidden to speak, considering that many persons saw me at that time. There I was commanded to stand upon a pulpit of wood which stood in the middle of the temple, before the figure and remembrance of the goddess; my vestment was of fine linen, covered and embroidered with flowers; I had a precious cope upon my shoulders, hanging down behind me to the ground, whereon were beasts wrought of divers colours, as Indian dragons, and Hyperborean griffins, whom in form of birds the other part of the world doth engender: the priests commonly call such a habit an Olympian stole. In my right hand I carried a lighted torch, and a garland of flowers was upon my head, with white palm-leaves sprouting out on every side like rays; thus I was adorned like unto the sun, and made in fashion of an image, when the curtains were drawn aside and all the people compassed about to behold me. Then they began to solemnise the feast, the nativity of my holy order, with sumptuous banquets and pleasant meats: the third day was likewise celebrated with like ceremonies, with a religious dinner, and with all the consummation of the adept order. Now when I had continued there some days, conceiving a marvellous pleasure and consolation in beholding ordinarily the image of the goddess, because of the benefits, beyond all esteem or reward, which she had brought me, at length she admonished me to depart homeward, not without rendering of thanks, which although they were not sufficient, yet they were according to my power. Howbeit I could hardly be persuaded to break the chains of my most earnest devotion and to depart, before I had fallen prostrate before the face of the goddess and wiped her feet with my face, whereby I began so greatly to weep and sigh that my words were interrupted, and as devouring my prayer I began to say in this sort: "O holy and blessed dame, the perpetual comfort of human kind, who by Thy bounty and grace nourishest all the world, and bearest a great affection to the adversities of the miserable as a loving mother, Thou takest no rest night or day, neither art Thou idle at any time in giving benefits and succouring all men as well on land as sea; Thou art she that puttest away all storms and dangers from men's life by stretching forth Thy right hand, whereby likewise Thou dost unweave even the inextricable and entangled web of fate, and appeasest the great tempests of fortune, and keepest back the harmful course of the stars. The gods supernal do honour Thee; the gods infernal have Thee in reverence; Thou dost make all the earth to turn, Thou givest light to the sun, Thou governest the world, Thou treadest down the power of hell. By Thy mean the stars give answer, the seasons return, the gods rejoice, the elements serve: at Thy commandment the winds do blow, the clouds nourish the earth, the seeds prosper, and the fruits do grow. The birds of the air, the beasts of the hill, the serpents of the den, and the fishes of the sea do tremble at Thy majesty: but my spirit is not able to give Thee sufficient praise, my patrimony is unable to satisfy Thy sacrifices; my voice hath no power to utter that which I think of Thy majesty, no, not if I had a thousand mouths and so many tongues and were able to continue forever. Howbeit as a good religious person, and according to my poor estate, I will do what I may: I will always keep Thy divine appearance in remembrance, and close the imagination of Thy most holy godhead within my breast."

Dedicatory Inscription

N. N. dedicated this to Isis, Serapis, Anubis, and Carpocrates. I am Isis, the mistress of every land, and was taught by Hermes, and devised with Hermes the demotic letters, that all things might not be written with the same [letters]. I gave and ordained laws unto men, which no one is able to change. I am eldest daughter of Cronos. I am wife and sister of King Osiris. I am she that riseth in the star of the Dog god. I am she that is called goddess by women. For me was the city of Bubastis built. I divided the earth from the heaven. I showed the path of the stars. I ordered the course of the sun and moon. I devised business in the sea. I made strong the right. I brought together woman and man. I appointed unto women the new-born babe in the tenth month. I ordained that parents should be loved by children. I laid punishment upon those disposed without natural affection towards their parents. I made with my brother Osiris an end of the eating of men. I taught to honour images of the gods. I consecrated the precincts of the gods. I broke down the governments of tyrants. I compelled women to be loved by men. I made the right to be stronger than gold and silver. I ordained that the true should be thought good. I devised marriage contracts. I assigned to Greeks and barbarians their languages. I made the beautiful and the ill-favoured to be distinguished by nature. I laid [?] fear [?] of an oath upon . . . unjustly . . .

Letter Honoring Serapis

To Apollonius greeting [from] Zoilus the Aspendian, . . . of the . . . , who also was presented unto thee by the king's friends. It happened unto me, while I was serving the god Serapis for thy health and success with king Ptolemy, that Serapis warned me many a time in sleep that I should sail over to thee and signify to thee this answer: That there must be made for him by thee a temple of Serapis and a grove in the Greek quarter by the haven, and a priest must oversee it and sacrifice at the altar for you. And when I had besought the god Serapis that he would set me free from the work here, he cast me into a great sickness, insomuch that I stood also in jeopardy. But having prayed to him, if he would heal me, I said that I would endure my ministry and do that which was commanded by him. Now when I was quickly healed, there came a certain man from Cnidus, who took in hand to build a temple of Serapis in this place and had brought stones. But afterward the god forbade him to build and he departed. But when I was come unto Alexandria, and delayed to make intercession with thee concerning these things, save of the affair which thou hadst also promised unto me, again I relapsed four months; wherefore I could not straightway come unto thee. It is therefore well, O Apollonius, that thou follow the command by the god, that Serapis may be favourable unto thee and make thee much greater with the king and more glorious, together with the health of thy body. Be not stricken with terror of the expense, as being of great cost to thee; nay, it shall be to thee of great profit, for I will together oversee all these things.

FAREWELL.

MAGICAL INCANTATIONS

Found on scraps of papyrus, scratched on potsherds and recorded on inscriptions at the shrines of healing gods, hundreds of magical formulae and longer incantation texts have been found. Of those included here in translation, the first is a full incantation aimed at forcing a demon to assist in bringing together Urbanus—apparently sick with love, and the author or sponsor of the incantation—with Candida, his beloved. The second text is a more general appeal to the demons, phrased in the pompous, polysyllabic, word-coining style apparently admired by those addicted to magic.

The third actually describes a theurgic process by which the desired effect is to be brought about through the ritual slaying of a white cock. The situation implied in the fourth text is that a magician has been asked by someone who has seen a vision of a supernatural being what is the present and the potential significance of what he has been allowed to behold; the possibilities are nearly limitless, he is told. The magician revealing the methods of the prince of demons, Beelzeboul, is apparently a Jew, who in our fifth excerpt has disclosed the methods of his demonic highness in tricking and dominating foolish men.

The final brief document is an inscription dedicated to Aesclepius, the god of healing, and was found on the island in the Tiber at Rome where a shrine to him was located in ancient times and where in more recent times there is a hospital. The inscription attests the restoration of sight to the blind by the formerly blind himself.

I

> I adjure thee, demonic spirit, who dost rest here, with the sacred names Aoth Abaoth, by the God of Abraan and the Jao[1] of Jaku, the Jao Aoth Abath, the God of Israma: hearken to the glorious and fearful and great name, and hasten to Urbanus, whom Urbana bore, and bring him to Domitiana, whom Candida bore, so that he, loving, frantic, sleepless with love of her and desire, may beg her to return to his house and become his wife. I adjure thee by the great God, the eternal and almighty, who is exalted above the exalted Gods. I adjure thee by Him who created the heaven and the sea. I adjure thee by him who separates the devout ones. I adjure thee by him who divided his staff in the sea, that thou bring Urbanus, whom Urbana bore, and unite him with Domitiana, who Candida bore, so that he, loving, tormented, sleepless with desire of her and with love, may take her home to his house as his wife. I adjure thee by him who caused the mule not to bear. I adjure thee by him who divided the light from the darkness. I adjure thee by him who crusheth the rocks. I adjure thee by him who parted the mountains. I adjure thee by him who holdeth the earth

---

[1]The names of the deity ending in ⁼*oth*, but especially the name Jao (or Iao), recall Hebrew spelling and specifically the Hebrew name for God, Yah or Yahweh. The context of the incantation is clearly that of Roman paganism, but from hellenistic times on, there was widespread syncretism, according to which worshippers asserted the identity of the gods behind the diversity of the names.

upon her foundations. I adjure thee by the sacred Name which is not uttered; in the [— —] I will mention it and the demons will be startled, terrified and full of horror, that thou bring Urbanus, whom Urbana bore, and unite him as husband with Domitiana, who Candida bore, and that he loving may beseech her; at once! quick! I adjure thee by him who set a lamp and stars in the heavens by the command of his voice so that they might lighten all men. I adjure thee by him who shook the whole world, and causeth the mountains to fall and rise, who causeth the whole earth to quake, and all her inhabitants to return. I adjure thee by him who made signs in the heaven and upon the earth and upon the sea, that thou bring Urbanus, whom Urbana bore, and unite him as husband with Domitiana, whom Candida bore, so that he, loving her, and sleepless with desire of her, beg her and beseech her to return to his house as his wife. I adjure thee by the great God, the eternal and almighty, whom the mountains fear and the valleys in all the world, through whom the lion parts with the spoil, and the mountains tremble and the earth and the sea, [through whom] every one becomes wise who is possessed with the fear of the Lord, the eternal, the immortal, the all-seeing, who hateth evil, who knoweth what good and what evil happeneth in the sea and the rivers and the mountains and the earth, Aoth Abaoth; by the God of Abraan and the Jao of Jaku, the Jao Aoth Abaoth, the God of Israma, bring and unite Urbanus, whom Urbana bore, with Domitiana, whom Candida bore—loving, frantic, tormented with love and affection and desire for Domitiana, whom Candida bore; unite them in marriage and as spouses in love for the whole time of their life. So make it that he, loving, shall obey her like a slave, and desire no other wife or maiden, but have Domitiana alone, whom Candida bore, as his spouse for the whole time of their life, at once, at once! quick, quick!

II

I invoke you, ye holy ones, mighty, majestic, glorious Splendours, holy, and earth-born, mighty arch-demons; compeers of the great god; denizens of Chaos, of Erebus and of the unfathomable abyss; earth-dwellers, haunters of sky-depths, nook-infesting, murk-enwrapped; scanning the mysteries, guardians of secrets, captains of the hosts of hell; kings of infinite space, terrestrial overlords, globe-shaking, firm-founding, ministering to earth-quakes; terror-strangling, panic-striking, spindle-turning; snow-scatterers, rain-wafters, spirits of air; fire-tongues of summer-sun, tempest-tossing lords of fate; dark shapes of Erebus, senders of necessity; flame-fanning fire-darters; snow-compelling, dew-compelling; gale-raising, abyss-plumbing, calm-bestriding air-spirits; dauntless in courage, heart-crushing despots; chasm-leaping, overburdening, iron-nerved demons; wild-raging, unenslaved; watchers of Tartaros;[2] delusive fate-phantoms; all-seeing, all-hearing, all-conquering, sky-wandering vagrants; life-inspiring, life-destroying,

---

[2]*Tartaros* is the underworld, the abode of the dead, dark and chaotic.

primeval pole-movers; heart-jocund death-dealers; revealers of angles, justicers of mortals, sunless revealers, masters of daimons, air-roving, omnipotent, holy, invincible [magic words], perform my behests.

III

Keep yourself pure for seven days, and then go on the third day of the moon to a place which the receding Nile has just laid bare. Make a fire on two upright bricks with olive-wood, that is to say thin wood, when the sun is half-risen, after having before sunrise circumambulated the altar. But when the sun's disc is clear above the horizon, decapitate an immaculate, pure-white cock, holding it in the crook of your left elbow; circumambulate the altar before sunrise. Hold the cock fast by your knees and decapitate it with no one else holding it. Throw the head into the river, catch the blood in your right hand and drink it up. Put the rest of the body on the burning altar and jump into the river. Dive under in the clothes you are wearing, then stepping backwards climb on to the bank. Put on new clothes and go away without turning round. After that take the gall of a raven and rub some of it with the wing of an ibis on your eyes and you will be consecrated.

IV

This is the holy operation for winning a familiar spirit. The process shows that he is the god; a spirit of the air was he whom you saw. He will perform at once any commission you may give him. He will send dreams, he will bring you women and men without need of a material link; he will remove, he will subdue, he will hurl winds up from the bosom of the earth; he will bring gold, silver, bronze, and give it to you, if you need it; he will also free from bonds the prisoner in chains, he opens doors, he renders you invisible, so that no human soul can see you; he will bring fire, carry water, bring wine, bread, and any other food you want: oil, vinegar, everything except fish, as many vegetables as you want; but as for pork, you must never command him to bring that. And if you wish to give a banquet, state your intention and order him to make ready with all speed any suitable place you have chosen for it. He will forthwith build round it a room with a gilded ceiling, and you will see its walls shining with marble, and you will partly believe it to be a reality and partly only an illusion. And he will provide precious wine too, such as is necessary to the spendour of the banquet, and he will hastily summon demons and provide you with servants in livery. All this he will do in the twinkling of an eye. . . . He can bind ships and loose them again; he can ban wicked demons in any quantity; he can soothe wild animals and instantly break the teeth of wild reptiles; he can send dogs to sleep and make them noiseless; he can transform into any shape or form as a winged creature, a water-creature, a four-footed beast or a reptile.

He will carry you through the air and throw you down again into the waves of the sea and the ocean streams; he will make rivers and seas fast in a moment, so that you can walk on them upright, if you wish . . . and if you wish to draw down the stars, and make warm cold, and cold warm, he will do it for you; he will make lights shine and go out; he will shake walls and reduce them by fire; he will be serviceable to you in all that you may desire, you happy mystic of holy magic.

V

And I summoned again to stand before me *Beelzeboul*, the prince of demons, and I sat him down on a raised seat of honour, and said to him: "Why are thou alone, prince of the demons?" And he said to me: "Because I alone am left of the angels of heaven that came down. For I was first angel in the first heaven, being entitled *Beelzeboul*. And now I control all those who are bound in *Tartarus*. . ."

I Solomon said unto him: "*Beelzeboul*,[3] what is thy employment?" And he answered me: "I destroy kings. I ally myself with foreign tyrants. And my own demons I set on to men, in order that the latter may believe in them and be lost. And the chosen servants of God, priests and faithful men, I excite unto desires for wicked sins, and evil heresies, and lawless deeds; and they obey me, and I bear them on to destruction. And I inspire men with envy, and murder, and for wars and sodomy, and other evil things. And I will destroy the world. . . ." I said to him: "Tell me by what angel thou art frustrated." And he answered: "By the holy and precious name of the Almighty God, called by the Hebrews by a row of numbers,[4] of which the sum is 644, and among the Greeks it is *Emannuel*. And if one of the Romans adjure me by the great name of the power Eleêth, I disappear at once."

I Solomon was astounded when I heard this; and I ordered him to saw up Theban marbles. And when he began to saw the marbles, the other demons cried out with a loud voice, howling because of their king *Beelzeboul*.

---

[3]"Beelzeboul" is one of a series of variant spellings for the chief of demons. It has been conjectured that originally this name was *Baal* (or Beel—*shamayim*, meaning "lord of the heavens," but that it was corrupted to Baal-zebul, meaning "lord of the dung," or Baal-zebub, meaning "lord of the flies," after the deity worshipped in the Philistine city of Ekron who had the power to drive away insects.

[4]Since in both Hebrew and Greek letters were used for numerals, the practice developed of attaching significance to the sum of the numerical values of the letters in a word or a name. Then the sum could be used by those in the know for the name or word thus represented. A similar practice lies behind the mysterious 666, used in Rev. 13 as a cryptic reference to the blasphemous "beast",—probably one of the Roman emperors.

But I Solomon questioned him, saying: "If thou wouldst gain a respite, discourse to me about the things in heaven." And *Beelzeboul* said: "Hear, O king, if thou burn gum, and incense, and bulbs of the sea, with nard and saffron, and light seven lamps in an earthquake, thou wilt firmly fix thy house. And if, being pure, thou light them at dawn in the sun alight, then wilt thou see the heavenly dragons, how they wind themselves along and drag the chariot of the sun." And I Solomon, having heard this, rebuked him, and said: "Silence for the present, and continue to saw marbles as I commanded thee."

VI

To Valerius Aper, a blind soldier, the god[6] revealed that he should go and take blood of a white cock, together with honey, and rub them into an eyesalve and anoint his eyes three days. And he received his sight, and came and gave thanks publicly to the god.

THE CHURCH IN THE APOSTOLIC AGE

For information concerning the history of the church after the period of the New Testament and for the fate of the apostles and others mentioned in the New Testament we are largely dependent on the writings of

Asclepius, the god of healing, restoring a patient while the concerned friends or family look on. (Source: National Museum, Athens)

Eusebius of Caesarea (264–349) in his *Ecclesiastical History*. For much of his material he draws on legends or traditions written by or attributed to leaders of the church in the second century. Because nearly all the works he mentions are otherwise lost, we are indebted to him for the material he has preserved, but we are often in no position to evaluate it.

What is excerpted here are passages in which he tells where the apostles went, how they met death, and what writings they left behind, if any. In discussing the origins of the gospels, he makes an attempt to account for the differences among them, thus setting an early example for critical historical study of the New Testament, even though modern critics are often unconvinced by his arguments.

Eusebius: Ecclesiastical History

XV . . . At that same time also JAMES,[1] who was called the brother of the Lord, inasmuch as the latter too was styled the child of Joseph, and Joseph was called the father of Christ, for the Virgin was betrothed to him when, before they came together, she was discovered to have conceived by the Holy Spirit, as the sacred writing of the Gospels teaches—this same James, to whom the men of old had also given the surname of Just for his excellence of virtue, is narrated to have been the first elected to the throne of the bishopric of the Church in Jerusalem. Clement in the sixth book of the *Hypotyposes* adduces the following: "For," he says, "PETER and JAMES and JOHN after the Ascension of the Saviour did not struggle for glory, because they had previously been given honour by the Saviour, but chose James the Just as bishop of Jerusalem." The same writer in the seventh book of the same work says in addition this about him, "After the Resurrection the Lord gave the tradition of knowledge to James the Just and John and Peter, these gave it to the other Apostles and the other Apostles to the seventy, of whom Barnabas also was one. Now there were two Jameses, one James the Just, who was thrown down from the pinnacle of the temple and beaten to death with a fuller's club, and the other he who was beheaded." Paul also mentions the same James the Just when he writes, "And I saw none other of the Apostles save James the brother of the Lord."

At this time too the terms of our Saviour's promise to the king of the Osrhoenes were receiving fulfilment. THOMAS was divinely moved to send THADDAEUS to Edessa[2] as herald and evangelist of the teaching concerning Christ, as we have shown just previously from the writing preserved there. Where he reached the place Thaddaeus healed Abgar by the word of Christ, and amazed all the inhabitants by his strange miracles. By the mighty influence of his deeds he brought them to reverence the power of Christ, and made them disciples of the saving

---

[1] James, the brother of Jesus; not to be confused with James the son of Zebedee and brother of John.

[2] A city in Northern Syria.

teaching. From that day to this the whole city of Edessenes has been dedicated to the name of Christ, thus displaying no common proof of the beneficence of our Saviour to them. Of such evil was SIMON[3] the father and fabricator, and the Evil Power, which hates that which is good and plots against the salvation of men, raised him up at that time as a great antagonist for the great and inspired Apostles of our Saviour. Nevertheless the grace of God which is from heaven helped its ministers and quickly extinguished the flames of the Evil One by their advent and presence, and through them humbled and cast down "every high thing that exalteth itself against the knowledge of God." Wherefore no conspiracy, either of Simon, or of any other of those who arose at that time, succeeded in those Apostolic days; for the light of the truth and the divine Logos himself, which had shone from God upon men by growing up on the earth and dwelling among his own Apostles, was overcoming all things in the might of victory. The aforesaid sorcerer, as though the eyes of his mind had been smitten by the marvellous effulgence of God when he had formerly been detected in his crimes in Judaea by the Apostle PETER, at once undertook a great journey across the sea, and went off in flight from east to west, thinking that only in this way could he live as he wished. He came to the city of the Romans, where the power which obsessed him wrought with him greatly, so that in a short time he achieved such success that he was honoured as a god by the erection of a statue by those who were there. But he did not prosper long. Close after him in the same reign of Claudius the Providence of the universe in its great goodness and love towards men guided to Rome, as against a gigantic pest on life, the great and mighty Peter, who for his virtues was the leader of all the other Apostles. Like a noble captain of God, clad in divine armour, he brought the costly merchandise of the spiritual light from the east to the dwellers in the west, preaching the Gospel of the light itself and the word which saves souls, the proclamation of the Kingdom of Heaven. XV. Thus when the divine word made its home among them the power of Simon was extinguished and perished immediately, together with the fellow himself.

But a great light of religion shone on the minds of the hearers of PETER, so that they were not satisfied with a single hearing or with the unwritten teaching of the divine proclamation, but with every kind of exhortation besought Mark whose Gospel is extant, seeing that he was Peter's follower, to leave them a written statement of the teaching given them verbally, nor did they cease until they had persuaded him, and so became the cause of the Scripture called the Gospel according to Mark. And they say that the Apostle, knowing by the revelation of the spirit to him what had been done, was pleased at their zeal, and ratified the scripture for study in the churches. Clement quotes the story in the sixth book of the *Hypotyposes*, and the bishop of Hierapolis, named Papias, confirms him. He also says that Peter mentions MARK in his first Epistle, and that he composed this in Rome itself, which they say that he himself indicates, referring to the city

---

[3]Simon Magus (the Magician), mentioned in Acts 8:9 ff., and considered by early Christian writers to have been the father of heresies, especially of Gnosticism.

metaphorically as Babylon, in the words, "the elect one in Babylon greets you, and Marcus my son."

XVI. They say that this MARK was the first to be sent to preach in Egypt the Gospel which he had also put into writing, and was the first to establish churches in Alexandria itself. The number of men and women who were there converted at the first attempt was so great, and their asceticism was so extraordinarily philosophic, that Philo thought it right to describe their conduct and assemblies and meals and all the rest of their manner of life.

When PAUL appealed to Caesar and was sent over to Rome by Festus the Jews were disappointed of the hope in which they had laid their plot against him and turned against JAMES, the brother of the Lord, to whom the throne of the bishopric in Jerusalem had been allotted by the Apostles. The crime which they committed was as follows. They brought him into the midst and demanded a denial of the faith in Christ before all the people, but when he, contrary to the expectation of all of them, with a loud voice and with more courage than they had expected, confessed before all the people that our Lord and Saviour Jesus Christ is the son of God, they could no longer endure his testimony, since he was by all men believed to be most righteous because of the height which he had reached in a life of philosophy and religion, and killed him, using anarchy as an opportunity for power since at that moment Festus had died in Judaea, leaving the district without government or procurator. The manner of James's death has been shown by the words of Clement already quoted, narrating that he was thrown from the battlement and beaten to death with a club, but Hegesippus, who belongs to the generation after the Apostles, gives the most accurate account of him speaking as follows in his fifth book: "The charge of the Church passed to James the brother of the Lord, together with the Apostles. He was called the 'Just' by all men from the Lord's time to ours, since many are called James, but he was holy from his mother's womb. He drank no wine or strong drink, nor did he eat flesh; no razor went upon his head; he did not anoint himself with oil, and he did not go to the baths. He alone was allowed to enter into the sanctuary, for he did not wear wool but linen, and he used to enter alone into the temple and be found kneeling and praying for forgiveness for the people, so that his knees grew hard like a camel's because of his constant worship of God, kneeling and asking forgiveness for the people. So from his excessive righteousness he was called the Just and Oblias, that is in Greek, 'Rampart of the people and righteousness,' as the prophets declare concerning him.

And many were convinced and confessed at the testimony of James and said, 'Hosanna to the Son of David.' Then again the same Scribes and Pharisees said to one another, 'We did wrong to provide Jesus with such testimony, but let us go up and throw him down that they may be afraid and not believe him.' And they cried out saying, 'Oh, oh, even the just one erred.' And they fulfilled the Scripture written in Isaiah, 'Let us take the just man for he is unprofitable to us. Yet they shall eat the fruit of their works.' So they went up and threw down the Just, and they said to one another, 'Let us stone James the

Just,' and they began to stone him since the fall had not killed him, but he turned and knelt saying, "I beseech thee, O Lord, God and Father, forgive them, for they know not what they do." And while they were thus stoning him one of the priests of the sons of Rechab, the son of Rechabim, to whom Jeremiah the prophet bore witness, cried out saying, 'Stop! what are you doing? The Just is praying for you.' And a certain man among them, one of the laundrymen, took the club with which he used to beat out the clothes, and hit the Just on the head, and so he suffered martyrdom. And they buried him on the spot by the temple, and his gravestone still remains by the temple. He became a true witness both to Jews and to Greeks that Jesus is the Christ, and at once Vespasian began to besiege them."

XXV. When the rule of Nero was now gathering strength for unholy objects he began to take up arms against the worship of the God of the universe. It is not part of the present work to describe his depravity: many indeed have related his story in accurate narrative, and from them he who wishes can study the perversity of his degenerate madness, which made him compass the unreasonable destruction of so many thousands, until he reached that final guilt of sparing neither his nearest nor dearest, so that in various ways he did to death alike his mother, brothers, and wife, with thousands of others attached to his family, as though they were enemies and foes. But with all this there was still lacking to him this—that it should be attributed to him that he was the first of the emperors to be pointed out as a foe of divine religion. This again the Latin writer Tertullian mentions in one place as follows: "Look at your records: there you will find that Nero was the first to persecute this belief when, having overcome the whole East, he was specially cruel in Rome against all. We boast that such a man was the author of our chastisement; for he who knows him can understand that nothing would have been condemned by Nero had it not been great and good."

In this way then was he the first to be heralded as above all a fighter against God, and raised up to slaughter against the Apostles. It is related that in his time PAUL was beheaded in Rome itself, and

Nero, whose full title (in abbreviations) is here given: Nero Claudius Caesar Augustus Germanicus. It was under Nero (54–68 A.D. that the first persecution of Christians in Rome, and that Peter and Paul were martyred, according to ancient Christian tradition.

that PETER likewise was crucified, and the title of "Peter and Paul," which is still given to the cemeteries there, confirms the story, no less than does a writer of the Church named Caius, who lived when Zefyrinus was bishop of Rome. Caius in a written discussion with Proclus, the leader of the Montanists, speaks as follows of the places where the sacred relics of the Apostles in question are deposited: "But I can point out the trophies of the Apostles, for if you will go to the Vatican or to the Ostian Way you will find the trophies of those who founded this Church." And that they both were martyred at the same time DIONYSIUS, bishop of Corinth, affirms in this passage of his correspondence with the Romans: "By so great an admonition you bound together the foundations of the Romans and Corinthians by Peter and Paul, for both of them taught together in our Corinth and were our founders, and together also taught in Italy in the same place and were martyred at the same time."

Such was the condition of things among the Jews, but the holy Apostles and disciples of our Saviour were scattered throughout the whole world, THOMAS, as tradition relates, obtained by lot Parthia, ANDREW Scythia, JOHN Asia[4] (and he stayed there and died in Ephesus), but PETER seems to have preached to the Jews of the Dispersion in Pontus and Galatia and Bithynia, Cappadocia, and Asia, and at the end he came to Rome and was crucified head downwards, for so he had demanded to suffer. What need be said of PAUL, who fulfilled the gospel of Christ from Jerusalem to Illyria and afterward was martyred in Rome under Nero?

ROM. 15:
19

Now it would be clear from Paul's own words and from the narrative of Luke in the Acts that Paul, in his preaching to the Gentiles,

---

[4]The Roman province of Asia; what is now the western edge of Turkey.

The stone slab resting over the tomb believed to be that of Paul. It is among the few bits remaining from the church built on the ancient road to Ostia, port of Rome, in the time of Constantine to honor the apostle who was martyred on this spot according to ancient tradition.

laid the foundations of the churches from Jerusalem round about unto Illyricum. And from the Epistle which we have spoken of as indisputably PETER's, in which he writes to those of the Hebrews in the Dispersion of Pontus and Galatia, Cappadocia, Asia, and Bithynia, it would be clear from his own words in how many provinces he delivered the word of the New Testament by preaching the Gospel of Christ to those of the circumcision. But it is not easy to say how many of these and which of them were genuinely zealous and proved their ability to be the pastors of the churches founded by the Apostles, except by making a list of those mentioned by Paul. For there were many thousands of his fellow-workers and, as he called them himself, fellow-soldiers, of whom the most were granted by him memorial past forgetting, for he recounts his testimony to them unceasingly in his own letters, and, moreover, Luke also in the Acts gives a list of those known to him and mentions them by name. Thus TIMOTHY is related to have been the first appointed bishop of the diocese of Ephesus, as was TITUS of the churches in Crete. Luke, who was by race an Antiochian and a physician by profession, was long a companion of Paul, and had careful conversation with the other Apostles, and in two books left us examples of the medicine for souls which he had gained from them—the Gospel, which he testifies that he had planned according to the tradition received by him by those who were from the beginning, and Acts of the Apostles which he composed no longer on the evidence of hearing but of his own eyes. And they say that Paul was actually accustomed to quote from LUKE's Gospel since when writing of some Gospel as his own he used to say, "According to my Gospel." Of the other followers of Paul there is evidence that Crescens was sent by him to Gaul, and Linus, who is mentioned in the second Epistle to Timothy as present with him in Rome has already been declared to have been the first after Peter to be appointed to the bishopric of the Church in Rome. Of CLEMENT too, who was himself made the third bishop of the church of Rome, it is testified by Paul that he worked and strove in company with him. In addition to these Dionysius, one of the ancients, the pastor of the diocese of the Corinthians, relates that the first bishop of the Church at Athens was that member of the Areopagus, the other DIONYSIUS, whose original conversion after Paul's speech to the Athenians in the Areopagus Luke described in the Acts.[5]

COL. 4: 14

LK. 1: 1-4

PHIL. 4: 3

. . . the people of the church in Jerusalem were commanded by an oracle given by revelation before the war to those in the city who were worthy of it to depart and dwell in one of the cities of Perea which they called Pella.[6] To it those who believed on Christ migrated from Jerusalem, that when holy men had altogether deserted the royal capital of the Jews and the whole land of Judaea, the judgement of God might at last overtake them for all their crimes against the Christ

MK. 13: 14 (?)

---

[5]Acts 17:34.

[6]A hellenistic city on the eastern side of the upper Jordan Valley, and a part of the loose federation of cities known as Decapolis. Recently excavated, it contains extensive Roman remains and evidence of having continued as a center of Christianity down to the sixth century, when the Muslim invasion of Palestine occurred.

and his Apostles, and all that generation of the wicked be utterly blotted out from among men. Those who wish can retrace accurately from the history written by Josephus how many evils at that time overwhelmed the whole nation in every place and especially how the inhabitants of Judea were driven to the last point of suffering, how many thousands of youths, women, and children perished by the sword, by famine, and by countless other forms of death; they can read how many and what famous Jewish cities were besieged, and finally how terrors and worse than terrors were seen by those who fled to Jerusalem as if to a mighty capital; they can study the nature of the whole war, all the details of what happened in it, and how at the end the abomination of desolation spoken of by the prophets was set up in the very temple of God, for all its ancient fame, and it perished utterly and passed away in flames.

After the martyrdom of JAMES and the capture of Jerusalem which immediately followed, the story goes that those of the Apostles and of the disciples of the Lord who were still alive came together from every place with those who were, humanly speaking, of the family of the Lord, for many of them were then still alive, and they all took counsel together as to whom they ought to adjudge worthy to succeed James, and all unanimously decided that SIMEON the son of CLOPAS,[7] whom the scripture of the Gospel also mentions, was worthy of the throne of the diocese there. He was, so it is said, a cousin of the Saviour, for Hegesippus relates that Clopas was the brother of Joseph, (XII.) and in addition that Vespasian, after the capture of Jerusalem, ordered a search to be made for all who were of the family of David, that there might be left among the Jews no one of the royal family and, for this reason, a very great persecution was again inflicted on the Jews.

XVIII. At this time, the story goes, the Apostle and Evangelist JOHN was still alive, and was condemned to live in the island of Patmos for his witness to the divine word. At any rate Irenaeus, writing about the number of the name ascribed to the anti-Christ in the so-called Apocalypse of John, states this about John in so many words in the fifth book against Heresies. "But if it had been necessary to announce his name plainly at the present time, it would have been spoken by him who saw the apocalypse. For it was not seen long ago but almost in our own time, at the end of the reign of Domitian."[8]

The same Domitian gave orders for the execution of those of the family of David and an ancient story goes that some heretics accused the grandsons of JUDAS (who is said to have been the brother, according to the flesh, of the Saviour) saying that they were of the family of David and related to the Christ himself. Hegesippus relates this exactly as follows. XX. "Now there still survived of the family of the Lord grandsons of Judas, who was said to have been his brother according to the flesh, and they were related as being of the family of David. These the officer brought to Domitian Caesar, for, like Herod, he was afraid of the coming of the Christ. He asked them if they were

JUDE 1

---

[7]In Luke 24:18.
[8]That is, prior to A.D. 96.

of the house of David and they admitted it. Then he asked them how much property they had, or how much money they controlled, and they said that all they possessed was nine thousand denarii between them, the half belonging to each, and they stated that they did not possess this in money but it was the valuation of only thirty-nine plethra of ground on which they paid taxes and lived on it by their own work." They then showed him their hands, adducing as testimony of their labour the hardness of their bodies, and the tough skin which had been embossed on their hands from their incessant work. They were asked concerning the Christ and his kingdom, its nature, origin, and time of appearance, and explained that it was neither of the world nor earthly, but heavenly and angelic, and it would be at the end of the world, when he would come in glory to judge the living and the dead and to reward every man according to his deeds. At this Domitian did not condemn them at all, but despised them as simple folk, released them, and decreed an end to the persecution against the church. But when they were released they were the leaders of the churches, both for their testimony and for their relation to the Lord, and remained alive in the peace which ensued until Trajan. Hegesippus tells this; moreover, Tertullian also has made similar mention of Domitian. "Domitian also once tried to do the same as he, for he was a Nero in cruelty, but I believe, inasmuch as he had some sense, he stopped at once and recalled those whom he had banished."

At this time that very disciple whom Jesus loved, JOHN, at once Apostle and Evangelist, still remained alive in Asia and administered the churches there, for after the death of Domitian, he had returned from his banishment on the island. And that he remained alive until this time may fully be confirmed by two witnesses, and these ought to be trustworthy for they represent the orthodoxy of the church, no less persons than Irenaeus and Clement of Alexandria. The former of these writes in one place in the second of his books *Against the Heresies*, as follows: "And all the presbyters who had been associated in Asia with JOHN, the disciple of the Lord, bear witness to his tradition, for he remained with them until the times of Trajan." And in the third book of the same work he makes the same statement as follows: "Now the church at Ephesus was founded by Paul, but John stayed there until the times of Trajan, and it is a true witness of the tradition of the Apostles."

Clement indicates the same time, and in the treatise to which he gave the title *Who is the rich man that is saved*, adds a narrative most acceptable to those who enjoy hearing what is fine and edifying. Take and read here what he wrote. "Listen to a story which is not a story but a true tradition of JOHN the Apostle preserved in memory. For after the death of the tyrant he passed from the island of Patmos to Ephesus, and used also to go, when he was asked, to the neighbouring districts of the heathen, in some places to appoint bishops, in others to reconcile whole churches, and in others to ordain some one of those pointed out by the Spirit."

But come, let us indicate the undoubted writings of this Apostle. Let the Gospel according to him be first recognized, for it is read in all the churches under heaven. Moreover, that it was reasonable for the ancients to reckon it in the fourth place after the other three may be explained thus. Those inspired and venerable ancients, I mean Christ's Apostles, had completely purified their life and adorned their souls with every virtue, yet were but simple men in speech. Though they were indeed bold in the divine and wonder-working power given them by the Saviour, they had neither the knowledge nor the desire to represent the teachings of the Master in persuasive or artistic language, but they used only the proof of the Spirit of God which worked with them, and the wonder-working power of Christ which was consummated through them. Thus they announced the knowledge of the Kingdom of Heaven to all the world and cared but little for attention to their style. And this they did inasmuch as they were serving a greater, superhuman ministry. Thus PAUL, the most powerful of all in the preparation of argument and the strongest thinker, committed to writing no more than short epistles, though he had ten thousand ineffable things to say, seeing that he had touched the vision of the third heaven, had been caught up to the divine paradise itself, and was there granted the hearing of ineffable words. Nor were the other pupils of our Saviour without experience of the same things—the twelve Apostles and the seventy disciples and ten thousand others in addition to them. Yet nevertheless of all those who had been with the Lord only MATTHEW and JOHN have left us their recollections, and tradition says that they took to writing perforce. MATTHEW had first preached to Hebrews, and when he was on the point of going to others he transmitted in writing in his native language the Gospel according to himself, and thus supplied by writing the lack of his own presence to those from whom he was sent, and MARK and LUKE had already published the Gospels according to them, but JOHN, it is said, used all the time a message which was not written down, and at last took to writing for the following cause. The three gospels which had been written down before were distributed to all including himself; it is said that he welcomed them and testified to their truth but said that there was only lacking to the narrative the account of what was done by Christ at first and at the beginning of the preaching. The story is surely true. It is at least possible to see that the three evangelists related only what the Saviour did during one year after John the Baptist had been put in prison and that they stated this at the beginning of their narrative. At any rate, after the forty days' fast and the temptation which followed, Matthew fixes the time described in his own writing by saying that "hearing that John had been betrayed, he retreated" from Judaea "into Galilee." Similarly MARK says, "and after John was betrayed Jesus came into Galilee." And Luke, too, makes a similar observation before beginning the acts of Jesus saying that Herod added to the evil deeds which he had done by "shutting up John in prison." They say accordingly that for this reason the apostle John was asked to relate in his own gospel the period passed over in silence by the former evangelists and the things done during it by the Saviour (that is to say, the events before the imprisonment of the Baptist), and that he indicated this at one time by saying, "this beginning of miracles did Jesus," at another by mentioning the Baptist in the midst of the acts of Jesus as at that time still baptizing at Aenon

II COR.
12:2-4

MT. 4:12

LK. 3:
19-20

JN. 3:
22-24

near Salem, and that he makes this plain by saying, "for John was not yet cast into prison." Thus JOHN in the course of his gospel relates what Christ did before the Baptist had been thrown into prison, but the other three evangelists narrate the events after the imprisonment of the Baptist. If this be understood the gospels no longer appear to disagree, because that according to John contains the first of the acts of Christ and the others the narrative of what he did at the end of the period, and it will seem probable that John passed over the genealogy of our Saviour according to the flesh, because it had been already written out by Matthew and Luke, and began with the description of his divinity since this had been reserved for him by the Divine Spirit as for one greater than they.

The above must suffice us concerning the writing of the Gospel according to JOHN, and the cause for that according to Mark has been explained above. LUKE himself at the beginning of his treatise prefixed an account of the cause for which he had made his compilation, explaining that while many others had somewhat rashly attempted to make a narrative of the things of which he had himself full knowledge, he felt obliged to release us from the doubtful propositions of the others and related in his own gospel the accurate account of the things of which he had himself firmly learnt the truth from his profitable intercourse and life with Paul and his conversation with the other apostles.

Meaning in History

What combines the otherwise diverse writings grouped in this section is that all of them are concerned with the meaning of history. In the Book of Jubilees we have a midrashic retelling and expansion of the biblical narratives. The points at which the scriptural accounts have been modified are especially significant: Enoch, who merits only passing mention in the text of Genesis (5: 21–24), figures prominently as the source and channel of special divine wisdom concerning the future of the creation; Noah's struggles in the flood are the work of demonic powers, not merely the consequence of human disobedience as the Genesis account indicates; the trials of Israel in Egypt are likewise the result of the evil schemes of Mastema, demonic prince, rather than of the ill will of Pharaoh; the Isaac story is combined with the biblical account in Genesis 49 of Jacob's blessing his twelve sons in order to give special place to Levi and Judah, progenitors of the anointed priest and king expected in Essene (Qumran) eschatology. And obedience to the law of Moses is expanded so that the sabbath observance becomes linked with the movement of history through cycles of years, culminating in the Great Sabbath era, the New Age.

Philo's *On the Virtues* also retells the biblical narrative, but his aim is to show that the goal of the faithful is to obtain release from earthly, bodily existence, so that by attuning one's soul to the harmony of the celestial bodies (obvious neo-Pythagorean influence), one may leave behind the limitations of the body and enter immortality. Philo's outlook is not wholly antihistorical, however—he does foresee a glorious future for the nation Israel. But it is clear that for him the primary hope is to gain immortal life.

The author of IV Maccabees is interested primarily in the hellenistic goals of the attainment of virtue, which for him is the life of reason. He retells the story of the Maccabean struggle, showing that the successful resistance of the Maccabees was not merely a result of bravery, but of their allowing reason to be the dominant force in life.

The Fourth Eclogue of Virgil is an enigma; it is impossible to determine what the poet's precise aim was or what lies behind the veiled allusions and imagery. He probably wrote in praise of Caesar Augustus and in the hope that the new era that began with him would culminate in the renewal of the creation. Lily Ross Taylor's[1] plausible proposal is that the "new child" of this eclogue combines elements of Aion (meaning "age"; an abstract divinity compounded of Egyptian and Iranian elements), Horus from Egypt, and Mithra from Iran. The poem's perspective on history has been shaped by the Jewish Sibylline Oracles, which had been growing by accretion since the second century B.C. The Greek and Roman Sibylls, whose oracles were highly regarded and often consulted in Rome, were prophetesses, the counterparts of the Hebrew prophets. Alexandrine Jews began to produce their own Sibylline Oracles which, though retaining many aspects of pagan mythology and hellenistic history, set forth eschatological views like those of the later Hebrew prophets and predicted the coming of the Messiah. The fact that Virgil would espouse such hopes and express them in terms drawing from such a wide range of cultural traditions is itself testimony both to the syncretism that characterized the period and to the widespread longing for a new beginning.

JEWISH APOCALYPTIC:
[JUBILEES]

The writer, probably an Essene (or a member of a similar, earlier group), retells the history of Israel from creation to the giving of the Law at Sinai, but he places the whole narrative in a cosmic setting, according

---

[1] *The Divinity of the Roman Emperor* (Middletown, Conn.: American Philological Association, 1931), pp. 113–14.

to which the orderly movement of the heavenly bodies is a sign of the orderly movement of history toward its divinely determined goal: the establishment of God's rule on the earth, with the anointed king (from the tribe of Judah) and the anointed priest (from the tribe of Levi) exercising authority in God's stead.

The text is an expanded version (midrash) of the book of Genesis and parts of Exodus. Heavy emphasis is placed on chronology as the evidence of the outworking of the divine plan. The assurance that God has given to the writer (or his community) the true interpretation of scripture and of the history of Israel rests on the fact that their calendar is superior to the basically lunar calendar then in use among Jews, which was in constant need of adjustment as it became out of phase with the solar year. The book of Jubilees seems to have been produced or preserved by a dissident Jewish sect—an impression that receives support from the fact that several fragments of the book were found at Qumran among the Dead Sea Scrolls.

PROLOGUE

This is the history of the division of the days of the law and of the testimony, of the events of the years, of their [year] weeks, of their Jubilees throughout all the years of the world, as the Lord spake to Moses on Mount Sinai when he went up to receive the tables of the law and of the commandment, according to the voice of God as he said unto him, "Go up to the top of the Mount."

1:1–11; 26–29

(1) And it came to pass in the first year of the exodus of the children of Israel out of Egypt, in the third month, on the sixteenth day of the month, that God spake to Moses, saying: "Come up to Me on the Mount, and I will give thee two tables of stone of the law and of the commandment, which (2) I have written, that thou mayst teach them." And Moses went up into the mount of God, and the (3) glory of the Lord abode on Mount Sinai, and a cloud overshadowed it six days. And He called to Moses on the seventh day out of the midst of the cloud, and the appearance of the glory of the (4) Lord was like a flaming fire on the top of the mount. And Moses was on the Mount forty days and forty nights, and God taught him the earlier and the later history of the division of all the days (5) of the law and of the testimony. And He said: "Incline thine heart to every word which I shall speak to thee on this mount, and write them in a book in order that their generations may see how I have not forsaken them for all the evil which they have wrought in transgressing the covenant (6) which I establish between Me and thee for their generations this day on Mount Sinai. And thus it will come to pass when all these things come upon them, that they will recognise that I am more righteous than they in all their judgements and in all their actions, and

they will recognise that (7) I have been truly with them. And do thou write for thyself all these words which I declare unto thee this day, for I know their rebellion and their stiff neck, before I bring them into the land of which I sware to their fathers, to Abraham and to Isaac and to Jacob, saying: 'Unto your seed (8) will I give a land flowing with milk and honey.' And they will eat and be satisfied, and they will turn to strange gods, to [gods] which cannot deliver them from aught of their (9) tribulation: and this witness shall be heard for a witness against them. For they will forget all My commandments, [even] all that I command them, and they will walk after the Gentiles, and after their uncleanness, and after their shame, and will serve their gods, and these will (10) prove unto them an offence and a tribulation and an affliction and a snare. And many will perish and they will be taken captive, and will fall into the hands of the enemy, because they have forsaken My ordinances and My commandments, and the festivals of My covenant, and My sabbaths, and My holy place which I have hallowed for Myself in their midst, and My tabernacle, and My sanctuary, which I have hallowed for Myself in the midst of the land, that I should set my name (11) upon it, and that it should dwell [there].

(26) And do thou write down for thyself all these words which I declare unto thee on this mountain, the first and the last, which shall come to pass in all the divisions of the days in the law and in the testimony and in the weeks and the jubilees unto eternity, until I descend and dwell (27) with them throughout eternity." And He said to the angel of the presence: "Write for Moses from (28) the beginning of creation till My sanctuary has been built among them for all eternity. And the Lord will appear to the eyes of all, and all shall know that I am the God of Israel and the Father of all the children of Jacob, and King on Mount Zion for all eternity. And Zion and Jerusalem shall (29) be holy." And the angel of the presence who went before the camp of Israel took the tables of the divisions of the years—from the time of the creation—of the law and of the testimony of the weeks of the jubilees, according to the individual years, according to all the number of the jubilees [according to the individual years], from the day of the [new] creation when the heavens and the earth shall be renewed and all their creation according to the powers of the heaven, and according to all the creation of the earth, until the sanctuary of the Lord shall be made in Jerusalem on Mount Zion, and all the luminaries be renewed for healing and for peace and for blessing for all the elect of Israel, and that thus it may be from that day and unto all the days of the earth.

4:16–25

(16) And in the eleventh jubilee Jared took to himself a wife, and her name was Bâraka, the daughter of Râsujâl, a daughter of his father's brother, in the fourth week of this jubilee, and she bare him a son in the fifth week, in the fourth year of the jubilee, and (17) he called his

name Enoch.[1] And he was the first among men that are born on earth who learnt writing and knowledge and wisdom and who wrote down the signs of heaven according to the order of their months in a book, that men might know the seasons of the years according to the order of (18) their separate months. And he was the first to write a testimony, and he testified to the sons of men among the generations of the earth, and recounted the Sabbaths of the years (19) as we made [them] known to him. And what was and what will be he saw in a vision of his sleep, as it will happen to the children of men throughout their generations until the day of judgment; he saw and understood everything, and wrote his testimony, and placed the testimony on earth for all (20) the children of men and for their generations. And in the twelfth jubilee, in the seventh week thereof, he took to himself a wife, and her name was Ednî, the daughter of Dânêl, the daughter of his father's brother, and in the sixth year in this week she bare him a son and he called his name (21) Methuselah. And he was moreover with the angels of God these six jubilees of years, and they showed him everything which is on earth and in the heavens, the rule of the sun, and he wrote down (22) everything. And he testified to the Watchers, who had sinned with the daughters of men; for these had begun to unite themselves, so as to be defiled, with the daughters of men, and Enoch (23) testified against [them] all. And he was taken from amongst the children of men, and we conducted him into the Garden of Eden in majesty and honour, and behold there he writes down the (24) condemnation and judgment of the world, and all the wickedness of the children of men. And on account of it [God] brought the waters of the flood upon all the land of Eden; for there he was set as a sign and that he should testify against all the children of men, that he should recount all the (25) deeds of the generations until the day of condemnation.

10:1–14

(1) And in the third week of this jubilee the unclean demons began to lead astray the children of (2) the sons of Noah, and to make them to err and destroy them. And the sons of Noah came to Noah their father, and they told him concerning the demons which were leading astray and blinding and (3) slaying his sons' sons. And he prayed before the Lord his God, and said:

"God of the spirits of all flesh, who hast shown mercy unto me,
And hast saved me and my sons from the waters of the flood,
And hast not caused me to perish as Thou didst the sons of perdition;

For Thy grace has been great towards me,
And great has been Thy mercy to my soul;

Let Thy grace be lift up upon my sons,
And let not wicked spirits rule over them
Lest they should destroy them from the earth.

---

[1]Enoch, who rates only a few verses in the Bible (Gen. 5:19–24) captured the Hebrew imagination because he is not recorded as having died. Around him developed an extensive literature. See below pp. 180–191.

(4) But do Thou bless me and my sons, that we may increase and multiply and replenish the earth. (5) And Thou knowest how Thy Watchers, the fathers of these spirits, acted in my day: and as for these spirits which are living, imprison them and hold them fast in the place of condemnation, and let them not bring destruction on the sons of thy servant, my God; for these are malignant, and (6) created in order to destroy. And let them not rule over the spirits of the living; for Thou alone canst exercise dominion over them. And let them not have power over the sons of the righteous (7, 8) from henceforth and for evermore." And the Lord our God bade us to bind all. And the chief of the spirits, Mastema, came and said: "Lord, Creator, let some of them remain before me, and let them hearken to my voice, and do all that I shall say unto them; for if some of them are not left to me, I shall not be able to execute the power of my will on the sons of men; for these are for corruption and leading astray before my judgment, for great is the wickedness of the sons of men." (9) And He said: "Let the tenth part of them remain before him, and let nine parts descend into the (10) place of condemnation." And one of us He commanded that we should teach Noah all their (11) medicines; for He knew that they would not walk in uprightness, nor strive in righteousness. And we did according to all His words: all the malignant evil ones we bound in the place of condemnation, (12) and a tenth part of them we left that they might be subject before Satan on the earth. And we explained to Noah all the medicines of their diseases, together with their seductions, how he (13) might heal them with herbs of the earth. And Noah wrote down all things in a book as we instructed him concerning every kind of medicine. Thus the evil spirits were precluded from (14) [hurting] the sons of Noah.

31:5–26

(5) And Isaac said: "Let my son Jacob come, and let me see him before I die." And Jacob went to his father Isaac and to his mother Rebecca, to the house of his father Abraham, and he took two of his sons with him, Levi and Judah, and he came to his father Isaac and to his mother Rebecca. (6) And Rebecca came forth from the tower to the front of it to kiss Jacob and embrace him; for her spirit had revived when she heard: "Behold Jacob thy son has come"; and she kissed (7) him. And she saw his two sons, and she recognised them, and said unto him: "Are these thy sons, my son?" and she embraced them and kissed them, and blessed them, saying: "In you shall the (8) seed of Abraham become illustrious, and ye shall prove a blessing on the earth." And Jacob went in to Isaac his father, to the chamber where he lay, and his two sons were with him, and he took the hand of his father, and stooping down he kissed him, and Isaac clung to the neck of Jacob his son, (9) and wept upon his neck. And the darkness left the eyes of Isaac, and he saw the two sons of Jacob, (10) Levi, and Judah, and he said: "Are these thy sons, my son? for they are like thee." And he said unto him that they were truly his sons: "And thou hast truly seen that they are truly my sons." (11) And they came near to him, and he turned and kissed them and embraced them both together. (12) And the spirit of prophecy came down into his mouth, and he took Levi by right hand and (13) Judah by his left. And he

turned to Levi first, and began to bless him first, and said unto him:
"May the God of all, the very Lord of all the ages, bless thee and thy
children throughout all the (14) ages. And may the Lord give to thee
and to thy seed greatness and great glory, and cause thee and thy
seed, from among all flesh to approach Him to serve in His sanctuary
as the angels of the presence and as the holy ones. [Even] as they,
shall the seed of thy sons be for glory and greatness (15) and holiness,
and may He make them great unto all the ages. And they shall be
judges and princes, and chiefs of all the seed of the sons of Jacob;

They shall speak the word of the Lord in righteousness,
And they shall judge all His judgments in righteousness.

And they shall declare My ways to Jacob
And my paths to Israel.

The blessing of the Lord shall be given in their mouths
To bless all the seed of the beloved.

(16) Thy mother has called thy name Levi,
And justly has she called thy name;

Thou shalt be joined to the Lord
And be the companion of all the sons of Jacob;

Let His table be thine,
And do thou and thy sons eat thereof;

And may thy table be full unto all generations,
And thy food fail not unto all ages.

(17) And let all who hate thee fall down before thee,
And let all thy adversaries be rooted out and perish;

And blessed be he that blesses thee,
And cursed be every nation that curses thee."

(18) And to Judah he said:
"May the Lord give thee strength and power

To tread down all that hate thee;
A prince shalt thou be, thou and one of thy sons, over the sons of
    Jacob;

May thy name and the name of thy sons go forth and traverse every
    land and region.
Then shall the Gentiles fear before thy face,

And all the nations shall quake
(And all the peoples shall quake).

(19) In thee shall be the help of Jacob,
And in thee be found the salvation of Israel.

(20) And when thou sittest on the throne of honour of thy righteous-
    ness
There shall be great peace for all the seed of the sons of the beloved;

Blessed be he that blesseth thee,
And all that hate thee and afflict thee and curse thee
Shall be rooted out and destroyed from the earth and be accursed."

(21) And turning he kissed him again and embraced him, and rejoiced greatly; for he had seen the (22) sons of Jacob his son in very
truth. And he went forth from between his feet and fell down and
bowed down to him, and he blessed them and rested there with Isaac
his father that night, and they (23) ate and drank with joy. And he
made the two sons of Jacob sleep, the one on his right hand and the
(24) other on his left, and it was counted to him for righteousness. And
Jacob told his father everything during the night, how the Lord had
shown him great mercy, and how he had prospered [him in] all (25)
his ways, and protected him from all evil. And Isaac blessed the God
of his father Abraham, who (26) had not withdrawn his mercy and
his righteousness from the sons of his servant Isaac.

48:1–19

(1) And in the sixth year of the third week of the forty-ninth jubilee thou didst depart and dwell in the land of Midian five weeks and
one year. And thou didst return into Egypt in the second week in the
second year in the fiftieth jubilee. And thou thyself knowest what He
spake unto thee on (2) Mount Sinai, and what prince Mâstêma desired
to do with thee when thou wast returning into Egypt (3) [on the way
when thou didst meet him at the lodging-place]. Did he not with all
his power seek to slay thee and deliver the Egyptians out of thy hand
when he saw that thou wast sent to execute (4) judgment and vengeance on the Egyptians? And I delivered thee out of his hand, and thou
didst perform the signs and wonders which thou wast sent to perform
in Egypt against Pharaoh, and (5) against all his house, and against
his servants and his people. And the Lord executed a great vengeance
on them for Israel's sake, and smote them through (the plagues of)
blood and frogs, lice and dog-flies, and malignant boils breaking forth
in blains; and their cattle by death; and by hailstones, thereby He
destroyed everything that grew for them; and by locusts which devoured the residue which had been left by the hail, and by darkness;
and [by the death] of the first-born of (6) men and animals, and on
all their idols the Lord took vengeance and burned them with fire.
And everything was sent through thy hand, that thou shouldst declare
(these things) before they were done, and thou didst speak with the
king of Egypt before all his servants and before his people. (7) And
everything took place according to thy words; ten great and terrible
judgments came on the (8) land of Egypt that thou mightest execute
vengeance on it for Israel. And the Lord did everything for Israel's
sake, and according to His covenant, which He had ordained with
Abraham that He (9) would take vengeance on them as they had
brought them by force into bondage. And the prince Mâstêma stood
up against thee, and sought to cast thee into the hands of Pharaoh,
and he helped (10) the Egyptian sorcerers, and they stood up and

wrought before thee. The evils indeed we permitted (11) them to work, but the remedies we did not allow to be wrought by their hands. And the Lord smote them with malignant ulcers, and they were not able to stand, for we destroyed them so that (12) they could not perform a single sign. And notwithstanding all (these) signs and wonders the prince Mâstêma was not put to shame because he took courage and cried to the Egyptians to pursue after thee with all the powers of the Egyptians, with their chariots, and with their horses, and with all the (13) hosts of the peoples of Egypt. And I stood between the Egyptians and Israel, and we delivered Israel out of his hand, and out of the hand of his people, and the Lord brought them through the (14) midst of the sea as if it were dry land. And all the peoples whom he brought to pursue after Israel, the Lord our God cast them into the midst of the sea, into the depths of the abyss beneath the children of Israel, even as the people of Egypt had cast their children into the river. He took vengeance on 1,000,000 of them, and one thousand strong and energetic men were destroyed on (15) account of one suckling of the children of thy people which they had thrown into the river. And on the fourteenth day and on the fifteenth and on the sixteenth and on the seventeenth and on the eighteenth the prince Mâstêma was bound and imprisoned behind the children of Israel that he (16) might not accuse them. And on the nineteenth we let them loose that they might help the (17) Egyptians and pursue the children of Israel. And he hardened their hearts and made them stubborn, and the device was devised by the Lord our God that He might smite the Egyptians and (18) cast them into the sea. And on the fourteenth we bound him that he might not accuse the children of Israel on the day when they asked the Egyptians for vessels and garments, vessels of silver, and vessels of gold, and vessels of bronze, in order to despoil the Egyptians in return for the bondage in (19) which they had forced them to serve. And we did not lead forth the children of Israel from Egypt empty-handed.

50:1–13

(1) And after this law I made known to thee the days of the Sabbaths in the desert of Sin[ai], which is between Elim and Sinai. (2) And I told thee of the jubilee years in the sabbaths of years: but the year thereof have I not told thee till ye enter the land which ye are to possess. (3) And the land also shall keep its sabbaths while they dwell upon it, and they shall know the jubilee year. (4) Wherefore I have ordained for thee the year-weeks and the years and the jubilees: there are forty-nine jubilees from the days of Adam until this day, and one week and two years: and there are yet forty years to come [lit., "distant"] for learning the commandments of the Lord, until they pass over into the land of Canaan, crossing the Jordan to the west. (5) And the jubilees shall pass by, until Israel is cleansed from all guilt of fornication, and shall be no more a Satan or any evil one, and the land shall be clean from that time for evermore.

(6) And behold the commandment regarding the Sabbaths—I have written [them] down for thee—and all the judgments of its laws. (7)

Six days shalt thou labour, but on the seventh day is the Sabbath of the Lord your God. In it ye shall do no manner of work, ye and your sons, and your men-servants and your maid-servants, and all your cattle and the sojourner also who is with you. (8) And the man that does any work on it shall die: whoever desecrates that day, whoever lies with [his] wife, or whoever says he will do something on it, that he will set out on a journey thereon in regard to any buying or selling: and whoever draws water thereon which he had not prepared for himself on the sixth day, and whoever takes up any burden to carry it out of his tent or out of his house shall die. Ye shall do no work whatever on the Sabbath day save what ye have prepared for yourselves on the sixth day, so as to eat, and drink, and rest, and keep Sabbath from all work on that day, and to bless the Lord your God, who has given you a day of festival and a holy day: and a day of the holy kingdom, for all Israel is this day among their days forever. (10) For great is the honour which the Lord has given to Israel that they should eat and drink and be satisfied on this festival day, and rest thereon from all labour which belongs to the labour of the children of men, save burning frankincense and bringing oblations and sacrifices before the Lord for days and for Sabbaths. (11) This work alone shall be done on the Sabbath-days in the sanctuary of the Lord your God; that they may atone for Israel with sacrifice continually from day to day for a memorial well-pleasing before the Lord, and that He may receive them always from day to day according as thou hast been commanded. (12) And every man who does any work thereon, or goes on a journey, or tills (his) farm, whether in his house or any other place, and whoever lights a fire, or rides on any beast, or travels by ship on the sea, and whoever strikes or kills anything, or slaughters a beast or a bird, or whoever catches an animal or a bird or a fish, or whoever fasts or makes war on the Sabbaths: (13) The man who does any of these things on the Sabbath shall die, so that the children of Israel shall observe the Sabbaths according to the commandments regarding the Sabbaths of the land, as it is written in the tablets, which He gave into my hands that I should write out for thee the laws of the seasons, and the seasons according to the division of their days.

JEWISH MYSTICAL:

[PHILO OF ALEXANDRIA]

Philo, On the Virtues (Based on Deut. 34)

XI:66–75

Here we have the first proof of the kindness (66) and faithfulness which he [Moses] showed to all his compatriots, but there is another not inferior to it. When his disciple, Joshua, who modelled himself on his master's characteristics with the love which they deserved, had been approved by divine judgement as best fitted to command, Moses was not depressed as another might have been because the choice had not fallen on his sons or nephews, but was filled with intense joy, to think that the nation would be in the (67) charge of one excelling in every way, since he knew that one in whom God is well pleased must needs be of a noble character. So taking Joshua by the right hand he brought him forward to where the multitude was congregated. He had no tremors at the thought of his own end, but had added other new joys to the old, for he had not only the memory of earlier felicities, which every kind of virtue had given him, filling him to overflowing with delight, but also the hope of coming immortality as he passed from the corruptible life to the incorruptible. Thus with a face beaming with the gladness of his soul, he said brightly and cheerfully, "The time has come for me to depart (68) from the life of the body, but here is a successor to take charge of you, chosen by God," and he at once proceeded to recite the messages declaring God's approval, to which they gave credence; then turning (69) his eyes on Joshua he bade him be of good courage and mighty in wise policy, initiate good plans of action and carry out his decisions with strong and resolute thinking to a happy conclusion. For though he to whom he addressed these words did not perhaps need the exhortation, Moses would not keep hidden the personal friendship and patriotism which urged him like a spur to lay bare what he thought would be profitable. Also he had received the divine command (70) that he should exhort his successor and create in him the spirit to undertake the charge of the nation with a high courage, and not to fear the burden of sovereignty. Thus all future rulers would find a law to guide them right by looking to Moses as their archetype and model, and none would grudge to give good advice to their successors, but all would train and school their souls with admonitions and exhortations. For a good man's exhortation can (71) raise the disheartened, lift them on high and establish them superior to occasions and circumstances, and inspire them with a gallant and dauntless spirit.

Having discoursed thus suitably to his subjects and (72) the heir of his headship, he proceeded to hymn God in a song in which he rendered the final thanksgiving of his bodily life for the rare and extraordinary gifts with which he had been blest from his birth to his old age. He convoked a divine assemblage of the (73) elements of all existence and the chiefest parts of the universe, earth and heaven, one the home of mortals, the other the house of immortals. With these around him he sang his canticles with every kind of harmony and sweet music in the ears of both mankind and ministering angels: of men that as disciples they (74) should learn from him the lesson of like thankfulness of heart: of angels as watchers, observing, as themselves masters of melody, whether the song had any discordant note, and scarce able to credit that any man imprisoned in a corruptible body could like the sun and moon and the most sacred choir of the other stars attune his soul to harmony with God's instrument, the heaven and the whole universe. Thus in (75) his post amid the ethereal choristers the great Revealer blended with the strains of thankfulness to God his own true feelings of affection to the nation, therein joining with his arraignment of them for past sins his admonitions for the present occasion and calls to a sounder mind, and his exhortations for the future expressed in hopeful words of comfort which needs must be followed by their happy fulfilment.

XII:76–79

When he had ended his anthems, a blend we (76) may call them of religion and humanity, he began to pass over from mortal existence to life immortal and gradually became conscious of the disuniting of the elements of which he was composed. The body, the shell-like growth which encased him, was being stripped away and the soul laid bare and yearning for its natural removal hence. Then after accomplishing (77) the preparations for his departure he did not set out for his new home until he had honoured all the tribes of his nation with the content of his benedictions, mentioning the founders of the tribes by name. That these benedictions will be fulfilled we must believe, for he who gave them was beloved of God the lover of men and they for whom he asked were of noble lineage and held the highest rank in the army led by the Maker and Father of all. (The prayers were requests (78) for true goods, not only that they should have them in this mortal life but much more when the soul is set free from the bonds of the flesh.) For Moses (79) alone, it is plain, had grasped the thought that the whole nation from the very first was akin to things divine, a kinship most vital and a far more genuine tie than that of blood, and, therefore, he declared it the heir of all good things that human nature can contain. What he had himself he gave them ready for their use, what he did not possess he supplicated God to grant them, knowing that though the fountains of His grace are perennial they are not free for all, but only to suppliants. And suppliants are all those who love a virtuous life, to whom it is permitted to quench their thirst for wisdom with water drawn from the fountains of true holiness.

HELLENISTIC ETHICAL:

[IV MACCABEES]

The author, a hellenized Jew, possibly from Alexandria, seeks to show that the inspired Law of Moses is wholly compatible with the Stoic virtues of reason, self-control, and triumph over the passions. He retells the story of the Maccabean struggle against the Seleucids, but is not interested in the events themselves as much as in their demonstration of the fact that reason can be victorious over the body and its passions.

IV MACCABEES: 1:1–27

(1) Philosophical in the highest degree is the question I propose to discuss, namely whether the Inspired Reason is supreme ruler over the passions; and to the philosophy of it I would seriously entreat (2) your earnest attention. For not only is the subject generally necessary as a branch of knowledge, but it includes the praise of the (3) greatest

of virtues, whereby I mean self-control. That is to say, (4) if Reason is proved to control the passions adverse to temperance, gluttony and lust, it is also clearly shown to be lord over the passions, like malevolence, opposed to justice, and over those opposed to manliness, namely rage and pain and fear.

(5) But, some may ask, if the Reason is master of the passions, why does it not control forgetfulness and ignorance? their object (6) being to cast ridicule. The answer is that Reason is not master over defects inhering in the mind itself, but over the passions *or moral defects* that are adverse to justice and manliness and temperance and judgement; and its action in their case is not to extirpate the passions, but to enable us to resist them successfully.

(7) I could bring before you many examples, drawn from various sources, where Reason has proved itself master over the passions, (8) but the best instance by far that I can give is the noble conduct of those who died for the sake of virtue, Eleazar, and the Seven (9) Brethren and the Mother. For these all by their contempt of pains, yea, even unto death, proved that Reason rises superior to the (10) passions. I might enlarge here in·praise of their virtues, they, the men with the Mother, dying on this day we celebrate for the love of moral beauty and goodness, but rather would I felicitate them (11) on the honours they have attained. For the admiration felt for their courage and endurance, not only by the world at large but by their very executioners, made them the authors of the downfall of the tyranny under which our nation lay, they defeating the tyrant by their endurance, so that through them was their country purified. (12) But I shall presently take opportunity to discuss this, after we have begun with the general theory, as I am in the habit of doing, and I will then proceed to their story, giving glory to the all-wise God.

(13) Our enquiry, then, is whether the Reason is supreme master (14) over the passions. But we must define just what the Reason is and what passion is, and how many forms of passion there are, and whether (15) the Reason is supreme over all of them. Reason I take to be the (16) mind preferring with clear deliberation the life of wisdom. Wisdom I take to be the knowledge of things, divine and human, and of their (17) causes. This I take to be the culture acquired under the Law, through which we learn with due reverence the things of God and for our worldly profit the things of man.

(18) Now wisdom is manifested under the forms of judgement and (19) justice, and courage, and temperance. But judgement *or self-control* is the one that dominates them all, for through it, in truth, Reason (20) asserts its authority over the passions. But of the passions there are two comprehensive sources, namely, pleasure and pain, and either (21) belongs essentially also to the soul as well as to the body. And with respect both to pleasure and pain there are many cases where (22) the passions have certain sequences. Thus while desire goes before (23) pleasure, satisfaction follows after, and while fear goes before (24) pain, after pain comes sorrow. Anger, again, if a man will retrace the course of his feelings, is a passion in which are blended both (25) pleasure and pain. Under pleasure, also, comes that moral debasement (26) which exhibits the widest variety of the passions. It manifests (27) itself in the soul as ostentation, and covetous-

ness, and vain-glory, and contentiousness, and backbiting, and in the body as eating of strange meat, and gluttony, and gormandizing in secret.

IV MACCABEES: 17:11–24

(11, 12) For truly it was a holy war which was fought by them. For on that day virtue, proving them through endurance, set before them (13) the prize of victory in incorruption in everlasting life. But the first in the fight was Eleazar, and the mother of the seven sons (14) played her part, and the brethren fought. The tyrant was their adversary and the world and the life of man were the spectators. (15) And righteousness won the victory, and gave the crown to her athletes. (16) Who but wondered at the athletes of the true Law? Who were not (17, 18) amazed at them? The tyrant himself and his whole council admired their endurance, whereby they now do both stand beside the throne (19) of God and live the blessed age. For Moses says, "All also who (20) have sanctified themselves are under thy hands." And these men, therefore, having sanctified themselves for God's sake, not only have received this honour, but also *the honour* that through them the (21) enemy had no more power over our people, and the tyrant suffered (22) punishment, and our country was purified, they having as it were become a ransom for our nation's sin; and through the blood of these righteous men and the propitiation effected by their death, the divine Providence (23) delivered Israel that had previously been evil. For when the tyrant Antiochus saw the heroism of their virtue, and their endurance under the tortures, he publicly held up their endurance (24) to his soldiers as an example; and he thus inspired his men with a sense of honour and heroism on the field of battle and in the *labours of* besieging, so that he plundered and overthrew all his enemies.

IV MACCABEES: 18:1–4

(1) O Israelites, children born of the seed of Abraham, obey this Law, and be righteous in all ways, recognizing that Inspired Reason (2) is lord over the passions, and over pains, not only from within, but from without ourselves; by which means those men, delivering up (3) their bodies to the torture for righteousness' sake, not only won the admiration of mankind, but were deemed worthy of a divine inheritance. (4) And through them the nation obtained peace and restoring the observance of the Law in our country hath captured the city from the enemy.

ROMAN ESCHATOLOGICAL:

[VIRGIL, ECLOGUE IV]

SICILIAN Muses, let us sing a somewhat loftier strain. Not all do the orchards please and the lowly tamarisks. If our song is of the woodland, let the woodland be worthy of a consul.

Now is come the last age of the song of Cumae; the great line of the centuries begins anew. (5) Now the Virgin returns, the reign of Saturn returns; now a new generation descends from heaven on high. Only do thou, pure Lucina, smile on the birth of the child, under whom the iron brood shall first cease, and a golden race spring up throughout the world! Thine own Apollo now is king! (10)

And in thy consulship, Pollio, yea in thine, shall this glorious age begin, and the mighty months commence their march; under thy sway, and lingering traces of our guilt shall become void, and release the earth from its continual dread. (15) He shall have the gift of divine life, shall see heroes mingled with gods, and shall himself be seen of them, and shall sway a world to which his father's virtues have brought peace.

But for thee, child, shall the earth untilled pour forth, as her first pretty gifts, straggling ivy with foxglove everywhere, and the Egyptian bean blended with the smiling acanthus. (20) Uncalled, the goats shall bring home their udders swollen with milk, and the herds shall fear not huge lions; unmasked, thy cradle shall pour forth flowers for thy delight. (25) The serpent; too, shall perish, and the false poison-plant shall perish; Assyrian spice shall spring up on every soil.

(26) But soon as thou canst read of the glories of heroes and thy father's deeds, and canst know what valour is, slowly shall the plain yellow with the waving corn, on wild brambles shall hang the purple grape, and the stubborn oak shall distil dewy honey. Yet shall some few traces of olden sin lurk behind, to call men to essay the sea in ships, to gird towns with walls, and to cleave the earth with furrows. A second Tiphys shall then arise, and a second Argo to carry chosen heroes; a second warfare, too, shall there be, and again shall a great Achilles be sent to Troy.

(37) Next, when now the strength of years has made thee man, even the trader shall quit the sea, nor shall the ship of pine exchange wares; every land shall bear all fruits. The earth shall not feel the harrow, nor the vine the pruning-hook; the sturdy ploughman, too, shall now loose his oxen from the yoke. Wool shall no more learn to counterfeit varied hues, but of himself the ram in the meadows shall change his fleece, now to sweetly blushing purple, now to a saffron yellow; of its own will shall scarlet clothe the grazing lambs.

(46) "Ages such as these, glide on!" cried to their spindles the Fates, voicing in unison the fixed will of Destiny!

(48) Enter on thy high honours—the hour will soon be here—O thou dear offspring of the gods, mighty seed of a Jupiter to be! Behold the world bowing with its massive dome—earth and expanse of sea and heaven's depth! Behold, how all things exult in the age that is at hand! O that then the last days of a long life may still linger for me, with inspiration enough to tell of thy deeds! Not Thracian Orpheus, not Linus shall vanquish me in song, though his mother be helpful to the one, and his father to the other, Calliope to Orpheus, and fair Apollo to Linus. Even Pan, were he to contend with me and Arcady be judge, even Pan, with Arcady for judge, would own himself defeated.

(60) Begin, baby boy, to know thy mother with a smile—to thy mother ten months have brought the weariness of travail. Begin, baby boy!

LITERARY TEXTS AND FOLK-LITERARY SOURCES

Literary Texts

WISDOM AND ITS MEDIATORS

In the hellenistic period the exposure of Jews to Greek culture produced an ambivalence within the Jewish community. On the one hand there was an enormous .appeal of both the intellectual and the more superficial aspects of hellenistic world, which led some Jews to adopt Greek modes of dress and recreation in defiance of the Law of Moses, and induced others to study Greek philosophy in order to discover how it might be correlated with the revealed truths of Mosaic Law. But on the other hand, many Jews stiffened their opposition to hellenistic ways, and concentrated their attention on the study of the Law. In the so-called wisdom literature of Judaism from this period, both tendencies are evident.

The *Wisdom of Jesus Ben Sira* (or Jesus Sirach, but usually known simply as Ecclesiasticus, from the title given in Latin versions of the collection of late, post-biblical Jewish writings commonly called *The Apocrypha*), is the oldest surviving, and perhaps the very first documentation we have for the scribal movement, members of which devoted themselves to the study of the Law of Moses and to interpreting its truths for their contemporaries. Ben Sira was a teacher, and it has been conjectured that his book is a poeticized transcript of some of his lectures.[1] For him wisdom consists in devotion to the teachings of the scriptures— the books of Moses, as well as the prophetic writings, the psalms, and the proverbs —and the appropriation of their truths in the light of a commonsense assessment of life based on experience itself. Thus Ben Sira comes down on the side of Jewish distinctiveness, though without dogmatically narrow limitation to the words of the Law, on which the Sadducees were later to insist. The excerpts from the *Wisdom of Jesus Ben Sira* given here include the wisdom of pursuing wisdom, the place of man in the creation, the preferential nature of the scribe's place in society, and finally the praise of men of the past, ranging from obscure artisans whose work binds society together to the recently deceased Simon the High Priest (ca. 200 B.C.), whose splendor Ben Sira depicts.

The *Wisdom of Solomon* affirms the uniqueness of Jewish knowledge of truth even while showing the correlation between the revealed wisdom of God of which "Solomon" speaks and the truth as perceived by the great philosophers of the Greek tradition. The book implies that its author is the historical Solomon (the king of Israel who built the temple in Jerusalem) addressing his fellow kings, but it was composed in Greek, depends on the Greek translation of the Bible rather than on the Hebrew text, and utilizes many of the technical terms of Greek philosophy for which there would be no exact equivalents in Hebrew. Building on a theme that appears in the canonical book of Proverbs (8:22–31), which was also traditionally assigned to Solomon, the author describes Wisdom in an almost personified form as the agent of God in creating and ordering the world. What is distinctive about the development of this idea in the excerpt from *Widom of Solomon* is that some of the technical terms of the Platonic doctrine of the creation of the world are used there, although in keeping with the Jewish tradition, the relationship with wisdom is allegorized on the analogy of a lover and his beloved. The mood of the work, then, is one of Jewish piety, rational striving for understanding of metaphysical problems about the creation of the world and the origin of evil, and a mystical religious longing.

Wisdom of Ben Sira

15:1–20

The man who fears the Lord will do this,
  and he who holds to the law will obtain wisdom.

---

[1]Proposed by R. H. Pfeiffer, *History of New Testament Times* (New York: Harper, 1949), p. 367.

She will come to meet him like a mother,
    and like the wife of his youth she will welcome him.
She will feed him with the bread of understanding,
    and give him the water of wisdom to drink.
He will lean on her and will not fall,
    and he will rely on her and will not be put to shame.
She will exalt him above his neighbors,
    and will open his mouth in the midst of the assembly.
He will find gladness and a crown of rejoicing,
    and will acquire an everlasting name.
Foolish men will not obtain her,
    and sinful men will not see her.
She is far from men of pride,
    and liars will never think of her.

A hymn of praise is not fitting on the lips of a sinner,
    for it has not been sent from the Lord.
For a hymn of praise should be uttered in wisdom,
    and the Lord will prosper it.

Do not say, "Because of the Lord I left the right way";
    for he will not do what he hates.
Do not say, "It was he who led me astray";
    for he has no need of a sinful man.
The Lord hates all abominations,
    and they are not loved by those who fear him.
It was he who created man in the beginning,
    and he left him in the power of his own inclination.
If you will, you can keep the commandments,
    and to act faithfully is a matter of your own choice.
He has placed before you fire and water:
    stretch out your hand for whichever you wish.
Before a man are life and death,
    and whichever he chooses will be given to him.
For great is the wisdom of the Lord;
    he is mighty in power and sees everything;
His eyes are on those who fear him,
    and he knows every deed of man.
He has not commanded anyone to be ungodly,
    and he has not given anyone permission to sin.

16:26–17:32

The works of the Lord have existed from the beginning by his creation,
    and when he made them, he determined their divisions.
He arranged his works in an eternal order,
    and their dominion for all generations;
they neither hunger nor grow weary,
    and they do not cease from their labors.
They do not crowd one another aside,
    and they will never disobey his word.
After this the Lord looked upon the earth,
    and filled it with his good things;

with all kinds of living beings he covered its surface,
    and to it they return.

(17) The Lord created man out of earth,
    and turned him back to it again.
He gave to men few days, a limited time,
    but granted them authority over the things upon the earth.
He endowed them with strength like his own,
    and made them in his own image.
He placed the fear of them in all living beings,
    and granted them dominion over beasts and birds.
He made for them tongue and eyes;
    he gave them ears and a mind for thinking.
He filled them with knowledge and understanding,
    and showed them good and evil.
He set his eye upon their hearts
    to show them the majesty of his works.
And they will praise his holy name,
    to proclaim the grandeur of his works.
He bestowed knowledge upon them,
    and allotted to them the law of life.
He established with them an eternal covenant,
    and showed them his judgments.
Their eyes saw his glorious majesty,
    and their ears heard the glory of his voice.
And he said to them, "Beware of all unrighteousness."
    And he gave commandment to each of them concerning his
    neighbor.
Their ways are always before him,
    they will not be hid from his eyes.
He appointed a ruler for every nation,
    but Israel is the Lord's own portion.
All their works are as the sun before him,
    and his eyes are continually upon their ways.
Their iniquities are not hidden from him,
    and all their sins are before the Lord.
A man's almsgiving is like a signet with the Lord,
    and he will keep a person's kindness like the apple of his eye.
Afterward he will arise and requite them,
    and he will bring their recompense on their heads.
Yet to those who repent he grants a return,
    and he encourages those whose endurance is failing.
Turn to the Lord and forsake your sins;
    pray in his presence and lessen your offenses.
Return to the Most High and turn away from iniquity,
    and hate abominations intensely.
Who will sing praises to the Most High is Hades,
    as do those who are alive and give thanks?
From the dead, as from one who does not exist, thanksgiving has
    ceased;
    he who is alive and well sings the Lord's praises.
How great is the mercy of the Lord,
    and his forgiveness for those who turn to him!

For all things cannot be in men,
    since a son of man is not immortal.
What is brighter than the sun? Yet its light fails.
    So flesh and blood devise evil.
He marshals the host of the height of heaven;
    but all men are dust and ashes.

38:24–39:11

The wisdom of the scribe depends on the opportunity of leisure;
    and he who has little business may become wise.
How can he become wise who handles the plow,
    and who glories in the shaft of a goad,
who drives oxen and is occupied with their work,
    and whose talk is about bulls?
He sets his heart on plowing furrows,
    and he is careful about fodder for the heifers.
So too is every craftsman and master workman
    who labors by night as well as by day;
those who cut the signets of seals,
    each is diligent in making a great variety;
he sets his heart on painting a lifelike image,
    and he is careful to finish his work.
So too is the smith sitting by the anvil,
    intent upon his handiwork in iron;
the breath of the fire melts his flesh,
    and he wastes away in the heat of the furnace;
he inclines his ear to the sound of the hammer,
    and his eyes are on the pattern of the object.
He sets his heart on finishing his handiwork,
    and he is careful to complete its decoration.
So too is the potter sitting at his work
    and turning the wheel with his feet;
he is always deeply concerned over his work,
    and all his output is by number.
He moulds the clay with his arm
    and makes it pliable with his feet;
he sets his heart to finish the glazing,
    and he is careful to clean the furnace.

All these rely upon their hands,
    and each is skilful in his own work.
Without them a city cannot be established,
    and men can neither sojourn nor live there.
Yet they are not sought out for the council of the people,
    nor do they attain eminence in the public assembly.
They do not sit in the judge's seat,
    nor do they understand the sentence of judgment;
they cannot expound discipline or judgment,
    and they are not found using proverbs.
But they keep stable the fabric of the world,
    and their prayer is in the practice of their trade.

(39) On the other hand he who devotes himself
    to the study of the law of the Most High
will seek out the wisdom of all the ancients,
    and will be concerned with prophecies;
he will preserve the discourse of notable men
    and penetrate the subtleties of parables;
he will seek out the hidden meanings of proverbs
    and be at home with the obscurities of parables.
He will serve among great men
    and appear before rulers;
he will travel through the lands of foreign nations,
    for he tests the good and the evil among men.
He will set his heart to rise early to seek the Lord who made him,
    and will make supplication before the Most High;
he will open his mouth in prayer
    and make supplication for his sins.

If the great Lord is willing,
    he will be filled with the spirit of understanding;
he will pour forth words of wisdom
    and give thanks to the Lord in prayer.
He will direct his counsel and knowledge aright,
    and meditate on his secrets.
He will reveal instruction in his teaching,
    and will glory in the law of the Lord's covenant.
Many will praise his understanding,
    and it will never be blotted out;
his memory will not disappear,
    and his name will live through all generations.
Nations will declare his wisdom,
    and the congregation will proclaim his praise;
if he lives long, he will leave a name greater than a thousand,
    and if he goes to rest, it is enough for him.

44:1–15

Let us now praise famous men,
    and our fathers in their generations.
The Lord apportioned to them great glory,
    his majesty from the beginning.
There were those who ruled in their kingdoms,
    and were men renowned for their power,
giving counsel by their understanding,
    and proclaiming prophecies;
leaders of the people in their deliberations
    and in understanding of learning for the people,
    wise in their words of instruction;
those who composed musical tunes,
    and set forth verses in writing;
rich men furnished with resources,
    living peaceably in their habitations—

all these were honored in their generations,
and were the glory of their times.
There are some of them who have left a name,
so that men declare their praise.
And there are some who have no memorial,
who have perished as though they had not lived;
they have become as though they had not been born,
and so have their children after them.
But these were men of mercy,
whose righteous deeds have not been forgotten;
their prosperity will remain with their descendants,
and their inheritance to their children's children.
Their descendants stand by the covenants;
their children also, for their sake.
Their posterity will continue forever,
and their glory will not be blotted out.
Their bodies were buried in peace,
and their name lives to all generations.
Peoples will declare their wisdom,
and the congregation proclaims their praise.

50:1–17

The leader of his brethren and the pride of his people
was Simon the high priest, son of Onias,
who in his life repaired the house
and in his time fortified the temple.
He laid the foundations for the high double walls,
the high retaining walls for the temple enclosure.
In his days a cistern for water was quarried out,
a reservoir like the sea in circumference.
He considered how to save his people from ruin,
and fortified the city to withstand a siege.
How glorious he was when the people gathered round him
as he came out of the inner sanctuary!
Like the morning star among the clouds,
like the moon when it is full;
like the sun shining upon the temple of the Most High,
and like the rainbow gleaming in glorious clouds;
like roses in the days of the first fruits,
like lilies by a spring of water,
like a green shoot on Lebanon on a summer day;
like fire and incense in the censer,
like a vessel of hammered gold adorned with all kinds of precious
stones;
like an olive tree putting forth its fruit,
and like a cypress towering in the clouds.
When he put on his glorious robe
and clothed himself with superb perfection
and went up to the holy altar,
he made the court of the sanctuary glorious.

And when he received the portions from the hands of the priests,
    as he stood by the hearth of the altar
with a garland of brethren around him,
    he was like a young cedar on Lebanon;
and they surrounded him like the trunks of palm trees,
    all the sons of Aaron in their splendor,
with the Lord's offering in their hands,
    before the whole congregation of Israel.
Finishing the service at the altars,
    and arranging the offering to the Most High, the Almighty,
he reached out his hand to the cup
    and poured a libation of the blood of the grape;
he poured it out at the foot of the altar,
    a pleasing odor to the Most High, the King of all.
Then the sons of Aaron shouted,
    they sounded the trumpets of hammered work,
they made a great noise to be heard
    for remembrance before the Most High.
Then all the people together made haste
    and fell to the ground upon their faces
to worship their Lord,
    the Almighty, God Most High.

Wisdom of Solomon

7:15–8:16

May God grant that I speak with judgment
and have thoughts worthy of what I have received,
for he is the guide even of wisdom
and the corrector of the wise.
For both we and our words are in his hand,
as are all understanding and skill in crafts.
For it is he who gave me unerring knowledge of what exists,
to know the structure of the world and the activity of the elements;
the beginning and end and middle of times,
the alternations of the solstices and the changes of the seasons,
the cycles of the year and the constellations of the stars,
the natures of animals and the tempers of wild beasts,
the powers of spirits and the reasonings of men,
the varieties of plants and the virtues of roots;
I learned both what is secret and what is manifest,
for wisdom, the fashioner of all things, taught me.

For in her there is a spirit that is intelligent, holy,
unique, manifold, subtle,
mobile, clear, unpolluted,
distinct, invulnerable, loving the good, keen,
irresistible, beneficent, humane,
steadfast, sure, free from anxiety,

all-powerful, overseeing all,
and penetrating through all spirits
that are intelligent and pure and most subtle.
For wisdom is more mobile than any motion;
because of her pureness she pervades and penetrates all things.
For she is a breath of the power of God,
and a pure emanation of the glory of the Almighty;
therefore nothing defiled gains entrance into her.
For she is a reflection of eternal light,
a spotless mirror of the working of God,
and an image of his goodness.
Though she is but one, she can do all things,
and while remaining in herself, she renews all things;
in every generation she passes into holy souls
and makes them friends of God, and prophets;
for God loves nothing so much as the man who lives with wisdom.
For she is more beautiful than the sun,
and excels every constellation of the stars.
Compared with the light she is found to be superior,
for it is succeeded by the night,
but against wisdom evil does not prevail.

(8) She reaches mightily from one end of the earth to the other,
and she orders all things well.

I loved her and sought her from my youth,
and I desired to take her for my bride,
and I became enamored of her beauty.
She glorifies her noble birth by living with God,
and the Lord of all loves her.
For she is an initiate in the knowledge of God,
and an associate in his works.
If riches are a desirable possession in life,
what is richer than wisdom who effects all things?
And if understanding is effective,
who more than she is fashioner of what exists?
And if anyone loves righteousness,
her labors are virtues;
for she teaches self-control and prudence,
justice and courage;
nothing in life is more profitable for men than these.
And if any one longs for wide experience,
she knows the things of old, and infers the things to come;
she understands turns of speech and the solutions of riddles;
she has foreknowledge of signs and wonders
and of the outcome of seasons and times.
Therefore I determined to take her to live with me,
knowing that she would give me good counsel
and encouragement in cares and grief.
Because of her I shall have glory among the multitudes
and honor in the presence of the elders, though I am young.
I shall be found keen in judgment,

and in the sight of rulers I shall be admired.
When I am silent they will wait for me,
and when I speak they will give heed;
and when I speak at greater length
they will put their hands on their mouths.
Because of her I shall have immortality,
and leave an everlasting remembrance to those who come after me.
I shall govern peoples,
and nations will be subject to me;
dread monarchs will be afraid of me when they hear of me;
among the people I shall show myself capable, and courageous in war.
When I enter my house, I shall find rest with her,
for companionship with her has no bitterness,
and life with her has no pain, but gladness and joy.

JEWISH INTERPRETATION OF SCRIPTURE:

[SOME DEFINITIONS OF TERMS]

TARGUM

Because the ordinary spoken language of Palestine was Aramaic—although Hebrew was used for religious ceremonial purposes and Greek for public and commercial communication—it was necessary to provide for the mass of worshipping Jews interpretive translations of the Hebrew scriptures into Aramaic. Such a translation was known as a *targum* (plural, *targumim*). Although the targum followed the Hebrew text verse by verse, it was more often a paraphrase than a translation. This interpretive process probably took formal shape in connection with the synagogue, where the public reading of the Hebrew scripture in the synagogue was followed by an impromptu interpretation in the Aramaic vernacular. The targumic tradition survives, therefore, in several different written traditions, each of which aims to preserve a particular oral interpretation of scripture. Like all the other forms of rabbinic interpretation of scripture, the targumim developed along different lines in Babylon and in Jerusalem, although the relative ease of movement between these two widely separated centers of Jewish life resulted in considerable mutual influence. The surviving targumic materials are of late date (after the sixth century A.D.), but they incorporate older material that reaches back to the first century A.D. One such complete targum on the entire Pentateuch (the first five books of the Hebrew Bible, often referred to as Torah) is called *pseudo-Jonathan*, as a result of its having been wrongly attributed to a certain Jonathan ben Uzziel, a pupil of Hillel (the most important of the liberal teachers, fl. after 30 B.C.). Excerpts from Targum Pseudo-Jonathan are given after the present section on term definitions.

HALAKAH AND HAGGADAH

Exposition of scripture was in some cases devoted to strictly legal interpretation: this was called *halakah*. Other interpretation of biblical themes or more general religious ideas, however, consisted of stories, parables, biographical anecdotes, sometimes of moral value and sometimes recounted out of a simple human interest: this was known as *haggadah*. Both these terms refer to the content of the scriptural interpretation, in contrast to the terms *midrash* and *mishnah*, which are categories of interpretive method.

MISHNAH

Although the Law of Moses was said by Jewish tradition to have been given complete by God to Moses on Sinai, the books of Moses in their present form developed and were edited repeatedly over a period of centuries. Only in the fifth century B.C. or somewhat later did the Torah receive approximately the form in which we now know it. But once the content of the Law of Moses was fixed and no longer subject to revision, Jewish teachers began to expand and add to the written Law a growing body of oral interpretation in which new applications of the ancient precepts were offered and new institutions dealt with that were not anticipated in the ancient laws themselves. In order to lend authority to the oral law, the tradition developed that it was as old as the written law and had actually been given orally to Moses at the same time he received the written Torah. The name *mishnah* is given to the material, interpretive and homiletical, as it developed down to the end of the second century A.D. by which time it was arranged in topical form, by subject matter. The official interpreters of the Law, who lived in the last two centuries of this period—after Hillel, about A.D. 10 and before A.D. 220—are known as the *Tannaim*. Obviously it is this phase of scriptural interpretation, which is chiefly halakhic, that has more direct bearing than any other rabbinic exposition on the thought of the New Testament writers.

MIDRASH SIFRE ON NUMBERS

In contrast to mishnah, which is legal tradition originally oral in nature and functioning as an expansion of the Torah, *midrash* is a general term for exposition of scripture and is arranged on the basis of the biblical text, verse by verse. Some *midrashim* are devoted almost entirely to the exposition of the legal portions of scripture; others are hortatory or merely entertaining (in other words, some are *halakah*, some are *hag-*

gadah). Two examples will be given, one of each type. *Midrash Sifre to Numbers* is attributed to the School of Ishmael (second century A.D.), and is mostly halakhic. The other selections are from the *Mechilta*, a midrash on Exodus and one of the oldest preserved midrashim, although in its present form it is thought to have come from the School of Ishmael as well, because it quotes with great frequency the rabbis of that group. The *Mechilta* is mostly haggadic. Its attempt to trace its claim to authority in interpretation back through generations of teachers stands in sharp contrast to Jesus', "You have heard it said of old ... but I say to you ..." (Mt. 5: 21 ff.).

ALLEGORICAL INTERPRETATION OF SCRIPTURE: PHILO

Although there are allegorical passages in the rabbinic sources, it was Philo of Alexandria whose exposition of the Jewish scriptures was almost wholly allegorical in method. Philo's religious views were dominated by the hybrid philosophical views that prevailed in Alexandria: the metaphysical views were Platonic in origin; the views of the natural world as ruled by Reason were Stoic, as were the main ethical virtues. But the whole of his religious outlook and therefore of his allegorical method of interpretation was placed in a mystical-religious framework. In this way, for example, it was possible for Philo to equate the Ultimate Unity behind the manifold world of appearances with the One God affirmed in the Shema: "Hear, O Israel, Yahweh our God is one (Deut. 6:4)."

NON-RABBINIC MIDRASH: GENESIS APOCRYPHON

The exposition of scripture was carried on around the beginning of our era by interpreters who were not included among or even hostile toward the rabbis whose teachings of the Law were recognized by or included in the official body of oral law and scriptural exposition. Two quite different examples of the nonrabbinic exposition will be given: the first is a curious document, unknown until a copy was found among the first of the Dead Sea Scrolls to be discovered, and consisting of a midrashic expansion of the book of Genesis. It retells the story, elaborating details of human interest, such as Sarah's beauty, and explaining supernatural events in terms that were meaningful to the writer's own time, such as the demonic origin of the plagues that fell upon Egypt when Pharaoh took Abraham's wife, Sarah, into his household. The details of the elaborated narrative resemble closely those of such apocalyptic writings as the Book of Enoch, so that it is extremely likely that the *Genesis Apocryphon*, as scholars call this midrash, was written by Essenes, together with the books of Enoch and Jubilees.

BIBLICAL ANTIQUITIES OF PSEUDO-PHILO

In the existing version, *The Biblical Antiquities of Pseudo-Philo*, which were wrongly attributed to Philo of Alexandria, recount Israel's history from creation to the time of David, although the original may have carried the story even farther. Some of the details are an expansion of scripture; others have no basis in the scriptural account. The *Antiquities* is therefore partly targumic and partly haggadic midrash, developing its own expansion of scripture. Although it was attributed to Philo, it was written in Greek (or possibly translated from a Hebrew original into Greek) sometime in the first century A.D. It represents, therefore, a very early exegetical tradition.

PARAPHRASES AND EXPANSION OF THE SCRIPTURAL NARRATIVES

The four excerpts are from the Targum of Pseudo-Jonathan, which includes early material even though it assumed its present form in the seventh century or later. The first excerpt is a slight expansion of the creation story of Genesis III; the second is chiefly significant because it mentions Enoch as a personal mediator of the will of God, similar to Christian conceptions of Jesus; the third has some legendary touches, as in the mention of Abraham's using the altar earlier employed for worship by Adam and Noah, and in the enlargement on the role of angels; the fourth manifests the strong messianic interests of the period, with the explicit expectations of the kingly son of Judah who is to establish the divine rule.

Targum of Pseudo-Jonathan

GENESIS III: 1–24

(1) *Now the serpent was* wiser for evil *than any beast of the field which the Lord God had made. And he said unto the woman,* "Is it in truth that the Lord *God hath said, Ye shall not eat of any tree of the garden?*"
(2) *And the woman said unto the serpent,* "Of the other *fruit of the trees of the garden we may eat:*
(3) *but of the fruit of the tree which is in the midst of the garden,* the Lord *God hath said, Ye shall not eat of it, neither shall ye touch it, lest ye die.*"
(4) *And the serpent* acting as an informer to its creator *said unto the woman:* "You will not die at all for every craftsman hates his fellow-craftsman.
(5) It is revealed before the Lord that *in the day* on which you eat of

it, *your eyes shall be* enlightened, *and ye shall be as* the mighty angels who are wise (enough) to distinguish between *good and evil.*"

(6) *And the woman saw* Sammael, the angel of death, and she was afraid, and she knew *that the tree was good for food, and that* it was a remedy for the enlightenment of *the eyes, and that the tree was to be desired to make one wise, she took of the fruit thereof, and did eat; and she gave also unto her husband with her, and he did eat.*

(7) *And the eyes of them both were opened, and they knew that they were naked,* stripped of the clothing of onyx in which they had been created, and they saw their shame; *and they sewed fig leaves together, and made themselves aprons.*

(8) *And they heard the voice of* the word of *the Lord God walking in the garden in the* resting-time *of the day. And* Adam *and his wife hid themselves from the presence of the Lord God amongst the trees of the garden.*

(9) *And the Lord God called unto* Adam *and said unto him*: "Is not all the world which I have created open before me, the darkness the same as the light? So how can you think in your heart to hide yourself from before me? Can I not see the place in which you are hiding? And where are the commandments which I commanded you?"

(10) *And he said,* "I heard the voice of your word *in the garden, and I was afraid, because I was naked,* and the laws which you commanded me I have transgressed, *and I hid myself* for shame."

(11) *And he said,* "Who told thee that thou wast naked, except *thou hast eaten of* the fruit of *the tree, whereof I commanded thee that thou shouldest not eat?*"

(12) *And* Adam *said* "The woman whom thou gavest to be with me, she gave me of* the fruit of *the tree, and I did eat.*"

(13) *And the Lord God said unto the woman,* "What is this thou hast done?" *And the woman said,* "The serpent beguiled me with his cleverness and deceived me with his wickedness, *and I did eat.*"

(14) *And the Lord God* brought the three of them to judgment, and he *said unto the serpent,* "Because thou hast done this, cursed art thou above all cattle, and above every beast of the field; upon thy belly shalt thou go,* and your feet will be cut off, and your skin you will cast off once in every seven years, and the poison of death will be in your mouth, *and dust shalt thou eat all the days of thy life*:

(15) *and I will put enmity between thee and the woman, and between* the seed of your offspring and the seed of her offspring; and it shall be that when the offspring of the woman keep the commandments of the Law, they will aim right [at you] and they will smite you on the *head*; but when they abandon the commandments of the Law, you will aim right [at them], and you will wound them in the *heel*. However, for them there will be a remedy, but for you there will be none, and in the future they will make peace with the heel in the days of the king, Messiah."

(16) *Unto the woman he said,* "I will greatly multiply thy sorrow by the blood of your virginity *and thy conception; in sorrow thou shalt bring forth children; and thy desire shall be to thy husband, and he shall rule over thee* for good and for ill."

(17) *And unto Adam he said,* "Because thou hast hearkened unto the

word *of thy wife, and hast eaten of* the fruit of *the tree, of which I commanded thee, saying, Thou shalt not eat of it; cursed is the ground* because it did not show forth your guilt; *in toil shalt thou eat of it all the days of thy life; thorns also and thistles shall it bring forth* and increase on account of you; *and thou shalt eat the herb* which is on the face *of the field.*"

(18) Adam answered and said "I pray by the mercies which are before you, O Lord, that we may not be reckoned as cattle to eat grass in the open field. Let us stand up and labour with the labour of the hands, and eat food from the food of the earth, and in this way let there be a distinction before you between the children of men and the cattle."

(19) "*In the sweat of* the palm of your hands *shalt thou eat* food *till thou return unto the* dust from which you were created. *For dust thou art, and unto dust shalt thou return,* and from the dust you will arise in the future to render reckoning and account for all that you have done, on the day of the great judgment."

(20) *And* Adam *called his wife's name Eve, because she was the mother of all the sons of men.*

(21) *And the Lord God made for Adam and for his wife* glorious garments from the skin cast off by the serpent on the skin of their flesh, instead of their onyx which had been cast away; and he *clothed them.*

(22) *And the Lord God said* to the angels who minister before him, "Behold, Adam is unique in the world as I am in the heavens above; and in the future there will arise from him men who know how to distinguish between *good and evil.* If he had kept the commandments which I commanded him he would have lived and flourished as the tree of life forever; but in fact he has not kept what I commanded him, so we are going to decree against him and we forbid him the garden of Eden before he stretches out his hand and takes for himself from the fruit of the tree of life. For if he eats from it he will *live* and flourish *forever.*"

(23) So *the Lord God* took him out of *the garden of Eden,* and he went and dwelt on mount Moriah, *to till the ground from whence he was created.*

(24) *So he drove* Adam *out and he* set the glory of his Shekina[1] to *the east of the garden of Eden* between the two Cherubim. Before God created the world he created the Law, he prepared the garden of Eden for the righteous that they might eat and be satisfied with the fruit of the tree, because they would have observed in their lives the instruction of the Law (in this world) and would have maintained the commandments; and he prepared Gehinnom for the wicked which is like the sharp sword devouring with two edges, and he pre-

---

[1]In order to bridge the gap between the created world and Yahweh, who was increasingly conceived in post-exilic Judaism as utterly transcendent, the rabbis spoke of the manifestations of God as quasi-personified agents created to accomplish God's will. One such agent was the *shekinah* (lit., "dwelling place") or divine presence. Often identified with the cloud of glory that filled the innermost court of the temple built by Solomon (I Kings 8:10–11), *shekinah* was often used as a circumlocution for the divine name, which was considered by the rabbis as too holy to be pronounced or written.

pared within flashing sparks of fire and burning coals for the judgment of the wicked who rebelled in their lives against the instruction of the Law. Better is the Law to one who observed it and walks in the paths of the way of life, than the fruit of the tree of life; for the word of the Lord prepared it for man to keep it, that he may be established in the world to come.

GENESIS V: 1–3; 22–24

(1) *This is the book of the* genealogy of the *generations of Adam. In the day that* the Lord *created* Adam, *in the likeness of* the Lord *made he him;*

(2) *male* with female parts *created he them; and blessed them* in the name of his word, *and called their name Adam, in the day when they were created.*

(3) *And Adam lived an hundred and thirty years, and begat* Seth who resembled his likeness and his appearance. For before that time, Eve had borne Cain who was not from him [Adam] and did not resemble him, and Abel was killed at the hands of Cain, and Cain was cast out, and his descendants were not recorded in the book of the genealogy of Adam. And after that there was born one who resembled him, and he *called his name Seth.*

(22) *And Enoch* served before the Lord in uprightness *after he begat Methuselah three hundred years, and begat sons and daughters:*

(23) *and all the days of Enoch* with the dwellers on earth *were three hundred sixty and five years:*

(24) *and Enoch* served before the Lord in uprightness, and, behold, *he was not* with the dwellers on earth, for he was withdrawn and went up to the firmament by the word before the Lord, and his name was called Metatron[2] the great scribe.

GENESIS XXII: 1–21

(1) *And it came to pass after these things, that* Isaac and Ishmael were disputing. Ishmael said: "It is right for me to be the heir of my father, since I am his first-born son." But Isaac said: "It is right for me to be the heir of my father, since I am the son of Sarah his wife, but you are the son of Hagar, the handmaid of my mother." Ishmael answered and said: "I am more righteous than you because I was circumcised when thirteen years old; and if it had been my wish to refuse I would not have handed myself over to be circumcised." Isaac answered and said: "Am I not now thirty-seven years old? If the Holy One, blessed be he, demanded all my members I would not hesitate." Immediately, these words were heard before the Lord of the universe, and immediately, the word of the Lord tested *Abraham, and said unto him,* "Abraham"; and he said, "Here am I."

---

[2]Metatron figures frequently in later Jewish speculation about the communication and interpretation of the divine will.

(2) *And he said, "Take now thy son, thine only son, whom thou lovest,
even Isaac, and get thee into the land of* worship; *and offer him there
for a burnt offering upon one of the mountains which I will tell thee of."*
(3) *And Abraham rose early in the morning and he saddled his ass,
and took two of his young men,* Eliezer and Ishmael, *with him, and
Isaac his son; and he clave the wood* of the olive and the fig and the
palm which are proper *for the burnt offering, and rose up, and went
unto the place of which* the Lord *had told him.*
(4) *On the third day Abraham lifted up his eyes, and saw* the cloud
of glory smoking on the mountain, and he recognised it *afar off.*
(5) *And Abraham said unto his young men, "Abide ye here with the
ass, and I and the lad will go yonder* to find if what I was assured—
'so shall thy seed be'—will be established; *and we will worship* the
Lord of the universe, *and come again to you."*
(6) *And Abraham took the wood of the burnt offering, and laid it upon
Isaac his son; and he took in his hand the fire and the knife; and they
went both of them together.*
(7) *And Isaac spake unto Abraham his father, and said, "My father":
and he said, "Here am I, my son." And he said, "Behold the fire and
the wood: but where is the lamb for a burnt offering?"*
(8) *And Abraham said: "The Lord will choose for himself the lamb for
a* burnt offering, my son." *So they went both of them* with a single
heart *together.*
(9) *And they came to the place which God had told him of; and Abraham built the altar there* which Adam had built, which had been destroyed by the waters of the flood and which Noah had rebuilt. It had
been destroyed in the generation of the division. And he *laid the wood
in order, and bound Isaac his son, and laid him on the altar, upon the
wood.*
(10) *And Abraham stretched forth his hand, and took the knife to slay
his son.* Isaac answered and said to his father: "Bind me well that I
may not struggle at the anguish of my soul, and that a blemish may
not be found in your offering, and that I may not be cast into the
depth of destruction." The eyes of Abraham looked at the eyes of
Isaac, but the eyes of Isaac looked at the angels on high: Isaac saw
them but Abraham did not see them. The angels on high answered,
"Come and see these two unique men in the earth; the one slaughters
and the other is slaughtered. The one who slaughters does not hesitate, the one to be slaughtered stretches out his neck."
(11) *And the angel of the Lord called unto him out of heaven, and
said* to him, *"Abraham, Abraham": and he said, "Here am I"*
(12) *And he said, "Lay not thine hand upon the lad, neither do thou
anything evil unto him: for now* it is revealed before me *that thou
fearest the Lord, seeing thou has not withheld thy son, thine only son,
from me."*
(13) *And Abraham lifted up his eyes, and looked, and behold,* that one
ram which created in the evening of the completion of the world
caught in the thicket of a tree *by his horns: and Abraham went and
took the ram, and offered him up for a burnt offering in the stead of
his son.*
(14) *And Abraham* give thanks and prayed there in *that place,* and

said: "When I prayed for mercy from before you, O Lord, it was revealed before you that there was no deviousness in my heart, and I sought to perform your decree with joy, that when the descendants of Isaac, my son, shall come to the hour of distress, you may remember them, and answer them, and deliver them; and that all generations to come may say, In this mountain Abraham bound Isaac, his son, and there the Shekina *of the Lord* was revealed to him."

(15) *And the angel of the Lord called unto Abraham a second time out of heaven*

(16) *and said, "By* my word *have I sworn, saith the Lord, because thou hast done this thing, and hast not withheld thy son, thine only son:*

(17) *that in blessing I will bless thee, and in multiplying I will multiply thy seed as the stars of the heaven, and as the sand which is upon the seashore; and thy* sons *shall possess the* cities of their *enemies;*

(18) *and* because of the merit of your sons *shall all the nations of the earth be blessed; because thou hast obeyed my voice."*

(19) And the angels on high led Isaac and brought him to the school of Shem the great, and he was there three years. And on the same day *Abraham returned unto his young men, and they rose up and went together to Beer-sheba; and Abraham dwelt at Beer-sheba.*

(20) *And it came to pass after these things,* after Abraham had bound Isaac, that Satan came and told Sarah that Abraham had slaughtered Isaac; and Sarah rose up and cried out and was choked and died because of the anguish. And Abraham came and rested on the way, and *it was told Abraham, saying, Behold, Milcah, she also hath borne children;* she is granted easement through the merit of her sister to bear sons *unto thy brother Nahor;*

(21) *Uz his firstborn, and Buz his brother, and Kemuel* the master of the Aramaean diviners.

GENESIS XLIX: 1–28

(1) *And Jacob called unto his sons, and said:* "Purify yourselves from uncleanness, and I will show you hidden secrets and unknown ends, the recompense of the reward of the just, and the retribution of the wicked, and the security of Eden, what it is." The twelve tribes of Israel gathered themselves as one around the golden bed on which he lay: and after the glory of the Shekina of the Lord had been revealed to him, the time when the king, Messiah, was going to come was concealed from him; and then he said, "Come, *that I may tell you that which shall befall you in the latter days.*

(2) *Assemble yourselves, and hear, ye sons of Jacob; and* receive instruction from *Israel your father.*

(3) *Reuben, thou art my first-born,* the *beginning* of the *might* of my generation and the first outpouring of my imagination full of desire. To you belonged the birthright and the chief priesthood and the kingdom, but because you sinned, my son, the birthright has been given to Joseph, the kingdom to Judah, and the priesthood to Levi.

(4) I will liken you to a small garden into which enter torrents rushing and strong, and it is not able to endure them, and it is swamped. So

you have been carried away, Reuben, my son; in that you have sinned, do not do so again, and your sin will be forgiven you; for it is reckoned to you as though you went to the woman with whom your father had lain, at the time when you disturbed *my* bed, when you went to it. (5) *Simeon and Levi are brethren* alike in every way. Sharp weapons for violence, it is this by which they may be recognised.

(6) In their counsel *my soul* has taken no pleasure, and in their gathering to destroy Shechem my honour was not involved; *for in their anger they* killed the king and rulers, and of their own freewill they split open the fortified wall of their enemy."

(7) Jacob said, "The stronghold of Shechem was cursed when they entered it to destroy[3] it in their anger which was relentless, and (cursed) their hatred against Joseph, because it was adamant." Jacob said, "If both of them dwell together as one, there is no king or ruler who can stand before them. *I will divide* the inheritance of the sons of Simeon into two parts. One part shall come from the inheritance of the sons of Judah, one part shall be among the rest of the tribes of *Jacob*, and I will scatter the tribe of Levi among all the tribes of *Israel*. (8) *Judah*, you acknowledged what happened with Tamar, therefore your brothers shall acknowledge you, and they shall be called Jehudain after your name. Your hands will take revenge for you on your enemies, shooting arrows at them when they turn their necks before you. And *thy father's sons* will be ever quick to give you their greeting in advance of your own.

(9) I will liken you, Judah my son, to a *whelp*, the young one of lions, because from the killing of Joseph my son your soul departed, and in the judgment of Tamar you spared her. He is at ease and rests in confidence *as a lion*, and like a strong lion when he is resting *who shall rouse him up*?

(10) Kings and rulers shall not cease *from* the house of *Judah*, nor scribes teaching the law from his seed, until the time when the king, Messiah,[4] shall *come*, the youngest of his sons; and because of him *the peoples* shall flow together.

(11) How noble is the king, Messiah, who is going to rise from the house of Judah. He has girded his loins and come down, setting in order the order of battle with his enemies and killing kings with their rulers (and there is not a king or a ruler who shall stand before him), reddening the mountains with the blood of their slain. With his garments dipped in blood, he is like one who treads grapes in the press. (12) More noble are the eyes of the king, Messiah, like sparkling *wine*, than to see the uncovering of nakedness and the shedding of innocent blood, his *teeth* are cleaner than *milk*, not for eating the torn or the stolen. And thus his mountains are red, and his press red from wine,

---

[3]The warfare of Simeon and Levi against Shechem to avenge the abuse of their sister Dinah is described in Genesis 34.

[4]Although some texts from this period (e.g., some of the Dead Sea Scrolls and the Testaments of the Twelve Patriarchs) expect an anointed king as well as an anointed priest in the end time, this targum envisions only the descendant of Judah as the messianic king. See K. G. Kuhn, "The Two Messiahs of Aaron and Israel," in *The Scrolls and the New Testament*, K. Stendhahl, ed. New York: Harper and Row, 1956), pp. 54–64.

and his hills are white from the corn and from the tents of the flocks. (13) *Zebulun shall dwell* on the shores *of the sea*, and he will have authority over the harbours, subduing the domains of the sea with *ships; and his border* will extend as far as *Zidon.*

(14) *Issachar* longs for the law. He is a strong tribe knowing the determined times, and he lies down *between the* borders of his brothers. (15) *And he saw the resting place* of the world to come, *that it is good*, and the portion of the land of Israel, that it is pleasant, therefore he bent his shoulders to labour in the law, and to him shall his brothers offer gifts.

(16) From the house of *Dan* there is going to arise a man who will judge his people with the judgment of truth; *as one* the tribes of Israel will listen to him.

(17) He will be a chosen man, and he will arise from the house of *Dan*, being like the venomous snake which lies at the parting of *the way*, and like the head of the *serpent* which hides on *the path* and *biteth the horse* in its *heel*, and it falls. And in his terror *his rider* is thrown off *backward* on his back. So will Samson the son of Manoah kill all the mighty men of the Philistines, both horsemen and men on foot, and he will hamstring their horses and throw their riders on to their backs."

(18) Jacob, when he saw Gideon the son of Joash, and Samson the son of Manoah, who were established to be deliverers, said: "I do not await the deliverance of Gideon, and I do not look out for the deliverance of Samson, because their salvation, being temporal, will not last. But I wait for your *salvation,* and look out for it, O Lord, because your salvation is eternal.

(19) The tribes of *Gad*, well-armed, will cross, with the rest of the tribes, the streams of Arnon, and they will subdue before them the inhabitants of the land. And they will return armed at the end with great riches, and they will dwell securely beyond the crossing of the Jordan. For as they desire, so will it be to them, and they will receive their possession.

(20) Happy is *Asher,* how rich are his fruits! His land produces spices and the roots of frankincense, and his border will produce the delicacies of kings, and he utters thanks and praises for them before the Lord of the universe.

(21) *Naphtali* is a swift messenger, like *a hind* which runs on the tops of the mountains, bringing good news. He brought the news that Joseph was still alive. He went at speed to Egypt and brought the title deed of the field of the double cave, in which Esau has no part. And when he opens his mouth in the company of Israel, his voice will be chosen out of all voices.

(22) My son, whom I brought up, *Joseph*, you my son who became great and strong: the end was upon you to be strong and to subdue your inclination in the case of your mistress and in the case of your brothers. I will liken you to a vine planted by streams of water which sends out its roots and splits the sharp rocks, and with her branches subdues all the barren trees. Even so, Joseph my son, you subdued by your wisdom and your good deeds all the sorcerers of Egypt. And when praises were sung before you, the daughters of the rulers walked on the walls and threw before you rings and necklaces of gold to make

you raise your eyes to them, but you did not raise your eyes to [any] one of them to be united with them in the day of great judgment.

(23) And all the sorcerers of Egypt were bitter and angry against him, so they brought information to Pharaoh hoping to bring him down from [his place of] honour. They spoke against him slanderously, which is as wounding as arrows.

(24) And the strength of his member reverted [through penitence] to its former state so as not to lie with his mistress, and *his hands* were strengthened from the imagining of seed, and he subdued his inclination because of the firm training which he received from *Jacob*. And for that reason he became worthy to be a leader and to have his name engraved with theirs on the stones *of Israel*.

(25) From the word of the *God of thy father* will be your *help*, and he who is called *'Almighty' shall bless thee, with blessings* which come down from the dew of heaven from above, and from the good *blessings* of the streams *of the deep* which come up and make the plant grow from below. Blessed are *the breasts* from which you were suckled and *the womb* in which you lay.

(26) *The blessings of thy father* will be added to *the blessings* by which my fathers Abraham and Isaac blessed me, which the princes of this world, Ishmael and Esau and all the sons of Qeturah, desired. All these blessings will be united and be made a diadem of majesty for *the head of Joseph, and on the crown* of the man who became a chief man and a ruler in Egypt, and attentive to in the glory of his *brethren.*

(27) *Benjamin is* a strong tribe like *a wolf* with his prey. In his land the Shekina of the ruler of the world will dwell, and in his possession will be built the house of the sanctuary. *In the morning* the priests will offer the lamb regularly until the fourth hour *and at even* they will offer the second lamb and in the evening they will *divide* what is left, the remainder of the offerings, and they will eat each man his own part."

(28) *All these are the twelve tribes of Israel*, all of them righteous as one: *and this is it that their father spake unto them and blessed them; everyone according to his blessing he blessed them.*

Midrash Sifre on Numbers 113

THE SABBATH-BREAKER (NUM. 15: 32–36)

And while the children of Israel were in the wilderness they found a man gathering sticks upon the Sabbath Day. Scripture relates this incident to show up Israel's lack of piety: they kept only one Sabbath, the second they profaned. *And they who found him gathering sticks, brought him unto Moses* [v. 33]. Why is it repeated? It implies that the man had been warned beforehand concerning works of this kind that are prohibited on the Sabbath. Hence the rule concerning all those chief works, which, according to the torah, are not to be done on the Sabbath, that a warning must be given first /if the person breaking them is to be punished/.

R. Isaac says: "It is not at all necessary [to deduce it from this passage]. It stands to reason [we can deduce it by inference]: if idolatry, which is such a grave sin, is only punished after due warning, much more so must it be with other transgressions."

[The rest of the text is defective.]

And they put him in ward. This suggests that all criminals who are to be executed must first be put in ward.

Because it had not been declared what should be done to him. But does it not say "all those who profane the Sabbath should surely die" [Ex. xxxi. 14]? The meaning is: Moses did not know by what *manner of death* he should die, until he was told directly by the mouth of Holiness.

And the Lord said to Moses: The man shall surely be put to death. This is a law for all generations.

All the congregation shall stone him. This means: he should be stoned in the *presence* of the whole congregation. Thou sayest that it means in their *presence*, but perhaps it is to be understood literally [that they should all stone him]? It says: "The hand of THE WITNESSES shall be on him first to kill him."

And the whole congregation brought him without the camp and stoned him to death with stones. From here it can be inferred that criminals who are to be executed should be put to death outside the court.

And stoned him to death with stones. Here it says "with *stones*," and in another passage it says, "and they stoned him with *a stone*" [Lev. xxiv. 23]; how should these passages be reconciled? The house of stoning [the stoning-place] was twice the height of a man. One of the witnesses pushed him [the criminal] from behind, so he fell face downward. He was then turned on his back. If he died from this fall, it was sufficient; if not, the second witness took the stone and dropped it on his heart. If this caused death, it was sufficient; if not, he was stoned by the whole congregation of Israel, as it is said: *"The hand of the witnesses should be the first to kill him and the hand of the whole people last"* [Deut. xiii. 10]. Thus *both* passages are in harmony with one another.

As the Lord commanded Moses. He [Moses] said to them: "Stone him!" and they stoned him. "Hang him!" and they hanged him. Concerning the hanging, we should know nothing, were it not for Deut. xxi.22: *"If there be found in man a sin which causes death, and he is executed, then he shall be hanged on a tree."* Thus R. Eliezer. R. Hidka said: "I had a fellow student, one of the disciples of R. Akiba, and he said: 'Moses knew that the penalty for him who gathers wood on the Sabbath was to be death, but he did not know what manner of death he should die.'"

76

AND WHEN YE GO TO WAR IN YOUR LAND AGAINST THE ADVERSARY THAT OPPRESSES YOU [Num. x. 9]. Both offensive and defensive warfare are meant [lit., "whether they come against you or ye come against them"].

AGAINST THE ADVERSARY THAT OPPRESSES YOU. This refers to the war of Gog and Magog [i.e., the future Messianic war, Ezek. xxxviii]. Thou sayest, it refers to the war of Gog and Magog, but perhaps it refers to all other wars mentioned in torah? It goes on to say here: "And ye shall be saved from your enemies." Come and see: which war is it [of which it can be said] that it will result in Israel's victory and which will not be followed by a renewed subjection [to the empires]? It can only be the war of Gog and Magog. Again it says: "And Yahweh will go out and fight against those nations" [Zech. xiv. 3]. What follows? "And the Lord will be king over the whole earth" [9].

111–112 PROPITIATION FOR SINS OF IGNORANCE

And when ye shall err and not observe all these commandments [Num. xv. 22–31]

This refers to idolatry. Thou sayest, "to idolatry," but maybe it refers to any Commandment of the Law? When it says [v.24]: "That if *it* has been hidden from the eyes of the community, and done unwittingly;" Scripture singles out one Commandment as being something unique, so it must be idolatry. When, also, it says here: "When ye shall err and not observe *all these Commandments*," a comparison is made between *all* the Commandments and the *one Commandment*, namely, as he who transgresses against all the Commandments of the torah, throws off the yoke /of God/, and destroys the covenant /of God with Israel, or with Abraham/, and "uncovers faces in the torah," so the transgressor of *the one Commandment* referred to in the passage is also one who breaks the yoke, and destroys the covenant, and treats the torah irreverently; and this must refer to an idolater, as it is said in connexion with idolatry, "to break his *covenant*"; and "covenant" is always "words of the *covenant*" [Deut. xxviii.69] Rabbi says: "The 'all' here and the 'all' there are akin to one another: as there it is connected with idolatry, so also here."

Which the Lord spoke to Moses. How can it be inferred that he who is given over to idolatry, denies all the Ten Words? Because it says /here, in connexion with idolatry/: "*which the Lord spoke to Moses,*" and in connexion with the Decalogue it also says [Ex. xxi. I]: "*And the Lord spoke* all these words, saying; 'I am the Lord thy God, thou shalt have none other Gods but Me.'"

Whence is it further to be inferred that he who worships idols denies all that was commanded to Moses [not only the Decalogue, which God spoke directly]? Because it says: "*All that the Lord God has commanded through Moses.*" He also breaks that which was commanded to the prophets, because it says: "*From the day when the Lord commanded*" [i.e., all Commandments are included]. Also that which was commanded to the Patriarchs, because it says: "For your generations." And when did the Holy One, blessed be He, begin to give Commandments to the Patriarchs? Since the time when it is said concerning Adam: "And the Lord *commanded* Adam." Thus, Scripture intimates that he who professes idolatry denies the Ten Words; the

Commandments given through Moses; the Commandments given through the Prophets; and the Commandments given to the Patriarchs. And he who *denies* idolatry, professes the whole torah.

If it be done unwittingly, etc., the priest shall make atonement for all the congregation of the house of Israel. How is it to be inferred from this that if one of the twelve tribes was prevented from bringing the Sacrifice it frustrated the Atonement? Because it says: "and the priest shall make atonement *for all the congregation of Israel, then shall they be forgiven.*" Are we to understand that sacrifice as a means of atonement is efficacious for sins committed *wilfully* as well as unintentionally? /No,/ because it says: "For it was in *error*" [a sin-offering is brought only for sins committed in ignorance, *not for wilful sins*]. R. Eliezer says: "/*On the contrary*/, this passage implies that the sins of the community *as a whole* [in contrast to the sins of the individual], even when done wilfully, are as if they were done unintentionally /and are atoned for by sacrifice/."

And it shall be forgiven. This [the masculine verb] implies only men. How then do we know that it refers to women also? Because it says: "*And it shall be forgiven to the whole congregation of the children of Israel.*"

And to the stranger [proselyte]. As Israel is specified, the proselytes must be specially mentioned. It is always the case in Scripture when Israel is specified, the proselytes must be expressly included (otherwise *we* would exclude them].

112

And if one person sin unwittingly [Num. xv. 27]. This is to exclude intentional sin /from sacrificial atonement/.

And the priest shall make atonement for the soul that erreth. The sins in his hand [i.e., his sins] have caused him to come to the "house of sin-offering" [unintentional sin is a revelation of sub-conscious sinfulness].

When he sinneth unwittingly. This [the repetition] is to exclude [from the necessity of a sacrifice] the "niceties" of idolatry [i.e., acquiescence in contemporary heathen customs, not directly idolatrous]. For otherwise we might have deduced by inference that those should also be included; for if the niceties of other Commandments, which, compared with idolatry, are "light," man is obliged [to bring a sacrifice in case of unintentional transgression], much more so should it be the case in connexion with idolatry.

And it shall be forgiven him. Perfect forgiveness, like all forgiveness [mentioned] in the torah.

Ye shall have one law for him that is home born among the sons of Israel and for the stranger. Why this repetition? Since we should otherwise have inferred that as Gentiles are put upon equal terms with the Israelites with regard to idolatry, they are also their equals in cases of unintentional idol worship; but now we learn that only the Israelites bring [a sacrifice] in such a case.

That doth aught unwittingly. R. Judah ben Bethyra says: "[This additional expression is to include] any sin which, if committed intentionally, is punished by 'Karet,' and if done in ignorance requires a sin-offering, as in the case of the sin of idolatry."

But the soul that doeth aught with a high hand [intentionally]; this is he who treats the torah irreverently, like Manasseh the son of Hezekiah.

The same blasphemeth the Lord. For he [Manasseh] used to sit and discuss scandalous homilies before God. Said he: "He (God) had nothing else to write in the torah than, 'And Reuben went in the days of harvest and found mandrakes in the field, etc.' [Gen. xxx. 14]; and He had nothing else to write than, 'And the children of Lotan were Kor and Heman'!" [Gen. xxxvi. 22]. Concerning him it is clearly stated in tradition: *"Thou sittest and speakest against thy brother, thou slanderest thine own mother's son; these things hast thou done and I kept silence, thou thoughtest that I was as thyself"* [Ps. 1. 20,21]. God said unto him: "Dost thou think that the ways of God are like the ways of man? I will reprove thee."

Isaiah [also] came and explicitly stated in tradition: "*Woe* unto them that draw iniquity with cords of vanity, and sin as it were with a cart rope" [Isa. v. 18]; [which means]: the beginning of sin is like one strand of a spider's web, but its end is like unto a cart rope, [meaning, either that the will is weakened by small offences, or that *one* sin is followed by many]. Rabbi says: "He who fulfils *one* Commandment for its own sake [not from selfish motives] should not rejoice merely because of that particular Commandment, for the end will be that this *one* good deed will be followed by many others; and he who breaks *one* Commandment, should not merely be perturbed because of that sin, for the end will be that *one* sin will be followed by many others. *One* good deed will bring forth another.

He blasphemeth [*megaddeph*] *the Lord.* R. El'azar ben Azaryah says: "It is like unto a man saying to his neighbour: 'thou hast scooped out [the first meaning of *gadef*] the dish and lessened it [the dish itself].'" Isi ben Akabya says: "It is like unto a man who says to his neighbour: 'Thou hast scratched out the whole dish and left nothing in it.'"

The soul shall be utterly cut off. "Cut off" means ceasing to be [total annihilation is implied].

From among his people. But the people will be at peace [the whole people is not responsible for the *intentional* idolatry of the individual].

Because he has despised the word of the Lord and has broken His Commandment. "Despised the word of the Lord" refers to a Sadducee; "and has broken His Commandment"—to an Epicurean. Another explanation:— "*Because he has despised the word of the Lord,*" —is he who treats the torah irreverently; "*And hath broken His Commandment*" is he who breaks the covenant of the flesh [i.e., who opposes circumcision]. Hence R. El'azar of Modi'im says: "He who profanes the holy things [the Sanctuary], and despises the *festivals*, and breaks the covenant of Abraham our father [*circumcision*], even if he has in his hand many good deeds, is worthy to be thrust out of the world" [i.e., of the world to come]. If he says: "I accept the whole torah, with the exception of *this* word," of him it is said: "For he despised the word of the Lord." If he says, "The whole torah was spoken by the mouth of Holiness, and this word Moses himself said," he despises the word of the Lord.

Another interpretation: "*For he has despised the word of the Lord.*" R. Meir says: "This is he who studies [the word of God], but does not teach others." [He "despises" the word in not being eager to spread it.] R. Nathan says: "It is he who does not consider the words of the torah at all" [the indifferent]. R. Ishamel says: "This passage speaks of idolatry, because it says, 'he despises *the word* of the Lord,' which means, he despises the *first word* [Commandment] which was spoken to Moses direct, by the Mouth of the Power, namely, 'I am the Lord thy God, thou shalt have no other gods before me' " [Ex. xx. 2].

That soul shall utterly be cut off [hikareth tikareth, infinitive with imperfect]. The first word refers to this world, and the second to *the world to come.* Thus R. Akiba. R. Ishmael said to him: "[Do you deduce from hikareth tikareth]? You might as well add the words in the preceding verse: 'and that soul shall be cut off,' and say that there are three 'cuttings off' from three worlds!" [It is a fanciful exegesis], for the torah speaks in the tongues of men.

His iniquity shall be upon him. Death atones for all sinners, except idolaters. It is similar to the expression [Ezek. xxxii. 27] "their iniquities shall be upon their bones." Perchance this also refers to an idolater who repents? It says here: "His iniquity shall be upon him," but not when he repents. [When he repents his sin is no more.] Similarly it says [Deut. xxxii. 5]: "*They have dealt corruptly with him and they are not his children, it is their blemish,*" which means, when their blemish is still in them [when they have not repented of their sin] they are not His children, but when their blemish is not any more in them, they are His children.

R. Ishmael says: "*His iniquity shall be upon him.*" What are we to learn from these words? Since it says: "*He visits the sins of the fathers upon the children*" [Ex. xx. 5], we might think that these words refer also to idolatry, therefore it says here: "*His iniquity shall be upon him;*" the iniquity hangs upon *him* [the idolater], but is not visited upon his descendants of the third and fourth generations. R. Nathan says: "It is a good sign if a man is punished by God [immediately] after his death. If he died without being lamented, or without being buried, or if a wild animal devoured him, or if rain-storms came upon him—it is a good sign, because it means that he has been punished already [in this world] soon after his death." And, although there is no direct proof from Scripture for this, there is a suggestion: "*At that time . . . they shall bring out the bones of the kings of Judah . . . and they shall spread them before the sun, etc.*"

Said R. Shimeon ben El'azar: "With this argument I have proved the fallacy of the books of the Sadducees,[1] who say that the dead

---

[1] Sadducees were a conservative Jewish group drawn from the wealthy and especially the priestly families. They rejected any traditions other than those documented in the written Torah or Law of Moses. Hence the oral tradition so important for the rabbis and probably the prophetic and poetic parts of the larger Jewish Bible as well were unacceptable to the Sadducees. This meant that their religion had no place for such Pharisaic doctrines as those concerning angels and demons, resurrection and judgment.

[will] not live [again]; for said I to them: it says: *'That soul shall utterly be cut off, his iniquity shall be upon him,'* which last words must mean that the *soul* will have to give an account in the Day of Judgment."

Mechilta on Exodus

I AM THE LORD THY GOD [EXODUS 20.2] Why were the Ten Commandments not said at the beginning of the torah? They give a parable.[2] To what may this be compared? To the following: A king who entered a province, and said to the people: May I be your king? But the people said to him: Have you done anything good for us that you should rule over us? What did he do then? He built the city wall for them, he brought in the water supply for them, and he fought their battles. Then when he said to them: May I be your king? They said to him: Yes, yes. Likewise, God. He brought the Israelites out of Egypt, divided the sea for them, sent down manna for them, brought up the well for them, brought the quails for them. He fought for them the battle with Amalek. Then He said to them: I am to be your king. And they said to Him: Yes, yes. Rabbi says: This proclaims the excellence of Israel. For when they all stood before mount Sinai to receive the Torah they all made up their mind alike to accept the reign of God joyfully. . . .

I AM THE LORD THY GOD: Why is this said? For this reason. At the sea He appeared to them as a mighty hero doing battle, as it is said, THE LORD IS A MAN OF WAR [EXODUS 15.3]. At Sinai He appeared to them as an old man full of mercy. It is said AND THEY SAW THE GOD OF ISRAEL etc. [EXODUS 24.10]. And of the time after they had been redeemed what does it say? AND THE LIKE OF THE VERY HEAVEN FOR CLEARNESS [ibid.]. Again it says: I BEHELD TILL THRONES WERE PLACED [DANIEL 7.9] and it also says A FIERY STREAM ISSUED AND CAME FORTH BEFORE HIM etc. [ibid. v.10]. Scripture, therefore, would not let the nations of the world have an excuse for saying that there are two Powers, but declares, I AM THE LORD THY GOD. I am He who was in EGYPT and I am He who was at the sea. I am He who was at Sinai. I am He who was in the past and I am He who will be in the future. I am He who is in this world and I am He who will be in the world to come, as it is said, SEE NOW THAT I, EVEN, I AM HE, etc. [DEUT. 32.39]. And it says, EVEN TO OLD AGE I AM THE SAME [ISAIAH 46.4]. And it says, THUS SAITH THE LORD, KING OF ISRAEL, AND HIS REDEEMER THE LORD OF HOSTS: I AM THE FIRST AND I AM THE LAST [ibid. 44.6]. And it says, WHO HATH WROUGHT AND DONE IT? HE THAT CALLED THE GENERATIONS FROM THE BEGINNING. I, THE LORD, WHO AM THE FIRST, etc. [ibid. 41.4]. Rabbi Nathan says: From this one can cite a refutation of the heretics who say: There are

---

[2]Parable is here an illustrative story, but the Semitic word *mashal*, which is usually translated as parable, can mean riddle, enigma, or proverbial saying.

two Powers. For when the Holy One, blessed be He, stood up and exclaimed: I AM THE LORD THY GOD was there any one who stood up to protest against Him? . . .

Another Interpretation: I AM THE LORD THY GOD. When the Holy One, blessed be He, stood up and said I AM THE LORD THY GOD, the earth trembled, as it is said LORD, WHEN THOU DIDST GO FORTH OUT OF SEIR, WHEN THOU DIDST MARCH OUT OF THE FIELD OF EDOM, THE EARTH TREMBLED [JUDGES 5.4]. And it goes on to say: THE MOUNTAINS QUAKED AT THE PRESENCE OF THE LORD [ibid. v.5]. And it also says: THE VOICE OF THE LORD IS POWERFUL: THE VOICE OF THE LORD IS FULL OF MAJESTY etc. [PSALM 29.4] up to AND IN HIS PALACE EVERY ONE SAYS "GLORY" [ibid. v.9]. And their houses even were filled with the splendor of the Shekinah [the Divine Presence]. At that time all the kings of the nations of the world assembled and came to Baalam the son of Beon. They said to him: Perhaps God is about to destroy His world by a flood. He said to them. Fools that you are! Long ago God swore to Noah that He would not bring a flood upon the world, as it is said FOR THIS IS THE WATERS OF NOAH UNTO ME: FOR I HAVE SWORN THAT THE WATERS OF NOAH SHOULD NO MORE GO OVER THE EARTH [ISAIAH 54.9]. They then said to him: Perhaps He will not bring a flood of water, but He may bring a flood of fire. But he said to them: He is not going to bring a flood of water or a flood of fire. It is simply that the Holy One, blessed be He, is going to give the Torah to His people. For it is said THE LORD WILL GIVE STRENGTH UNTO HIS PEOPLE etc. [PSALM 29.11]. As soon as they heard this from him, they all turned back and went each to his place.

And it was for the following reason that the nations[3] of the world were asked to accept the Torah: In order that they should have no excuse for saying: Had we been asked we would have accepted it. For, behold, they were asked and they refused to accept it, for it is said, AND HE SAID, "THE LORD CAME FROM SINAI" etc. [DEUT. 33.2]. He appeared to the children of Esau the wicked and said to them: Will you accept the Torah? they said to Him: What is written in it? He said to them: THOU SHALT NOT MURDER [DEUT. 5.17]. They then said to Him: The very heritage which our father left us was: AND BY THY SWORD SHALT THOU LIVE [Gen. 27.40]. He then appeared to the children of Amon and Moab. He said to them: Will you accept the Torah? They said to Him: What is written in it? He said to them: THOU SHALT NOT COMMIT ADULTERY [DEUT. 5.17]. They, however, said to Him that they were all of them children of adulterers, as it is said THUS WERE BOTH THE DAUGHTERS OF LOT WITH CHILD BY THEIR

---

[3]Nations or Gentiles. Judaism was increasingly concerned with its place among the religions of the world. Accordingly, there were two powerful and contradictory tendencies at work within Judaism of this period: (1) a concern to maintain separate Jewish identity, and (2) eagerness to demonstrate the universality of Israel's faith.

FATHER [GEN. 19.36]. Then He appeared to the children of Ishmael. He said to them: Will you accept the Torah? They said to Him: What is written in it? He said to them: THOU SHALT NOT STEAL [DEUT. 5.17]. They then said to Him: The very blessing that had been pronounced upon our father was: AND HE SHALL BE AS A WILD ASS OF A MAN: HIS HAND SHALL BE UPON EVERY-THING. [GEN. 16.12]. . . . But when He came to the Israelites and AT HIS RIGHT HAND WAS A FIERY LAW UNTO THEM [DEUT. 33.22], they all opened their mouths and said ALL THAT THE LORD HAS SPOKEN WILL WE DO AND OBEY [Exodus 24.7]. . . . Rabbi Simon ben Eleazar says: If the sons of Noah could not endure the seven commandments enjoined upon them, how much less could they have endured all the commandments of the Torah! To give a parable. A king had appointed two administrators. One was appointed over the store of straw and the other was appointed over the treasure of silver and gold. The one appointed over the store of straw was held in suspicion. But he used to complain about the fact that they had not appointed him over the treasure of silver and gold. The people then said to him: "Reka!"[4] If you were under suspicion in connection with the store of straw how could they trust you with the treasure of silver and gold! Behold, it is a matter of reasoning by the method of *kai vachomer* [a logical rule: from light to heavy]: If the sons of Noah could not endure the seven commandments enjoined upon them, how much less could they have endured all the commandments of the Torah!

MT. 5:
22

Why was the Torah not given in the land of Israel? In order that the nations of the world should not have the excuse for saying: Because it was given in Israel's land, therefore we have not accepted it. Another reason: To avoid causing dissension among the tribes. Else one might have said: In my territory the Torah was given. And the other might have said: In my territory the Torah was given. Therefore, the Torah was given in the desert, publicly and openly, in a place belonging to no one. To three things the Torah is likened: To the desert, to fire, and to water. This is to tell you that just as these three things are free to all who come into the world, so also are the words of the Torah free to all who come into the world.

Allegorical Interpretation of Scripture:

Philo of Alexandria: On the Cherubim

In the tractate here excerpted, Philo is explaining by his allegorical method the "real" significance of the biblical description of the ark of the covenant, the sacred box in which the stone tablets of the Mosaic Law were kept, and atop which were the winged sphinxes known as

---

[4] *Reka*, from a root found in Hebrew and Aramaic meaning "empty," and used therefore as an epithet, "empty-headed." It occurs in Mt. 5:22 as a term of insult.

Cherubim. Understood literally, a pious Jew might have had difficulty in accepting the biblical condoning of representational art work, which conflicted with the prohibition against "graven images," but Philo saw in the Cherubim as prescribed in the Law of Moses profound philosophical and mystical meaning. (See also Philo's interpretation of Deut. 34, in the section dealing with meaning in history, pp. 109–11.)

SEC. VII, VIII, AND IX PHILO OF ALEXANDRIA (ON THE CHERUBIM)

VII. We must now examine what is symbolized by (21) the Cherubim and the sword of flame which turns every way. I suggest that they are an allegorical figure of the revolution of the whole heaven. For the movements assigned to the heavenly spheres are of two opposite kinds, in the one case an unvarying course, embodying the principle of sameness, to the right, in the other a variable course, embodying the principle of otherness, to the left. The outermost (22) sphere, which contains what are called the fixed stars, is a single one and always makes the same revolution from east to west. But the inner spheres, seven in number, contain the planets and each has two motions of opposite nature, one voluntary, the other under a compelling force. Their involuntary motion is similar to that of the fixed stars, for we see them pass every day from east to west, but their own proper motion is from west to east, and it is in this that we find the revolutions of the seven governed also by certain lengths of time. (23) These lengths are the same in the case of three whose course is equal, and these three which have the same rate of speed are known as the Sun, the Morning-star, and the Sparkler [Mercury]. The others have unequal courses and different lengths of time in revolution, though these too preserve a definite proportion to each other and above-named three.

(24) One of the Cherubim then symbolizes the outermost sphere of the fixed stars. It is the final heaven of all, the vault in which the choir of those who wander not move in a truly divine unchanging rhythm, never leaving the post which the Father who begat them has appointed them in the universe. The other of the Cherubim is the inner contained sphere, which through a sixfold division He has made into seven zones of regular proportion and fitted each planet into one of them. He has set each star in its proper zone as a driver in a chariot, and yet He has in no case trusted the reins to the driver, fearing that their rule might be one of discord, but He has made them all dependent on Himself, holding that thus would their march be orderly and harmonious. For when God is with us all we do is worthy of praise; all that is done without Him merits blame.

VIII. This then is one interpretation of the (25) allegory of the Cherubim, and the flaming turning sword represents, we must suppose, their movement and the eternal revolution of the whole heaven. But perhaps on another interpretation the two Cherubim represent the two hemispheres. For we read that the Cherubim stand face to face with their wings inclining to the mercy-seat [Exod. xxx.19]. And so, too, the hemispheres are opposite to each other and stretch out to the earth, the centre of all things, which actually parts them. And as this alone in all the universe stands firm, it has been rightly named by men of old the standing-place, and it stands thus, that the revolution of each of the hemispheres may circle round one fixed centre and thus be wholly harmonious. The flaming sword on this interpretation is the Sun, that packed mass of flame, which is the swiftest of all existing things and whirls round the whole universe in a single day.

IX. But there is a higher thought than these. It comes from a voice in my own soul, which oftentimes is God-possessed and divines where it does not know. This thought I will record in words if I can. The voice told me that while God is indeed one, His highest and chiefest powers are two, even goodness and sovereignty. Through His goodness He begat all that is, through His sovereignty He rules what He has begotten. And in the midst between the two there is a third which unites them, Reason, for it is through reason that God is both ruler and good. Of these two potencies, sovereignty and goodness, the Cherubim are symbols, as the fiery sword is the symbol of reason. For exceeding swift and of burning heat is reason and chiefly so the reason of the [Great] Cause, for it alone preceded and outran all things, conceived before them all, manifest above them all.

O then, my mind, admit the image unalloyed of the two Cherubim, that having learnt its clear lesson of the sovereignty and beneficence of the Cause, thou mayest reap the fruits of a happy lot. For straightway thou shalt understand how these unmixed potencies are mingled and united, how, where God is good, yet the glory of His sovereignty is seen amid the beneficence, how, where He is sovereign, through the sovereignty the beneficence still appears. Thus thou mayest gain the virtues begotten of these potencies, a cheerful courage and a reverent awe towards God. When things are well with thee, the majesty of the sovereign king will keep thee from high thoughts. When thou sufferest what thou wouldest not, thou wilt not despair of betterment, remembering the loving-kindness of the great and bountiful God. And for this cause is the sword a sword of flame, because in their company reason the measure of things must follow, reason with its fierce and burning heat, reason that ever moves with unswerving zeal, teaching thee to choose the good and eschew the evil.

Non-Rabbinic Midrash:

The Genesis Apocryphon

Among the Dead Sea Scrolls was found a paraphrase on and expansion of the book of Genesis, of which Column XX of the scroll, based on Genesis 12:10–20, is given here in the translation of Y. Yadin. The story recounts how Abraham and Sarah took refuge in Egypt during a famine in Palestine and dwells at length on the beauty of Sarah, a fact that is simply stated without elaboration in the biblical account. More significant is the dualistic element that the expositor has introduced by attributing the plague to an evil spirit. (The point of this is obscured in Yadin's

The site of the Dead Sea community during the excavations. In the background is the Dead Sea itself. The ruins include the pools, the community refectory, the remains of the scrollery where the documents were copied or composed. The small openings in the cliff at the lower right are entrances to Cave Four, where many of the fragments of scrools were found. Some scholars think that this was the main repository for the community's library. (*Source*: Israel Department of Antiquities and Museums.)

translation, which has been slightly modified to bring out the real force of vs. 29.)

MIDRASH ON GENESIS, COLUMN XX: 1–34

(1) . . . .

(2) . . .   . . .   "How . . . and [how] beautiful the look of her face . . . and how

(3) . . .   . . . fine is the hair of her head, how fair indeed are her eyes and how pleasing her nose and all the radiance

(4) of her face . . . how beautiful her breasts and how lovely all her whiteness. Her arms goodly to look upon, and her hands how

(5) perfect . . . all the appearance of her hands. How fair her palms and how long and fine all the fingers of her hands. Her legs

(6) how beautiful and how without blemish her thighs. And all maid-

ens and all brides that go beneath the wedding canopy are not more fair than she. And above all

(7) women is she lovely and higher is her beauty than that of them all, and with all her beauty there is much wisdom in her. And the tip of her hands

(8) is comely." And when the King heard the words of HRQNWS[1] and the words of his two companions, for all three spoke as one man, he desired her exceedingly and he sent

(9) at once to bring her to him and he looked upon her and marvelled at all her loveliness and took her to him to wife and sought to slay me. And Sarai spoke

(10) to the King, saying, "He is my brother," that it might be well with me [that I might profit thereby]. And I, Abram, was saved because of her and was not slain. And I wept, I,

(11) Abram, with grievous weeping, I and with me, Lot, my brother's son, wept that night when Sarai was taken from me by force.

(12) That night I prayed and entreated and begged and said in sorrow, as my tears fell, "Blessed art Thou, Most High God, Lord of all

(13) worlds, because Thou art Lord and Master of all and ruler of all the kings of earth, all of whom Thou judgest. Behold now

(14) I cry before Thee, my Lord, against Pharaoh-Zoan, King of Egypt, because my wife has been taken from me by force. Do Thou judge him for me and let me behold Thy mighty hand

(15) descend upon him and all his household and may he not this night defile my wife. And men shall know, my Lord, that Thou art the Lord of all the kings

(16) of earth." And I wept and grieved. That night the Most High God sent a pestilential spirit to afflict him and all his household, a spirit

(17) that was evil. And it smote him and all his house and he could not come near her nor did he know her and he was with her

(18) two years. And at the end of two years the plagues and the afflictions became grievous and strong in him and in all his house. And he sent

(19) and called for all the wise men of Egypt and all the wizards and all the physicians of Egypt, if perchance they might heal him from that pestilence, him and

(20) his house. And all the physicians and wizards and wise men could not rise up to heal him, for the wind smote them all

(21) and they fled. Then came to me HRQNWS and besought me to come and to pray for

(22) the king and to lay my hands upon him that he might live, for in the dream. . . . And Lot said unto him, "Abram, my uncle, cannot pray

(23) for the King while Sarai, his wife, is with him. Go now and tell

---

[1] The name transliterated as HRQNWS is not found in the biblical text, but sounds like Hyrcanos, a common name of the Hasmonean times, and therefore perhaps an indication of the date of origin of this document: late second to early first century B.C.

the King to send away his wife to her husband and he will pray for him and he will live."

(24) And when HRQNWS heard these words of Lot he went and said to the King, "All these plagues and afflictions

(25) with which my lord, the King, is plagued and afflicted, are for the sake of Sarai, the wife of Abram. Restore her, Sarai, to Abram, her husband,

(26) and the plague will depart from thee and the evil will pass away." And he called me to him and said to me, "What hast thou done unto me for the sake of [Sara]i, that thou hast told

(27) me 'She is my sister,' and she is indeed thy wife, and I took her to me to wife. Behold thy wife who is with me, go thy way and depart from

(28) all the land of Egypt. And now pray for me and all my house that this evil wind may depart from us." And I prayed for . . . this

(29) swiftly [?] and I laid my hand upon his head and the plague departed from him and the evil spirit was brought under control and he lived. And the King rose and said unto

(30) me . . . and the King swore to me with and oath that cannot (be changed).

(31) . . . And the King gave him a large . . .   . . . and much clothing of fine linen and purple . . .   . . .

(32) before her, and also Hagar . . . and appointed men for me who would take (me) out . . .

(33) And I, Abram, went forth, exceedingly rich in cattle and also in silver and in gold, and I went up out (of Egypt and Lot),

(34) the son of my brother, with me. And Lot also had great possessions and took unto himself a wife from . . .

Midrash Pesher

A distinctive type of midrashic exposition of scripture was found among the Dead Sea Scrolls. Most of the interpretive passages begin with the term, "its interpretation is" (*peshru*, in Hebrew). But the meaning that is set forth is not that intended by the original writer, but a special hidden meaning, intended for the elect community that believes itself to be living in the End Time and to whom the secrets of the divine plan have alone been vouchsafed. To accomplish this interpretive process the expositor feels free to alter the text, to redistribute the letters so as to give other meanings than those usually understood, and to supply different vowels to the consonantal Hebrew text where the resultant meaning is more to the interpreter's purpose. The orientation of the interpretation is overwhelmingly eschatological in bent, and the community can read its own history from the words of scripture. The similarities of this method to the interpretation of scripture by the New Testament writers is evident.

COMMENTARY ON HABAKKUK 1–6 (FROM DEAD SEA SCROLLS)

(1) And God told Habakkuk to write the things that were to come upon the last generation,[1] but the consummation of the period he did not make known to him. (2) And as for what it says, *that he may run who reads it*, this means the teacher of righteousness,[2] to whom God made known all the mysteries of the words of his servants the prophets.

(3) *For still the vision is for an appointed time; it hastens to the period and does not lie.* This means that the last period extends over and above all that the prophets said; for the mysteries of God are marvelous. *If it tarries, wait for it, for it will surely come; it will not delay.* This means the men of truth, the doers of the law, whose hands do not grow slack from the service of the truth, when the last period is stretched out over them. For all the periods of God will come to their fixed term, as he decreed for them in the mysteries of his wisdom.

(4) *Behold, puffed up, not upright is his soul in him.* This means that they make double the judgment upon themselves; they do not win acceptance when they are judged, for their souls are not upright. *But the righteous shall live by his faith.* This means all the doers of the law in the house of Judah, whom God will rescue from the house of judgment because of their labor and their faith in the teacher of righteousness.

(5) *Moreover wealth is treacherous, an arrogant man, and will not abide. His greed is as wide as Sheol; and he like death has never enough. To him are gathered all the nations, and to him are assembled all the people. (6) Shall not all of them take up their taunt against him, in scoffing derision of him, and say, "Woe to him who heaps up, but it is not his own! How long will he load himself with pledges?"*

This means the wicked priest,[3] who was named according to the truth when he first took office; but when he had begun to rule in Israel, his heart was lifted up, and he forsook God and betrayed the statutes because of wealth. He plundered and assembled the wealth of men of violence who rebelled against God. He took the wealth of peoples, adding to himself iniquity and guilt; and ways of abominations he wrought, in all impurity of uncleanness.

Biblical Antiquities of Pseudo-Philo

The next excerpt is a continuous expansion of the text of Torah, written for narrative and homiletical rather than for legal purposes, and is

---

[1]The community is convinced that it is living in the last generation of the present age and that it alone will survive into the Age to Come.

[2]Better, the One who Teaches Rightly. See the Rule of the Community for the sect's account of his role in founding the community. He was the one who gave them the clues to understand the scriptures.

[3]Various conjectures have been advanced as to who the Wicked Priest is, but it was presumably one of the Hasmonean King-Priests of the period around 100 B.C.

hence haggadic in nature. It was probably composed in Hebrew or Aramaic, but was translated into Greek and then into the Latin version in which it is alone extant. Although the date cannot be determined with certainty, it was likely written in the first century A.D., sometime after the fall of Jerusalem.

The first selection is a slightly expanded version of the flood in the days of Noah. But the second narrative is based on the story of the Tower of Babel (Genesis 11), to which have been added elements from the story of Abraham but also from the account (Daniel 3) of God's delivering from the fiery furnace the faithful Hebrews who risked death rather than accede to the pagan king's demand that they participate in idolatrous practices. That issue would be a live one during the period between the first and second Jewish revolts against the Romans.

Even though there is no hint of a doctrine of the resurrection of the dead in the book of Genesis, Pseudo-Philo finds it there in his expanded version of Genesis (3:10), just as the early Christians found support for the doctrine in their reading of the Old Testament. The advice to stand firm for the faith in the face of impending persecution (VI; 1–18) sounds like the apocalyptic sections of the gospels (Mk. 13) and Revelation.

III: 1–11

(1) And it happened when men had begun to multiply on the earth, that beautiful daughters were born to them. And the sons of God saw the daughters of men, that they were very beautiful; they took wives for themselves of all that they had chosen.

(2) And God said: "My spirit will not judge among all these men forever, because they are flesh; but their years will be 120"; at which he set the limits of life; "and in their hands the law will not be extinguished."

(3) And God saw that among all the dwellers on earth evil works were put into effect, and since they thought about wickedness all their days, he said, "I will destroy man and everything which has come to life in the earth, because it repents me that I have made him."

(4) But Noe found favour and pity before the Lord; and these are his generations. Noe, who was a just man and undefiled in his own generation, was pleasing to God. To him God said, "The time of all men living on the earth has come, because their works are very evil. And now, make for yourself an ark of cedar wood, and thus shall you make it: its length shall be 300 cubits, and its width 50 cubits, and its height 30 cubits. And you shall enter into the ark, yourself and your wife and your sons and your sons' wives with you, and I will make my covenant with you, that I will destroy all the dwellers on earth. But of the clean animals and of the clean birds of the sky you shall take them seven by seven, male and female, that their seed may be able to bring life to the earth. Of the unclean animals and of the unclean birds you shall take them for yourself two by two, male and female. You shall take provision for yourself and for them."

(5) So Noe did what God commanded him, and he entered into the ark, himself and all his sons with him. And it happened after seven days that the water of the flood began to be on the earth. And in that day all the depths were opened and the great fountain and the cataracts of heaven, and there was rain on the earth for forty days and forty nights.

(6) It was then 1652 years since God had made heaven and earth, on the day when the earth was destroyed together with its inhabitants because of the wickedness of their works.

(7) And with the flood continuing 150 days on the earth, Noe alone was left, and those who were with him in the ark. And when God remembered Noe, he made the water diminish.

(8) And it happened on the ninetieth day that God dried the earth and said to Noe: "Go out of the ark, you and all who are with you, and increase and multiply in the earth." So Noe went out of the ark, himself and his sons and his sons' wives, and all the beasts and reptiles and birds and cattle he brought out with him, just as God had commanded him. Then Noe built an altar to the Lord, and he took of all the clean animals and birds, and offered burnt offerings on the altar, and it was acceptable to the Lord as an odour of rest.

(9) And God said, "I will not again curse the earth for man, since the image of man's heart has left him from his youth; and therefore I will not again destroy all living things as I have done. But it will be that when the dwellers on earth have sinned, I will judge them by famine or sword or fire or death, and there will be earthquakes, and they will be scattered to uninhabited parts. But I will not again destroy the earth with a flood of water, and in all the days of the earth seed-time and harvest, cold and heat, summer and autumn, day and night will not cease, as long as I remember those who dwell on the earth, until the times are complete.

(10) But when the years of the world are complete, then will light cease and darkness be extinguished, and I will give life to the dead, and I will raise up those who sleep from the earth. The nether world will pay its debt, and destruction make good its part, that I may pay to each one according to his works and according to the fruit of his imaginings, as I judge between soul and body. And the world shall cease and death shall be extinguished, and the nether world shall close his mouth. And the earth will not be without birth, nor barren for those dwelling in it. And none shall be defiled once they have been justified in me. And there will be another earth and another heaven, an everlasting habitation."

(11) And the Lord again spoke to Noe and his sons: "Behold, I will make my covenant with you and with your seed after you, and I will not add again to destroy the earth with the water of a flood. And everything which moves and lives shall be for you as food. Nevertheless flesh with the blood of life you shall not eat. For he who sheds the blood of man, at the hand of God his blood shall be shed, since God made man in his own image. But as for you, increase and multiply and fill the earth, as the multitude of fishes multiplying themselves in the waves."

VI: 1–18

(1) Then those who had been divided, all the dwellers on earth, assembled after that and dwelt together. And they set forth from the East and found a plain in the land of Babylon, and, dwelling there, they said each to his neighbour: "See, it is going to come about that we shall be scattered, each from his own brother, and in the last days we will be fighting one against another. Now, therefore, come, and let us build for ourselves a tower, whose top shall reach to heaven, and we shall make for ourselves a name and a glory on earth."

(2) And they said each one to his neighbour: "Let us take bricks and write each of us our own names on the bricks and burn them with fire; and it will be that they will be thoroughly baked into clay and brick."

(3) So they took, each of them, their bricks, except for twelve men who refused to do so; and these are their names: Abraham, Nachor, Loth, Ruge, Tenute, Zaba, Armodat, Jobab, Esar, Abimahel, Saba, Ausin.

(4) And the people of the land seized them, and brought them to their rulers and said to them: "These are the men who have transgressed our plans and refuse to walk in our ways." So the leaders said to them: "Why have you refused to set out each one of you his brick with the people of the land?" Then they answered saying to them, "We do not set out bricks with you, nor do we join our intentions with yours. One God we know and him do we worship. Even if you set us in the fire with your bricks we will not consent to you."

(5) Then the angered leaders said, "As they have spoken so do to them: it shall be that unless they consent with you in setting forth bricks, you shall consume them in fire with your bricks."

(6) Then Jectan, who was the first ruler of the leaders, replied: "Not so; there shall be given them a space of seven days, and it shall be that if they turn away from their most evil decisions and are willing to set forth bricks with you, they shall live. But if not, they shall be burned according to your decision." But he sought how he might save them from the hands of the people, since he was of their tribe, and served God.

(7) With these words he took them and shut them up in the king's house. And when evening was come he ordered fifty men, mighty in courage, to be called to him, and said to them: "Go, and take those men tonight who are shut up in my house, and put provisions for them from my house on ten pack-animals, and bring those men to me; and take their provisions with the pack-animals to the mountains, and wait with them there. And understand that if anyone knows what I have said to you, I will burn you with fire."

(8) So the men went and did everything which their leader had commanded them. And they brought the men to his house by night, and taking their provisions they put them on pack-animals and led them to the mountains as he had ordered them.

(9) Then the ruler called those twelve men to himself and said to

them: "Be of good courage and fear not, for you are not going to die. For God is strong in whom you trust, and therefore be firm in him, who will set you free and save you. And now understand, I have given orders to fifty men to lead you out, with provisions taken from my house. Go to the mountains and hide yourselves in a valley, and I will give you fifty other men to lead you out thither. So go and hide yourselves there in the valley, having water to drink flowing down from the rock, and keep yourselves there for thirty days, until the hatred of the people of the land abates and until God sends his wrath upon them and shatters them. For I know that the plan of wickedness which they have plotted to do will not endure, since their thinking is empty. And it shall be, when seven days have passed and they look for you, that I shall say to them: 'The door of the prison, in which they were shut up, was broken, so they have gone out and have fled in the night, and I have sent a hundred men to look for them.' And I will turn them away from their present fury."

(10) Then eleven of the men replied to him saying, "Your servants have found favour in your eyes, because we have been set free from the hands of these proud men."

(11) But Abraham alone was silent, so the leader said to him: "Why do you not reply to me, Abraham, servant of God?" Abraham replied and said: "Suppose I flee today to the mountains: if I escape the fire, wild animals may emerge from the mountains and come and devour us, or our food may run out and we shall die of hunger; and we shall be found fleeing before the people of the earth and falling in our sins. And now, as he lives in whom I trust, I will not move from my place in which they have put me. And if there be any sin of mine so that I am utterly consumed [in the fire], God's will be done." Then the leader said to him: "Your blood be on your own head if you are unwilling to go with them. But if you are willing to go you will be free. So if you wish to stay, stay as you will." Then Abraham said, "I will not go, here I will stay."

(12) Then the leader took the eleven men and sent fifty others with them, and gave them orders saying, "Wait as well in the mountains for fifteen days with those fifty who have been sent on ahead, and when you come back, say, We did not find them, just as I have told the earlier men. And know that if anyone disobeys any of these words which I have spoken to you he shall be burned with fire." So when the men had gone, he took Abraham alone and shut him up where he had been imprisoned before.

(13) After seven days had gone by the people assembled and spoke to their leader saying, "Hand over to us the men who refused to join in our plans and we will burn them with fire." And they sent authorities to bring them, and they found none except Abraham. And the whole assembly said to their leaders, "The men whom you imprisoned have fled, eluding our intention."

(14) Then Fenech and Nembroth said to Jectan: "Where are the men whom you imprisoned?" He said: "They completely broke their bonds in the night. But I have sent a hundred men to look for them, not only shall they burn them with fire but they shall give their bodies to the birds of the air, and thus shall they destroy them."

(15) At that they said to him, "Then let us burn this one who was found." And they took Abraham, and led him to their leaders; and they said to him, "Where are those who were with you?" And he said, "I was sleeping soundly one night; when I woke I could not find them."

(16) So they took him and built a furnace and set it alight. And they put bricks burnt with fire into the furnace. Then Jectan, stupefied, took Abraham and put him with the bricks in the fire of the furnace.

(17) But God caused a great earthquake, and the fire, leaping up from the furnace, burst into flames and sparks of flame, and it burnt up all those standing around in sight of the furnace. And all those who were burnt up in that day were 83,500. But on Abraham there was not any sign of hurt in the burning of the fire.

(18) So Abraham arose from the furnace and the fiery furnace fell down; and Abraham was saved, and he went to the eleven men who had hidden themselves in the mountains, and he told them everything that had happened to him. And they came down with him from the mountains rejoicing in the name of the Lord, and no one met them to terrify them that day. And they called that place by the name of Abraham, and in the Chaldaean language Deli, which means God.

JEWISH LEGAL INTERPRETATION

"Moses received Torah (the Law) from Sinai and delivered it to Joshua, and Joshua to the Elders, and the Elders to the Prophets, and the Prophets delivered it to the men of the Great Synagogue" from Sayings of the Fathers (1:1). On the basis of this tradition, the rabbis sought to show a direct link between Moses, through whom the Law was first given, and themselves, as the heirs of the study of the Law that was said to have been launched by Ezra after the Jews returned from captivity in Babylon and re-established their institutions in Jerusalem. There is very little historical evidence concerning the Great Synagogue, though the assembly for the reading and study of the Law in Nehemiah 9 and 10 may be a parallel tradition pointing to the same events. How long such an assembly lasted we have no way of determining, but it was later appealed to by the rabbis as the basis for authorizing their interpretations of the Law. The presupposition underlying the tradition of links going back to Moses is that Torah contained in direct expression or in interpretive potential all that Israel had needed or would ever need for its legal guidance. The task of the student of the Law was to unfold the potential significance, not to innovate for unforeseen circumstances.

What is given in the section below is of two types: (1) brief excerpts from a wide range of sources dealing with several subjects of importance for Jews in this period: how to deal with proselytes (Gentiles who wanted to become members of the Jewish covenant community); the relation of poverty and wealth to goodness; how one is to gauge the authority of an interpretation of the Law; what is the authority of the oral law; and (2) two extended sections of the tractate *Sanhedrin* (from Nezikin), one dealing with judicial procedure and the other with the death penalty—subjects of special significance for anyone interested in the gospel accounts of the trial and death of Jesus.

Concerning Proselytes

RABBINIC WRITINGS

R. Huna narrated: "An astrologer who had become a proselyte to Judaism consulted his horoscope before departing on a journey. The reading showed that he would meet with danger, and he was minded to delay his voyage. Then his courage rose within him, and he said to himself: 'Did I not join the nation of Israel because I am convinced that God protects those who believe and trust in Him?'

"He departed on his way, and in a lonely spot encountered some wild beasts. He was about to leave them his donkey, but the beasts ran away.

"Why did the proselyte meet with danger? Because he had consulted the horoscope. Why was he saved? Because he trusted in the Lord."

TJ SHABBAT, 8D

A gentile asked Shammai to accept him as a proselyte on the condition that he learn the Written Law only. The rabbi refused.

The man then went to Hillel with the same proposal. Hillel had him circumcised, and commenced to teach him the Hebrew alphabet. In the course of time the proselyte was taught the Scriptures and then was told to learn the explanations of the Oral Law.

When he remonstrated, Hillel said: "You trusted me in what I taught you before. Why, then, dost thou not trust me now?"

TB SHABBAT, 31A, ABBREVIATED

When a man comes in these times seeking to become a proselyte, he is asked: "What is your motive in presenting yourself to become a proselyte? Do you not know that in these times the Israelites are afflicted, distressed, downtrodden, torn to pieces, and that suffering is their lot?"

If he answer: "I know; and I am unworthy [to share their sufferings]," they accept him at once, and acquaint him with some of the lighter and some of the weightier commandments; they instruct him regarding the sin he may commit in such matters as picking up the forgotten sheaf, reaping the corner of the field, and the poor tithe. They acquaint him also with the penalties attached to the commandments and with the reward of keeping them. This discourse should not go too much into particulars."

TB YEBAMOT, 46B

Rab said: "Even those who become proselytes from motives of self-interest are proselytes. This is the rule. They are not to be repelled as proselytes are repelled at the outset, but received; and they must have friendly treatment, for perhaps after all they have become proselytes for God's sake."

TJ KIDDUSHIN, 65B

A certain philosopher who was converted by the constancy of the martyrs, Rabbi Hanina ben Teradion and his wife and daughter, and was sentenced to the same fate, said: "You have told me good news. Tomorrow my portion will be with them in the World-to-Come."

SIFRE DEUT., 307

Rabbi Nathan used to say: "Do not throw up to your fellow a blemish you have yourself. If you insult a man because he is a proselyte, he can retort: 'The Scripture says: "For ye were aliens." '"

Rabbi Simeon ben Yohai said: "It says: 'And those that love Him are like the sun when it rises in its power' (Judges 5, 31). Which is greater: he who loves the king, or he whom the king loves? You must say, he whom the king loves. And it is said of God, 'And He loveth a proselyte [Deut. 10:18].'"

MECHILTA MISHPATIM, 18

Rabbi Simeon ben Yohai said: "Our father Abraham was not circumcised till he was ninety-nine years old. If he had been circumcised at twenty or at thirty, a man could have become a proselyte only at a lower age than twenty or thirty; therefore, God postponed it in his case till he arrived at the age of ninety-nine, in order not to bolt the door in the face of proselytes who come."

MECHILTA MISHPATIM, 18

When Aquila, the nephew of Emperor Hadrian, desired to become a proselyte to Judaism, he said to the Emperor: "I wish to engage in business. Can you advise me how to buy?"

The Emperor replied: "Go about and see what merchandise is very cheap in the present market, and then buy. It will surely rise in price if you wait long enough."

Aquila departed, and underwent circumcision. When he acquainted his uncle of his deed, the Emperor wished to know who had enjoined him to do this.

"Thou art the man," Aquila replied. "Israel is the cheapest nation today; hence I bought my way into it."

"What will you gain?"

"The ability to learn Torah."

"But why must you circumcise for that?"

Aquila said: "Can anyone in your army gain distinction unless he proves his loyalty and readiness to sacrifice himself for you? By the same token, no one can gain distinction in the knowledge of the Torah, unless he shows readiness to shed his blood for God."

TANHUMA, MISHPATIM

Rabbi Johanan said: " 'The proselyte shall not lodge without; I will open my doors to the wayfarer [Job 31, 32].' This is a text proving the rule that proselytes should be held back with the weaker left hand and drawn near with the right. Men should not do like Elisha, who thrust Gehazi away with both hands."

TJ SANHEDRIN, 29B

The rabbis say: "If a proselyte takes it upon himself to obey all the words of the Torah except one single commandment, he is not to be received."

SIFRA, KEDOSHIM, 8

One who brings a foreigner near and makes a proselyte of him is as if he created him.

BERESHIT RABBAH, 39

ACTS 15:
19-21

Rabbi Johanan said: "Seven laws are binding on the descendants of Noah [Gentiles]: establishment of courts of justice; blasphemy prohibition; prohibition of the worship of other gods, of murder, of incest and adultery, of theft and robbery, and of eating the flesh of a living animal before it dies."

TB SANHEDRIN, 56A

Rabbi Nehemiah said: "Those who became proselytes for the love of a Jewess or out of fear of Jews and proselytes for the sake of bettering their lot should not be accepted. Genuine proselytes are those who become Israelites, though there be nothing to gain thereby."

TB YEBAMOT, 24B

MT. 1:5

Said R. Alexander: "God saith to the Gentiles: 'Be not afraid to come near Me even if thou hast offended greatly. Have I not accepted in My fold Rahab, the harlot, who married Joshua and had fine descendants? Have I not received Jethro, the Pagan Priest, whose daughter married Moses, our greatest man? Have I not promised that the Messiah will descend from Ruth, the Moabitess?' "

PESIKTA RABBATI, 41, 3

MT 8:
5-12

Rabbi Jose ben Halafta taught: "In the Time-to-Come [the Messianic Age] the heathen will come to Israel as proselytes."

TB ABODAH ZARA, 3B

Rabbi Meir said: " 'Ye shall therefore keep My statutes and My ordinances, which, if a man do, he shall live by them [Lev. 18:5].' It is not said that priests, Levites and Israelites shall live by them, but 'a man'; therefore, even a Gentile."

TB SANHEDRIN, 59A

Rabbi Joshua ben Hananiah said: "It is written [Psalm 9:18]: 'The wicked shall return to Sheol, all the Gentiles, who forgot God.' This implies that there are righteous men in the nations of the world [the Gentiles], who have a portion in the World-to-Come."

MT. 7
26-29

TOS SANHEDRIN, 13, 2

Rabbi Jose ben Halafta said: "A proselyte who embraces Judaism is like a new-born child. God cannot therefore now chastise him for deeds done or duties neglected before his new birth."

JN. 3:

TB YEBAMOT, 48B

Aquila the Proselyte came to Rabbi Eliezer and said: "Is this the love with which God loves the proselyte, that He supplies him with bread and raiment [Deut. 10:18]? Is this all He gives the proselyte? I have many pheasants and many raiments of peacock color, yet even my slaves do not hold them to be of importance." Rabbi Eliezer rebuked Aquila and he departed.

The Proselyte went to Rabbi Joshua, who sought to appease him, saying: "Bread includes spiritual food, and raiment includes the Tallit of the learned doctors. And, when a proselyte was not only rich in material possessions but also in spiritual wealth, the High Priest himself was happy to have him marry his daughter, and he might even see his grandson officiate as the High Priest."

The students said: "Were it not for Rabbi Joshua's patience in dealing with him, Aquila might have returned to paganism." And they said: "He that is slow to anger is better than the mighty."

BERESHIT RABBAH, 70

An old man met Elijah and asked him: "Will there be any non-Jews in the Messianic Era?"

Elijah replied: "Yes, all the nations who have persecuted and done evil unto Israel will behold Israel's rejoicing and then will perish from envy, but those who did not persecute Israel will live throughout the entire Era and labor for Israel [Isaiah 61:5]. And at the conclusion of the Messianic period in the new World-to-Come, then too, they will not share equally with Israel. If the uncircumcised could not eat of the Pascal Lamb with Israel, how much the more logical is it to say that they will not enjoy the Holy of Holies that will then come. A distinct section will be set aside for them apart from Israel."

LK. 13
28-30

TANNA DE-BE EILYAHU
RABBAH, 22

The Rabbis have taught: "For the sake of peaceful intercourse or for the sake of the Torah whose ways are ways of peace, the non-Jewish poor may gather unharvested produce left over in Jewish fields, in the same fashion as the Jewish poor. The non-Jewish poor shall receive food and garments from Jewish charity funds the same as Jews. If the non-Jewish sick have no friends, they should be visited the same as the Jewish sick. If no one claims the body of the non-Jewish dead, they should be buried by Jews, the same as the Jewish dead. When a Jew sees a non-Jew at work in the field, he should greet him with words of blessing, even in the forbidden seventh year when a Jewish worker should be shunned."

MK. 15: 42-46

TB GITTIN, 61A

Even an idolator who studies Torah is like the High Priest.

TB BABA KAMMA, 38A

A foreigner came to Shammai, saying, "Make a proselyte of me, on condition that you teach me the whole of the Torah while I stand on one foot."

Shammai drove him off with a measuring-stick he had in his hand. Thereupon he repaired to Hillel with the same proposition.

Hillel received him as a proselyte and taught him: "What you do not like to have done to you, do not do to your fellow. This is the whole of the Torah; the rest is the explanation of it. Go, learn it."

MT. 7:12

TB SHABBAT, 31A

The Poor, the Rich, and the Wicked

When the poor man, the rich man, and the wicked stand in Judgement, the poor man will be asked: "Why have you not learned and obeyed the Torah?"

If he says: "I was forced to earn a livelihood," he is asked: "Art thou poorer than Hillel, who studied amid the direst poverty?"

If the rich man, in answer to the same question, says: "I was too concerned with my many affairs of business," he is told: "Art thou richer than Rabbi Eliezer ben Harsom, who owned a thousand villages but left the management to others that he might study day and night?"

If the wicked man in reply declares: "My passion was over-strong within me," they say to him: "Was it stronger within thee than within the lonely youth, Joseph, the son of Jacob? If one mortal can conquer the circumstances of his life and attain goodness, others can do so, for Joseph was human like his fellow-beings."

TB YOMA, 35B

Authority in Interpretation

We learnt elsewhere: If he cut it[1] into separate tiles, placing sand between each tile: R. Eliezer declared it clean, and the Sages declared

---

[1]The immediate question under discussion is whether a certain kind of oven, called a *taboun*, constructed of pieces of tile and sand with inner and outer layers of mortar is clean according to Jewish law. Rabbi Eliezer says that each component is not in itself a utensil, and that therefore the laws do not apply. Others held that the

it unclean; [59b] and this was the oven of 'Aknai. Why [the oven of] 'Aknai?—Said Rab Judah in Samuel's name: [It means] that they encompassed it with arguments as a snake, and proved it unclean. It has been taught: On that day R. Eliezer brought forward every imaginable argument, but they did not accept them. Said he to them: "If the *halachah* agrees with me, let this carob-tree prove it!" Thereupon the carob-tree was torn a hundred cubits out of its place—others affirm, four hundred cubits. "No proof can be brought from a carob-tree," they retorted. Again he said to them: "If the *halachah* agrees with me, let the stream of water prove it!" Whereupon the stream of water flowed backwards. "No proof can be brought from a stream of water," they rejoined. Again he urged: "If the *halachah* agrees with me, let the walls of the schoolhouse prove it," whereupon the walls inclined to fall. But R. Joshua rebuked them, saying: "When scholars are engaged in a *halachic* dispute, what have ye to interfere?" Hence they did not fall, in honour of R. Joshua, nor did they resume the upright, in honour of R. Eliezer; and they are still standing thus inclined. Again he said to them: "If the *halachah* agrees with me, let it be proved from Heaven!" Whereupon a Heavenly Voice cried out: Why do ye dispute with R. Eliezer, seeing that in all matters the *halachah* agrees with him!" But R. Joshua arose and exclaimed: "*It is not in heaven.*" What did he mean by this?—Said R. Jeremiah:" That the Torah had already been given at Mount Sinai; we pay no attention to a Heavenly Voice, because Thou hast long since written in the Torah at Mount Sinai, *After the majority must one incline.*"

LK. 17:«

MK. 1:1

TB BABA MAZIA 59B

Oral Law

To study the Torah is more important than to honor parents.

MK. 7: 9-13

TB MEGILLAH, 16B

The Torah was given to Moses chiefly in writing, a small portion in oral form.

TB GITTIN, 60B

As the sea has little waves between the large ones, so the Torah has many details of Oral Law affecting commandments of the Written Law.

SHEKALIM, 6, 1

---

mortar unified the whole, and that therefore the laws did apply. Mention of "Aknai," which is presumably the name of a rabbi but also the word for snake, leads into a pun in which the antagonists compare their opponent's argumentation to the writhings of a snake. The inability to resolve the issue by rational means raises the question as to what objective basis there is for deciding among competing interpretive claims. The appeal then shifts to external evidence.

Torah that is not a tradition is not Torah.

TB V. SHABBAT, 19, 6

Two Torahs were given to Israel—one in written and one in oral form.

SIFRA, BEHUKOTAI

He who abides by the precepts of the Sages is called modest and holy.

TB YEBAMOT, 20; NIDDAH, 12

When the wall of the vineyard fell, the vineyard was destroyed.

ABOT DE-R. NATHAN, 24

When Moses received the Oral Law, he asked permission to write it down. God replied: "A time will come when the Gentiles will translate the written Torah and say: 'We are the true Israel, we are the true sons of God.' And then Israel will say: 'We are the keepers of God's secret Law, and the people to whom God has entrusted His Tradition are his true sons.' "

PESIKTA RABBATI, 5

Moses was amazed when it was vouchsafed to him to listen to Rabbi Akiba discovering in his laws meanings of which he had never thought.

TB MENAHOT, 29B

"Doing depends upon learning, not learning upon doing."
At a conference of Rabbis at Lydda, the question was propounded: "Is study the greater thing, or doing?"
The decision was unanimous in favor of study, on the ground that study leads to doing.

TB KIDDUSHIN, 40B

Rabbi Meir advised: "Be not much engaged in business, and busy yourself with the Torah, and be lowly in spirit before every man. If you give yourself a vacation from study, you will find many reasons for wasting your time; but, if you study industriously, He has a great reward to give you."

ABOT, 4, 10

RAISING THE VOICE

Beruriah, the wife of Rabbi Meir, noticed a student studying in silence. She declared: "We read; 'Ordered in all things and sure [II

Samuel, 23:5].' If the Torah is studied properly with all thy faculties, it is sure to be remembered."

Samuel said to Rab Judah: "Shinenna [diligent student], open thy mouth and read, open thy mouth and learn, so that thou mayest live long and remember well."

TB 'ERUBIN, 54

A Rabbi narrated: "While travelling, a man met me and continued on the way with me. He said: 'Rabbi, it is my belief that only the Torah was given on Mount Sinai, but not the Mishnah.'

"I replied: 'Nay, my son, both were given to Moses on Mount Sinai. Are you open to reason?'

" 'Yes,' he answered.

"I said: 'When you recite a definite number of benedictions in the Amidah, is the number inscribed in the Torah? When you hold Services, is the procedure definitely inscribed in the Torah? In every Mitzvah you must refer to the Traditional Law concerning the manner of its performance. Therefore, the Traditional or Oral Law must have originated at Mount Sinai.' "

ELIYAHU ZUTA, 2

Judicial Procedures

MISHNAH SANHEDRIN, 3:5–5:5

(3:5) A friend or an enemy [is disqualified]. By friend is meant a man's groomsman, and by enemy any that through enmity has not spoken with him for three days. They replied: Israelites should not be suspected for such a cause.

(6) How did they prove witnesses? They brought them in and admonished them; then they put them all forth and kept back the chief among them and said to him, "Say, how dost thou know that he is in debt to the other?" If he said, "He said to me 'I am in debt to him,' or 'Such-a-one said to me that he was in debt to him,' he has said nothing: he must be able to say, 'In our presence he acknowledged to the other that he owed him 200 zuz.' " Afterward they brought in the second witness and proved him. If their words were found to agree together, the judges discussed the matter. If two said, "He is not guilty," and one said, "He is guilty," he is not guilty; if two said, "He is guilty," and one said, "He is not guilty," he is guilty; if one said, "He is not guilty," and one said, "He is guilty," and even if two declared him not guilty or two declared him guilty while one said, "I do not know, they must add the judges."

MK. 14: 55-56

(7) When the judges reached their decision they brought in the suitors. The chief among the judges says, "Thou, such-a-one, art not guilty," or "Thou, such-a-one, art guilty." And whence do we know that after one of the judges has gone forth he may not say, "I declare him not guilty and my fellows declare him guilty; but what may I do, for my fellows outvoted me?" Of such a one it is written, *Thou shalt*

not go up and down as a talebearer among thy people; and it also says,
He that goeth about as a talebearer revealeth secrets (but he that is of
a faithful spirit concealeth the matter).

(8) So long as a suitor can produce any proof the court may reverse
the verdict. If they had said, "Bring all the proofs that thou hast
within thirty days," and he brought them within the thirty days, the
court may reverse the verdict; but (if he brought any proof) after the
thirty days, the court cannot reverse the verdict. Rabban Simeon b.
Gamaliel said: "What should he do that did not find it within thirty
days but found it after thirty days?" If they had said to him, "Bring
witnesses," and he said, "I have no witnesses," or [if they said], "Bring
proof," and he said, "I have no proof," and he later found proof or
found witnesses, then they are in no wise valid. Rabban Simeon b.

MT. 26:
59-61

Gamaliel said: What should he do that did know ˜that he had witnesses, then found witnesses, or that did not know that he had proof,
then found proof? If they had said to him, "Bring witnesses," and he
said, "I have no witnesses," or, "Bring proof," and he said, "I have no
proof," but, when he saw that he would be accounted guilty, he said,
"Come near, such-a-one and such-a-one, and bear witness for me!" or
if he brought forth some proof from his wallet, then it is in no wise
valid.

(4:1) Non-capital and capital cases are alike in examination and
inquiry, for it is written, *Ye shall have one manner of law.* In what do
non-capital cases differ from capital cases? Non-capital cases [are
decided] by three and capital cases by three and twenty [judges].
Non-capital cases may begin either with reasons for acquittal or for
conviction, but capital cases must begin with reasons for acquittal and
may not begin with reasons for conviction. In non-capital cases they
may reach a verdict either of acquittal or of conviction by the decision
of a majority of one; but in capital cases they may reach a verdict of
acquittal by the decision of a majority of two. In non-capital cases
they may reverse a verdict either [from conviction] to acquittal or
[from acquittal] to conviction; but in capital cases they may reverse
a verdict [from conviction] to acquittal but not [from acquittal] to
conviction. In non-capital cases all may argue either in favour of conviction or of acquittal; but in capital cases all may argue in favour
of acquittal but not in favour of conviction. In non-capital cases he
that had argued in favour of conviction may afterward argue in favour
of acquittal, or he that had argued in favour of acquittal may afterward argue in favour of conviction; in capital cases he that had argued in favour of conviction may afterward argue in favour of acquittal, but he that had argued in favour of acquittal cannot afterward
change and argue in favour of conviction. In non-capital cases they

MT. 26:
17

hold the trial during the daytime and the verdict may be reached during the night; in capital cases they hold the trial during the daytime

MT. 26:
20

and the verdict also must be reached during the daytime. In non-
capital cases the verdict, whether of acquittal or of conviction, may

MT. 26:
59

be reached the same day; in capital cases a verdict of acquittal may
be reached on the same day, but a verdict of conviction not until the

MT. 26:
66

following day. Therefore trials may not be held on the eve of a Sabbath or on the eve of a Festival-day.

MT. 27:
1-2

(2) In non-capital cases concerning uncleanness and cleanness [the

judges declare their opinion] beginning from the eldest, but in capital cases they begin from [them that sit at] the side. All [of the family stocks] are qualified to try non-capital cases; but all are not qualified to try capital cases, but only priests, Levites, and Israelites that may give [their daughters] in marriage into the priestly stock.

(3) The Sanhedrin was arranged like the half of a round threshing-floor so that they all might see one another. Before them stood the two scribes of the judges, one to the right and one to the left, and they wrote down the words of them that favoured acquittal and the words of them that favoured conviction. R. Judah says: There were three: one wrote down the words of them that favoured acquittal, and one wrote down the words of them that favoured conviction, and the third wrote down the words both of them that favoured acquittal and of them that favoured conviction.

(4) Before them sat three rows of disciples of the Sages, and each knew his proper place. If they needed to appoint [another as a judge], they appointed him from the first row, and one from the second row came into the first row, and one from the third row came into the second; and they chose yet another from the congregation and set him in the third row. He did not sit in the place of the former, but he sat in the place that was proper for him.

(5) How did they admonish the witnesses in capital cases? They brought them in and admonished them [saying], "Perchance ye will say what is but supposition or hearsay or at secondhand, or [ye may say in yourselves], "We heard it from a man that was trustworthy." Or perchance ye do not know that we shall prove you by examination and inquiry? Know ye, moreover, that capital cases are not as non-capital cases: in non-capital cases a man may pay money and so make atonement, but in capital cases the witness is answerable for the blood of him [that is wrongfully condemned] and the blood of his posterity [that should have been born to him] to the end of the world. For so have we found it with Cain that slew his brother, for it is written, *The bloods of thy brother cry*. It says not "The blood of thy brother," but *The bloods of thy brother*—his blood and the blood of his posterity. [Another saying is: *Bloods of thy brother*—because his blood was cast over the trees and stones.] Therefore but a single man was created in the world, to teach that if any man has caused a single soul to perish from Israel Scripture imputes it to him as though he had caused a whole world to perish; and if any man saves alive a single soul from Israel, Scripture imputes it to him as though he had saved alive a whole world. Again [but a single man was created] for the sake of peace among mankind, that none should say to his fellow, "My father was greater than thy father"; also that the heretics should not say, "There are many ruling powers in heaven." Again [but a single man was created] to proclaim the greatness of the Holy One, blessed is he; for man stamps many coins with the one seal and they are all like one another; but the King of kings, the Holy One, blessed is he, has stamped every man with the seal of the first man, yet not one of them is like his fellow. Therefore every one must say, For my sake was the world created. And if perchance ye would say, Why should we be at these pains?—was it not once written, *He being a witness, whether he hath seen or known (if he do not utter it, then shall he bear his in-*

MT. 27: 25

iquity)? And if perchance ye would say, Why should we be guilty of the blood of this man?—was it not once written, *When the wicked perish there is rejoicing?*

(5:1) They used to prove witnesses with seven inquiries: In what weeks of years? In what year? In what month? On what date in the month? On what day? In what hour? In what place? /R. Jose says: [They asked only], On what day? In what hour? In what place?/ [Moreover they asked]: Do ye recognize him? Did ye warn him? If a man had committed idolatry [they asked the witnesses], What did he worship? and, How did he worship it?

(2) The more a judge tests the evidence the more is he deserving of praise: Ben Zakkai once tested the evidence even to the inquiring about the stalks of figs. Wherein do the inquiries differ from the cross-examination? If to the inquiries one [of the two witnesses] answered, "I do not know," their evidence becomes invalid; but if to the cross-examination one answered, "I do not know," or if they both answered, "We do not know," their evidence remains valid. Yet if they contradict one another, whether during the inquiries or the cross-examination, their evidence becomes invalid.

(3) If one said, "On the second of the month," and the other said, "On the third," their evidence remains valid, since one may have known that the month was intercalated and the other did not know that the month was intercalated; but if one said, "On the third," and the other said, "On the fifth," their evidence becomes invalid. If one said, "At the second hour," and the other said, "At the third," their evidence remains valid; but if one said, "At the third hour," and the other said, "At the fifth," their evidence becomes invalid. R. Judah says: "It remains valid"; but if one said, "At the fifth hour," and the other said, "At the seventh," their evidence becomes invalid since at the fifth hour the sun is in the east and at the seventh it is in the west.

(4) They afterward brought in the second witness and proved him. If their words were found to agree together they begin [to examine the evidence] in favour of acquittal. If one of the witnesses said, "I have somewhat to argue in favour of his acquittal," or if one of the disciples said, "I have somewhat to argue in favour of his acquittal," they bring him up and set him among them and he does not come down from thence the whole day. If there is aught of substance in his words they listen to him. Even if the accused said, "I have somewhat to argue in favour of my acquittal," they listen to him, provided that there is aught of substance in his words.

MK. 15:1   (5) If they found him innocent they set him free; otherwise they leave his sentence over until the morrow. [In the meantime] they went together in pairs, they ate a little [but they used to drink no wine the whole day], and they discussed the matter all night, and early on the morrow they came to the court. He that favoured acquittal says: "I declared him innocent [yesterday] and I still declare him innocent"; and he that favoured conviction says, "I declared him guilty [yesterday] and I still declare him guilty." He that had favoured conviction may now acquit, but he that had favoured acquittal may not retract and favour conviction. If they erred in the matter the scribes of the judges must put them in remembrance. If they [all] found him innocent they set him free; otherwise they decide by vote. If twelve favour acquittal and eleven favour conviction, he is declared innocent; if twelve favour conviction and eleven favour acquittal, or, even if eleven favour acquittal and eleven favour conviction and one says, "I do not know," or even if twenty-two favour acquittal or favour conviction and one says, "I do not know," they must add to the number of judges. Up to what number may they add to them? By two at a time up to one and seventy. If then thirty-six favour acquittal and thirty-five favour conviction, he is declared innocent; if thirty-six favour conviction and thirty-five favour acquittal, they debate one with another until one of them that favoured conviction approves of the words of them that favour acquittal.

Death Penalty

MISHNAH SANHEDRIN

(6:1) When sentence [of stoning] has been passed they take him forth to stone him. The place of stoning was outside [far away from] the court, as it is written, *Bring forth him that hath cursed without the camp.* One man stands at the door of the court with a towel in his hand, and another, mounted on a horse, far away from him [but near enough] to see him. If [in the court] one said, "I have somewhat to argue in favour of his acquittal," that man waves the towel and the horse runs and stops him [that was going forth to be stoned]. Even if he himself said, "I have somewhat to argue in favour of my acquittal," they must bring him back, be it four times or five, provided that there is aught of substance in his words. If then they found him innocent they set him free; otherwise he goes forth to be stoned. A herald goes out before [calling], "Such-a-one, the son of such-a-one, is going forth to be stoned for that he committed such or such an offence. Such-a-one and such-a-one are witnesses against him. If any man knoweth aught in favour of his acquittal let him come and plead it."

(2) When he was about ten cubits from the place of stoning they used to say to him, "Make thy confession," for such is the way of them that have been condemned to death to make confession, for every one that makes his confession has a share in the world to come. For so have we found it with Achan. Joshua said to him, *My son, give, I pray thee, glory to the Lord, the God of Israel, and make confession unto him, and tell me now what thou hast done; hide it not from me. And Achan answered Joshua and said, Of a truth I have sinned against the Lord, the God of Israel, and thus and thus have I done.* Whence do we learn that his confession made atonement for him? It is written, *And Joshua said, Why hast thou troubled us? The Lord shall trouble thee this day—this day* thou shalt be troubled, but in the world to come thou shalt not be troubled. If he knows not how to make his confession come thou shalt not be troubled. If he knows not how to make his confession they say to him, "Say, May my death be an atonement for all my sins." R. Judah says: "If he knew that he was

MT. 15: 21-24

MT. 27: 32

MT. 21: 39

MK. 15: 4, 5

MK. 15: 26

condemned because of false testimony he should say, 'Let my death be an atonement for all my sins excepting this sin.'" They said to him: "If so, every one would speak after this fashion to show his innocence."

MK. 15:
20, 24

(3) When he was four cubits from the place of stoning they stripped off his clothes. A man is kept covered in front and a woman both in front and behind. So R. Judah. But the Sages say: A man is stoned naked but a woman is not stoned naked.

(4) The place of stoning was twice the height of a man. One of the witnesses knocked him down on his loins; if he turned over on his heart the witness turned him over again on his loins. If he straightway died it sufficed; but if not, the second [witness] took the stone and dropped it on his heart. If he straightway died, that sufficed; but if not, he was stoned by all Israel, for it is written, *The hand of the witnesses shall be first upon him to put him to death and afterward the hand of all the people.* All that have been stoned must be hanged. So R. Eliezer. But the Sages say: None is hanged save the blasphemer and the idolator. A man is hanged with his face to the people and a woman with her face towards the gallows. So R. Eliezer. But the Sages say: A man is hanged but a woman is not hanged. R. Eliezer said to them: Did not Simeon ben Shetah hang women in Ashkelon? They answered: He hanged eighty women, whereas two ought not to be judged in the one day. How did they hang a man? They put a beam into the ground and a piece of wood jutted from it. The two hands [of the body] were brought together and [in this fashion] it was hanged. R. Jose says: The beam was made to lean against a wall and one hanged the corpse thereon as the butchers do. And they let it down at once: if it remained there overnight a negative command

MK. 15:
42

JN. 19:31

is thereby transgressed, for it is written, *His body shall not remain all night upon the tree, but thou shalt surely bury him the same day; for he that is hanged is a curse against God*; as if to say: Why was this one hanged? Because he blessed the Name, and the Name of Heaven was found profaned.

(5) R. Meir said: When man is sore troubled, what says the Shekinah? My head is ill at ease, my arm is ill at ease. If God is sore troubled at the blood of the ungodly that is shed, how much more at the blood of the righteous? Furthermore, every one that suffers his dead to remain overnight transgresses a negative command; but if he had

MK. 15:
43-46

suffered it to remain by reason of the honour due it, to bring for it a coffin and burial clothes, he does not thereby commit transgression. They used not to bury him in the burying-place of his fathers, but two burying-places were kept in readiness by the court, one for them that were beheaded or strangled, and one for them that were stoned or burnt.

(6) When the flesh had wasted away they gathered together the bones and buried them in their own place. [After he was put to death] the kinsmen came and greeted the judges and the witnesses as if to say, "We have naught against you in our hearts, for ye have judged the judgement of truth." And they used not to make [open] lamenta-

tion but they went mourning, for mourning has place in the heart alone.

(7:1) The court had power to inflict four kinds of death-penalty: stoning, burning, beheading, and strangling. R. Simeon says: [Their order of gravity is] burning, stoning, strangling, and beheading. This is the ordinance of them that are to be stoned.

MK. 14: 64

MK. 15: 15

(2) The ordinance of them that are to be burnt [is this]: They set him in dung up to his knees and put a towel of coarse stuff within one of soft stuff and wrap it around his neck; one [witness] pulled one end towards him and the other pulled one end towards him until he opened his mouth; a wick was kindled and thrown into his mouth, and it went down to his stomach and burnt his entrails. R. Judah says: If thus he died at their hands they would not have fulfilled the ordinance of burning; but, rather, they must open his mouth with tongs by force and kindle the wick and throw it into his mouth, and it goes down to his stomach and burns his entrails. R. Eliezer b. Zadok said: It happened once that a priest's daughter committed adultery and they encompassed her with bundles of branches and burnt her. They said to him: Because the court at that time had not right knowledge.

(3) The ordinance of them that are to be beheaded [is this]: they used to cut off his head with a sword as the government does. R. Judah says: This is shameful for him; but, rather they lay his head on a block and cut it off with an axe. They said to him: There is no death more shameful than this. The ordinance of them that are to be strangled [is this]: they set him in dung up to his knees and put a towel of coarse stuff within one of soft stuff and the other pulled one end towards him, until his life departed.

(4) These are they that are to be stoned: he that has connexion with his mother, his father's wife, his daughter-in-law, a male, or a beast, and the woman that suffers connexion with a beast, and the blasphemer and the idolator, and he that offers any of his seed to Molech, and he that has a familiar spirit and the soothsayer, and he that profanes the Sabbath, and he that curses his father or his mother, and he that has connexion with a girl that is betrothed, and he that beguiles [others to idolatry], and he that leads [a whole town] astray, and the sorcerer and a stubborn and rebellious son. He that has connexion with his mother is thereby culpable both by virtue of the law of the mother and of the father's wife. R. Judah says: He is culpable by virtue of the law of the mother only. He that has connexion with his father's wife is thereby culpable both by virtue of the law of the father's wife and of another man's wife, whether in his father's lifetime or after his father's death, whether after bethrothal [only] or after wedlock. He that has connexion with his daughter-in-law is thereby culpable both by virtue of the law of the daughter-in-law and of another man's wife, whither in his son's lifetime or after his son's death, whether after betrothal [only] or after wedlock. He that has connexion with a male or with a beast, and she that suffers connexion with a beast [their death is] by stoning. If it is the man that has sinned how has the beast sinned? But inasmuch as an offence has be-

fallen a man by reason of it, therefore Scripture has said that it shall be stoned. Another saying is: Lest the beast should go through the market and they say, This is the beast by reason of which such-a-one was stoned.

JN. 19:7

(5) "The blasphemer" is not culpable unless he pronounces the Name itself. R. Joshua b. Karha says: On every day [of the trial] they examined the witnesses with a substituted name [such as] 'May Jose smite Jose.' When sentence was to be given they did not declare him guilty of death [on the grounds of evidence given] with the substituted name, but they sent out all the people and asked the chief among the witnesses and said to him, "Say expressly what thou heardest," and he says it; and the judges stand up on their feet and rend their garments, and they may not mend them again. And the second witness says, "I also heard the like," and the third says, "I also heard the like."

MK. 14: 61-64

MK. 14: 56

(6) "The idolator" [is culpable] no matter whether he worships or sacrifices or burns incense or pours out a libation or bows himself down to it or accepts it as his god or says to it, Thou art my god. But he that puts his arms around it or kisses it or sweeps it or besprinkles it or washes it or anoints it or clothes it or shoes it transgresses [only] a negative command. He that makes a vow in its name or takes an oath in its name transgresses a negative command. But if a man excretes to Baal Peor [he is to be stoned, because] this is how it is worshipped. He that throws a stone at a *Merkolis* [is to be stoned, because] this is how it is worshipped.

(7) "He that offers any of his seed to Molech" is not culpable unless he gives up [the child] to Molech and passes him through the fire: if he gave him up to Molech but did not pass him through the fire, or if he passed him through the fire but did not give him up to Molech, he is not culpable; he must both give him up to Molech and pass him through the fire. "He that has a familiar spirit" (such is the Python which speaks from his armpits), "and the soothsayer" (such is he that speaks with mouth), these are [to be put to death] by stoning, and he that inquires of them transgresses against a warning.

(8) "He that profanes the Sabbath" [is liable, after warning, to death by stoning] if he committed an act which renders him liable to Extirpation if he acted wantonly or, or to a Sin-offering if he acted in error. "He that curses his father or his mother" is not culpable unless he curses them with the Name. If he cursed them with a substituted name R. Meir declares him culpable but the Sages declare him not culpable.

(9) "He that has connexion with a girl that is betrothed" is not culpable unless she is still in her girlhood, and a virgin, and betrothed, and still in her father's house. If two had connexion with her the first is [liable to death] by stoning, but the second [only] by strangling.

(10) "He that beguiles [others to idolatry]"—such is a common man that beguiles another common man. If he said to another, "There is a god in such a place that eats this, drinks that, does good in this way and does harm in that way"—they may not place witnesses in hiding against any that become liable to the death-penalties enjoined in the Law save in this case alone. If he spoke [after this fashion] to two,

and they are such that can bear witness against him, they bring him to the court and stone him. If he spoke so to one only he may reply, "I have companions that are so minded"; and if the other was crafty and would not speak before them, witnesses may be placed in hiding behind a wall. Then he says to the other, "Say [again] what thou didst say to me in private," and the other speaks to him [as before] and he replies, "How shall we leave our God that is in Heaven and go and worship wood and stone?" If he retracted it shall be well with him, but if he said, "It is our duty and it is seemly so to do," they that are behind the wall bring him to the court and stone him. If a man said, "I will worship [another god]" or "I will go and worship it" or "Let us go and worship it," or "I will sacrifice to it" or "I will go and sacrifice to it" or "Let us go and sacrifice to it," or "I will burn incense to it," or "I will go and burn incense to it" or "Let us go and burn incense to it," or "I will make a libation to it" or "I will go and make a libation to it" or "Let us go and make a libation to it," or "I will bow myself down before it" or "I will go and bow myself down before it" or "Let us go and bow ourselves down before it," [such a one is culpable]. "He that leads [a whole town] astray" is he that says, "Let us go and worship idols."

(11) "The sorcerer"—he that performs some act is culpable, and not he that [only deceives the eyes]. R. Akiba in the name of R. Joshua says: If two were gathering cucumbers [by sorcery] one gatherer may not be culpable and the other gatherer may be culpable: he that [indeed] performed the act is culpable, but he that [only] deceived the eyes is not culpable. MK. 3: 22-30

ESCHATOLOGICAL TEXTS

After the shock of the fall of Jerusalem to the Babylonians and the subsequent capitivity of the Jewish people, the return to the land and the reestablishment of the Jewish commonwealth there did not bring about the establishment of the universal rule of God through the Scion of David that the prophets Isaiah and Micah had foretold. The Maccabean revolt established the Hasmonean family on the throne of Palestine for a century, but it became hopelessly corrupt and worldly in the final decades. In reaction to these disillusioning national experiences, the faith of the covenant people, if it was to survive at all, had two lines of development open to it: it could repeat the hopes of the ancient prophets, and leave to God the time and circumstances under which the promises would be fulfilled, or it could assess the national calamities as the work of a demonic power opposed to God and shift the sphere of the final triumph of God from the chronological future to the cosmic realms.

The Pharisees in the first century B.C. took the first of these options. Documentation of their outlook has survived in a pseudonymous work known as the *Psalms of Solomon*. But other groups—chiefly the Essenes—adopted a dualistic view. They taught that God had revealed to them the secret schedule for the outworking of His plan, by which the evil powers would be overcome and His rule established. They did not expect the restoration of the whole of the Jewish people, but rather the vindication of a small faithful remnant, which was of course identical with the sect of Jews that produced this literature. The second of these points of view found expression in a distinctive type of literature, highly figurative and even enigmatic in style, filled with veiled references to historical events, structured around a series of events that would lead up to the final conflict that would usher in the New Age. All was predetermined, but only those within the group were able to decipher the revelations (in Greek, *Apocalypse*) and to interpret the scriptures in the appropriate way so as to discern there the movement of the divine purpose. The oldest of the apocalypses is the Book of Daniel, although there are apocalyptic passages in Zechariah, Isaiah, and Ezekiel.

The mainstream of Judaism largely repudiated the apocalytic tradition after it was adapted for its own purposes by the Christian community. The language of the gospels and Paul, not to mention the book of Revelations, is filled with apocalyptic concepts and expressions. But the church preserved many of the originally Jewish apocalyptic writings, translating them into various languages. Then when the Dead Sea Scrolls began to come to light in the 1950s, fragments of known apocalyptic writings appeared among the scrolls, and previously unknown apocalypses were found as well. The excerpts given below include portions of three long-known writings—The Testaments of the Twelve Patriarchs, Enoch, and IV Ezra—in addition to parts of several of the Dead Sea Scrolls.

Pharisaic Nationalistic Texts:

The Psalms of Solomon

The Psalms of Solomon seem to have been written by Pharisees, who longed for the establishment of the Davidic ruler as God's anointed vicegerent over Israel, but who did not see in the Hasmonean dynasty the hand of God. The Psalms allude to the death of Pompey, who took over Palestine for the Romans in 63 B.C., and therefore probably were written about the middle of the first century B.C. There are no predictions about the trials that the faithful will undergo before the messianic era comes, nor are there any cryptic chronological clues as to when that event will occur, so the Psalms entirely lack the characteristic features of apocalyptic writings. There is instead unswerving confidence that God will establish the Davidic Messiah (no mention is made, as at Qumran, of an anointed priest as well), and through him God will exercise authority over all the nations. This will occur, the Psalmist declares (17:24), "At the time in the which thou seest, O God . . ."

17:1–38

(17:1) Lord, Thou art our King forever and ever,
    For in Thee, O God, doth our soul glory.
(2) How long are the days of man's life upon the earth?
    As are his days, so is the hope [set] upon him.
(3) But we hope in God, our deliverer;
For the might of our God is forever with mercy,
(4) And the kingdom of our God is forever over the nations in judgement.

(5) Thou, O Lord, didst choose David [to be] king over Israel,
    And didst swear to him concerning his seed that never should his kingdom fail before thee.
(6) But, for our sins, sinners rose up against us;
    They assailed us and thrust, us out;
    What Thou hadst not promised to them, they took away [from us] with violence.
(7) They in no wise glorified Thy honourable name;
    They set a [worldly] monarchy in place of [that which was] their excellency;
(8) They laid waste the throne of David in tumultous arrogance.

But Thou, O God, didst cast them down, and remove their seed from the earth,
(9) In that there rose up against them a man that was alien to our race.
(10) According to their sins didst Thou recompense them, O God;
    So that it befell them according to their deeds.
(11) God showed them no pity;
    He sought out their seed and let not one of them go free.
(12) Faithful is the Lord in all His judgements
    Which He doeth upon the earth.
(13) The lawless one laid waste our land so that none inhabited it,
    They destroyed young and old and their children together.
(14) In the heat of His anger He sent them away even unto the west,
    And [He exposed] the rulers of the land unsparingly to derision.
(15) Being an alien the enemy acted proudly,
    And his heart was alien from our God.
(16) And all . . . Jerusalem,
    As also the nations . . .
(17) And the children of the covenant in the midst of the mingled peoples . . .
    There was not among them one that wrought in the midst of Jerusalem mercy and truth.
(18) They that loved the synagogues of the pious fled from them,
    As sparrows that fly from their nest.
(19) They wandered in deserts that their lives might be saved from harm,
    And precious in the eyes of them that lived abroad was any that escaped alive from them.

(20) Over the whole earth were they scattered by lawless [men].

(21) For the heavens withheld the rain from dropping upon the earth,
Springs were stopped [that sprang] perennial[ly] out of the deeps,
[that ran down] from lofty mountains.
For there was none among them that wrought righteousness, and
justice;
From the chief of them to the least [of them] all were sinful;

(22) The king was a transgressor, and the judge disobedient, and the
people sinful.

MK. 11:
10

(23) Behold, O Lord, and raise up unto them their king, the son of
David,

MT. 21:9

At the time in the which Thou seest, O God, that he may reign
over Israel Thy servant.

(24) And gird him with strength, that he may shatter unrighteous
rulers,

(25) And that he may purge Jerusalem from nations that trample [her]

MK. 11:
15-17

down to destruction.

Wisely, righteously (26) he shall thrust out sinners from [the]
inheritance,
He shall destroy the pride of the sinner as a potter's vessel.
With a rod of iron he shall break in pieces all their substance,

(27) He shall destroy the godless nations with the word of his mouth;
At his rebuke nations shall flee before him,
And he shall reprove sinners for the thoughts of their heart.

MT. 24:
31

(28) And he shall gather together a holy people, whom he shall lead
in righteousness,
And he shall judge the tribes of the people that has been sanctified
by the Lord his God.

(29) And he shall not suffer unrighteousness to lodge anymore in their
midst,
Nor shall there dwell with them any man that knoweth wickedness,

(30) For he shall know them, that they are all sons of their God.
And he shall divide them according to their tribes upon the land,

(31) And neither sojourner nor alien shall sojourn with them anymore.
He shall judge peoples and nations in the wisdom of his righteousness.

SELAH

(32) And he shall have the heathen nations to serve him under his
yoke;
And he shall glorify the Lord in a place to be seen of [?] all the
earth;

(33) And he shall purge Jerusalem, making it holy as of old:

MK. 11:
17

(34) So that nations shall come from the ends of the earth to see his
glory,

MT. 28:
19

Bringing as gifts her sons who had fainted,

LK. 24:
37

(35) And to see the glory of the Lord, wherewith God hath glorified
her.
And he [shall be] a righteous king, taught of God, over them.

MT. 21:
1-9

(36) And there shall be no unrighteousness in his days in their midst,
For all shall be holy and their king the anointed of the Lord.

JN. 12:13

(37) For he shall not put his trust in horse and rider and bow,
Nor shall he multiply for himself gold and silver for war,

Nor shall he gather confidence from [?] a multitude [?] for the day
   of battle.
(38) The Lord Himself is his king, the hope of him that is mighty
   through [his] hope in God.

Apocalyptic Texts

Testaments of the Twelve Patriarchs

These writings have long been known and widely read in the eastern
churches. Based on Genesis 49, in which the dying Jacob makes specific
pronouncements and predictions concerning each of his twelve sons, this
writing purports to be the last will and testament of each of his sons.
Some scholars think that it received its present form considerably later,
and there do seem to be some specifically Christian interpolations in the
text. But at Qumran fragments of several parts of this writing have been
found, including the Testaments of Naphtali and Levi. Of special importance is the belief expressed in the Testament of the XII that there will
be in the End Time *two* anointed ones (Messiahs): The king, from the
tribe of Judah, and the priest, from the tribe of Levi. Of the two, the
priest has precedence.

Testaments of the Twelve Patriarchs

TESTAMENT OF LEVI, 4:1–5:7

(1) Now, therefore, know that the Lord shall execute judgement upon
   the sons of men.
Because when the rocks are being rent,
And the sun quenched,
And the waters dried up,
And the fire cowering,
And all creation troubled,
And the invisible spirits melting away,
And Hades taketh spoils through the visitations of the Most High,
Men will be unbelieving and persist in their iniquity.
On this account with punishment shall they be judged.
(2) [Therefore] the Most high hath heard thy prayer,
To separate thee from iniquity, and that thou shouldst become to Him   MK. 1:11
   a son,
And a servant, and a minister of His presence.   MK. 10:
(3) The light of knowledge shalt thou light up in Jacob,   45
And as the sun shalt thou be to all the seed of Israel.
Until the Lord shall visit all the Gentiles in His tender mercies forever.   MK. 11:
(4) And there shall be given to thee a blessing, and to all thy seed,   17
                                                                        MT. 24:
                                                                        14

(5) [And] therefore there have been given to thee counsel and
     understanding,
That thou mightst instruct thy sons concerning this;
(6) Because they that bless Him shall be blessed,
And they that curse Him shall perish.

(5:1) And thereupon the angel opened to me the gates of heaven, and
I saw the holy temple, and upon (2) a throne of glory the Most High.
And He said to me: Levi, I have given thee the blessings of the
(3) priesthood until I come and sojourn in the midst of Israel. Then
the angel brought me down to the earth, and gave me a shield and a
sword, and said to me: Execute vengeance on Shechem because
(4) of Dinah, thy sister, and I will be with thee because the Lord
hath sent me. And I destroyed at (5) that time the sons of Hamor,
as it is written in the heavenly tables. And I said to him: I pray (6)
thee, O Lord, tell me Thy name, that I may call upon Thee in a day
of tribulation. And he said: I am the angel who intercedeth for the
nation of Israel that they may not be smitten utterly, (7) for every
evil spirit attacketh it. And after these things I awakened, and blessed
the Most High, and the angel who intercedeth for the nation of Israel
and for all the righteous.

9:1–10:5

(1, 2) And after two days I and Judah[1] went up with our father
Jacob to Isaac our father's father. And my father's father blessed me
according to all the words of the visions which I had seen. And (3)
he would not come with us to Bethel. [And when we came to Bethel],
my father saw a vision (4) concerning me, that I should be their priest
unto God. And he rose up early in the morning, (5) and paid tithes of
all [to the Lord] through me. And [so] we came to Hebron to dwell
there. (6) And Isaac called me continually to put me in remembrance
of the law of the Lord, even as the (7) angel of the Lord showed unto
me. And he taught me the law of the priesthood, of sacrifices, (8)
whole burnt-offerings, first-fruits, freewill-offerings, peace-offerings.
And each day he was instructing (9) me, and was busied on my behalf
before the Lord, and said to me: Beware of the spirit of (10) fornication; for this shall continue and shall by thy seed pollute the holy
place. Take, therefore, to thyself a wife without blemish or pollution,
while yet thou art young, and not of the race of (11) strange nations.
And before entering into the holy place, bathe; and when thou offer-
est the (12) sacrifice, wash; and again, when thou finishest the sacrifice, wash. Of twelve trees having leaves (13) offer to the Lord, as
Abraham taught me also. And of every clean beast [and bird] offer a
(14) sacrifice to the Lord. And of all thy first-fruits and of wine offer
the first, as a sacrifice to the Lord God; and every sacrifice thou shalt
salt with salt.

---

[1]Throughout, there is special prominence given to the two sons, Levi and Judah,
from whom the two messiahs are to come.

(10:1) Now, therefore, observe whatsoever I command you, children; for whatsoever things I have (2) heard from my fathers [I have declared unto you. And behold] I am clear from your ungodliness and transgression, which ye shall commit in the end of the ages [—against the Saviour of the world, Christ, acting godlessly—],[2] deceiving Israel, and stirring up against it great evils from the (3) Lord. And ye shall deal lawlessly together with Israel, so He shall not bear with Jerusalem because of your wickedness; but the veil of the temple shall be rent, so as not to cover your (4) shame. And ye shall be scattered as captives among the Gentiles, and shall be for a reproach (5) and for a curse there. For the house which the Lord shall be called Jerusalem, as is contained in the book of Enoch[3] the righteous.

MK. 15: 38

15:1–16:5

(1) Therefore the temple, which the Lord shall choose, shall be laid waste through your uncleanness, (2) and ye shall be captives throughout all nations. And ye shall be an abomination unto them, and ye (3) shall receive reproach and everlasting shame from the righteous judgement of God. And all who hate (4) you shall rejoice at your destruction. And if you were not to receive mercy through Abraham, Isaac, and Jacob, our fathers, not one of our seed should be left upon the earth.

MK. 13:2

(16:1) And now I have learnt that for seventy weeks[4] ye shall go astray, and profane the priesthood, and (2) pollute the sacrifices. And ye shall make void the law, and set at nought the words of the prophets by evil perverseness. And ye shall persecute righteous men, and hate the godly; the words of the (3) faithful shall ye abhor. And a man who reneweth the law in the power of the Most High, ye shall call a deceiver; and at last ye shall rush upon him—to slay him, not knowing his dignity, taking (4) innocent blood through wickedness upon your heads. And your holy places shall be laid waste (5) even to the ground because of him. And ye shall have no place that is clean; but ye shall be among the Gentiles a curse and a dispersion until He shall again visit you, and in pity shall receive you through faith and water.

MT. 27: 19, 24

18:1–14

(1) And after their punishment shall have come from the Lord, the priesthood shall fail.

---

[2]Probably a Christian interpolation, although the present wording may replace an original reference to the two anointed ones (in Greek, *christoi*).

[3]The reference indicates that the Testaments of the XII and Enoch likely originated in the same circles.

[4]This reference goes back to Jeremiah 25:12 where the interval between the punishment of the nation and its deliverance is seventy years. In Dan. 9:24, however, the predicted period has been expanded to seventy "weeks" of years ($70 \times 7 = 490$). Probably this allusion to the corruption of the nation and its priesthood was written in the declining decades of the Hasmonean era, that is, after 100 B.C.

(2) Then shall the Lord praise up a new priest.[5]
And to him all the words of the Lord shall be revealed;
And he shall execute a righteous judgement upon the earth for a
  multitude of days.
(3) And his star shall arise in heaven as of a king.
Lighting up the light of knowledge as the sun the day,
And he shall be magnified in the world.
(4) He shall shine forth as the sun on the earth,
And shall remove all darkness from under heaven,
And there shall be peace in all the earth.
(5) The heavens shall exult in his days,
And the earth shall be glad,
And the clouds shall rejoice;
(And the knowledge of the Lord shall be poured forth upon the
  earth, as the water of the seas);
And the angels of the glory of the presence of the Lord shall
  be glad in him.
(6) The heavens shall be opened.
And from the temple of glory shall come upon him sanctification,
With the Father's voice as from Abraham to Isaac.
(7) And the glory of the Most High shall be uttered over him,
And the spirit of understanding and sanctification shall rest
  upon him [in the water].
(8) For he shall give the majesty of the Lord to His sons in
  truth for evermore;
And there shall none succeed him for all generations forever.
(9) And in his priesthood the Gentiles shall be multiplied in
  knowledge upon the earth,
And enlightened through the grace of the Lord:
In his priesthood shall sin come to an end,
And the lawless shall cease to do evil.
[And the just shall rest in him.]
(10) And he shall open the gates of paradise,
And shall remove the threatening sword against Adam.
(11) And he shall give to the saints to eat from the tree of life,
And the spirit of holiness shall be on them.
(12) And Beliar[6] shall be bound by him,
And he shall give power to His children to tread upon the evil
  spirits.
(13) And the Lord shall rejoice in His children,
And be well pleased in His beloved ones forever.
(14) Then shall Abraham and Isaac and Jacob exult,

---

[5]The new priest refers to the Zadokite priesthood, as they styled themselves, who
were established by the Teacher of Righteousness—or more accurately, the One who
Teaches Rightly—the founder of the Qumran community that settled on the shores
of the Dead Sea. They were awaiting the fulfillment of God's time before He would
restore them to the true and pure priestly service of God in Jerusalem.

[6]Beliar (sometimes spelled Belial) was the chief opponent of God, the ruler of the
demonic powers, roughly equivalent to Satan (meaning Adversary). The creation was
to be under the sway of Beliar until the Rule of God was reestablished in the End
Time.

And I will be glad,
And all the saints shall clothe themselves with joy.

TESTAMENT OF JUDAH, 1:1–6

(1, 2) The copy of the words of Judah, what things he spake to his sons before he died. They gathered (3) themselves together, therefore, and came to him, and he said to them: Hearken, my children, to Judah your father. I was the fourth son born to my father Jacob; and Leah my mother named (4) me Judah, saying, I give thanks to the Lord, because He hath given me a fourth son also. I was (5) swift in my youth, and obedient to my father in everything. And I honoured my mother and my (6) mother's sister. And it came to pass, when I became a man, that my father blessed me, saying Thou shalt be a king, prospering in all things.

21:1–22:3

(1) And now, my children, I command you, love Levi,[7] that ye may abide, and exalt not yourselves (2) against him, lest ye be utterly destroyed. For to me the Lord gave the kingdom, and to him the (3) priesthood, and He set the kingdom beneath the priesthood. To me He gave the things upon the (4) earth; to him the things in the heavens. As the heaven is higher than the earth, so is the priesthood of God higher than the earthly kingdom, unless it falls away through sin from the Lord and is (5) dominated by the earthly kingdom—. For the angel of the Lord said unto me: The Lord chose him rather than thee, to draw near to Him, and to eat of His table and to offer Him the first-fruits of the choice things of the sons of Israel; but thou shalt be king of Jacob.

HEB. 9: 11, 23-26

(6) And thou shalt be amongst them as the sea. For as, on the sea, just and unjust are tossed about, some taken into captivity while some are enriched, so also shall every race of men be in thee: some shall be impoverished, being taken captive, and others grow rich by plundering the possessions of others.
(7) For the kings shall be as sea-monsters.
They shall swallow men like fishes:
The sons and daughters of freemen shall they enslave;
Houses, lands, flocks, money shall they plunder:
(8) And with the flesh of many shall they wrongfully feed the ravens
      and the cranes;
—And they shall advance in evil, in covetousness uplifted,—
(9) And there shall be false prophets like tempests,
And they shall persecute all righteous men.

(22:1) And the Lord shall bring upon them divisions one against
      another
And there shall be continual wars in Israel;

MK. 13: 7-8

---

[7]Judah, the king-designate, is to cooperate with the priestly son of Levi.

(2) And among men of another race[8] shall my kingdom be brought
to an end,
Until the salvation of Israel shall come,

ROM. 11:
25-27

Until the appearing of the God of righteousness,
That Jacob and all the Gentiles may rest in peace.
(3) And he shall guard the might of my kingdom forever;
For the Lord sware to me with an oath that He would not destroy
the kingdom from my seed forever.

TESTAMENT OF NAPHTALI, 8:1–10

(1) And lo! my children, I have shown unto you the last times, how
everything shall come to pass in (2) Israel. Do ye also, therefore,
charge your children that they be united to Levi and to Judah;
For through them shall salvation arise unto Israel,
And in them shall Jacob be blessed.

MK. 1:
2-3

(3) For through their tribes shall God appear [dwelling among men][9]
on earth,
To save the race of Israel,

(CF.
MAL.
3:1)

And to gather together the righteous from amongst the Gentiles.
(4) If ye work that which is good, my children,
Both men and angels shall bless you;

MT. 1:23

And God shall be glorified among the Gentiles through you,
And the devil shall flee from you,
And the wild beasts shall fear you—,
And the Lord shall love you,
[And the angels shall cleave to you].
(5) As a man who has trained a child well is kept in kindly
remembrance;
So also for a good work there is a good remembrance before God.
(6) But him that doeth not that which is good,
Both angels and men shall curse,
And God shall be dishonoured among the Gentiles through him,
And the devil shall make him as his own peculiar instrument,
And every wild beast shall master him,
And the Lord shall hate him.
(7) For the commandments of the law are two fold,
And through prudence must they be fulfilled.

I COR.
7:5

(8) For there is a season for a man to embrace his wife,
And a season to abstain therefrom for his prayer.
(9) So, then, there are two commandments; and, unless they be done
in due order, they bring (10) very great sin upon men. So also is it
with the other commandments. Be ye therefore wise in God, my
children, and prudent, understanding the order of His commandments,
and the laws of every word, that the Lord may love you.

I Enoch

The book known to scholars as I Enoch is a collection of writings
based on the speculation in post-exilic Judaism concerning Enoch (Gen-

---

[8]Possibly a reference to the Romans, who seized control of Jerusalem in 63 B.C.
[9]Probably a Christian interpolation.

esis 5:18–24). The biblical account implies that he did not die, declaring instead that he "walked with God." Pious speculation led therefore to the conclusion that he had been taken directly into the presence of God at the end of his earthly life, that he had been granted special knowledge of the divine secrets, including the future of the world, and that there was a role for him yet to fulfill at the End Time.

The Enochic literature was probably influenced by Babylonian astrology, in that it lays stress on the movement of the heavenly bodies and on the correspondence between the celestial order and the divinely intended earthly order. If the divine will were truly obeyed, earth would be as orderly as heaven. Meanwhile, attainment of the longed-for goal was promised in the secrets revealed by Enoch to the chosen community. The writings therefore describe the journeys of Enoch over heaven and earth and transmit in enigmatic form the content of the visions and revelations which he has received. Five major segments of the book are apparent:

1) Heavenly Journeys (ch. 1–36)
2) Similitudes or Parables (ch. 37–71)
3) Movements of the Heavenly Bodies (ch. 72–82)
4) Dream Visions (ch. 83–90)
5) Apocalypse of Weeks (ch. 91–108)

Excerpts are given below from the first four sections, although the material from the Parables is placed last because some scholars suspect it is later than the rest and—some have claimed—of Christian origin. There is, however, nothing distinctively Christian about it, although it does use the term "Son of Man" that is common in the gospel tradition. Parts of the four other sections of Enoch have been found at Qumran, but not of the Parables, and this has been taken as further evidence of their late date. The argument is not conclusive, and the term seems to build on the phrase as it appears in Ezekiel (where it means simply "a man") and Daniel 7, where "one like a son of man" is the divine agent in establishing God's kingdom.

The most obscure part of the book is the Dream Visions, in which in allegorical form the author retells the biblical story of the creation and fall of man, of the founding of the nation, of the exodus and the wilderness wandering. Probably the "sheep" (leader) of 89:38f. was the Teacher, and the two leaders may well be the anointed king and priest of the End Time.

2:1–4; 5:1–9

(1) Observe ye everything that takes place in the heaven, how they do not change their orbits, and the luminaries which are in the heaven, how they all rise and set in order each in its season, and transgress (2) not against their appointed order. Behold ye the earth, and give heed to the things which take place upon it from first to last,

how steadfast they are, how none of the things upon earth (3) change, but all the works of God appear to you. Behold the summer and the winter, how the whole earth is filled with water, and clouds and dew and rain lie upon it.

(3) Observe and see how [in winter] all the trees seem as though they had withered and shed all their leaves, except fourteen trees, which do not lose their foliage but retain the old foliage from two to three years till the new comes.

(4) And again, observe ye the days of summer how the sun is above the earth over against it. And you seek shade and shelter by reason of the heat of the sun, and the earth also burns with glowing heat, and so you cannot tread on the earth, or on a rock by reason of its heat.

(5:1) Observe ye how the trees cover themselves with green leaves and bear fruit: wherefore give ye heed and know with regard to all His works, and recognize how He that liveth forever hath made them so.

(2) And all His works go on thus from year to year forever, and all tasks which they accomplish for Him, and their tasks change not, but according as God hath ordained so is it done.

(3) And behold how the sea and the rivers in like manner accomplish and change not their tasks from His commandments.

(4) But ye ye have not been steadfast, nor done the commandments
     of the Lord,
But ye have turned away and spoken proud and hard words
With your impure mouths against His greatness.
Oh, ye hard-hearted, ye shall find no peace.
(5) Therefore shall ye execrate your days,
And the years of your life shall perish,
And the years of your destruction shall be multiplied in eternal
     execration,
And ye shall find no mercy.

(6a) In those days ye shall make your names eternal execration unto
     all righteous,
(b) And by you shall all who curse, curse,
And all the sinners and godless shall imprecate by you,
(c) And for you the godless there shall be a curse.
(d) And all the . . . shall rejoice,
(e) And there shall be forgiveness of sins,
(f) And every mercy and peace and forebearance:
(g) There shall be salvation unto them, a goodly light.
(i) And for all of your sinners there shall be no salvation,
(j) But on you all shall abide a curse.
MT. 5:5   (7a) But for the elect there shall be light and joy and peace,
(b) And they shall inherit the earth.

MT. 11:   (8) And then there shall be bestowed upon the elect wisdom,
25-26   And they shall all live and never again sin,

Either through ungodliness or through pride:
But they who are wise shall be humble.

(9) And they shall not again transgress,
Nor shall they sin all the days of their life.

24:1–25:7

(1) And from thence I went to another place of the earth, and he showed me a mountain range of (2) fire which burnt day and night. And I went beyond it and saw seven magnificent mountains all differing from the other, and the stones [thereof] were magnificent and beautiful, magnificent as a whole, of glorious appearance and fair exterior: three towards the east, one founded on the other, and three towards the south, one upon the other, and deep rough ravines, no one of which (3) joined with any other. And the seventh mountain was in the midst of these, and it excelled them (4) in height, resembling the seat of a throne: and fragrant trees encircled the throne. And amongst them was a tree such as I had never yet smelt, neither was any amongst them nor were others like it: it had a fragrance beyond all fragrance, and its leaves and blooms and wood wither not forever: (5) and its fruit is beautiful, and its fruit resembles the dates of a palm. Then I said: "How beautiful is this tree, and fragrant, and its leaves are fair, and its blooms very delightful in appearance." (6) Then answered Michael, one of the holy and honoured angels who was with me and was their leader.

REV. 20: 11

REV. 22: 2

(25:1) And he said unto me: "Enoch, why dost thou ask me regarding the fragrance of the tree, (2) and why dost thou wish to learn the truth?" Then I answered him saying: "This high mountain which thou hast seen, whose summit is like the throne of God, is His throne, where the Holy Great One, the Lord of Glory, the Eternal King, will sit, when He shall come down to visit (4) the earth with goodness. And as for this fragrant tree no mortal is permitted to touch it till the great judgement, when He shall take vengeance on all and bring [everything] to its consummation (5) forever. It shall then be given to the righteous and holy. Its fruit shall be for food to the elect: it shall be transplanted to the holy place, to the temple of the Lord, the Eternal King.

(6) Then shall they rejoice with joy and be glad,
And into the holy place shall they enter;
And its fragrance shall be in their bones,
And they shall live a long life on earth,
Such as thy fathers lived:
And in their days shall no sorrow or plague
Or torment or calamity touch them."

(7) Then blessed I the God of Glory, the Eternal King, who hath prepared such things for the righteous, and hath created them and promised to give to them.

81:1–10

(1) And he said unto me:
"Observe, Enoch, these heavenly tablets,[1]
And read what is written thereon,
And mark every individual fact."

(2) And I observed the heavenly tablets, and read everything which was written [thereon] and understood everything, and read the book of all the deeds of mankind, and of all the children of flesh (3) that shall be upon the earth to the remotest generations. And forthwith I blessed the great Lord the King of glory forever, in that He has made all the works of the world,

And I extolled the Lord because of His patience,
And blessed Him because of the children of men.

(4) And after that I said:
"Blessed is the man who dies in righteousness and goodness,
REV. 14:   Concerning whom there is no book of unrighteousness written,
13   And against whom no day of judgement shall be found."

(5) And those seven holy ones brought me and placed me on the earth before the door of my house, and said to me: "Declare everything to thy son Methuselah, and show to all thy children that no (6) flesh is righteous in the sight of the Lord, for He is their Creator. One year we will leave thee with thy son, till thou givest thy [last] commands, that thou mayst teach thy children and record [it] for them, and testify to all thy children; and in the second year they shall take thee from their midst.

(7) Let thy heart be strong,
For the good shall announce righteousness to the good;

The righteous with the righteous shall rejoice,
And shall offer congratulation to one another.

(8) But sinners shall die with the sinners,
And the apostate go down with the apostate.

(9) And those who practise righteousness shall die on account of the deeds of men,
And be taken away on account of the doings of the godless."

(10) And in those days they ceased to speak to me, and I came to my people, blessing the Lord of the world.

85:1–89:41

(1, 2) And after this I saw another dream, and I will show the whole dream to thee, my son. And Enoch lifted up [his voice] and

---

[1]Perhaps a reference to the tablets of the kind received by Moses from God on Mt. Sinai, but here the implication is that the whole course of history has been written down as a sign that it has all been predetermined by God.

spake to his son Methuselah: "To thee, my son, will I speak: hear my (3) words—incline thine ear to the dream-vision of thy father. Before I took thy mother Edna, I saw in a vision on my bed, and behold a bull came forth from the earth, and that bull was white; and after it came forth a heifer, and along with this [latter] came forth two bulls, one of them black and (4) the other red. And that black bull gored the red one and pursued him over the earth, and thereupon (5) I could no longer see that red bull. But that black bull grew and that heifer went with him, and (6) I saw that many oxen proceeded from him which resembled and followed him. And that cow, that first one, went from the presence of that first bull in order to seek that red one, but found him (7) not, and lamented with a great lamentation over him and sought him. And I looked till that first (8) bull came to her and quieted her, and from that time onward she cried no more. And after that she bore another white bull, and after him she bore many bulls and black cows.

(9) And I saw in my sleep that white bull likewise grow and become a great white bull, and from him which resembled them, one following the other, [even] many.

(86:1) And again I saw with mine eyes as I slept, and I saw the heaven above, and behold a star fell (2) from heaven,[2] and it arose and ate and pastured amongst those oxen. And after that I saw the large and the black oxen, and behold they all changed their stalls and pastures and their cattle, and began (3) to live with each other. And again I saw in the vision, and looked towards the heaven, and behold I saw many stars descend and cast themselves down from heaven to that first star, and they became (4) bulls amongst those cattle and pastured with them [amongst them]. And I looked at them and saw, and behold they all let out their privy members, like horses, and began to cover the cows of the oxen, (5) and they all became pregnant and bare elephants, camels, and asses. And all the oxen feared them and were affrighted at them, and began to bite with their teeth and to devour, and to gore with their (6) horns. And they began, moreover, to devour those oxen; and behold all the children of the earth began to tremble and quake before them and to flee from them.

(87:1) And again I saw how they began to gore each other and to devour each other, and the earth (2) began to cry aloud. And I raised mine eyes again to heaven, and I saw in the vision, and behold there came forth from heaven beings who were like white men: and four went forth from that place (3) and three with them. And those three that had last come forth grasped me by my hand and took me up, away from the generations of the earth, and raised me up to a lofty place, and showed me (4) a tower raised high above the earth, and all the hills were lower. And one said unto me: "Remain here till thou seest everything that befalls those elephants, camels, and asses, and the stars and the oxen, and all of them." MT. 4:8

---

[2]The star fallen is probably an allusion to the story told in Gen. 6 of the illicit intercourse between the "sons of God and the daughters of men." This idea was modified by the concept of the Fallen Angel (in Isa. 14:12) who came to be identified with Satan or Beliar. The point is that evil originated with the coming of the Fallen Angel among men.

(88:1) And I saw one of those four who had come forth first, and he seized that first star which had fallen from the heaven, and bound it hand and foot and cast it into an abyss: now that abyss was (2) narrow and deep, and horrible and dark. And one of them drew a sword, and gave it to those elephants and camels and asses: then they began to smite each other, and the whole earth quaked (3) because of them. And as I was beholding in the vision, lo, one of those four who had come forth stoned [them] from heaven, and gathered and took all the great stars whose privy members were alike those of horses, and bound them all hand and foot, and cast them in an abyss of the earth.

(89:1) And one of those four went to that white bull and instructed him in a secret, without his being terrified: he was born a bull and became a man,[3] and built for himself a great vessel and dwelt thereon; (2) and three bulls dwelt with him in that vessel and they were covered in. And again I raised mine eyes towards heaven and saw a lofty roof, with seven water torrents thereon, and those torrents (3) flowed with much water into an enclosure. And I saw again, and behold fountains were opened on the surface of that great enclosure, and that water began to swell and rise upon the surface, (4) and I saw that enclosure till all its surface was covered with water. And the water, the darkness, and mist increased upon it; and as I looked at the height of that water, that water had risen above the height of that enclosure, and was streaming over that enclosure, and it stood upon the earth. (5) And all the cattle of that enclosure were gathered together until I saw how they sank and were (6) swallowed up and perished in that water. But that vessel floated on the water, while all the oxen and elephants and camels and asses sank to the bottom with all the animals, so that I could no longer (7) see them, and they were not able to escape, [but] perished and sank into the depths. And again I saw in the vision till those water torrents were removed from that high roof, and the chasms (8) of the earth were levelled up and other abysses were opened. Then the water began to run down into these, till the earth became visible; but that vessel settled on the earth, and the darkness (9) retired and light appeared. But that white bull which had become a man came out of that vessel, and the three bulls with him, and one of those three was white like that bull, and one of them was red as blood, and one black: and that white bull departed from them.

(10) And they began to bring forth beasts of the field and birds, so that there arose different genera: lions, tigers, wolves, dogs, hyenas, wild boars, foxes, squirrels, swine, falcons, vultures, kites, (11) eagles, and ravens; and among them was born a white bull. And they began to bite one another; but that white bull which was born from him begat a wild ass and a white bull with it, and the (12) wild asses multiplied. But that bull which was born from him begat a black wild boar and a white (13) sheep; and the former begat many boars, but that sheep[4] begat twelve sheep. And when those twelve sheep had

---

[3]Noah; the story in Gen. 7–8 about him and the ark is here given in veiled, allegorical form.

[4]Jacob (the black boar is his brother, Esau); the twelve sheep are his sons, who in turn are the progenitors of the twelve tribes of Israel.

grown, they gave up one of them to the asses, and those asses again gave up that sheep (14) to the wolves, and that sheep grew up among the wolves. And the Lord brought the eleven sheep to live with it and to pasture with it among the wolves; and they multiplied and became many (15) flocks of sheep. And the wolves began to fear them, and they oppressed them until they destroyed their little ones, and they cast their young into a river of much water: but those sheep began to (16) cry aloud on account of their little ones, and to complain unto their Lord. And a sheep which had been saved from the wolves fled and escaped to the wild asses; and I saw the sheep how they lamented and cried, and besought their Lord with all their might, till that Lord of the sheep descended (17) at the voice of the sheep from a lofty abode, and came to them and pastured them. And He called that sheep which had escaped the wolves, and spake with it concerning the wolves that it should (18) admonish them not to touch the sheep. And the sheep went to the wolves according to the word of the Lord, and another sheep met it and went with it, and the two went and entered together into the assembly of those wolves, and spake with them and admonished them not to touch the (19) sheep from henceforth. And thereupon I saw the wolves, and how they oppressed the sheep exceedingly (20) with all their power; and the sheep cried aloud. And the Lord came to the sheep and they began to smite those wolves: and the wolves began to make lamentation; but the sheep became (21) quiet and forthwith ceased to cry out. And I saw the sheep till they departed from amongst the wolves; but the eyes of the wolves were blinded, and those wolves departed in pursuit of the sheep (22) with all their power. And the Lord of the sheep[5] went with them, as their leader, and all His sheep (23) followed Him: and His face was dazzling and glorious and terrible to behold. But the wolves (24) began to pursue those sheep till they reached a sea of water. And that sea was divided, and the water stood on this side and on that before their face, and their Lord led them and placed Himself between (25) them and the wolves. And as those wolves did not yet see the sheep, they proceeded into the midst of that sea, and the wolves followed the sheep, and those wolves ran after them into that sea. (26) And when they saw the Lord of the sheep, they turned to flee before His face, but that sea gathered itself together, and became as it had been created, and the water swelled and rose till it covered (27) those wolves. And I saw till all the wolves who pursued those sheep perished and were drowned.

(28) But the sheep escaped from that water and went forth into a wilderness, where there was no water and no grass; and they began to open their eyes and to see; and I saw the Lord of the sheep (29) pasturing them and giving them water and grass, and that sheep going and leading them. And that (30) sheep ascended to the summit of that lofty rock, and the Lord of the sheep sent it to them. And after that I saw the Lord of the sheep who stood before them, and His appearance was great and (31) terrible and majestic, and all those sheep saw Him and were afraid before His face. And they all feared and trembled because of Him, and they cried to that sheep with them

---

[5]The story is that of the Exodus, in which the "Lord of the Sheep" (= God? Moses?) leads the Israelites out of Egypt.

which was amongst (32) them: "We are not able to stand before our Lord or to behold Him." And that sheep which led them again ascended to the summit of that rock, but the sheep began to be blinded and to wander (33) from the way which he had showed them, but that sheep knew not thereof. And the Lord of the sheep was wrathful exceedingly against them, and that sheep discovered it, and went down from the summit of the rock, and came to the sheep, and found the greatest part of them blinded and fallen (34) away. And when they saw it they feared and trembled at its presence, and desired to return to their (35) folds. And that sheep took other sheep with it, and came to those sheep which had fallen away, and began to slay them; and the sheep feared its presence, and thus that sheep brought back those (36) sheep that had fallen away, and they returned to their folds. And I saw in this vision till that sheep became a man and built a house for the Lord of the sheep, and placed all the sheep in that house. (37) And I saw till this sheep which had met that sheep which led them fell asleep:[6] and I saw till all the great sheep perished and little ones arose in their place, and they came to a pasture, and (38) approached a stream of water. Then that sheep, their leader which had become a man, withdrew (39) from their and fell asleep, and all the sheep sought it and cried over it with a great crying. And I saw till they left off crying for that sheep and crossed that stream of water, and there arose the two sheep as leaders[7] in the place of those which had led them and fallen asleep [lit., "had fallen asleep and led (40) them"]. And I saw till the sheep came to a goodly place, and a pleasant and glorious land, and I saw till those sheep were satisfied; and that house stood amongst them in the pleasant land.

(41) And sometimes their eyes were opened, and sometimes blinded, till another sheep arose and led them and brought them all back, and their eyes were opened.

90:28–42

(28) And I stood up to see till they folded up that old house;[8] and carried off all the pillars, and all the beams and ornaments of the house were at the same time folded up with it, and they carried (29) it off and laid it in a place in the south of the land. And I saw till the Lord of the sheep brought a new house greater and loftier than that first, and set it up in the place of the first which had been folded up: all its pillars were new, and its ornaments were new and larger than those of the first, the old one which He had taken away, and all the sheep were within it.

(30) And I saw all the sheep which had been left, and all the

HEB. 8: 13

---

[6]The sheep that fell asleep is Moses, whose death was regarded as mysterious and whose burial was in an unknown place (Deut. 34:6).

[7]Probably the anointed king and the anointed priest: the Two Messiahs, as expected by some of the later prophets and by the Dead Sea community.

[8]The Jerusalem temple is here described as destroyed only to be replaced by one that God himself builds. In it and around it gather all the nations of the world to be judged in the Last Day.

beasts on the earth, and all the birds of the heaven, falling down and doing homage to those sheep and making petition to and obeying (31) them in everything. And thereafter those three who were clothed in white and had seized me by my hand who had taken me up before, and the hand of that ram also seizing hold of me, they (32) took me up and set me down in the midst of those sheep before the judgement took place. And those (33) sheep were all white, and their wool was abundant and clean. And all that had been destroyed and dispersed, and all the beasts of the field, and all the birds of the heaven, assembled in that house, and the Lord of the sheep rejoiced with great joy because they were all good and had returned to (34) His house. And I saw till they laid down that sword, which had been given to the sheep, and they brought it back into the house, and it was sealed before the presence of the Lord, and all the sheep (35) were invited into that house, but it held them not. And the eyes of them all were opened, and they (36) saw the good, and there was not one among them that did not see. And I saw that that house was large and broad and very full.

(37) And I saw that a white bull[9] was born, with large horns, and all the beasts of the field and all the (38) birds of the air feared him and made petition to him all the time. And I saw till all their generations were transformed, and they all became white bulls; and the first among them became a lamb, and that lamb became a great animal and had great black horns on its head; and the Lord of the sheep (39) rejoiced over it and over all the oxen. And I slept in their midst: and I awoke and saw everything. (40) This is the vision which I saw while I slept, and I awoke and blessed the Lord of righteousness and (41) gave Him glory. Then I wept with a great weeping and my tears stayed not till I could no longer endure it: when I saw, they flowed on account of what I had seen; for everything shall come and (42) be fulfilled, and all the deeds of men in their order were shown to me. On that night I remembered the first dream, and because of it I wept and was troubled—because I had seen that vision.

PARABLES OF ENOCH 71:1–17

(1) And it came to pass after this that my spirit was translated	REV. 4:
And it ascended into the heavens:[10]	1 ff.
And I saw the holy sons of God.	
They were stepping on flames of fire:	
Their garments were white—and their raiment—,	DAN. 12:
And their faces shone like snow.	3
(2) And I saw two streams of fire,	
And the light of the fire shone like hyacinth,	

---

[9]The Messiah or the Founder of the Elect Community in the New Age.

[10]It is noteworthy that the divine deliverances and transformations described in Enoch up to this point all take place on earth. The final judgment scene in the Parables of Enoch, on the other hand, occurs in heaven. This shift in locale may be added confirmation of a different author and a different time of origin of this section.

And I fell on my face before the Lord of Spirits.

(3) And the angel Michael—one of the archangels—seized me by my
    right hand,
And lifted me up and led me forth into all the secrets,
And he showed me all the secrets of righteousness.

(4) And he showed me all the secrets of the ends of the heaven,
And all the chambers of all the stars, and all the luminaries,
Whence they proceed before the face of the holy ones.

(5) And he translated my spirit into the heaven of heavens,
And I saw there as it were a structure built of crystals,
And between those crystals tongues of living fire.

(6) And my spirit saw the girdle which girt that house of fire,
And on its four sides were streams full of living fire,
And they girt that house.

(7) And round about were Seraphin, Cherubin, and Ophannin:
And these are they who sleep not
And guard the throne of His glory.

(8) And I saw angels who could not be counted,
A thousand thousands, and ten thousand times ten thousand,
Encircling that house.

And Michael, and Raphael, and Gabriel, and Phanuel,
And the holy angels who are above the heavens,
Go in and out of that house.

(9) And they came forth from that house,
And Michael and Gabriel, Raphael and Phanuel,
And many holy angels without number.

REV. 1:   (10) And with them the Head of Days,[11]
13-16   His head white and pure as wool,
           And His raiment indescribable.

(11) And I fell on my face,
And my whole body became relaxed,
And my spirit was transfigured;

And I cried with a loud voice,
. . . with the spirit of power,
And blessed and glorified and extolled.

REV. 5:   (12) And these blessings which went forth out of my mouth were
11   well pleasing before that Head of (13) Days. And that Head of Days
           came with Michael and Gabriel, Raphael and Phanuel, thousands and
           ten thousands of angels without number.[12]

---

[11]God depicted as an old man. See Daniel 7.
[12]There probably was a passage at this point, but now lost, in which Enoch asked
about the identity of the Son of Man.

(14) And he [i.e., the angel] came to me and greeted me with His
　　　voice, and said unto me:
"This is the Son of Man who is born unto righteousness,
And righteousness abides over him,

And the righteousness the Head of Days forsakes him not."
(15) And he said unto me:
"He proclaims unto thee peace in the name of the world to come;
For from hence has proceeded peace since the creation of the world,
And so shall it be unto thee forever and forever and ever.

(16) And all shall walk in his ways since righteousness never forsaketh   I THESS.
　　　him: 4:13-17
With him will be their dwelling-places, and with him their heritage,
And they shall not be separated from him forever and ever and ever.

(17) And so there shall be length of days with that Son of Man,
And the righteous shall have peace and an upright way
In the name of the Lord of Spirits forever and ever."

IV Ezra

This apocalypse is usually thought to have received its present form
in the first century A.D., but it surely incorporates older material. It has
been preserved by Christians, who gave it their own distinctive beginning and end, but the central sections retain their original Jewish quality. The excerpt from 4:22 to 5:13 makes the point that was of prime
importance for the Jewish—and later on, the Christian—apocalyptic sects
that the trials they were about to undergo or were in fact already passing
through were divinely ordained as the birthpangs of the New Age. The
Eagle Vision of Chapter 11 alludes to four beasts seen in visions by
Daniel, but the final beast is not the hellenistic rulers as in Daniel (8:21
ff.) but Rome, which is of course most appropriately portrayed as an
eagle. This vision need not have originated later than the first century
B.C., sometime after the Romans took over Palestine. The vision of the
Man in Chapter 13 is closely related to the Son of Man in the Parables
of Enoch, and shows kinship with the triumphant Son of Man in the New
Testament book of Revelation (1:13).

4:22–43

(22) Then answered I and said: I beseech thee, O Lord, wherefore
have I been endowed with an (23) understanding to discern? For I
meant not to ask about the ways above but of those things we daily
experience;

Why is Israel to the heathen given over for reproach,
　　　thy beloved people to godless tribes given up?

The Law of our fathers has been brought to destruction,
    the written covenant exist no more;
(24) We vanish from the world as locusts,
    our life is as a breath.

(25) We indeed are not worthy to obtain mercy; but what will he do for his own name whereby we are called? It is about these things that I have asked.

(26) Then he answered me and said: If thou survive thou shalt see, and if thou livest long thou shalt marvel; for the age is hastening fast to its end.

(27) Because it is unable to bear the things promised in their season to the righteous; for this age is full of sorrow and impotence.

(28) For the evil concerning which thou askest me is sown, but the ingathering of it is not yet (29) come. Unless, therefore, that which is sown be reaped, and unless the place where the evil is sown (30) shall have passed away, the field where the good is sown cannot come. For a grain of evil seed was sown in the heart of Adam from the beginning, and how much fruit of ungodliness has it produced unto this time, and shall yet produce until the threshing-floor come!

ROM. 5: 12-14

MT. 3:12

(31) Reckon up, now, in thine own mind: if a grain of evil seed has produced so much fruit of (32) ungodliness, when once the ears of the good seed shall have been sown without number, how great a floor shall they be destined to fill?

(33) Then I answered and said: How long and when shall these things [be coming to pass]? For our years are few and evil.

MK. 13: 32

(34) And he answered me and said: Thy haste may not exceed that of the Most High; for thou art hastening for thine own self, but the Exalted One on behalf of many.

(35) Were not these questions of thine asked by the souls of the righteous in their chambers?

How long are we [to remain] here? When cometh the fruit upon the threshing-floor of our reward?

ROM. 11: 25-27

(36) And to them the archangel Jeremiel made reply, and said: Even when the number of those like yourself is fulfilled!

For he has weighed the age in the balance,
    (37) And with measure has measured the times,
    And by number has numbered the seasons:
Neither will he move nor stir things,
    till the measure appointed be fulfilled.

(38, 39) Then I answered and said: O Lord my Lord, but behold we are all full of ungodliness. Is it, perchance, on our account that the threshing-floor of the righteous is kept back—on account of the sins of the dwellers upon earth?

(40) So he answered me and said: Go and ask the woman who is pregnant, when she has completed her nine months, if her womb can keep the birth any longer within her?

(41) Then said I: No, Lord, it cannot. And he said to me: The

underworld and the chambers of (42) souls are like the womb: for just
as she who is in travail makes haste to escape the anguish of the (43)
travail; even so do these places hasten to deliver what has been entrusted to them from the beginning. Then to thee it shall be showed
concerning those things that thou desirest to see.

ROM. 8:
22

MK. 13:
20

4:51–5:13

(51) Then I made supplication, and said: Thinkest thou that I shall
live until those days? Who shall be [live] in those days?

(52) He answered me, and said: —As for the signs concerning
which thou askest me, I may tell thee of them in part; but—concerning
thy life I have not been sent to speak to thee, nor have I any knowledge [thereof].

(5:1) Concerning the signs, however:
Behold, the days come when the inhabitants of earth shall be
seized with great panic,

I THESS.
4:15

MK. 13–
24

REV. 6:
15-17

And the way of truth shall be hidden,
    and the land be barren of faith.

(2) And iniquity shall be increased above that which thou thyself
now seest or that thou hast heard of (3) long ago. And the land that
thou seest now to bear rule shall be a pathless waste; and men (4)
shall see it forsaken: if the Most High grant thee to live, thou shalt
see it after the third [period] in confusion.

Then shall the sun suddenly shine forth by night
    and the moon by day:
(5) And blood shall trickle forth from wood,
    and the stone utter its voice:
The peoples shall be in commotion,
    the outgoings of the stars shall change.

REV. 6:
12 ff.

MK. 13:
24-25

(6) And one whom the dwellers upon earth do not look for shall wield
sovereignty, and the birds shall take to general flight,
(7) and the sea shall cast forth its fish.
And one whom the many do not know will make his voice heard by
night; and all shall hear his voice.

EZEK.
38:20

(8) And the earth o'er wide regions shall open,
and fire burst forth for a long period:

The wild beasts shall desert their haunts, and women bear monsters.
And one-year-old children shall speak with their voices; pregnant
women shall bring forth (22) untimely births at three or four months,
and these shall live and dance. And suddenly shall the sown places
appear unsown, and the full storehouses shall suddenly be found
empty.

(9) Salt waters shall be found in the sweet; friends shall attack one another suddenly.

MK. 13:
12

(10) Then shall intelligence hide itself,
> and wisdom withdraw to its chamber.—
> by many shall be sought and not found.

(11) And righteousness and incontinency shall be multiplied upon the earth. One land shall also ask another and say: Is Righteousness— that doeth the right—passed through thee? And it shall answer, No.

(12) And it shall be
In that time men shall hope and not obtain,
> shall labour and not prosper.

(13) Such are the signs I am permitted to tell thee; but if thou wilt pray again, and weep as not, and fast seven days, thou shalt hear again greater things than these.

11:1–11

(1) And it came to pass the second night that I saw a dream: and lo! there came up from the sea (2) an eagle which had twelve [?] feathered wings, and three heads. And I beheld, and lo! he spread his wings over the whole earth, and all the winds of heaven blew on him, and [the clouds] were (3) gathered together [unto him]. And I beheld, [and lo!] out of his wings there grew anti-wings; (4) and they became wings petty and small. But his heads were at rest; the middle head was greater (5) than the other heads, yet it rested with them. And I beheld, and lo! the eagle flew with his wings (6) to reign over the earth and over them that dwell therein. And I beheld how all things under heaven were subject unto him, and no one spake against him—not even one of the creatures upon (7) earth. And I beheld, and lo! the eagle rose upon his talons, and uttered his voice to his wings, (8, 9) saying, Watch not all at once: sleep every one in his place, and watch by course: but let the heads (10) be preserved for the last. And I beheld, and lo! the voice proceeded not from his heads, but from (11) the midst of his body. And I numbered his anti-wings, and lo! there were eight.

11:38–46

(38, 39) Hear, thou Eagle—I will talk with thee; the Most High saith to thee: Art thou not it that remainest of the four beasts which I made to reign in my world, that the end of my times might (40) come through them? Thou, however, the fourth, who art come, hast overcome all the beasts that are past;

DAN.
7:2 ff.

Thou hast wielded power over the world with great terror,
> and over all the inhabited earth with grievous oppression;

Thou hast dwelt so long in the civilized world with fraud,
(41) and hast judged the earth, [but] not with faithfulness:
(42) For thou hast afflicted the meek,
and oppressed the peaceable;
Thou hast hated the upright,
and loved liars;
Thou hast destroyed the strongholds of the fruitful,
and laid low the walls of such as did thee no harm—
(43) And so thine insolence hath ascended to the Most High, ISA. 14:
and thy pride to the Mighty One. 12-15
(44) Then the Most High regarded his times— EZEK.
And lo! they were ended; 28:17-18
And his ages—
[and] they were fulfilled.
(45) Therefore shalt thou disappear, O thou Eagle,
and thy horrible wings,
and thy little wings most evil,
thy harm-dealing heads,
thy hurtful talons,
and all thy worthless body!

(46) And so the whole earth, freed from thy violence, shall be refreshed again, and hope for the judgement and mercy of him that made her.

13:1–13

(1, 2) And it came to pass after seven days that I dreamed a dream by night: [and I beheld,] and lo! (3) there arose a violent wind from the sea, and stirred all its waves. And I beheld, and lo! [the wind caused to come up out of the heart of the seas as it were the form of a man. And I beheld and lo!] this Man flew with the clouds of heaven. And wherever he turned his countenance to (4) look everything seen by him trembled; and whithersoever the voice went out of his mouth, all that (5) heard his voice melted away, as the wax melts when it feels EZEK. 38 the fire. And after this I beheld, and lo! there was gathered together from the four winds of heaven an innumerable multitude of men (6) DAN. to make war against the Man that came up out of the sea. And I be- 2:35, 45 held, and lo! he cut out for (7) himself a great mountain and flew up upon it. But I sought to see the region or place from whence the (8) mountain had been cut out; and I could not. And after this I beheld, and lo! all who were gathered together against him to wage war with him were seized with great fear; yet they dared to fight. (9) And lo! when he saw the assault of the multitude as they came he neither REV. 19: lifted his hand, nor held (10) spear nor any warlike weapon; but I 12-15 saw only how he sent out of his mouth as it were a fiery stream, and out of his lips a flaming breath, and out of his tongue he shot forth a REV. 1: storm of (11) sparks. And these were all mingled together—the fiery 16 stream, the flaming breath, and the . . . storm, and fell upon the assault of the multitude which was prepared to fight, and burned them all up, so that suddenly nothing more was to be seen of the innumerable multitude save only (12) dust of ashes and smell of smoke. When I saw this I was amazed. Afterwards I beheld the same Man come down from the mountain, and call unto him another multitude which was peaceable. (13) Then drew nigh unto him the faces of many men, some of whom were glad, some sorrowful; while some were in bonds, some brought others who should be offered.

13:25–40a, 47

(25) These are the interpretations of the vision: Whereas thou didst see a Man coming up from (26) the heart of the Sea: this is he whom the Most High is keeping many ages [and] through whom (27) he will deliver his creation, and the same shall order the survivors. And whereas thou didst see (28) that out of his mouth there came wind, and fire, and storm; and whereas he held neither spear, nor any war-like weapon, but destroyed the assault of that multitude which had come to fight against (29) him—this is the interpretation: Behold, the days come when the Most High is about to deliver them (30, 31) that are upon earth. And there shall come astonishment of mind upon the dwellers on earth: and they shall plan to war one against another, city against city, place against place, people against (32) people, and king-dom against kingdom. And it shall be when these things shall come to pass, and the signs shall happen which I showed thee before, then shall my Son be revealed whom thou didst see as (33) a Man ascend-ing. It shall be, when all the nations hear his voice, every man shall leave his own (34) land and the warfare which they have one against another; and an innumerable multitude shall be (35) gathered to-gether, as thou didst see, desiring to come and to fight against him. But he shall stand (36) upon the summit of Mount Sion. And Sion shall come and shall be made manifest to all men, (37) prepared and builded, even as thou didst see the mountain cut out without hands. But he, my Son, shall reprove the nations that are come for their un-godliness—which things [i.e., the rebukes] are (38) like unto a storm; and shall reproach them to their face with their evil thoughts and with the tortures with which they are destined to be tortured—which are compared unto a flame; and then (39) shall he destroy them without labour by the Law which is compared unto fire. And whereas thou didst see that he summoned and gathered to himself another multi-tude which was peaceable—(40) These are the ten tribes which were led away captive out of their own land in the days of Josiah the king,[1] which [tribes] Salmanassar the king of the Assyrians led away captive;

(47) There they have dwelt until the last times; and now, when they are about to come again, the Most High will again stay the springs of the River, that they may be able to pass over. Therefore thou didst see a multitude (48) gathered together in peace.

JN. 6:62

MK. 14:
62

REV. 19:
11-21

REV. 21:
24

---

[1]The author of this apocalypse seeks to give the weight of antiquity to his writing by suggesting that it dates from the time of Josiah, King of Judah, in the 7th Cen-tury B.C.

Qumran Texts:

The Dead Sea Scrolls

These documents of sectarian Judaism date from the first century A.D. and in some cases even earlier, but they were unknown until about 1950, when the first of them came to the attention of the scholarly world after being discovered by an Arab goatherd in a cave overlooking the north-western shore of the Dead Sea. Published first by American and then by Israeli scholars, the larger remains have all appeared, but there are hundreds of fragments as yet unpublished and in some cases probably undeciphered. The popular and scholarly publications concerning these sensational finds are enormous in quantity, and a separate scholarly journal, *Révue de Qumran* (the local Arab name for the cave site), is being published.

The chief importance of the scrolls lies in their providing us with access to nonrabbinic thought and hopes in Palestine in the first century. Because it was rabbinic Judaism that came to dominate, all other evidence was lost. A few documents found in a storage room of a synagogue in Cairo around the turn of this century were thought by some to be forgeries, but they now are recognized to be copies of the writings from the Dead Sea caves.

Among the documents preserved is one that traces the history of the sect, which considered its members to be the heirs of the New Covenant, the elect community chosen by God to establish the proper priesthood and the pure worship of God in the renovated temple in Jerusalem. The teacher of righteousness, or better, the One who Teaches Rightly, showed them the way. Once the community was established in the wilderness (Damascus), it had to develop rigid rules in order to preserve its purity. A copy of the Rule of the Community was found, and is excerpted here. It culminates in a fine hymn of praise to God for his faithfulness in calling the elect.

Another group of writings consists of a set of hymns in which God is praised, or in which the writer—some scholars think the Teacher himself —reviews his tribulations, but rejoices in God nonetheless. One of these Thanksgiving Psalms is given in this section. And finally, the members of the community believed that at the End of Days there would be a great conflict between them and their enemies, but at the same time a battle between the powers of God and those of Beliar, His cosmic enemy.

Portions of this work, called the War of the Sons of Light and the Sons of Darkness, are given, with the climax in the great eschatological hymn of victory.

Although there is no evidence that Jesus was a member of this community, as has often been proposed, or that his followers were adherents of this sect, there is considerable similarity between the self-understanding of the community at Qumran and the earliest church, and the outlook of both groups is very similar concerning the conflict between God and his Adversary and the resolution of the struggle in the coming of the New Age.

THE DAMASCUS DOCUMENT

I. And now listen, all you who know righteousness and understand the works of God. For he has a controversy with all flesh, and will execute judgment upon all who despise him. For when those who forsook him trespassed, he hid his face from Israel and from his sanctuary, and gave them up to the sword; but when he remembered the covenant of the ancients, he left a remnant to Israel and did not give them up to destruction. And in the period of the wrath—three hundred and ninety years, when he gave them into the hand of Nebuchadnezzar, king of Babylon—he visited them and caused to sprout from Israel and Aaron a root of planting to inherit his land and to grow fat in the goodness of his soil. Then they perceived their iniquity and knew that they were guilty men; yet they were like men blind and groping for the way for twenty years. And God observed their works, that they sought him with a perfect heart; and he raised up for them a teacher of righteousness to lead them in the way of his heart. And he made known to later generations what he did to a later generation, to a congregation of treacherous men, those who turned aside out of the way.

This was the time concerning which it was written, "Like a stubborn heifer, Israel was stubborn," when arose the man of scorn, who preached to Israel lying words and led them astray in a trackless wilderness, so that he brought low their iniquitous pride, so that they turned aside from the paths of righteousness, and removed the landmark which the forefathers had fixed in their inheritance, so making the curses of his covenant cleave to them, delivering them to the sword that wreaks the vengeance of the covenant. For they sought smooth things, and chose illusions, and looked for breaches, and chose the fair neck; and they justified the wicked and condemned the righteous, transgressed the covenant, and violated the statute. And they banded together against the life of the righteous, and all who walked uprightly their soul abhorred, and they pursued them with the sword and exulted in the strife of the people. Then was kindled the wrath of God against their congregation, laying waste all their multitude; and their deeds were uncleanness before him.

II. And now listen to me, all you who have entered the covenant, and I will uncover your ears as to the ways of the wicked. God loves the knowledge of wisdom; and sound wisdom he has set before him;

prudence and knowledge minister to him. Longsuffering is with him, and abundance of pardon to forgive those who turn from transgression, but power and might and great wrath with flames of fire by all the angels of destruction upon those who turn aside from the way and abhor the statute, so that they shall have no remnant of survival.

For God did not choose them from the beginning of the world, but before they were established he knew their works and abhorred their generations from of old, and he hid his face from the land and from his people until they were consumed; for he knew the years of abiding and the number and explanation of their periods for all who exist in the ages, and the things that come to pass even to what will come in their periods for all the years of eternity.

But in all of them he raised up for himself men called by name, in order to leave a remnant to the land, and to fill the face of the world with their seed. And he caused them to know by his anointed his Holy Spirit and a revelation of truth; and in the explanation of his name are their names. But those he hated he caused to go astray.

III. And now, my sons, listen to me, and I will uncover your eyes to see and understand the works of God, and to choose what he likes and reject what he hates; to walk perfectly in all his ways, and not to go about with thoughts of a guilty impulse and eyes of fornication; for many went astray in them, and mighty men of valor stumbled in them, formerly and until now. In their walking in the rebelliousness of their hearts the watchers of heaven fell; in it they were caught who did not keep the commandment of God, and their children, whose height was like the loftiness of the cedars, and whose bodies were like the mountains, fell thereby. Yea, all flesh that was on the dry land fell; yea, it perished; and they were as though they had not been, because they did their own will and did not keep the commandment of their Maker, until his anger was kindled against them.

IV. In it the sons of Noah and their families went astray; in it they were cut off. Abraham did not walk in it, and he was accounted as God's friend, because he kept the commandments of God and did not choose the will of his own spirit. And he passed on the commandment to Isaac and Jacob, and they kept it and were recorded as friends of God and possessors of the covenant forever.

The sons of Jacob went astray in them and were punished according to their error, and their sons in Egypt walked in the stubbornness of their hearts, taking counsel against the commandments of God and doing each what was right in his own eyes. They ate blood, and he cut off their males in the desert. And he said to them in Kadesh, "Go up and take possession of the land," but they hardened their spirit and did not listen to the voice of their Maker, the commandments of their Teacher, but murmured in their tents.

Then the anger of God was kindled against their congregation; their children perished by it, their kings were cut off by it, and their mighty men perished by it; and their land was made desolate by it. By it the first that entered the covenant became guilty, and they were delivered to the sword, because they forsook the covenant of God and chose their own will, and went about after the stubbornness of their heart, each doing his own will.

V. But with those who held fast to the commandments of God,

those who were left of them, God established his covenant for Israel to eternity, revealing to them hidden things in which all Israel had gone astray. His holy Sabbaths and his glorious festivals, his righteous testimonies and his true ways, and the desires of his will, by which, if a man does them, he shall live, he opened up before them. And they dug a well for many waters, and he who despises them shall not live. But they defiled themselves with the transgression of man, and in the ways of the unclean woman, and they said, "That is for us." But God

ACT 15:
16

AMOS 9:
12

in his wondrous mysteries forgave their iniquity and pardoned their transgression, and he built for them a sure house in Israel, the like of which has not existed from of old or until now. Those who hold fast to it are for eternal life, and all the glory of man is theirs; as God established it for them by the prophet Ezekiel, saying, "The priests and the Levites and the sons of Zadok, who kept the charge of my sanctuary when the sons of Israel went astray from me, they shall offer to me fat and blood."

VI. The priests are the captivity of Israel who went forth from the land of Judah, and the Levites are those who joined them; and the sons of Zadok are the elect of Israel, those called by name, who will abide at the end of days. Behold the explanation of their names according to their generations, and the period of their abiding, and the number of their distresses, and the years of their sojourning, and the explanation of their works, the first saints whom God forgave, and who justified the righteous and condemned the wicked.

All who come after them must do according to the explanation of the law in which the forefathers were instructed until the completion of the period of these years. According to the covenant which God established with the forefathers to forgive their sins, so God will forgive them. And at the completion of the period to the number of these years they shall no more join themselves to the house of Judah, but everyone must stand up on his watchtower. The wall has been built; the decree is far away.

.   .   .

VIII. In the period of the destruction of the land arose the removers of the landmark and led Israel astray. And the land became desolate, because they spoke rebellion against the commandments of God by Moses, and also by the holy anointed ones; and they prophesied falsehood to turn away Israel from following God.

But God remembered the covenant of the forefathers, and raised up from Aaron men of understanding, and from Israel wise men. And he made them listen, and they dug the well. "A well which princes dug, which the nobles of the people delved with the staff." The well is the law, and those who dug it are the captivity of Israel, who went out from the land of Judah and sojourned in the land of Damascus, all of whom God called princes, because they sought him, and their glory was not rejected in the mouth of anyone. And the staff [or legislator] is he who studies the law, as Isaiah said, "He produces an instrument for his work." And the nobles of them people are those who come to dig the well with the staves [or rules] which the staff [or legislator] prescribed to walk in during the whole period of wickedness; and without them they shall not attain to the arising of him who will teach righteousness at the end of days.

And all who have been brought into the covenant not to come into the sanctuary to kindle fire on his altar in vain shall become those who shut the door, as God said, "Who among you will shut his door, so that you will not kindle fire on my altar in vain?"—unless they observe to do according to the explanation of the law for the period of wickedness; and to separate from the sons of the pit; and to keep away from the unclean wealth of wickedness acquired by vowing and devoting and by appropriating the wealth of the sanctuary; and not to rob the poor of his people, so that widows become their spoil, and they murder the fatherless; and to make a separation between the unclean and the clean, and to make men know the difference between the holy and the common; and to keep the Sabbath day according to its explanation, and the festivals and the day of the fast, according to the decision of those who entered the new covenant in the land of Damascus; to contribute their holy things according to their explanation; to love each his brother as himself; and to hold fast the hand of the poor and the needy and the proselyte; and to seek everyone the peace of his brother; for a man shall not trespass against his next of kin; and to keep away from harlots according to the ordinance; to rebuke each his brother according to the commandment, and not to bear a grudge from day to day; and to separate from all uncleannesses according to their ordinances; for a man shall not make abominable his holy spirit, as God separated for them.

For all who walk in these things in perfection of holiness, according to all his teaching, God's covenant stands fast, to make them live to a thousand generations.

. . .

When the two houses of Israel separated, Ephraim departed from Judah; and all who turned back were given over to the sword, but those who stood firm escaped to the land of the north, as it says, "And I will exile the *sikkuth* of your king and the *kiyyun* of your images from the tents of Damascus." The books of the law are the booth of the king, as it says, "And I will raise up the booth of David that is fallen"; the king is the assembly; and the *kiyyun* of the images are the books of the prophets, whose words Israel despised; and the star is the interpreter of the law who came to Damascus, as it is written, "A star shall come forth out of Jacob, and a sceptre shall rise out of Israel." The sceptre is the prince of the whole congregation. And when he arises, he "shall break down all the sons of Seth."

And such shall be the judgment of everyone who rejects the former ones and the latter ones; those who have taken idols into their hearts and walked in the stubbornness of their hearts. They have no share in the house of the law. According to the judgment of their fellows who turned back with the men of scorn shall they be judged, for they spoke error against the statutes of righteousness and rejected the firm covenant which they had established in the land of Damascus, that is,

AMOS 9: 12

NUM. 24:17

the new covenant. And neither they nor their families shall have a share in the house of the law.

From the day of the gathering in of the unique teacher until the annihilation of all the men of war who returned with the man of the lie will be about forty years; and in that period will be kindled the anger of God against Israel, as it says, "There is no king and no prince and no judge, and none who rebuke in righteousness." Those who repented of the transgressions of Jacob have kept the covenant of God.

Then each will speak to his neighbor, to strengthen one another, that their steps may hold fast to the way of God; and God will listen to their words and hear, and a book of remembrance will be written before him for those who fear God and think of his name, until salvation and righteousness are revealed for those who fear God. Then you shall again discern between the righteous and the wicked, between him who serves God and him who does not serve him. And he will show kindness to thousands, to those who love him and keep his commandments, to a thousand generations, after the manner of the house of Peleg, who went out from the holy city and leaned upon God during the period when Israel transgressed and polluted the sanctuary; but they turned to God. And he smote the people with few words. All of them, each according to his spirit, shall be judged in the holy council. And all who have broken through the boundary of the law, of those who entered the covenant, at the appearing of the glory of God to Israel shall be cut off from the midst of the camp, and with them all who condemn Judah in the days of its trials.

But all who hold fast to these ordinances, going out and coming in according to the law, and who listen to the voice of a teacher and confess before God, "We have sinned, we have done wickedly, both we and our fathers, in walking contrary to the statutes of the covenant; right and true are thy judgments against us"; all who do not lift a hand against his holy statutes and his righteous judgments and his true testimonies; who are instructed in the former judgments with which the men of the community were judged; who give ear to the voice of a Teacher of Righteousness and do not reject the statutes of righteousness when they hear them—they shall rejoice and be glad, and their hearts shall be strong, and they shall prevail over all the sons of the world, and God will forgive them, and they shall see his salvation, because they have taken refuge in his holy name.

THE RULE OF THE COMMUNITY

... the order of the community; to seek God ...; to do what is good and upright before him as he commanded through Moses and through all his servants the prophets; to love all that he has chosen and hate all that he has rejected; to be far from all evil and cleave to all good works; to do truth and righteousness and justice in the land; to walk no longer in the stubbornness of a guilty heart and eyes of fornication, doing all evil; to bring all those who have offered themselves to do God's statutes into a covenant of steadfast love; to be united in the counsel of God and to walk before him perfectly with regard to all the things that have been revealed for the appointed times of their testimonies; to love all the sons of light, each according to his lot in the counsel of God, and to hate all the sons of darkness, each according to his guilt in vengeance of God.

And all who have offered themselves for his truth shall bring all their knowledge and strength and wealth into the community of God, to purify their knowledge in the truth of God's statutes, and to distribute their strength according to the perfection of his ways and all their property according to his righteous counsel; not to transgress in any one of all the words of God in their periods; not to advance their times or postpone any of their appointed festivals; not to turn aside from his true statutes, going to the right or to the left.

And all who come into the order of the community shall pass over into the covenant before God, to do according to all that he has commanded, and not to turn away from following him because of any dread or terror or trial or fright in the dominion of Belial. And when they pass into the covenant, the priests and the Levites shall bless the God of salvation and all his works of truth; and all those who are passing into the covenant shall say after them, "Amen! Amen!"

The priests shall recount the righteous acts of God in his mighty works and tell all the acts of steadfast love and mercy upon Israel; and the Levites shall recount the iniquities of the sons of Israel and all their guilty transgressions and sin in the dominion of Belial. Then all those who are passing into the covenant shall confess after them, saying, "We have committed iniquity, we have transgressed, we have sinned, we have done evil, we and our fathers before us, in walking contrary to the statutes of truth; but righteous is God, and true is his judgment on us and on our fathers; and the mercy of his steadfast love he has bestowed upon us from everlasting to everlasting."

Then the priests shall bless all the men of God's lot, who walk perfectly in all his ways, and shall say: "May he bless you with all good and keep you from all evil; may he enlighten your heart with life-giving prudence and be gracious to you with eternal knowledge; may he lift up his loving countenance to you for eternal peace." And the Levites shall curse all the men of Belial's lot and shall answer and say: "Accursed may you be in all your wicked, guilty works; may God make you a horror through all those that wreak vengeance and send after you destruction through all those that pay recompense; accursed may you be without mercy according to the darkness of your works, and may you suffer wrath in the deep darkness of eternal fire. May God not be gracious to you when you call, and may he not pardon, forgiving your iniquities; may he lift up his angry countenance for vengeance upon you, and may there be no peace for you at the mouth of all those that hold enmity!" And all who are passing over into the covenant shall say after those who bless and those who curse, "Amen! Amen!"

PSN. 106:2 ff.

And the priests and Levites shall continue and say: "Accursed for passing over with the idols of his heart may he be who comes into this covenant and sets the stumbling block of his iniquity before him, turning back with it, and when he hears the words of this covenant blesses himself in his heart, saying, 'May I have peace, because I walk in the stubbornness of my heart!' But his spirit will be swept away, the thirsty together with the sated, without pardon. The wrath of God and the jealousy of his judgments will burn in him to eternal destruction; and all the curses of this covenant will cleave to him; and God will set him apart for evil; and he will be cut off from the midst of all the sons of light, when he turns away from following God with his idols and the stumbling-block of his iniquity. He will put his lot in the midst of those accursed forever." And all who are coming into the covenant shall answer and say after them, "Amen! Amen!"

So shall they do year by year all the days of the dominion of Belial. The priests shall pass over first in order, according to their spirits, one after another; and the Levites shall pass over after them, and all the people shall pass over third in order, one after another, by thousands and hundreds and fifties and tens, so that every man of Israel may know his appointed position in the community of God for the eternal council. And none shall be abased below his appointed position or exalted above his allotted place; for they shall all be in true community and good humility and loyal love and righteous thought, each for his fellow in the holy council, and they shall be sons of the eternal assembly.

Everyone who refuses to enter God's covenant, walking in the stubbornness of his heart, shall not attain to his true community. For his soul has abhorred the discipline of knowledge, the judgments of righteousness he has not confirmed because of his apostasies; and with the upright he will not be reckoned. His knowledge and his strength and his wealth shall not come into the council of community, because in the traffic of wickedness is his devising, and there is pollution in his plans. He will not be justified while giving free rein to the stubbornness of his heart. In darkness he looks at the ways of light, and with the perfect he will not be reckoned. He will not be purified by atonement offerings, and he will not be made clean with the water for impurity; he will not sanctify himself with seas and rivers or be made clean with any water for washing. Unclean, unclean he will be all the days that he rejects the ordinances of God, not being instructed in the community of his counsel.

. . .

The instructor's duty is to make all the sons of light understand and to teach them in the history of all the sons of man as to all their kinds of spirits with their signs, as to their works in their generations, and as to the visitation of their afflictions together with the periods of their recompense. From the God of knowledge is all that is and that is to be; and before they came into being he established all their designing. And when they come into being for their testimony according to his glorious design, they fulfill their work; and nothing is to be changed. In his hand are the ordinances of all; and he provides for them in all their affairs.

He created man to have dominion over the world and made for him two spirits, that he might walk by them until the appointed time of his visitation; they are the spirits of truth and of error. In the abode of light are the origins of truth, and from the source of darkness are

II COR.
4:4

II
THESS.
2:7-10

the origins of error. In the hand of the prince of lights is dominion over all sons of righteousness; in the ways of light they walk. And in the hand of the angel of darkness is all dominion over the sons of error; and in the ways of darkness they walk. And by the angel of darkness is the straying of all the sons of righteousness, and all their sin and their iniquities and their guilt, and the transgressions of their works in his dominion, according to the mysteries of God, until his time, and all their afflictions and the appointed times of their distress in the dominion of his enmity. And all the spirits of his lot try to make the sons of light stumble; but the God of Israel and his angel of truth have helped all the sons of light. For he created the spirits of light and of darkness, and upon them he founded every work and upon their ways every service. One of the spirits God loves for all the ages of eternity, and with all its deeds he is pleased forever; as for the other, he abhors its company, and all its ways he hates forever.

And these are their ways in the world: to shine in the heart of man, and to make straight before him all the ways of true righteousness, and to make his heart be in dread of the judgments of God, and to induce a spirit of humility, and slowness to anger, and great compassion, and eternal goodness, and understanding and insight, and mighty wisdom, which is supported by all the works of God and leans upon the abundance of his steadfast love, and a spirit of knowledge in every thought of action, and zeal for righteous judgments, and holy thought with sustained purpose, and abundance of steadfast love for all the sons of truth, and glorious purity, abhorring all unclean idols, and walking humbly with prudence in all things, and concealing the truth of the mysteries of knowledge.

These are the counsels of the Spirit for the sons of the truth of the world and the visitation of all who walk by it, for healing and abundance of peace in length of days, and bringing forth seed, with all eternal blessings and everlasting joy in the life of eternity, and a crown of glory with raiment of majesty in everlasting light.

COL. 2:
2-3

I JN. 4:
1-6

But to the spirit of error belong greediness, slackness of hands in the service of righteousness, wickedness and falsehood, pride and haughtiness, lying and deceit, cruelty and great impiety, quickness to anger and abundance of folly and proud jealousy, abominable works in a spirit of fornication and ways of defilement in the service of uncleanness, and a blasphemous tongue, blindness of eyes and dullness of ears, stiffness of neck and hardness of heart, walking in all the ways of darkness and evil cunning. And the visitation of all who walk by it is for abundance of afflictions by all destroying angels, to eternal perdition in the fury of the God of vengeance, to eternal trembling and everlasting dishonor, with destroying disgrace in the fire of dark places. And all their periods to their generations will be in sorrowful mourning and bitter calamity, in dark disasters until they are destroyed, having no remnant or any that escape.

In these two spirits are the origins of all the sons of man, and in their divisions all the hosts of men have their inheritance in their generations. In the ways of the two spirits men walk. And all the performance of their works is in their two divisions, according to each man's inheritance, whether much or little, for all the periods of eternity. For

God has established the two spirits in equal measure until the last period, and has put eternal enmity between their divisions. An abomination to truth are deeds of error, and an abomination to error are all ways of truth. And contentious jealousy is on all their judgments, for they do not walk together.

But God in the mysteries of his understanding and in his glorious wisdom has ordained a period for the ruin of error, and in the appointed time of punishment he will destroy it forever. And then shall come out forever the truth of the world, for it has wallowed in the ways of wickedness in the dominion of error until the appointed time of judgment which has been decreed. And then God will refine in his truth all the deeds of a man, and will purify for himself the frame of man, consuming every spirit of error hidden in his flesh, and cleansing him with a holy spirit from all wicked deeds. And he will sprinkle upon him a spirit of truth, like water for impurity, from all abominations of falsehood and wallowing in a spirit of impurity, to make the upright perceive the knowledge of the Most High and the wisdom of the sons of heaven, to instruct those whose conduct is blameless. For God has chosen them for an eternal covenant, and theirs is all the glory of man; and there shall be no error, to the shame of all works of deceit.

There shall be in the council of the community twelve men, and there shall be three priests who are perfect in all that has been revealed of the whole law, to practice truth and righteousness and justice and loyal love and walking humbly each with his neighbor, to preserve faithfulness in the land with sustained purpose and a broken spirit, and to make amends for iniquity by the practice of justice and the distress of tribulation, and to walk with all by the standard of truth and by the regulation of the time.

When these things come to pass in Israel, the council of the community will be established in the truth for an eternal planting, a holy house for Israel, a foundation of the holy of holies for Aaron, true witnesses for justice and the elect by God's will, to make atonement for the land and to render to the wicked their recompense—this is the tested wall, a precious cornerstone; its foundations will not tremble or flee from their place—a most holy dwelling for Aaron with eternal knowledge for a covenant of justice and to offer a pleasing fragrance, and a house of perfection and truth in Israel to establish a covenant for eternal statutes. And they shall be accepted to make atonement for the land and to decide the judgment of wickedness, and there shall be no error. When these men have been prepared in the foundation of the community for two years with blameless conduct, they shall be separated in holiness in the midst of the council of the men of the community; and when anything which has been hidden from Israel is found by the man who is searching, it shall not be hidden from these men out of fear of an apostate spirit.

When these things come to pass for the community in Israel, by these regulations they shall be separated from the midst of the session of the men of error to go to the wilderness to prepare there the way of the LORD; as it is written, "In the wilderness prepare the way of the LORD; make straight in the desert a highway for our God." This is

I COR.
15:23-28

MT. 10:1

ACT. 6:
21

I PET.
2:4-8

ISZ. 40:
3

MK. 1:3

the study of the law, as he commanded through Moses, to do according to all that has been revealed from time to time, and as the prophets revealed by his Holy Spirit.

Any man of the men of the community, of the covenant of the community, who wilfully takes away a word from the whole commandment shall not touch the sacred food of the holy men; he shall not know any of their counsel until his works are cleansed from all error, so that he conducts himself blamelessly. Then he shall be admitted to the council as directed by the masters, and afterward he shall be registered in his position. According to this law shall it be done for everyone who is added to the community.

These are the ordinances by which the men of perfect holiness shall walk, each with his neighbor, everyone who enters the holy council, those who conduct themselves blamelessly as he commanded. Any man of them who·trangresses a word of the law of Moses overtly or with deceit shall be dismissed from the council of the community and shall not come back again; and none of the holy men shall participate in his wealth or in his counsel concerning anything. But if he acts unintentionally, he shall be separated from the sacred food and the council; and they shall interpret the ordinance that he shall not judge a man or be asked concerning any counsel for two years. If his conduct is perfect in the meeting, in interpretation, and in counsel as directed by the masters; if he has not again sinned unintentionally by the completion of his two years—because for one unintentional sin he shall be punished for two years—as for him who acts deliberately, he shall not come back again; only he who sins unintentionally shall be tested for two years, that his conduct and his counsel may be perfected under the direction of the masters—after that he shall be registered in his position for the holy community.

When these things come to pass in Israel according to all these regulations, for a foundation of a holy spirit, for eternal truth, for a ransom for the guilt of transgression and sinful faithlessness, and for acceptance for the land more than the flesh of whole burnt offerings and the fats of sacrifice, and an offering of the lips for justice like the pleasing quality of righteousness, and perfect conduct like a willing gift of an acceptable offering; at that time the men of the community shall be set apart, a house of holiness for Aaron, to be united as a holy of holies and a house of community for Israel, those who conduct themselves blamelessly.

THANKSGIVING PSALM (1)

Blessed art thou, O my God,
who openest to knowledge the heart of thy servant.
Direct in righteousness all his works
and establish the son of thy handmaid,
as thou didst accept the elect of mankind
to stand before thee forever.
For without thee conduct will not be blameless,
and apart from thy will nothing will be done.
It is thou that hast taught all knowledge;

MT. 11:
25

and everything that has come to pass has been by thy will.
And there is no other beside thee
to oppose thy counsel,
to understand all thy holy purpose,
to gaze into the depth of thy mysteries,
or to comprehend all thy marvels,
together with the strength of thy power.
Who is able to bear thy glory,
and what then is he,
the son of man, among thy marvelous works;
what shall one born of woman be accounted before thee?
As for him, he was kneaded from dust,
and the food of worms is his portion.
He is an emission of spittle, a cut-off bit of clay,
and his desire is for the dust.
What will clay reply, a thing formed by hand?
What counsel will it understand?

ROM. 3: 23-26

But as for me, my justification belongs to God,
and in his hand is the blamelessness of my conduct
together with the uprightness of my heart;
and in his righteousness my transgression will be wiped out.
For from the source of his knowledge he has opened up my light;
my eye has gazed into his wonders
and the light of my heart penetrates the mystery that is to be.
That which is eternal is the staff of my right hand;
on a strong rock is the way I tread;
before nothing will it be shaken.
For the faithfulness of God is the rock I tread,
and his strength is the staff of my right hand.
From the source of his righteousness is my judgment.

MT. 11: 27

A light is in my heart from his marvelous mysteries;
my eye has gazed on that which is eternal,

II COR. 4:6

sound wisdom which is hidden from the man of knowledge,
and prudent discretion from the sons of man,
a source of righteousness and reservoir of strength
together with a spring of glory hidden from the company of flesh.

MK. 4:11

To those whom God has chosen he has given them for an eternal
    possession;
he has given them an inheritance in the lot of the holy ones
and with the sons of heaven has associated their company
for a council of unity and a company of a holy building,
for an eternal planting
through every period that is to be.

THANKSGIVING PSALM (2)

I thank thee, O Lord,
because thou hast redeemed my soul from the pit;
from the Sheol of Abaddon
thou hast brought me up to an eternal height,
and I walk in an unsearchable plain.

I know that there is hope
for him whom thou hast formed from the dust
for an eternal company.
Thou hast purified the perverse spirit of a great sin,
to stand in his place with the army of the holy ones,
and to come together with the congregation of the sons of heaven.
Thou hast cast for man an eternal lot
with the spirits of knowledge,
to praise thy name together in joyful song
and to recount thy wonders in the presence of all thy works.
But I, a thing formed of clay, what am I?
A thing kneaded with water, for whom have I value,
and what strength have I?
For I took my stand in the border of wickedness,
and with the hapless in their lot;
but the poor man's soul was in dread, with great confusion;
engulfing destruction accompanied my steps;
when all the snares of the pit were opened,
and all the nets of wickedness were spread,
the seine of the hapless also on the face of the water;
when all the arrows of the pit flew, not turning aside,
and were loosed beyond hope;
when the line fell on judgment,
and the lot of anger on those who were forsaken;
a molten mass of wrath on dissemblers,
and a period of wrath for all worthlessness.
The cords of death surrounded me inescapably;
the torrents of Belial flowed over all the high banks.
Like a fire eating into all their springs,
destroying every green or dry tree in their channels,
it rushes about with flashes of flame,
until all who drink of them are no more;
into the walls of clay it eats,
and into the platform of the dry land.
The foundations of the mountains are given to the flames;
the roots of flint become torrents of pitch.
It devours to the great abyss;
the torrents of Belial burst into Abaddon;
the sentient beings of the abyss roar
with the noise of the eruptions of mire.
The earth cries aloud at the ruin
which has been wrought in the world;
all its sentient beings shout;
all who are upon it go mad
and melt in utter ruin.
For God thunders with the noise of his might,
and his holy dwelling re-echoes with his glorious truth;
the host of heaven utter their voice;
the eternal foundations melt and shake;
and the war of the mighty ones of heaven
rushes about in the world and turns not back

until the full end decreed forever;
and there is nothing like it.

The War of the Children of Light and the Children of Darkness

Discovered in the caves at Qumran in a nearly complete copy, as well as in some fragmentary copies, the War Scroll consists of an elaborate set of military preparations for the final battle at the end of the age between the evil forces of Belial and the elect community. Included in the work are prayers and praise for the eschatological fulfillment of God's promises to his chosen people. At stake is not merely the fate of the land of Palestine and the Jerusalem temple—though these are central to the values of the community—but the destiny of the whole cosmos, including the powers of good and evil. Since the visible manifestation of "the enemy" seems to be the Romans, who came to Palestine in force in 63 B.C., the writing must have originated after that date. Its main importance for the study of Christian origins is to demonstrate the apocalyptic view of history, which saw the historical forces as divided into two sharply differentiated groups (Sons of Light; Sons of Darkness); the course of history as filled with conflict and headed toward catastrophe; the goal of history as achieved through a coalition of human and divine forces (the elect and the angels), whose joint efforts would establish the divine rule in the cosmos.

WAR OF SONS OF LIGHT AND SONS OF DARKNESS

For thine is the battle, and by the strength of thy hand their corpses were scattered without burial. Goliath the Gittite, a mighty man of valor, thou didst deliver into the hand of thy servant David, because he trusted in thy great name and not in sword and spear, for thine is the battle; and he subdued the Philistines many times in thy holy name. Moreover by our kings thou didst save us many times, because of thy mercy and not according to our works, in which we acted wickedly, and the evil deeds of our transgressions. Thine is the battle, and from thee is power, and it is not ours; nor has our strength or the might of our hands done valiantly, but it is by thy strength and by the power of thy great might; as thou didst make known to us of old, saying, "A star shall come forth out of Jacob, and a scepter shall arise out of Israel, and it shall crush the forehead of Moab and break down all the sons of Sheth; and he shall go down from Jacob and destroy the remnant of Seir, and the enemy shall be dispossessed, and Israel shall do valiantly." By thy anointed ones, seers of testimonies, thou hast made known to us the ordering of the battles of thy hands, to fight against our enemies, to make the troops of Belial fall, seven nations of vanity, by the poor whom thou hast redeemed with strength and with peace, for marvelous power, and a melted heart, for a door

I SAM. 17

NUM. 24:17

of hope. And thou didst to them as to Pharaoh and the
chariots at the Red Sea. The stricken in spirit thou wil'
a flaming torch among sheaves, consuming wickedness,
turn back until guilt is destroyed. Of old thou didst cause us to ...
the appointed time of the power of thy hand against the Kittim, saying, "And Assyria shall fall by a sword, not of a man; and a sword,
not of man, shall devour him."

Rise, mighty one; bring back thy captives, man of glory!
Seize thy plunder, thou who doest valiantly!
Lay thy hand on the necks of thy enemies
and thy foot on the heaps of the slain;
smite the nations, thy adversaries,
and let thy sword consume guilty flesh!
Fill thy land with glory,
thy inheritance with blessing!
Let there be an abundance of cattle in thy territories,
silver and gold and precious stones in thy palaces.
Rejoice greatly, O Zion;
appear with glad shouts, O Jerusalem;
and exult, all ye cities of Judah!
Open the gate continually,
that the wealth of nations may be brought in to thee;
that their kings may minister to thee,
and all that have afflicted thee may bow down to thee
and lick the dust of thy feet.
O daughters of my people, cry aloud with the sound of a glad shout;
Adorn yourselves with glorious ornaments!

Today is his appointed time to lay low and to make fall the prince of
the dominion of wickedness; and he will send eternal help to the lot
he had redeemed by the power of the angel he has made glorious for
rule, Michael, in eternal light, to give light in joy to all Israel, peace
and blessing to the lot of God, to exalt among the gods the rule of
Michael and the dominion of Israel over all flesh. Righteousness shall
rejoice in the high places, and all the sons of his truth shall be joyful
in eternal knowledge. And you, sons of his covenant, be strong in the
crucible of God until he waves his hand and fills his crucibles with
his mysteries that you may stand.

POPULAR TALES AND BIOGRAPHICAL NARRATIVES

Popular "Lives" of Great Men

The biography, as a carefully sequential account of the life of a person, complete with attention to environmental influences and psychological development, is a relatively modern literary creation. In antiquity

authors preferred to string together brief anecdotal accounts, sometimes giving bits of narrative detail and at other times merely sayings or teachings of the hero. Known as a *chria*, the mode of biographical accounting is characteristic of nearly all the "lives" that have been preserved from the early centuries of the Roman empire and of the gospels as well. Diogenes Laertius was another who stitched together *chriae* concerning a number of philosophers, from which we have chosen typical examples depicting the life and teachings of Socrates (469–399 B.C.), and Diogenes of Sinope (412–323 B.C.), the outstanding representative of the Cynic School of philosophy.

In the rabbinic sources, there is almost no biographical interest, and most of the anecdotes that are included are edifying or amusing—sometimes both at once—concerning some activity or quality of one of the rabbis. Included here are some typical stories about the personalities of one of the most famous pairs of rabbis: Hillel and Shammai, of the first century A.D.

Even in the case of an extended work, such as Philostratus' *Life of Apollonius of Tyana* (late second century A.D.), the narrative is skimpy and the writing is sprinkled liberally with brief anecdotal accounts of the sage. In the *Life of Apollonius* Philostratus demonstrates his subject's superior wisdom and how it was rewarded by the gods and men. Lucian, on the other hand, offers in "Alexander the False Prophet" a delightful, cynically told story of an opportunist and trickster who makes his fortune by capitalizing on foolish, gullible people who are ready to believe anything. Reading these ancient "lives" should shed light on the distinctive features of the gospel accounts of Jesus, as well as showing the influences of contemporary literary styles on the writers of the gospels.

DIOGENES LAERTIUS: SOCRATES

Demetrius of Byzantium relates that Crito removed him from his workshop and educated him, being struck by his beauty of soul; that he discussed moral questions in the workshops and the market-place, being convinced that the study of nature is no concern of ours; and that he claimed that his inquiries embraced "Whatso'er is good or evil in an house;" that frequently, owing to his vehemence in argument, men set upon him with their fists or tore his hair out; and that for the most part he was despised and laughed at, yet bore all this ill-usage patiently. So much so that, when he had been kicked, and someone expressed surprise at his taking it so quietly, Socrates rejoined, "Should I have taken legal action against a donkey, supposing that he had kicked me?" Thus far Demetrius.

Unlike most philosophers, he had no need to travel, except when required to go on an expedition. The rest of his life he stayed at home and engaged all the more keenly in argument with anyone who would converse with him, his aim being not to alter his opinion but to get at the truth. They relate that Euripides gave him the treatise of Heraclitus and asked his opinion upon it, and that his reply was, "The part I understand is excellent, and so too is, I dare say, the part I do not understand; but it needs a Delian diver to get to the bottom of it."

He took care to exercise his body and kept it in good condition. At all events he served on the expedition to Amphipolis; and when in the battle of Delium Xenophon had fallen from his horse, he stepped in and saved his life. For in the general flight of the Athenians he personally retired at his ease, quietly turning round from time to time and ready to defend himself in case he were attacked. Again, he served at Potidaea, whither he had gone by sea, as land communications were interrupted by the war; and while there he is said to have remained a whole night without changing his position, and to have won the prize of valour.

He was a man of great independence and dignity of character. Pamphila in the seventh book of her Commentaries tells how Alcibiades once offered him a large site on which to build a house; but he replied, "Suppose, then, I wanted shoes and you offered me a whole hide to make a pair with, would it not be ridiculous in me to take it?" Often when he looked at the multitude of wares exposed for sale, he would say to himself, "How many things I can do without!" And he would continually recite the lines:

> The purple robe and silver's shine
> More fits an actor's need than mine.

Moreover, in his old age he learnt to play the lyre, declaring that he saw no absurdity in learning a new accomplishment. As Xenophon relates in the Symposium, it was his regular habit to dance, thinking that such exercise helped to keep the body in good condition. He used to say that his supernatural sign warned him beforehand of the future; that to make a good start was no trifling advantage, but a trifle turned the scale; and that he knew nothing except just the fact of ignorance. ... When Xanthippe first scolded him and then drenched him with water, his rejoinder was, "Did I not say that Xanthippe's thunder would end in rain?" When Alcibiades declared that the scolding of Xanthippe was intolerable, "Nay, I have got used to it," said he, "as to the continued rattle of a windlass. And you do not mind the cackle of geese." "No," replied Alcibiades, "but they furnish me with eggs and goslings." "And Xanthippe," said Socrates, "is the mother of my children." When she tore his coat off his back in the market-place and his acquaintances advised him to hit back, "Yes, by Zeus," said he, "in order that while we are sparring each of you may join in with 'Go it, Socrates!' 'Well done, Xanthippe!' " He said he lived with a shrew, as horsemen are fond of spirited horses, "but just as, when they have mastered these, they can easily cope with the rest, so I in the society of Xanthippe shall learn to adapt myself to the rest of the world."

.   .   .

The affidavit in the case, which is still preserved, says Favorinus, in the *Metroön*, ran as follows: "This indictment and affidavit is sworn by Meletus, the son of Meletus of Pitthos, against Socrates, the son of Sophroniscus of Alopece: Socrates is guilty of refusing to recognize the gods recognized by the state, and of introducing other new divinities. He is also guilty of corrupting the youth. The penalty demanded is death." The philosopher then, after Lysias had written a defence for him, read it through and said: "A fine speech, Lysias; it is not, however, suitable to me." For it was plainly more forensic than philosophical. Lysias said, "If it is a fine speech, how can it fail to suit you?" "Well," he replied, "would not fine raiment and fine shoes be just as unsuitable to me?"

Justus of Tiberias in his book entitled *The Wreath* says that in the course of the trial Plato mounted the platform and began: "Though I am the youngest, men of Athens, of all who ever rose to address you"—whereupon the judges shouted out, "Get down! Get down!" When therefore he was condemned by 281 votes more than those given for acquittal, and when the judges were assessing what he should suffer or what fine he should pay, he proposed to pay 25 drachmae. Eubulides indeed says he offered 100. When this caused an uproar among the judges, he said, "Considering my services, I assess the penalty at maintenance in the Prytaneum at the public expense."

Sentence of death was passed, with an accession of eighty fresh votes. He was put in prison, and a few days afterwards drank the hemlock, after much noble discourse which Plato records in the *Phaedo*...

So he was taken from among men; and not long afterwards the Athenians felt such remorse that they shut up the training grounds and gymnasia. They banished the other accusers but put Meletus to death; they honoured Socrates with a bronze statue, the work of Lysippus, which they placed in the hall of processions.

DIOGENES LAERTIUS: DIOGENES OF SINOPE

On reaching Athens he fell in with Antisthenes. Being repulsed by him, because he never welcomed pupils, by sheer persistence Diogenes wore him out. Once when he stretched out his staff against him, the pupil offered his head with the words, "Strike, for you will find no wood hard enough to keep me away from you, so long as I think you've something to say." From that time forward he was his pupil, and, exile as he was, set out upon a simple life.

Through watching a mouse running about, says Theophrastus in the Megarian dialogue, not looking for a place to lie down in, not afraid of the dark, not seeking any of the things which are considered to be dainties, he discovered the means of adapting himself to circumstances. He was the first, say some, to fold his cloak because he was obliged to sleep in it as well, and he carried a wallet to hold his victuals, and he used any place for any purpose, for breakfasting, sleeping, or conversing. And then he would say, pointing to the portico of Zeus and the Hall of Processions, that the Athenians had provided him with places to live in. He did not lean upon a staff until he grew infirm; but afterwards he would carry it everywhere, not indeed in the city, but when walking along the road with it and with his wallet; so say Olympiodorus, once a magistrate at Athens, Polyeuctus the orator, and Lysanias the son of Aeschrio. He had written to someone to try and procure a cottage for him. When this man was a long time about it, he took for his abode the tub in the Metroön, as he himself explains in his letters. And in summer he used to roll in it over hot sand, while in winter he used to embrace statues covered with snow, using every means of inuring himself to hardship.

He was great at pouring scorn on his contemporaries. The school of Euclides he called bilious, and Plato's lectures waste of time, the performances at the Dionysia great peep-shows for fools, and the demagogues the mob's lackeys. He used also to say that when he saw physicians, philosophers and pilots at their work, he deemed man the most intelligent of all animals; but when again he saw interpreters of dreams and diviners and those who attended to them, or those who were puffed up with conceit of wealth, he thought no animal more silly. He would continually say that for the conduct of life we need right reason or a halter.

One day, observing a child drinking out of his hands, he cast away the cup from his wallet with the words, "A child has beaten me in plainness of living." He also threw away his bowl when in like manner he saw a child who had broken his plate taking up his lentils with the hollow part of a morsel of bread. He used also to reason thus: "All things belong to the gods. The wise are friends of the gods, and friends hold things in common. Therefore all things belong to the wise.". . .

All the curses of tragedy, he used to say, had lighted upon him. At all events he was

> A homeless exile, to his country dead.
> A wanderer who begs his daily bread.

But he claimed that to fortune he could oppose courage, to convention nature, to passion reason. When he was sunning himself in the Craneum, Alexander came and stood over him and said, "Ask of me any boon you like." To which he replied, "Stand out of my light." Someone had been reading aloud for a very long time, and when he was near the end of the roll pointed to a space with no writing on it. "Cheer up, my men," cried Diogenes; "there's land in sight." To one who by argument had proved conclusively that he had horns, he said, touching his forehead, "Well, I for my part don't see any." In like manner, when somebody declared that there is no such thing as motion, he got up and walked about. When someone was discoursing on celestial phenomena, "How many days," asked Diogenes, "were you in coming from the sky?" A eunuch of bad character had inscribed on his door the words, "Let nothing evil enter." "How then," he asked, "is the master of the house to get in?" When he had anointed his feet with unguent, he declared that from his head the unguent passed into the air, but from his feet into his nostrils.

The musician who was always deserted by his audience he greeted with a "Hail chanticleer," and when asked why he so addressed him, replied, "Because your song makes everyone get up."

When someone reproached him with his exile, his reply was, "Nay, it was through that, you miserable fellow, that I came to be a philosopher." Again, when someone reminded him that the people of Sinope had sentenced him to exile, "And I them," said he, "to home-staying."

. . . Being asked whether he had any maid or boy to wait on him, he said "No." "If you should die, then, who will carry you out to burial?" "Whoever wants the house," he replied.

Being asked if the wise eat cakes, "Yes," he said, "cakes of all kinds, just like other men." Being asked why people give to beggars but not to philosophers, he said, "Because they think they may one day be lame or blind, but never expect that they will turn to philosophy." He was begging of a miserly man who was slow to respond; so he said, "My friend, it's for food that I'm asking, not for funeral expenses." Being reproached one day for having falsified the currency, he said, "That was the time when I was such as you are now; but such as I am now, you will never be."

Being asked whether death was an evil thing, he replied, "How can it be evil, when in its presence we are not aware of it?" When Alexander stood opposite him and asked, "Are you not afraid of me?" "Why, what are you?" said he, "a good thing or a bad?" Upon Alexander replying "A good thing," "Who then," said Diogenes, "is afraid of the good?" Education, according to him, is a controlling grace to the young, consolation to the old, wealth to the poor, and ornament to the rich. When Didymon, who was a rake, was once treating a girl's eye, "Beware," says Diogenes, "lest the oculist instead of curing the eye should ruin the pupil." On somebody declaring that his own friends were plotting against him, Diogenes exclaimed, "What is to be done then, if you have to treat friends and enemies alike?"
Being asked what was the most beautiful thing in the world, he replied, "Freedom of speech." On entering a boys' school, he found there many statues of the Muses, but few pupils. "By the help of the gods," said he, "schoolmaster, you have plenty of pupils."

RABBINIC ANECDOTES

MT. 7:12   RABBI ELIEZER SAYS: LET THE HONOR OF THY FELLOW BE AS DEAR TO THEE AS THINE OWN. BE NOT EASILY ANGERED. REPENT ONE DAY BEFORE THY DEATH.

LET THE HONOR OF THY FELLOW BE AS DEAR TO THEE AS THINE OWN: how so? This teaches that even as one looks out for his own honor, so should he look out for his fellow's honor. And even as no man wishes that his own honor be held in ill repute, so should he wish that the honor of his fellow shall not be held in ill repute.

Another interpretation. LET THE HONOR OF THY FELLOW BE AS DEAR TO THEE AS THINE OWN: For example, [even] when a man has had a million and then all his wealth is taken away, let him not discredit himself over so much as a perutah's worth.

BE NOT EASILY ANGERED: what is that? This teaches that one should be patient like Hillel the Elder and not short tempered like Shammai the Elder.   MT. 5:21

What was this patience of Hillel the Elder? The story is told:

Once two men decided to make a wager of four hundred zuz with each other. They said: "Whoever can put Hillel into a rage gets the four hundred zuz."

One of them went [to attempt it]. Now that day was a Sabbath eve, toward dusk, and Hillel was washing his head. The man came and knocked on his door. "Where's Hillel? Where's Hillel?" he cried.

Hillel got into a cloak and came out to meet him. "My son," he said, "what is it?"

The man replied: "I need to ask about a certain matter."

"Ask," Hillel said.

The man asked: "Why are the eyes of the Tadmorites bleary?"

"Because," said Hillel, "they make their homes on the desert sands which the winds come and blow into their eyes. That is why their eyes are bleary."

The man went off, waited a while, and returned and knocked on his door. "Where's Hillel?" he cried, "where's Hillel?"

Hillel got into a cloak and came out. "My son," he said, "what is it?"

The man replied: "I need to ask about a certain matter."

"Ask," Hillel said.

The man asked: "Why are the Africans' feet flat?"

"Because they dwell by watery marshes," said Hillel, "and all the time they walk in water. That is why their feet are flat."

The man went off, waited a while, and returned and knocked on the door. "Where's Hillel?" he cried, "where's Hillel?"

Hillel got into a cloak and came out. "What is it thou wishest to ask?" he inquired.

"I need to ask about some matter," the man said.

"Ask," Hillel said to him. In his cloak he sat down before him and said: "What is it?"

Said the man: "Is this how princes reply! May there be no more like thee in Israel!"

"God forbid!" Hillel said, "tame thy spirit! What dost thou wish?"

The man asked: "Why are the heads of Babylonians long?"

"My son," Hillel answered, "thou hast raised an important question. Since there are no skillful midwives there, when the infant is born, slaves and maidservants tend it on their laps. That is why the heads of Babylonians are long. Here, however, there are skillful midwives, and when the infant is born it is taken care of in a cradle and its head is rubbed. That is why the heads of Palestinians are round."

"Thou hast put me out of four hundred zuz!" the man exclaimed.
Said Hillel to him: "Better that thou lose four hundred zuz because of Hillel than that Hillel lose his temper."

What was this impatience of Shammai the Elder? The story is told:
A certain man once stood before Shammai and said to him: "Master, how many Torahs have you?"
"Two," Shammai replied, "one written and one oral."
Said the man: "The written one I am prepared to accept, the oral one I am not prepared to accept."
Shammai rebuked him and dismissed him in a huff.
He came before Hillel and said to him: "Master, how many Torahs were given?"
"Two," Hillel replied, "one written and one oral."
Said the man: "The written one I am prepared to accept, the oral one I am not prepared to accept."
"My son," Hillel said to him, "sit down."
He wrote out the alphabet for him [and pointing to one of the letters] asked him: "What is this?"
"It is 'aleph,' " the man replied.
Said Hillel: "This is not 'aleph but bet. What is that?" he continued.
The man answered: "It is bet."
"This is not bet," said Hillel, "but gimmel."
[In the end] Hillel said to him: "How dost thou know that this is 'aleph and this bet and this gimmel? Only because so our ancestors of old handed it down to us that this is 'aleph and this bet and this gimmel. Even as thou hast taken this in good faith, so take the other in good faith."

A certain heathen once passed behind a synagogue and heard a child reciting: And these are the garments which they shall make: a breastplate, and an ephod, and a robe [Exod. 28.4]. He came before Shammai and asked him: "Master, all this honor, whom is it for?"
Shammai said to him: "For the High Priest, who stands and serves at the altar."
Said the heathen: "Convert me on condition that thou appoint me High Priest, so I might serve at the altar."
"Is there no priest in Israel," Shammai exclaimed, "and have we no High Priests to stand and serve in high priesthood at the altar, that a paltry proselyte who has come with naught but his staff and bag should go and serve in high priesthood!" He rebuked him and dismissed him in a huff.
The heathen then came to Hillel and said to him: "Master, convert me on condition that thou appoint me High Priest, so that I might stand and serve at the altar."
"Sit down," Hillel said to him, "and I will tell thee something. If one wishes to greet a king of flesh and blood, is it not right that he learn how to make his entrances and exits?"
"Indeed," the heathen replied.
"Thou wishest to greet the King of kings of kings, the Holy One, blessed be He: is it not all the more right that thou learn how to enter

into the Holy of Holies, how to fix the lights, how to approach the altar, how to set the table, how to prepare the row of wood?"

Said the heathen: "Do what seems best in thine eyes."

First Hillel wrote out the alphabet for him and taught it to him. Then he taught him the book of Leviticus. And the heathen went on studying until he got to the verse, *And the common man that draweth nigh shall be put to death* [Num. 1:51]. Forthwith, of his own accord, he reasoned by inference as follows: "If Israel, who were called children of God and of whom the Shekinah said, *And ye shall be unto Me a kingdom of priests, and a holy nation* [Exod. 19:6], were nevertheless warned by Scripture, *And the common man that draweth nigh shall be put to death*, all the more I, a paltry proselyte, come with naught but my bag!" Thereupon that proselyte was reconciled of his own accord.

He came to Hillel the Elder and said to him: "May all the blessings of the Torah rest upon thy head! For hadst thou been like Shammai the Elder I might never have entered the community of Israel. The impatience of Shammai the Elder well nigh caused me to perish in this world and the world to come. Thy patience has brought me to the life of this world and the one to come."

It is said: To that proselyte were born two sons; one named Hillel and the other he named Gamaliel; and they used to be called "proselytes of Hillel."

REPENT ONE DAY BEFORE THY DEATH. Rabbi Eliezer was asked by his disciples: "Does, then, a man know on what day he will die, that he should know when to repent?"

"All the more," he replied; "let him repent today lest he die on the morrow; let him repent on the morrow lest he die the day after: and thus all his days will be spent in repentance."

Rabbi Yose bar Judah says in the name of Rabbi Judah son of Rabbi Il'ai who said it in the name of Rabbi Eliezer the Great: REPENT ONE DAY BEFORE THY DEATH. KEEP WARM AT THE FIRE OF THE SAGES. BEWARE OF THEIR GLOWING COAL LEST THOU BE SCORCHED: FOR THEIR BITE IS THE BITE OF A JACKAL AND THEIR STING THE STING OF A SCORPION—MOREOVER ALL THEIR WORDS ARE LIKE COALS OF FIRE.

FROM: THE FATHERS ACCORDING TO RABBI NATHAN (15)

PHILOSTRATUS: LIFE OF APOLLONIUS OF TYANA

VOL. I, BK. II, CH. XXXVIII–XL

XXXVIII When they [i.e., Apollonius and the King of India] had thus conversed, for by this time it was daylight, they sent out into the open. And Apollonius, understanding that the king had to give audience to embassies and such-like, said: "You then, O king, must attend to the business of state, but let me go and devote this hour to the Sun, for I must needs offer up to him my accustomed prayer." "And I pray he may hear your prayer," said the king, "for he will bestow his grace on all who find pleasure in your wisdom: but I will wait for you until you return, for I have to decide some cases in which your presence will very greatly help me."

APOLLONIUS then returned, when the day was already far advanced, and asked him about the cases which he had been judging; but he answered: "Today I have not judged any, for the omens did not allow me." Apollonius then replied and said: "It is the case then that you consult the omens in such cases as these, just as you do when you are setting out on a journey or a campaign." "Yes, by Zeus," he said, "for there is a risk in this case, too, of one who is a judge straying from the right line." Apollonius felt that what he said was true, and asked him again what the suit was which he had to decide; "For I see," he said, "that you have given your attention to it and are per-plexed what verdict to give." "I admit," said the king, "that I am per-plexed; and that is why I want your advice; for one man has sold to another land, in which there lay a treasure as yet undiscovered, and some time afterwards the land, being broken up, revealed a certain chest, which the person who sold the land says belongs to him rather than to the other, for that he would never have sold the land, if he had known beforehand that he had a fortune thereon; but the pur-chaser claims that he acquired everything that he found in land, which thenceforth was his. And both their contentions are just; and I shall seem ridiculous if I order them to share the gold between them, for any old woman could settle the matter in that way." Apollonius there-upon replied as follows: "The fact that they are quarrelling about gold shows that these two men are no philosophers; and you will, in my opinion, give the best verdict if you bear this in mind, that the gods attach the first importance and have most care for those who live a life of philosophy together with moral excellence, and only pay sec-ondary attention to those who have committed no faults and were never yet found unjust. Now they entrust to philosophers the task of rightly discerning things divine and human as they should be dis-cerned, but to those who merely are of good character they give enough to live upon, so that they may never be rendered unjust by actual lack of the necessaries of life. It seems then to me, O king, right to weigh these men in the balance, as it were, and to examine their respective lives; for I cannot believe that the gods would deprive the one even of his land, unless he had been a bad man, or that they would, on the other hand, bestow on the other even what was under the land, unless he had been better than the man who sold it." The two claimants came back the next day, and the seller was convicted of being a ruffian who had neglected the sacrifices, which it was his bounden duty to sacrifice to the gods on that land; but the other was found to be a decent man and a most devout worshipper of the gods. Accordingly, the opinion of Apollonius prevailed, and the better of the two men quitted the court as one on whom the gods had bestowed this boon.

LK. 12:
13 ff.

(XL) When the law-suit had been thus disposed of, Apollonius approached the Indian, and said: "This is the third day, O king, that you have made me your guest; and at dawn to-morrow I must quit your land in accordance with the law." "But," said the other, "the law does not yet speak to you thus, for you can remain on the morrow, since you came after midday." "I am delighted," said Apollonius, "with your hospitality, and indeed you seem to me to be straining the law for my sake." "Yes indeed, and I would I could break it," said the king, "in your behalf; but tell me this, Apollonius, did not the camels bring you from Babylon which they say you were riding?" "They did," he said, "and Vardan gave them us." "Will they then be able to carry you on, after they have come already so many stades from Babylon?" Apollonius made no answer, but Damis said: "O king, our friend here does not understand anything about our journey, nor about the races among which we shall find ourselves in future; but he regards our passage into India as mere child's play, under the impression that he will everywhere have you and Vardan to help him. I assure you, the true condition of the camels has not been acknowledged to you; for they are in such an evil state that we could carry them rather than they us, and we must have others. For if they collapse anywhere in the wilderness of India, we" he continued, "shall have to sit down and drive off the vultures and wolves from the camels, but no one will drive them off from us, for we shall perish too." The king answered accordingly and said, "I will remedy this, for I will give you other camels, and you need four I think, and the satrap ruling the Indus will send back four others to Babylon. But I have a herd of camels on the Indus, all of them white." "And," said Damis, "will you not also give us a guide, O king?" "Yes, of course," he answered, "and I will give a camel to the guide and provisions, and I will write a letter to Iarchas, the oldest of the sages, praying him to welcome Apollonius as not inferior to himself, and to welcome you also as philosophers and followers of a divine man." And forthwith the Indian gave them gold and precious stones and linen and a thousand other such things. And Apollonius said that he had enough gold already, because Vardan had given it to the guide on the sly; but that he would accept linen robes, because they were like the cloaks worn by the ancient and genuine inhabitants of Attica. And he took up one of the stones and said: "O rare stone, how opportunely have I found you, and how providentially!" detecting in it, I imagine, some secret and divine virtue. Neither would the companions of Damis accept for themselves the gold; nevertheless they took good handfuls of the gems, in order to dedicate them to the gods, whenever they should regain their own country.

LUCIAN OF SAMOSATA: ALEXANDER THE FALSE PROPHET

There was no slight difference of opinion between them on that score, but in the end Alexander won, and going to Chalcedon, since after all that city seemed to them to have some usefulness, in the temple of Apollo, which is the most ancient in Chalcedon, they buried bronze tablets which said that very soon Asclepius, with his father Apollo, would move to Pontus and take up his residence at Abonoteichus. The opportune discovery of these tablets caused this story to spread quickly to all Bithynia and Pontus, and to Abonoteichus sooner than anywhere else. Indeed, the people of that city immediately voted to build a temple and began at once to dig for the foundations. Then Cocconas was left behind in Chalcedon, composing equivocal, ambiguous, obscure oracles, and died before long, bitten, I think, by a viper. It was Alexander who was sent in first; he now wore his hair long, had falling ringlets, dressed in a parti-coloured tunic of white and purple, with a white cloak over it, and carried a falchion like that of Perseus, from whom he claimed descent on his mother's side. And although those miserable Paphlagonians knew that both his parents were obscure, humble folk, they believed the oracle when it said:

> Here in your sight is a scion of Perseus, dear
> unto Phoebus;
> This is divine Alexander, who shareth the blood of
> the Healer!

Podaleirius, the Healer, it would appear, was so passionate and amorous that his ardour carried him all the way from Tricca to Paphlagonia in quest of Alexander's mother!

An oracle by now had turned up which purported to be a prior prediction by the Sibyl:

> On the shores of the Euxine sea, in the neighborhood of
> Sinope,
> There shall be born, by a Tower, in the days of the Romans,
> a prophet;
> After the foremost unit and three times ten, he will shew
> forth
> Five more units besides, and a score told three times over,
> Matching, with places four, the name of a valiant defender!

Well, upon invading his native land with all this pomp and circumstance after a long absence, Alexander was a man of mark and note, affecting as he did to have occasional fits of madness and causing his mouth to fill with foam. This he easily managed by chewing the root of soapwort, the plant that dyers use; but to his fellow-countrymen even the foam seemed supernatural and awe-inspiring. Then, too, they had long ago prepared and fitted up a serpent's head of linen, which had something of a human look, was all painted up, and appeared very lifelike. It would open and close its mouth by means of horsehairs, and a forked black tongue like a snake's, also controlled by horsehairs, would dart out. Besides, the serpent from Pella was ready in advance and was being cared for at home, destined in due time to manifest himself to them and to take a part in their show—in fact, to be cast for the leading role.

When at length it was time to begin, he contrived an ingenious ruse. Going at night to the foundations of the temple which were just being excavated, where a pool of water had gathered which either issued from springs somewhere in the foundations themselves or had fallen from the sky, he secreted there a goose-egg, previously blown, which contained a snake just born; and after burying it deep in the mud, he went back again. In the morning he ran out into the market-place naked, wearing a loin-cloth (this too was gilded), carrying his falchion, and tossing his unconfined mane like a devotee of the Great Mother in the frenzy. Addressing the people from a high altar upon which he had climbed, he congratulated the city because it was at once to receive the god in visible presence. The assembly—for almost the whole city, including women, old men, and boys, had come running—marvelled, prayed and made obeisance. Uttering a few meaningless words like Hebrew or Phoenician, he dazed the creatures, who did not know what he was saying save only that he everywhere brought in Apollo and Asclepius. Then he ran at full speed to the future temple, went to the excavation and the previously improvised fountain-head of the oracle, entered the water, sang hymns in honour of Asclepius and Apollo at the top of his voice, and besought the god, under the blessing of Heaven, to come to the city. Then he asked for a libation-saucer, and when somebody handed him one, deftly slipped it underneath and brought up, along with water and mud, that egg in which he had immured the god; the joint about the plug had been closed with wax and white lead. Taking it in his hands, he asserted that at that moment he held Asclepius! They gazed unwaveringly to see what in the world was going to happen; indeed, they had already marvelled at the discovery of the egg in the water. But when he broke it and received the tiny snake into his hollowed hand, and the crowd saw it moving and twisting about his fingers, they at once raised a shout, welcomed the god, congratulated their city, and began each of them to sate himself greedily with prayers, craving treasures, riches, health, and every other blessing from him. But Alexander went home again at full speed, taking with him the new-born Asclepius, "born twice, when other men are born but once," whose mother was not Coronis, by Zeus, nor yet a crow, but a goose! And the whole population followed, all full of religious fervour and crazed with expectations.

For some days he remained at home, expecting what actually happened—that as the news spread, crowds of Paphlagonians would come running in. When the city had become over-full of people, all of them already bereft of their brains and sense, and not in the least like bread-eating humans, but different from beasts of the field only in their looks, he seated himself on a couch in a certain chamber, clothed in apparel well suited to a god, and took into his bosom his Asclepius from Pella, who, as I have said, was of uncommon size and beauty. Coiling him about his neck, and letting the tail, which was long, stream over his lap and drag part of its length on the floor, he concealed only the head at one side of his own beard, as if it certainly belonged to the creature that was in view.

Now then, please imagine a little room, not very bright and not admitting any too much daylight; also, a crowd of heterogeneous humanity, excited, wonder-struck in advance, agog with hopes. When they went in, the thing, of course, seemed to them a miracle, that the formerly tiny snake within a few days had turned into so great a serpent, with a human face, moreover, and tame! They were immediately crowded towards the exit, and before they could look closely were forced out by those who kept coming in, for another door had been opened on the opposite side as an exit. That was the way the Macedonians did, they say, in Babylon during Alexander's illness, when he was in a bad way and they surrounded the palace, craving to see him and say good-bye. This exhibition the scoundrel gave not merely once, they say, but again and again, above all if any rich men were newly arrived.

Again and again, as I said before, he exhibited the serpent to all who requested it, not in its entirety, but exposing chiefly the tail and the rest of the body and keeping the head out of sight under his arm. But as he wished to astonish the crowd still more, he promised to produce the god talking—delivering oracles in person without a prophet. It was no difficult matter for him to fasten cranes' windpipes together and pass them through the head, which he had so fashioned as to be lifelike. Then he answered the questions through someone else, who spoke into the tube from the outside, so that the voice issued from his canvas Asclepius.

These oracles were called autophones, and were not given to everybody promiscuously, but only to those who were noble, rich, and free-handed.

MIRACLE STORIES

The first group of miracle stories are derived from rabbinic sources and were told partly to amuse and partly to foster piety. The final excerpt, a pagan miracle story, is one of the clearest examples of the tendency in late antiquity to exalt certain men as possessing supernatural powers. This kind of tale was likely an influence on the later forms of miracle tradition that surrounded the figures of Jesus and the apostles in the second century and later, although its impact is already apparent in the more highly developed miracle stories within the gospels.

RABBINIC MIRACLE STORIES

Nahum was an exceedingly pious man who would always say, whatever befell him: "This, also, is for the best [Gam Zu Letobah]." In this way he received his nickname.

It became necessary for the leaders of Palestine to send a gift unto the Roman emperor. Nahum was chosen as messenger in the expectation that God would grant success to a man so righteous. For the purpose of the gift he was given a jewelled box with gems. At a tavern, while he slept, the inn-keeper emptied his guest's box and filled it with sand. When the Emperor's treasurer opened the casket, it was found to contain sand. Nahum was accused of disrespect for the Emperor and was led forth to execution. Nevertheless Nahum was heard to say: "This, also, is for the best."

God thereupon sent Elijah in the guise of a Roman patrician, who declared: "I have heard there is a tradition among the Jews that when Abraham in his battle against the four kings was short of ammunition and his sword became dull, he threw sand at the enemy, and it smote them like a sword. Let us try this sand; perhaps it has the same property." MK. 15: 35

The execution was delayed and the sand was tested; the results were admirable. A town which had resisted the Romans was compelled to surrender under the impact of the sand. Nahum was released and his pockets filled with gold. He halted at the same tavern and told the inn-keeper of the gift he had received in exchange for what he had brought. The inn-keeper carried to the palace a wagon-load of sand but, when it was tested, it proved to be no different from any other sand. The inn-keeper was executed for attempting to deceive the Emperor.

TAANIT, 21

It happened that the people said to Honi, the circle drawer etc. Once it happened that the greater part of the month of Adar had gone and yet no rain had fallen. The people sent a message to Honi the Circle Drawer. Pray that rain may fall. He prayed and no rain fell. He thereupon drew a circle and stood within it in the same way as the prophet Habakkuk had done, as it is said, *I will stand upon my watch, and set me upon the tower* etc. He exclaimed [before God], Master of the Universe, Thy children have turned to me because [they believe] me to be a member of Thy house. I swear by Thy great name that I will not move from here until Thou hast mercy upon Thy children! Rain began to drip and his disciples said to him, We look to you to save us from death; we believe that this rain came down merely to release you from your oath. Thereupon he exclaimed: It is not for this that I have prayed, but for rain [to fill] the cisterns, ditches and caves. The rain then began to come down with great force, every drop being as big as the opening of a barrel and the Sages estimated that no one drop was less than a *log*. His desciples then said to him: Master, we look to you to save us from death; we believe that the rain came down to destroy the world. Thereupon he exclaimed before [God], It is not for this that I have prayed, but for rain of benevolence, blessing and bounty. Then rain fell normally until the Israelites [in Jerusalem] were compelled to go up [for shelter] to the Temple Mount because of the rain. [His disciples] then said to him Master, in the same way as you have prayed for the rain to fall pray for the rain to cease. He replied: I have it as a tradition that we may not pray on account of an excess of good. Despite this bring unto me a bullock for a thanksgiving-offering. They brought unto him a bullock for a thanksgiving-offering and he laid his two hands upon it and said, Master of the Universe, Thy people

Israel whom Thou hast brought out from Egypt cannot endure an excess of good nor an excess of punishmnet; when Thou wast angry with them, they could not endure it; when Thou didst shower upon them an excess of good they could not endure it; may it be Thy will that the rain may cease and that there be relief for the world. Immediately the wind began to blow and the clouds were dispersed and the sun shone and the people went out into the fields and gathered for themselves mushrooms and truffles. Thereupon Simeon b. Shetah sent this message to him. Were it not that you are Honi I would have placed you under the ban; for were the years like the years [of famine in the time] of Elijah [in whose hands were the keys of Rain] would not the same of Heaven be profaned through you? But what shall I do unto you who actest petulantly before the Omnipresent and He grants your desire, as a son who acts petulantly before his father and he grants his desires; thus he says to him, give me nuts, almonds, peaches, and pomegranates and he gives them unto him. Of you Scripture says, *Let thy father and thy mother be glad, and let her that bore thee rejoice.*

Our Rabbis have taught: What was the message that the Sanhedrin sent to Honi the Circle-Drawer? [It was an interpretation of the verse:] *Thou shalt also decree a thing, and it shall be established unto thee, and light shall shine upon thy ways* etc. "Thou shalt also decree a thing": You have decreed [on earth] below and the Holy One, Blessed be He, fulfils your word [in heaven] above. "And light shall shine upon thy ways": You have illumined with your prayer a generation in darkness. *"When they cast thee down, thou shalt say: there is lifting up"*: You have raised with your prayer a generation that has sunk low. *"For the humble person He saveth"*: You have saved by your prayer a generation that is humiliated with sin. *He delivered him that is not innocent.* *"Yea, He shall be delivered through the cleanness of thy hands"*: You have delivered it through the work of your clean hands.

R. Johanan said: This righteous man [Honi] was throughout the whole of his life troubled about the meaning of the verse, *A Song of Ascents, When the Lord brought back those that returned to Zion, we were like unto them that dream.* Is it possible for a man to dream continuously for seventy years? One day he was journeying on the road and he saw a man planting a carob tree: he asked him, How long does it take [for this tree] to bear fruit? The man replied: Seventy years. He then further asked him: Are you certain that you will live another seventy years? The man replied I found [ready grown] carob trees in the world; as my forefathers planted these for me so I too plant these for my children.

Honi sat down to have a meal and sleep overcame him. As he slept a rocky formation enclosed upon him which hid him from sight and he continued to sleep for seventy years. When he awoke he saw a man gathering the fruit of the carob tree and he asked him, Are you the man who planted the tree? The man replied: I am his grandson. Thereupon he exclaimed: It is clear that I slept for seventy years. He then caught sight of his ass who had given birth to several generations of mules; and he returned home. He there enquired, Is the son of

Honi the Circle-Drawer still alive? The people answered him, His son is no more, but his grandson is still living. Thereupon he said to them: I am Honi the Circle-Drawer, but no one would believe him. He then repaired to the Beth Hamidrash and there he overheard the scholars say, The law is as clear to us as in the days of Honi the Circle-Drawer, for whenever he came to the Beth Hamidrash he would settle for the scholars any difficulty that they had. Whereupon he called out. I am he; but the scholars would not believe him nor did they give him the honour due to him. This hurt him greatly and he prayed [for death] and he died. Raba said: Hence the saying, Either companionship or death.

TAANITH 23

Honi ha-Maagal read the verse [Psalm 126:1]: "A Song of Ascents. When the Lord brought back those that returned to Zion, we were like unto them that dream." He said: "Is it possible that seventy years should be like a dream? Has anyone ever slept for seventy years?"

One day on the road he saw a man planting a carob tree. He said to him: "A carob tree brings forth no fruit for seventy years. Are you certain that you will live for seventy years?"

The man replied. "Did I find the world empty? As my fathers have planted for me, I am planting for my children."

Honi ate his food and fell asleep on the very spot where he had beheld the planter. A loose rock covered the sleeping man. Later he awakened and he beheld a man gathering the fruit of the carob tree. He said: "Who planted this tree?"

"My grandfather," answered the man.

Honi then understood that he had slept for seventy years. He went to his home and asked for the son of Honi. He was told that the son of Honi had died and that the grandson was now the owner of the house. He disclosed his identity, but no one believed him. He visited the House of Study and heard them say: "Today we understand that Halakah as if Honi himself were here to explain it to us."

But they also refused to believe him, and Honi prayed God to summon him into His Presence.

TAANIT, 23

R. Hanina ben Dosa was carrying some salt when rain began to fall. He said in prayer: "Everybody feels pleasant, but Hanina does not." The rain halted. Entering his home, he said: "Everybody feels unpleasant except Hanina." The rain came down once more.

R. Hanina entered his home and discovered his daughter in tears. By mistake she had poured vinegar into the lamp on Sabbath eve. He declared: "May He Who commanded the oil to burn, command also the vinegar to burn." The vinegar burned all day until after Habdalah.

People came to R. Hanina and said: "Your goats are doing damage."

He replied: "If my goats are causing damage, may they be eaten by wolves! If not, may each one bring in a wolf on his horns."

Each goat brought in a wolf.

Once a man left some hens at R. Hanina's door. He set them on their eggs, and, when he had too many chicks, he sold them and purchased goats. When, after considerable time had passed, a man informed him that he had left some hens with him by mistake, R. Hanina gave him the goats. These were the goats who brought in the wolves.

TAANIT, 24

ACT. 28:
1-6

Our Rabbis taught: In a certain place there was once a lizard which used to injure people. They came and told R. Hanina b. Dosa. He said to them: Show me its hole. They showed him its hole, and he put his heel over the hole, and the lizard came out and bit him, and it died. He put it on his shoulder and brought it to the Beth ha-Midrash and said to them: See, my sons, it is not the lizard that kills, it is sin that kills! On that occasion they said: Woe to the man whom a lizard meets, but woe to the lizard which R. Hanina b. Dosa meets!

BERAKOTH 33

MT. 8:
5-10

JN. 4:
46-54

Our Rabbis taught: Once the son of R. Gamaliel fell ill. He sent two scholars to R. Hanina b. Dosa to ask him to pray for him. When he saw them he went to an upper chamber and prayed for him. When he came down he said to them: Go, the fever has left him; They said to him: Are you a prophet? He replied: I am neither a prophet nor the son of a prophet, but I learnt this from experience. If my prayer is fluent in my mouth, I know that he is accepted: but if not, I know that he is rejected. They sat down and made a note of the exact moment. When they came to R. Gamaliel, he said to them: By the temple service! You have not been a moment too soon or too late, but so it happened: at that very moment the fever left him and he asked for water to drink.

On another occasion it happened that R. Hanina b. Dosa went to study Torah with R. Johanan ben Zakkai. The son of R. Johanan ben Zakkai fell ill. He said to him: Hanina my son, pray for him that he may live. He put his head between his knees and prayed for him and he lived. Said R. Johanan ben Zakkai: If Ben Zakkai had stuck his head between his knees for the whole day, no notice would have been taken of him. Said his wife to him: Is Hanina greater than you are? He replied to her: No; but he is like a servant before the king, and I am like a nobleman before a king.

R. Hiyya b. Abba said in the name of R. Johanan: A man should not pray save in a room which has windows, since it says, *Now his windows were open in his upper chamber towards Jerusalem.*

R. Kahana said: I consider a man impertinent who prays in a valley. R. Kahana also said: I consider a man impertinent who openly recounts his sins, since it is said, *Happy is he whose transgression is forgiven, whose sin is covered.*

BERAKOTH 34

PHILOSTRATUS: APOLLONIUS OF TYANA

VOL. II CH. XXXVIII

DAMIS says then that though Apollonius uttered many more discourses of the same kind, he was himself in despair of the situation, because he saw no way out of it except such as the gods have vouchsafed to some in answer to prayer, when they were in even worse straits. But a little before mid-day, he tells us that he said: "O man of Tyana,"— for he took a special pleasure, it appears, in being called by that name,—"what is to become of us?" "Why what has become of us already," Apollonius, "and nothing more, for no one is going to kill us." "And who," said Damis "is so invulnerable as that? But will you ever be liberated?" "So far as it rests with the verdict of the court," said Apollonius, "I shall be my own will, now and here." And with these words he took his leg out of the fetters and remarked to Damis: "Here is proof positive to you of my freedom, so cheer up." Damis says that it was then for the first time that he really and truly understood the nature of Apollonius, to wit that it was divine and superhuman, for without any sacrifice,—and how in prison could he have offered any?—and without a single prayer, without even a word, he quietly laughed at the fetters, and then inserted his leg in them afresh, and behaved like a prisoner once more.

PARABLES

Although the term *parable* is often used to translate the Semitic *mashal*, which can also mean "enigma," "riddle," or "obscure saying," as a brief narrative it functions as an extended metaphor and is a common feature in the rabbinic as well as the gospel tradition. Both have their antecedents in such Jewish traditions as the Parable of the Ewe Lamb (2 Samuel 12), by which the prophet Nathan rebukes David for stealing another man's wife, Bathsheba, or in the Song of the Vineyard (Isaiah. 5), in which the prophet announces God's intention to judge His disobedient people. On the whole, the parables of the rabbis are more direct in their point and less ambiguous than the parables preserved in the Jesus tradition; further, the rabbinic parables usually include an explanation, while in the gospel tradition the explanations are allegorical in nature (each point of the story has a counterpart in the explanation) and have almost certainly been added by the early church. Thus the Parable of the Sower (Mark 4:3–8) was intended as an encouragement to the early preachers of the gospel, and the Allegory of the Soils (Mark 4:13–20) is more of a warning to the hearers of that message. But among the rabbis, parable and explanation are directly linked. Some typical examples are given:

HOLD ON TO THE LIFELINE

When a passenger on the deck of a ship falls into the sea, the captain throws to him a line, crying, "Grasp it firmly and slacken not thy hold upon it at the peril of thy life!"

By the same token, amid the troubled seas of his earthly voyage, man should cling to the precepts of Torah and thereby remain attached to God. For thus he may truly live.

TANHUMA BUBER TO NUMBERS

CREDENTIALS AND CREDIBILITY

Rabbi Hananiah said: "The Sages are of greater importance than the prophets. It is like a king who sent ambassadors to a province. Concerning one, he sent word that he was not to be trusted without credentials, whereas the other was to be accredited without a token. Who was the greater?

MK. 8:12   "With respect to a prophet, God says: 'He giveth thee a sign or a
LK. 11:   token [Deut. 13:2].' "
29

"With respect to the Sages or Elders, God declares: 'According to the decision which they may say unto thee shalt thou do; thou shalt not depart from the sentence which they may tell thee, to the right or to the left [Deut. 17:11].' "

Y BERAKOT 1.5

THE FOXES AND THE FISHES

Papus ben Judah one day found Rabbi Akiba teaching the Torah in public, though this was prohibited by the Roman government.

"Art thou not afraid of the government?" inquired Papus.

"I will tell you a parable," replied the Rabbi. "Once while walking beside the river, a fox saw some fishes darting distractedly to and fro in the stream. 'From what, pray, are you fleeing?' the fox inquired.

"From the nets," they replied.

"Why, then," rejoined the fox, "do you not try the dry land with me, where you and I can live together?"

"Surely," exclaimed the fishes, "thou art not he of whom we have heard so much as the most cunning of animals. If we have cause to fear where it is natural for us to live, how much more reason have we to do so where we needs must die!"

"Just so," continued Akiba, "is it with us who study the Torah, in which it is written: 'For that is thy life, and the length of thy days [Deut 30:20]'; for, if we suffer while we study the Torah, how much more will we suffer if we neglect it!"

BERAKOT 61B

HELLENISTIC ETHICAL AND PHILOSOPHICAL TEXTS

Among Jews influenced by the synthesis of Platonic metaphysics, stoic ethics, and neo-Pythagorean speculation about numbers, Philo of Alexandria left the most extensive heritage (see his allegorical interpretation of the Cherubim on pp. 144–146. To a lesser extent, the Wisdom of Solomon shows kinship with the hybrid philosophy of the late hellenistic age. But as Christianity spread, it had to come to terms with lofty ethical notions and profound theorizing about the nature of things as these ideas were expressed by the great Greek philosophers and popularized by their followers and by epitomists who published in capsule form the teachings of others. One such prolific writer was Diogenes Laertius (3rd cent. A.D.) "lives" of philosophers included stories about and teachings of Zeno (b. 488 B.C.?), the founder of Stoicism, Socrates (469–399 B.C.), teacher of Plato, and Diogenes of Sinope (412–323 B.C.), a leading figure among the Cynics.* Both the content of their teaching and the style in which Diogenes Laertius describes their careers influenced the ways in which Christianity sought to communicate the life and meaning of Jesus and the apostles to prospective converts in the Roman world.

On the ethical side, the later Stoics, of whom Epictetus (b. 50 A.D.?) became a major figure, influenced Paul and his followers in the church in shaping new ethical perspectives for the nascent religion, Christianity. Especially noteworthy is the fact that Epictetus, though a man concerned about the practical affairs of life, approached everything with a mood of gratitude and devotion that was not incompatible with Christian views.

Diogenes Laertius: Zeno

An animal's first impulse, say the Stoics, is to self-preservation, because nature from the outset endears it to itself, as Chrysippus affirms in the first book of his work *On Ends*: his words are, "The dearest thing to every animal is its own constitution and its consciousness thereof"; for it was not likely that nature should estrange the living thing from itself or that she should leave the creature she has made without either estrangement from or affection for its own constitution. We are forced then to conclude that nature in constituting the animal

---

*Excerpts from Diogenes Laertius on Diogenes of Sinope and Socrates are given in the section on "Lives," pp. 212–16.

made it near and dear to itself; for so it comes to repel all that is injurious and give free access to all that is serviceable or akin to it.

As for the assertion made by some people that pleasure is the object to which the first impulse of animals is directed, it is shown by the Stoics to be false. For pleasure, if it is really felt, they declare to be a by-product, which never comes until nature by itself has sought and found the means suitable to the animal's existence or constitution; it is an aftermath comparable to the condition of animals thriving and plants in full bloom. And nature, they say, made no difference originally between plants and animals, for she regulates the life of plants too, in their case without impulse and sensation, just as also certain processes go on of a vegetative kind in us. But when in the case of animals impulse has been superadded, whereby they are enabled to go in quest of their proper aliment, for them, say the Stoics, Nature's rule is to follow the direction of impulse. But when reason by way of a more perfect leadership has been bestowed on the beings we call rational, for them life according to reason rightly becomes the natural life. For reason supervenes to shape impulse scientifically.

This is why Zeno was the first (in his treatise *On the Nature of Man*) to designate as the end "life in agreement with nature" (or living agreeably to nature), which is the same as a virtuous life, virtue being the goal towards which nature guides us. So too Cleanthes in his treatise *On Pleasure*, as also Posidonius, and Hecato in his work *On Ends*. Again, living virtuously is equivalent to living in accordance with experience of the actual course of nature, as Chrysippus says in the first book of his *De finibus*; for our individual natures are parts of the nature of the whole universe. And this is why the end may be defined as life in accordance with nature, or, in other words, in accordance with our own human nature as well as that of the universe,

ROM. 2:
14-15

a life in which we refrain from every action forbidden by the law common to all things, that is to say, the right reason which pervades all things, and is identical with this Zeus, lord and ruler of all that is. And this very thing constitutes the virtue of the happy man and the smooth current of life, when all actions promote the harmony of the spirit dwelling in the individual man with the will of him who orders the universe. Diogenes then expressly declares the end to be to act with good reason in the selection of what is natural. Archedemus says the end is to live in the performance of all befitting actions.

By the nature with which our life ought to be in accord, Chrysippus understands both universal nature and more particularly the nature of man, whereas Cleanthes takes the nature of the universe alone as that which should be followed, without adding the nature of the individual.

And virtue, he holds, is a harmonious disposition, choice-worthy for its own sake and not from hope or fear or any external motive. Moreover, it is in virtue that happiness consists; for virtue is the state of mind which tends to make the whole of life harmonious. When a

GAL. 5:
22-23

rational being is perverted, this is due to the deceptiveness of external pursuits or sometimes to the influence of associates. For the starting-points or nature are never perverse.

.   .   .

Amongst the virtues some are primary, some are subordinate to these. The following are the primary: wisdom, courage, justice, temperance. Particular virtues are magnanimity, continence, endurance, presence of mind, good counsel. And wisdom they define as the knowledge of things good and evil and of what is neither good nor evil; courage as knowledge of what we ought to choose, what we ought to beware of, and what is indifferent; justice . . . ; magnanimity as the knowledge or habit of mind which makes one superior to anything that happens, whether good or evil equally; continence as a disposition never overcome in that which concerns right reason, or a habit which no pleasures can get the better of; endurance as a knowledge or habit prompt to find out what is meet to be done at any moment; good counsel as knowledge by which we see what to do and how to do it if we would consult our own interests.

Similarly, of vices some are primary, others subordinate: e.g. folly, cowardice, injustice, profligacy are accounted primary; but incontinence, stupidity, ill-advisedness subordinate. Further, they hold that the vices are forms of ignorance of those things whereof the corresponding virtues are the knowledge.

GAL. 5: 19-21

Good in general is that from which some advantage comes, and more particularly what is either identical with or not distinct from benefit. Whence it follows that virtue itself and whatever partakes of virtue is called good in these three senses—viz. as being (1) the source from which benefit results; or (2) that in respect of which benefit results, e.g. the virtuous act; or (3) that by the agency of which benefit results, e.g. the good man who partakes in virtue.

Another particular definition of good which they give is "the natural perfection of a rational being *qua* rational." To this answers virtue and, as being partakers in virtue, virtuous acts and good men; as also its supervening accessories, joy and gladness and the like. So with evils: either they are vices, folly, cowardice, injustice, and the like; or things which partake of vice, including vicious acts and wicked persons as well as their accompaniments, despair, moroseness, and the like.

Again, some goods are goods of the mind and others external, while some are neither mental nor external. The former include the virtues and virtuous acts; external goods are such as having a good country or a good friend, and the prosperity of such. Whereas to be good and happy oneself is of the class of goods neither mental nor external. Similarly of things evil some are mental evils, namely, vices and vicious actions; others are outward evils, as to have a foolish country or a foolish friend and the unhappiness of such; other evils again are neither mental nor outward, e.g. to be yourself bad and unhappy.

ROM. 1: 18-21

Again, goods are either of the nature of ends or they are the means to these ends, or they are at the same time end and means. A friend and the advantages derived from him are means to good, whereas confidence, high-spirit, liberty, delight, gladness, freedom from pain, and every virtuous act are of the nature of ends.

All good (they say) is expedient, binding, profitable, useful, serviceable, beautiful, beneficial, desirable, and just or right. It is expedient, because it brings about things of such a kind that by their occurrence

PHIL. 4: 8-9

EPH. 4:3

we are benefited. It is binding, because it causes unity where unity is needed; profitable, because it defrays what is expended on the transaction. It is useful, because it secures the use of benefit; it is serviceable, because the utility it affords is worthy of all praise. It is beautiful, because the good is proportionate to the use made of it; beneficial, because by its inherent nature it benefits; choiceworthy, because it is such that to choose it is reasonable. It is also just or right, inasmuch as it is in harmony with law and tends to draw men together.

I COR.
12:11-12

.   .   .

Goods comprise the virtues of prudence, justice, courage, temperance, and the rest; while the opposites of these are evils, namely, folly, injustice, and the rest. Neutral (neither good nor evil, that is) are all those things which neither benefit nor harm a man: such as life, health, pleasure, beauty, strength, wealth, fair fame and noble birth, and their opposites, death, disease, pain, ugliness, weakness, poverty, ignominy, low birth, and the like.

The main, or most universal, emotions, according to Hecato in his treatise *On the Passions*, book ii., and Zeno in his treatise with the same title, constitute four great classes, grief, fear, desire or craving, pleasure. They hold the emotions to be judgements, as is stated by Chrysippus in his treatise *On the Passions*: avarice being a supposition that money is a good, while the case is similar with drunkenness and profligacy and all the other emotions.

And grief or pain they hold to be an irrational mental contraction. Its species are pity, envy, jealousy, rivalry, heaviness, annoyance, distress, anguish, distraction. Pity is a grief felt at undeserved suffering; envy, grief at others' prosperity; jealousy, grief at the possession by another of that which one desires for oneself; rivalry, pain at the possession by another of what one has oneself. Heaviness or vexation is grief which weighs us down, annoyance that which coops us up and straitens us for want of room, distress a pain brought on by anxious thought that lasts and increases, anguish painful grief, distraction irrational grief, rasping and hindering us from viewing the situation as a whole.

Fear is an expectation of evil. Under fear are ranged the following emotions: terror, nervous shrinking, shame, consternation, panic, mental agony. Terror is a fear which produces fright; shame is fear of disgrace; nervous shrinking is a fear that one will have to act; consternation is fear due to a presentation of some unusual occurrence; panic is fear with pressure exercised by sound; mental agony is fear when some issue is still in suspense.

I JN. 4:
18

Desire or craving is irrational appetency, and under it are ranged the following states: want, hatred, contentiousness, anger, love, wrath, resentment. Want, then, is a craving when it is balked and, as it were, cut off from its object, but kept at full stretch and attracted towards it in vain. Hatred is a growing and lasting desire or craving that it should go ill with somebody. Contentiousness is a craving or desire connected with partisanship; anger a craving or desire to punish one

ROM. 1:
24-32

who is thought to have done you an undeserved injury. The passion of love is a craving from which good men are free; for it is an effort to win affection due to the visible presence of beauty. Wrath is anger which has long rankled and has become malicious, waiting for its opportunity. . . .

I COR. 13:1–14:1

Now they say that the wise man is passionless, because he is not prone to fall into such infirmity. But they add that in another sense the term apathy is applied to the bad man, when, that is, it means that he is callous and relentless. Further, the wise man is said to be free from vanity; for he is indifferent to good or evil report. However, he is not alone in this, there being another who is also free from vanity, he who is ranged among the rash, and that is the bad man. Again, they tell us that all good men are austere or harsh, because they neither have dealings with pleasure themselves nor tolerate those who have. The term harsh is applied, however, to others as well, and in much the same sense as a wine is said to be harsh when it is employed medicinally and not for drinking at all.

I TIM. 5: 23

Again, the good are genuinely in earnest and vigilant for their own improvement, using a manner of life which banishes evil out of sight and makes what good there is in things appear. At the same time they are free from pretence; for they have stripped off all pretence or "make-up" whether in voice or in look. Free too are they from all business cares, declining to do anything which conflicts with duty. They will take wine, but not get drunk. Nay more, they will not be liable to madness either; not but what there will at times occur to the good man strange impressions due to melancholy or delirium, ideas not determined by the principle of what is choiceworthy but contrary to nature. Nor indeed will the wise man ever feel grief; seeing that grief is irrational contraction of the soul, as Apollodorus says in his *Ethics*.

EPH. 5: 18

They are also, it is declared, godlike; for they have a something divine within them; whereas the bad man is godless. And yet of this word—godless or ungodly—there are two senses, one in which it is the opposite of the term "godly," the other denoting the man who ignores the divine altogether: in this latter sense, as they note, the term does not apply to every bad man. The good, it is added, are also worshippers of God; for they have acquaintance with the rites of the gods, and piety is the knowledge of how to serve the gods. Further, they will sacrifice to the gods and they keep themselves pure; for they avoid all acts that are offences against the gods, and the gods think highly of them: for they are holy and just in what concerns the gods. The wise too are the only priests; for they have made sacrifices their study, as also the building of temples, purifications, and all the other matters appertaining to the gods.

I PET. 1: 3–4

.   .   .

The doctrine that the world is a living being, rational, animate and intelligent, is laid down by Chrysippus in the first book of his treatise *On Providence*, by Apollodorus in his *Physics*, and by Posidonius. It is a living thing in the sense of an animate substance endowed with sensation; for animal is better than non-animal, and nothing is better than the world, *ergo* the world is a living being. And it is endowed with soul, as is clear from our several souls being each a fragment of it.

Epictetus

Come, let us leave the chief works of nature, and consider merely what she does in passing. Can anything be more useless than the hairs on a chin? Well, what then? Has not nature used even these in the most suitable way possible? Has she not by these means distinguished between the male and the female? Does not the nature of each one among us cry aloud forthwith from afar, "I am a man; on this understanding approach me, on this understanding talk with me; ask for nothing further; behold the signs"? Again, in the case of women, just as nature has mingled in their voice a certain softer note, so likewise she has taken the hair from their chins. Not so, you say; on the contrary the human animal ought to have been left without distinguishing features, and each of us ought to proclaim by word of mouth, "I am a man." Nay, but how fair and becoming and dignified the sign is! How much more fair than the cock's comb, how much more magnificent than the lion's mane! Wherefore, we ought to preserve the signs which God has given; we ought not to throw them away; we ought not, so far as in us lies, to confuse the sexes which have been distinguished in this fashion.

Are these the only works of Providence in us? Nay, what language is adequate to praise them all or bring them home to our minds as they deserve? Why, if we had sense, ought we to be doing anything else, publicly and privately, than hymning and praising the Deity, and rehearsing His benefits? Ought we not, as we dig and plough and eat, to sing the hymn of praise to God? "Great is God, that He hath furnished us these instruments wherewith we shall till the earth. Great is God, that He hath given us hands, and power to swallow, and a belly, and power to grow unconsciously, and to breathe while asleep." This is what we ought to sing on every occasion, and above all to sing the greatest and divinest hymn, that God has given us the faculty to comprehend these things and to follow the path of reason. What then? Since most of you have become blind, ought there not to be someone to fulfil this office for you, and in behalf of all sing the hymn of praise to God? Why, what else can I, a lame old man, do but sing hymns to God? If, indeed, I were a nightingale, I should be singing as a nightingale; if a swan, as a swan. But as it is, I am a rational being, therefore I must be singing hymns of praise to God. This is my task; I do it, and will not desert this post, as long as it may be given me to fill it; and I exhort you to join me in this same song.

Do but keep in remembrance your general principles: "What is mine? What is not mine? What has been given me? What does God will that I do now, what does He not will?" A little while ago it was His will for you to be at leisure, to converse with yourself, to write about these things, to read, to listen, to prepare yourself; you had time sufficient for that. Now God says to you, "Come at length to the contest, show us what you have learned, how you have trained yourself. How long will you exercise alone? Now the time has come for you to discover whether you are one of the athletes who deserve victory, or belong to the number of those who travel about the world and are everywhere defeated." Why, then, are you discontented? No contest is held without turmoil. There must be many training-partners, many to shout applause, many officials, many spectators.—But I wanted to live a life of peace.—Wail, then, and groan, as you deserve to do. For what greater penalty can befall the man who is uninstructed and disobedient to the divine injunctions than to grieve, to sorrow, to envy, in a word to have no good fortune but only misfortune? Do you not wish to free yourself from all this?

And how shall I free myself?—Have you not heard over and over again that you ought to eradicate desire utterly, direct your aversion towards the things that lie within the sphere of the moral purpose, and these things only, that you ought to give up everything, your body, your property, your reputation, your books, turmoil, office, freedom from office? For if once you swerve aside from this course, you are a slave, you are a subject, you have become liable to hindrance and to compulsion, you are entirely under the control of others. Nay, the word of Cleanthes is ready at hand, GAL. 5:1

I COR. 9: 19

ROM. 8: 2

Lead thou me on, O Zeus, and Destiny.

Will ye have me go to Rome? I go to Rome. To Gyara? I go to Gyara. To Athens? I go to Athens. To prison? I go to prison. If but once you say, "Oh, when may a man go to Athens" you are lost. This wish, if unfulfilled, must necessarily make you unfortunate; if fulfilled, vain and puffed up over the wrong kind of thing; again, if you are hindered, you suffer a misfortune, falling into what you do not wish. Give up, then, all these things. "Athens is beautiful." But happiness is much more beautiful, tranquility, freedom from turmoil, having your own affairs under no man's control. "There is turmoil in Rome, and salutations." But serenity is worth all the annoyances. If, then, the time for these things has come, why not get rid of your aversion for them? Why must your needs bear burdens like a belabored donkey? Otherwise, I would have you see that you must be ever the slave of the man who is able to secure your release, to the man who is able to hinder you in everything, and you must serve him as an Evil Genius.

There is but one way to serenity (keep this thought ready for use at dawn, and by day, and at night), and that is to yield up all claim to the things that lie outside the sphere of the moral purpose, to regard nothing as your own possession; to surrender everything to the Deity, to Fortune; to yield everything to the supervision of those persons whom even Zeus has made supervisors; and to devote yourself to one thing only, that which is your own, that which is free from hindrance, and to read referring your reading to this end, and so to write and so to listen. That is why I cannot yet say that the man is industrious, until I know for what end he does so. For neither do you call a man ROM. 6: 15-19 industrious who loses sleep for the sake of a wench; no more do I. But if he acts this way for the sake of reputation, I call him ambitious; if for the sake of money, I call him fond of money, not fond of toil. If, however, the end for which he toils is his own governing principle, to have it be, and live continually, in accordance with nature, then and then only I call him industrious. For I would not have you men ever either praise or blame a man for things that may be either good or bad, but only for judgements. Because these are each man's own possessions, which make his actions either base or noble. Bearing all this in mind, rejoice in what you have and be satisfied with what the moment brings. If you see any of the things that you have learned and studied thoroughly coming to fruition for you in action, rejoice in these things. If you have put away or reduced a malignant disposition, and reviling, or impertinence, or foul language, or recklessness, or negligence; if you are not moved by the things that once moved you, or at least not to the same degree, then you can keep festival day after day; to-day because you behaved well in this action, to-morrow because you behaved well in another. How much greater cause for thanksgiving is this than a consulship or a governorship! These things come to you from your own self and from the gods. Remember who

II COR.
3:17

the Giver is, and to whom He gives, and for what end. If you are brought up in reasonings such as these, can you any longer raise the questions where you are going to be happy, and where you will please God? Are not men everywhere equally distant from God? Do they not everywhere have the same view of what comes to pass?

REVELATORY AND GNOSTIC TEXTS

The hellenistic drive to impose a single graecized culture on the world, combined with the Roman determination to bring it all under the dominance of Roman political power, proved to be profoundly disturbing to many people. Their old sense of local identity and of the continuity of local customs was shattered. The movement of life was no longer calculable, and submission to what was for many the alien forces of the hellenistic rulers and then of Rome seemed inevitable. The traditional religions were discredited because of their impotence in preserving the old ways.

In such a mood of uncertainty and insecurity, men turned to religious systems that claimed to have access to a truth that transcended time and space, and that guaranteed for its adherents participation in life beyond the material world and beyond death. The texts of these quasi-philosophical movements or religious groups have survived only in the later forms that they achieved in the second century A.D. and after. The intermediaries through whom the special revelation was believed to have come varied from group to group. Among the best known were Hermes, Solomon, and, in the avowedly Christian groups, Thomas the apostle.

Hermetica

In hellenistic times, the Egyptian god Thoth, whose roles were scribe of the gods and god of wisdom, was identified by the Greeks with Hermes, messenger of the Olympian gods of Greece. With the honorific title Trismegistos (thrice great), Hermes was the figure around whom there developed a vast body of writings known as the Hermetica. The oldest stratum, which can be traced back to the second century B.C., is astrological, the product of the combination of Babylonian astral observations and Greek skill in systematizing. But on the astrological base there was erected a great complex of (1) scientific knowledge about the properties—medicinal and otherwise—of plants and minerals, (2) cosmogonic speculation, and (3) mystical philosophy. The whole was presented as divine revelation mediated by Thoth (Hermes); it provided for those who were given access to this wisdom a sense of intimacy with the gods and a hope of eternal life. This material became the basis of further speculation of a popular philosophical sort, in which the gods function allegorically as symbols of the Divine Mind or other cosmic principles.

From this philosophizing stage of the development of the hermetic literature, the oldest datable evidence goes back to the first half of the second century A.D. Here the Egyptian base is almost entirely missing.

> The ideas are those of popular Greek philosophical thought, in a highly eclectic form, with a mixture of Platonism, Aristotelianism, and Stoicism, which was then greatly elaborated; here and there are traces of Judaism, and probably also a religious literature, the ultimate source of which is Iran. By contrast, there is no evidence of influence from Christianity or of neo-Platonism.

The question has sometimes been raised whether there was a hermetic religion, perhaps with cells of hermetics. There is evidence of a hermetic life-style, of a sacred literature, of a desire for separation from the world, of an appeal to those not yet converted to associate themselves with "the Way." But there are no ceremonial purifications and no practices to induce the epiphany of the god, so that hermeticism is not a mystery cult, but a mystery of the Word. Lacking originality, hermeticism is rather a mosaic of ancient ideas, often formulated by way of brief allusions, as would be the custom in a small in-group. The writings are as short on logic as they are on classical purity of language. A philosopher of the time would have been puzzled by the mechanical and incoherent way in which they were used. "Their popular appeal, in keeping with the spirit of the time in which they developed their present form (*i.e.*, second century A.D.), was based on the desire for an assured divine revelation, a fondness for the esoteric and the abstract, and a concern for the soul and its salvation. In these writings, man saw himself as in a mirror darkly, but even this dim self-vision enabled him to gain a sense of significance which separated him from the mass of the unenlightened and guaranteed his future."＊

CORPUS HERMETICUM: POIMANDRES

(1) One day, as I began to reflect on things that are,[1] my mind having been completely transported so that my bodily senses were in a trance as though I had been overcome by a surfeit of food or severe bodily fatigue, it seemed to me that there presented itself to me a being of such size as to be beyond measuring, calling me by name and saying: "What do you want to hear and perceive, and as you meditate, to learn and know?"

(2) And I said, "But indeed, who are you?"

"I am," he said, "Poimandres,[2] the Mind[3] of the One who is absolute. I know what you desire, and I am with you everywhere."

(3) I said, "I want to learn the things that are and to meditate upon their nature and to know God. O, how I want to hear!" I said. And he began to say to me, "Hold in your mind the things which you want to learn, and I shall teach you myself."

(4) When he had said this, he changed his appearance, and immediately all things opened before me in an instant, and I saw a limitless vision. All things became light, calm and joyous, and when I had seen, I was filled with love. And after a while there was darkness inclining downward which kept coming for a time, fearful and stygian, coiled about tortuously like a snake, as it seemed to me. Then the darkness was transformed into a sort of humid nature, unspeakably roiled, giving off a smoke as from a fire, and producing a sound, an unutterable wailing. Then it sent forth a cry inarticulately from within, as might be compared with the voice of a fire.

JN. 1:14   (5) And from this light the holy Word entered into nature, and an unmingled fire leapt forth from the humid nature up to the uppermost

---

＊This introduction is a translation and condensation by H. C. Kee of A. D. Nock's preface to *Corpus Hermeticum: Hermès Trismégiste*, Vol. I.: *Poimandrès et Traités II–XII*. Text established by A. D. Nock; translated into French by A.-J. Festugière. Paris: Société d'Édition "Les Belles Lettres," 1945, pp. i–vii.

[1]*That are*—The Hermetic literature preserves the classical philosophical distinction between being and becoming, so that the writer here contrasts the unchanging world of "being" with the ever-changing realm around and within that has no fixed state but is always "becoming" something different. Throughout the translation, "the things that are" refers to those persons or things that possess the true, immutable being.

[2]*Poimandres*, usually understood to mean "shepherd of men" (as though from *poimēn andres*), although other conjectural meanings based on Egyptian etymology have been advanced.

[3]*Mind* is here the translation for *nous*.

region. It was quick and keen and efficacious, and since the air was light, it followed the spirit,[4] mounting up to it to the fire from the earth and the water, so that it seemed to be suspended from the fire. The earth and the water remained by themselves unmixed, if one did not look at the earth from the water. And as they were being moved, through the Word[5] that was being borne along by the spirit they came to be heard. JN. 1:34

(6) Poimandres said to me, "Have you understood what this vision means?" And is said, "I shall know." "That light," he said, "is I, Mind, your God, who existed before the humid nature appeared out of the darkness. The luminous Word which proceeds from the darkness is the Son of God."[6] JN. 1:5 JN. 1:18

"What else?" said I.

"In this way know that what you see in yourself and hear is the Word of the Lord; the Mind is God the Father. They are not separable one from the other, for their unity is Life." JN. 8:12, 28, 47

"I give you thanks," said I.

"But mediate on the light and you shall know it."

(7) As he said these things, he remained facing me for a long time, so that I trembled at his appearance. And as he looked up, I saw in my mind the light which exists in the innumerable Powers and it became a cosmos[7] without limits, and the fire was overwhelmed by a great force; yet being overpowered, maintained stability. This I perceived in the things that I saw by the aid of Poimandres' Word.

(8) And as I was in a trance, he said again to me, "You saw in the Mind the archetypal form, the principle which is prior to the infinite beginning." Thus Poimandres spoke to me. I said, "These elemental realities, from whence do they exist?" And he replied to this, "By the will of God, which upon receiving the Word and beholding the good cosmos, imitates it, being fashioned as a cosmos by means of its own elemental realities and generative souls. JN. 1:1-3

(9) And the Mind of God, being bisexual, existing as Light and Life, engenders by the Word a second Mind, the Demiurge, who as God of fire and spirit fashions seven Agents, which encompass in their circles the sensible world, and their administration is called Destiny." JN. 1:4

[There follows a long passage of instructions about the nature of man; then Poimandres turns again to the subject of human destiny.]

---

[4]*Spirit* or *wind*, translating *pneuma*.

[5]*Word* here translates *logos*, the technical term for reason in Stoic philosophy, and the designation in the Gospel of John for the creative-redemptive agent of God (John 1).

[6]There is no clear evidence of Christian influence on the Hermetic literature, so that the use of such terms as "son of God" that are also found in the Christian tradition are probably to be accounted for as parallel developments out of the Jewish tradition.

[7]The Greek term is here simply transliterated into English, *cosmos*, on the assumption that it more accurately suggests the complex of the created universe than does the word "world," which can refer to the planet, or to the world-order.

(19) "[God] having thus spoken, Providence created sexual intercourse and established the generative actions, and caused all things to multiply according to their kind,[8] both those who through full self-knowledge come to abundant good, and those who, since they love the body because of erotic error, remain wandering in the darkness, suffering in their senses the things of death."

(20) "What sort of sin have the unknowing ones committed," I said, "that they should thus be denied immortality?"

"You who speak thus are like someone who did not reflect on what he saw and heard. Did I not tell you to meditate?"

"I meditate and I recall, and I give you thanks."

"If you meditate, who do you ask me why those who are worthy of death are in fact in death?"

"Because stygian darkness is the place of origin of the individual body, from it comes the humid nature, and from this nature the body subsists in the sensible world, and from the world flows forth death."

(21) "You have understood rightly, O man. But why does the Word of God say, 'The One who understands himself departs to himself?' "[9]

"Because," said I, "the Father of Totality exists out of Light and Life, and from Him man came into being."

JN. 1: 9-13 "You spoke well when you said that God the Father is Light and Life, and that from Him came man. If you learn that you are of Life and Light, and that you are constituted by these, you will return again into Life."

[Following a discourse on the nature of divine grace, Poimandres continues his description of the destiny of man.]

(24) Poimandres said, "First, by the dissolution of the material body, the body itself will be delivered up to transformation, and the appearance which it now has will become incapable of being perceived; your customary practices will no longer be performed, and the bodily senses will mount up to their sources, becoming part of and commingled with the Powers. And envy and desire will return to the irrational nature.[10]

JN. 6:62 (25) And finally man will thus fly up through the harmonious spheres:[11] in the first zone he will yield up the power of growth and diminution; in the second he will abandon the strategems of evil, so that deceit will no longer be operative; in the third the deceitfulness of desire will become inoperative; in the fourth the display of power will cease to exert itself; in the fifth, impious audacity will abandon its aggressive

---

[8]This sounds like an echo of the creation stories of Genesis 1 and 3.

[9]It is never clear in the Hermetic literature whether salvation is thought to take place in a heavenly realm or in the inner recesses of the human spirit. Using contemporary terminology, we might say that the Hermetic outlook is as much psychological as it is cosmological or theological.

[10]The nature that produced them.

[11]The so-called Ptolemaic set of successively larger spheres which were thought to surround the earth. Through them the soul must pass in order to reach the divine realities beyond the material world.

ways; in the sixth, evil schemes for gaining riches will be rendered powerless; and in the seventh zone, man will abandon ensnaring falsehood. And then, being stripped bare by the energies which are in the seven spheres, he will gain the ogdoadic nature,[12] possessing his own power, and he will sing praises to the Father with those who are.[13] Those who are shall rejoice together at his arrival, and when he has become like the other beings that are there, he shall hear also certain Powers which control the ogdoadic nature as they with sweet voices sing praise to God. And these shall then ascend to the Father, rank by rank, and they shall give themselves over to the Powers, and having become Powers, they shall become God. This is the good goal for those who possess knowledge: to be divinized. Finally, who do you hesitate? By my teaching you all things, have you not become a guide to those who are worthy, so that through you the human race might be saved by God?[14]

JN. 14:2

TRACTATE 9 OF THE CORPUS HERMETICUM,
CONCERNING SENSE AND PERCEPTION

The following excerpt is of special interest because it deals with the problem of the origins of evil, and manifests a dualistic outlook that attributes evil to the demonic powers.

(3) For Mind begets all concepts: good concepts, when it receives the seed from God; the contrary, when the seed comes from the demon. There is no part of the cosmos which is devoid of demons. ... The demon, by sneaking in, implants the seed of his power, and mind bears what has been implanted: adultery, murder, disrespect for parents, sacrilege, impiety, hanging [oneself] and jumping off a cliff, and all other such work of demons.

JN. 8:
44-47

(4) For the divine seeds are only a few, though they are great and beautiful and good: virtue and discretion and piety. Piety is the knowledge of God. Whoever knows Him has become full of all good things and thus is capable of divine perceptions, unlike the majority of people. On this account, those who are in the know are not pleasing to the majority, nor is the majority pleasing to them. They seem [to the majority] to be demented and are subjected to scorn; they are hated and treated with contempt and at times murdered. As I have said, evil ought to dwell here below in its own realm, for its realm is the earth, not the cosmos, as certain blasphemers sometimes say. The man of true piety toward God, on the other hand, is sustained in all things, since he is made aware through his knowledge. For to such a man all things are good, even though to others they may be evil. And even when he is conspired against, he elevates all things into the realm of knowledge, and thus from evil brings forth good alone.

I JN. 3:9

JN. 8:
31-32

[12]The eighth and ultimate sphere where Being dwells.
[13]See note 1.
[14]There is an evangelistic zeal evident here which seeks to convince others of the truth and thereby to liberate them from error.

The Odes of Solomon

The date, the provenance, and the original language of the Odes of Solomon cannot be determined with certainty. The two sure facts are that they are pseudonymous and that they were written about one millennium after the time of Solomon (10th century B.C.). It is probable that they were written in Greek somewhere in Syria about the year 100 A.D. But they may have incorporated older Semitic material, and they were very early translated into Syriac. Because the author knew the Jewish Bible in a Greek translation, the biblical idiom that is found throughout the Odes is not a result of awkwardly literal translation that betrays a Semitic original but is a sign of the way biblical modes of expression have shaped his own rhetoric and literary style. They may have been composed by a Jew and subsequently slightly christianized by an interpolator, or perhaps they were written by a Greek-speaking Jewish-Christian. Some scholars think the Odes are the creation of a Gnostic of the second century A.D., and were then utilized and adapted by Christians, and a recent thorough study of the Odes has led to the conclusion that they were written by a former Essene who converted to Christianity, and whose portrayal of Christ as Redeemer-Revealer is therefore strongly colored by imagery and perspectives known from the Qumran documents.[1] But whatever the circumstances of their origin, they are akin to the lengthy and prolix discourses of the Gospel of John, both in style and in the evident belief that truth is communicated to the elect through a revealer figure who has been sent by God (Ode VIII: 8–12).

ODE VIII

(1) Open ye, open ye your hearts to the exultation of the Lord:
And let your love abound from the heart, and even to the lips:
(2) To bring forth fruits to the Lord, a holy life,
And to talk watchfully in His light.
(3) Rise up and stand erect,
Ye who were sometimes brought low;
(4) Ye who were in silence, speak out,
[Now] that your mouth hath been opened.
(5) Ye who were despised, be lifted up;
Now that your righteousness has been lifted up;
(6) For the right hand of the Lord is with you;
And He will be your helper.
(7) And peace hath been prepared for you,
Before ever your war happened.

---

[1] J. H. Charlesworth, "Les Odes de Solomon et les manuscrites de la Mer Morte," Revue Biblique 77 (4), October 1970.

[Christ speaks]

(8) Hear the word of truth,
And receive the knowledge of the Most High
(9) Your flesh does not know what I am saying to you;
Nor your raiment what I am showing to you;
(10) Keep my secret, ye who are kept by it;
(11) Keep my faith, ye who are kept by it.
(12) And understand my knowledge,
Ye who know me in truth:
(13) Love me with affection,
Ye who love:
(14) For I do not turn away my face from them that are mine;
For I know them.
(15) Before they came into being,
I took knowledge of them,
And on their faces I set my seal.
(16) I fashioned their members;
My own breasts I prepared for them;
That they might drink my holy milk and live thereby.
(17) I took pleasure in them,
And I am not ashamed of them.
(18) For my workmanship are they,
And the strength of my thoughts:
(19) Who then shall stand up against my handiwork?
Or who is there that is not subject to them?
(20) I willed, and fashioned mind and heart;
And they are mine.
And by my own right hand I set my elect ones.
(21) And my righteousness goeth before them;
And they shall not be detached from my name:
For it is with them.

[The Odist]

(22) Pray and abide continually in the love of the Lord;
Ye beloved ones, in the Beloved;
And ye who are kept, in Him that lived [again];
And ye that are saved, in Him that was saved.
(23) And ye shall be found incorrupt in all ages,
To the name of your Father.
        Hallelujah.

ODE XII

(1) He hath filled me with words of truth,
That I may speak the same.
(2) And like the flow of waters, flows truth from my mouth,
And my lips showed forth its fruits.
(3) And it has caused its knowledge to abound in me,
Because the mouth of the Lord is the true Word,
And the door of His light;
(4) And the Most High hath given Him to His Worlds.
[Worlds] which are the interpreters of His own beauty,
And the repeaters of His praise,

And the confessors of His thought,
And the heralds of His mind,
And the instructors of His works.
(5) For the swiftness of the Word is inexpressible [?]
And like His expression [?] is His swiftness and His sharpness:
And His course has no limit.
(6) Never [doth the Word] fall, but ever it standeth;
His descent and His way are incomprehensible.
(7) For as His Work is, so is His limit;
For He is the light and the dawn of thought.
(8) And by him the worlds spake one to the other:
And those that were silent acquired speech.
(9) And from Him came love and concord;
And they spake one to the other what they had [to tell].
(10) And they were stimulated by the Word,
And they knew Him that made them.
Because they came into concord.
(11) For the mouth of the Most High spake to them;
And the interpretation of Himself had its course by Him.
(12) For the dwelling-place of the Word is man,
And His truth is love.
(13) Blessed are they who by it have comprehended everything,
And who have known the Lord by His truth.
Hallelujah

ODE XVI

(1) As the work of the husbandman is the ploughshare;
And the work of the steersman is the guidance of the ship:
So also my work is the Psalm of the Lord in His praises;
(2) My craft and my occupation are in His praises;
Because His love hath nourished my heart,
And even to my lips His fruits He poured out.
(3) For my love is the Lord
And therefore I will sing unto Him.
(4) For I am made strong in His praise,
And I have faith in Him.
(5) I will open my mouth,
And His spirit will utter in me
The glory of the Lord and His beauty;
(6) The work of His hands
And the fabric of His fingers;
(7) For the multitude of His mercies,
And the strength of His Word.
(8) For the Word of the Lord searches out the unseen thing,
And scrutinizes His thought.
(9) For the eye sees His works,
And the ear hears His thought.
(10) It is He who spread out the earth,
And settled the waters in the sea:
(11) He expanded the heavens,

And fixed the stars;

(12) And He fixed the creation and set it up:

And He rested from His works.

(13) And created things run in their courses,

And work their works:

And they know not how to stand [still] and to be idle.

(14) And the hosts are subject to His Word.

(15) The treasury of the light is the sun,

And the treasury of the darkness is the night.

(16) And He made the sun for the day that it might be bright;

But night brings darkness over the face of the earth:

(17) And [by] their reception one from the other

They speak the beauty of God.

(18) And there is nothing that is without the Lord;

For He was before anything came into being.

(19) And the Worlds were made by His Word,

And by the thought of His heart.

[Doxology]

(20) Glory and Honour to His name.

Hallelujah.

ODE XXII

(1) He who brings me down from on high;

And brings me up from the regions below;

(2) And who gathers the things that are betwixt,

And throws them to me;

(3) He who scattered my enemies

And my adversaries;

(4) He who gave me authority over bonds,

That I might loose them;

(5) He that overthrew by my hands the dragon with seven heads,

And set me at his roots that I might destroy his seed—

(6) Thou wast there and didst help me;

And in every place thy name was round about me.

(7) Thy right hand destroyed his wicked venom;

And thy hand levelled the way for those who believe in thee;

(8) And it chose them from the graves,

And separated them from the dead.

(9) It took dead bones,

And covered them with bodies;

(10) And they were motionless,

And it gave [them] energy for life.

(11) Thy way was without corruption and thy face;

Thou didst bring thy world to corruption;

That everything might be dissolved and renewed,

(12) And that the foundation for everything might be thy rock;

And on it thou didst build thy Kingdom;

And thou becamest the dwelling-place of the saints.

Hallelujah.

The Gospel of Thomas

Long known only by title from mention in ancient writings and in fragmentary form from ancient quotations, *The Gospel of Thomas* was discovered in a complete Coptic version (a language related to ancient Egyptian, but written for the most part in Greek letters) in upper Egypt in 1945. "Thomas," which seems at first to be the name of the purported writer, is actually a transliteration of the Aramaic word for twin, and is therefore the exact equivalent of the greek, Didymus (twin). The implication is that Judah, or Judas, the brother of Jesus is his twin, and that he has accordingly been granted access to esoteric information which he is now passing on to the readers of his gospel.

The book contains no narrative, no mention of the cross or resurrection, and no account of Jesus' activities, but consists entirely of a string of sayings (logia) joined together, usually by some such simple formula as "And Jesus said. . . ". Some of the logia are close to the sayings of Jesus found in the canonical gospels; some are slight modifications of known sayings; others bear little resemblance to the teachings of Jesus as reported in the four gospels of the New Testament. Similar collections of logia found more than fifty years ago in papyrus manuscripts from Egypt include writings that can now be shown to be copies of or earlier rescensions of the Gospel of Thomas, although in some cases sayings included

A papyrus fragment of a noncanonical gospel, akin to the synoptic gospels, but with traces of influence from the Gospel of John. It seems to be a mixture of oral tradition and imperfectly remembered traces of the canonical gospels. It is written on papyrus, a reed often used in antiquity as a writing material. The coarse fibers are visible in this picture.

in the Gospel of Thomas were probably also incorporated in (or copied from) such apocryphal works as the Gospel of the Hebrews and the Gospel of the Egyptians.

The Gospel of Thomas in the basic form that we now possess it was probably composed about the middle of the second century A.D., although it seems to have been a compilation of several sources or documents. It was written in a Greek-speaking Christian community—possibly in Egypt but more probably in Syria—at first in a more orthodox form, which was then modified by Gnostics in order to serve more effectively their interests. It is the Gnosticized version that is represented by the present Gospel of Thomas which is excerpted here.

The Gospel of Thomas

Here are the secret words which Jesus the Living spoke and which Didymus Jude Thomas wrote down.

And he said: "Whoever penetrates the meaning of these words will not taste death!"

(1) Jesus says: "Let him who seeks cease not to seek until he finds: when he finds he will be astonished; and when he is astonished he will wonder, and will reign over the universe!"

(2) Jesus says: "If those who seek to attract you say to you: 'See, the Kingdom is in heaven!' then the birds of heaven will be there before you. If they say to you: 'It is in the sea!' then the fish will be there before you. But the kingdom is within you and it is outside of you!"

(3) "When you know yourselves, then you will be known, and you will know that it is you who are the sons of the living Father. But if you do not know yourselves, then you will be in a state of poverty, and it is you (who will be) the poverty!"

(4) Jesus says: "Let the old man heavy with days hesitate not to ask the little child of seven days about the place of Life, and he will live! For it will be seen that many of the first will be last, and they will become a (single one!")

(5) Jesus says: "Know what is before your face, and what is hidden from you will be revealed to you. For nothing hidden will fail to be revealed!"

(6) His disciples asked and said to him:" Do you want us to fast? How shall we pray, how shall we give alms, what rules concerning eating shall we follow?" Jesus says: "Tell no lie, and whatever you hate, do not do: for all these things are manifest to the face of heaven; nothing hidden will fail to be revealed, and nothing disguised will fail before long to be made public!"

(7) Jesus says: "Blessed is the lion which a man eats so that the lion becomes a man. But cursed is the man whom a lion eats so that the man becomes a lion!"

(8) Then he says: "A man is like a skilled fisherman who cast his net into the sea. He brought it up out of the sea full of little fishes, and among them the skilled fisherman found one that was big and excel-

lent. He threw all the little fishes back into the sea; without hesitating he chose the big fish. He who has ears to hear, let him hear!"

(9) Jesus says: "See, the sower went out. He filled his hand and scattered (the seed). Some fell on the path: birds came and gathered them. Others fell on rocky ground: they found no means of taking root in the soil and did not send up ears of corn. Others fell among thorns; (these) stifled the grain, and the worm ate the (seed.) Others fell on good soil, and this (portion) produced an excellent crop: it gave as much as sixty-fold, and (even) a hundred and twenty-fold!"

(10) Jesus says "I have cast a fire onto the world, and see, I watch over it until it blazes up!"

(11) Jesus says: "This heaven will pass away, and the heaven which is above it will pass: but those who are dead will not live, and those who live will not die!"

(12) "Today you eat dead things and make them into something living: (but) when you will be in Light, what will you do then? For then you will become two instead of one; and when you become two, what will you do then?"

(13) The disciples say to Jesus:" We know that Thou wilt leave us: who will (then) be the great(est) over us?" Jesus says to them: "Wherever you go, you will turn to James the Just, for whose sake heaven as well as earth was produced."

(14) Jesus says to his disciples: "Compare me, and tell me whom I am like." Simon Peter says to him: "Thou art like a just angel" Matthew says to him: "Thou art like a wise man and a philosopher!" Thomas says to him: "Master, my tongue cannot find words to say whom thou art like." Jesus says: "I am no longer thy master; for thou hast drunk, thou art inebriated from the bubbling spring which is mine and which I sent forth." Then he took him aside; he said three words to him. And when Thomas came back to his companions, they asked him: "What did Jesus say to thee?" And Thomas answered them: "If I tell you (a single) one of the words he said to me, you will take up stones and throw them at me, and fire will come out of the stones and consume you!"

(23) The disciples say to Jesus: "Tell us what the Kingdom of heaven is like!" He says to them: "It is like a grain of mustard: it is smaller than all the (other) seeds, but when it falls on ploughed land it produces a big stalk and becomes a shelter for the birds of heaven."

(24) Mary says to Jesus: "Who are your disciples like?" He says to her: "They are like little children who have made their way into a field that does not belong to them. When the owners of the field come, they will say: 'Get out of our field!' They (then) will give up the field to those (people) and let them have their field back again."

(25) "That is why I tell you this: If the master of the house knows that the thief is coming, he will watch before he comes and will not allow him to force an entry into his royal house to carry off its furniture. You, then, be on the watch against the world. Gird your loins with great energy, so that the brigands do not find any way of reaching you; for they will find any place you fail to watch."

(26) "Let there be among you (such) a prudent man: when the fruit arrived, quickly, sickle in hand, he went and harvested it. He who has ears to hear, let him hear!"

(27) Jesus saw some children who were taking the breast: he said to his disciples: "These little ones who suck are like those who enter the Kingdom." They said to him: "If we are little, shall we enter the Kingdom?" Jesus says to them: "When you make the two (become) one, and when you make the inside like the outside and the outside like the inside, and the upper like the lower! And if you make the male and and female one, and when you put eyes in the place of an eye, and a hand in the place of a hand, and a foot in the place of a foot, and an image in the place of an image, then you will enter (the Kingdom!")

(28) Jesus says: "I will choose you, one from a thousand and two from ten thousand, and those (whom I have chosen) will be lifted up, being one!"

(29) His disciples say to him: "Instruct us about the place where thou art, for we must know about it. He says to them: "He who has ears, let him hear! If light exists inside a luminous one, then it gives light to the whole world; but if it does not give light (it means that it is) a darkness."

(30) Jesus says: "Love thy brother like thy soul; watch over him like the apple of thine eye."

(31) Jesus says: "The straw that is in thy brother's eye, thou seest; but the beam that is in thine own eye, then thou seest not! When thou hast cast out the beam that is in thine own eye, then thou wilt see to cast out the straw from thy brother's eye."

(32) "If you do not fast from the world, you will not find the Kingdom. If you do not make the Sabbath the (true) Sabbath, you will not see the Father."

(33) Jesus says: "I stood in the midst of the world, and in the flesh I manifested myself to them. I found them all drunk; I found none athirst among them. And my soul was afflicted for the children of men. Because they are blind in their heart and do not see, because they have come into the world empty, (that is why) they seek still to go out from the world empty. Because let someone come who will correct them! Then, when they have slept off their wine, they will repent."

(34) Jesus says: "If the flesh was produced for the sake of the spirit, it is a miracle. But if the spirit (was produced) for the sake of the body, it is a miracle of a miracle." But for myself(?) I marvel at that because the (. . . of) this (?) great wealth has dwelt in this poverty.

(35) Jesus says: "There where there are three gods, they are gods. Where there are two, or (else) one, I am with him."

(36) Jesus says: "A prophet is not accepted in his (own) city, and a doctor does not heal those who know him."

(37) Jesus says: "A city built on a high mountain, and which is strong, it is not possible that it should fall, and it cannot be hidden!"

(38) Jesus says: "What thou hearest with thine ear, and the other ear, proclaim from the roof-tops! For no one lights a lamp and puts it under a bushel or in a hidden place: but he puts it on the lamp stand so that all who come in or go out should see the light."

(39) Jesus says: "If a blind man leads another blind man, both of them fall into a ditch."

(40) Jesus says: "It is not possible for someone to enter the house of a

strong man and do him violence if he has not tied his hands; (only) then will he plunder his house."

(41) Jesus says: "Have no care, from morning to evening and from evening to morning about what you shall put on."

(42) His disciples say to him: "On what day wilt thou appear to us, and what day shall we see thee?" Jesus says: "When you strip yourselves without being ashamed, when you take off your clothes and lay them at your feet like little children and trample on them! Then (you will become) children of Him who is living, and you will have no more fear."

(69) He said: "An (important) man had a vineyard which he gave to cultivators so they should work it and he should receive the fruit from them. He sent his servant so that the cultivators should give him the fruit of the vineyard: (but) they seized his servant, beat him and almost killed him. The servant came back and told this to his master. His master said (to himself) 'Perhaps he did not recognize them?' He sent another servant: the cultivators beat this one also. Then the master sent his son: he said to himself: 'No doubt they will respect my child?' But when they realized that this was the heir to the vineyard, these cultivators seized him and killed him. He who has ears let him hear!"

(70) Jesus says: "Would that thou couldst tell me about the stone which the builders have rejected! It is that one, the cornerstone."

(112) Jesus says: "He who drinks from my mouth will become like me. As for me, I will become what he is, and what is hidden will be revealed to him."

(113) Jesus says: "The Kingdom is like a man who (has) a (hidden) treasure in his field and does not know it. He did not (find it before) he died, and he left his (property to his) son who did not know it (either). He took the field, sold it, and the man who bought it went to till it: (he found) the treasure, and he began to lend interest to those (whom he) wanted(?).

(114) Jesus says: "He who has found the world and become rich, let him renounce the world!"

(115) Jesus says: "The heavens and the earth will open(?) before you, and he who lives by Him who is living will not see death," because(?) Jesus says this: "He who keeps to himself alone, the world is not worthy of him."

(116) Jesus says: "Cursed is the flesh that depends on the soul, and cursed is the soul that depends on the flesh!"

(117) His disciples said to him: "On what day will the Kingdom come?" "It will not come when it is expected. No one will say: 'See, it is here!' or 'Look it is there!' but the Kingdom of the Father is spread over the earth and men do not see it."

(118) Simon Peter says to them: "Let Mary go out from our midst, for women are not worthy of life!" Jesus says: "See, I will draw her so as to make her male so that she also may become a living spirit like you males. For every woman who has become male will enter the Kingdom of heaven."

THE GOSPEL ACCORDING TO ST. THOMAS

The Acts of Thomas

Purporting to be an account of the divine choice of Thomas, the apostle, to evangelize the east as far as India, the Acts of Thomas is part legendary narrative and part esoteric information about the destiny of man. Written in Syria in the third century A.D., and surviving in both Greek and Syriac versions, the book does include references to authentic historical figures, such as Gundaphoras, a Parthian king of the first century of our era. But the book as a whole is a compilation of incidents and speeches chosen, or rather created for symbolic purposes, in order to communicate truth as the Gnostics viewed it. Accordingly the journeys and experiences of Thomas really are intended to depict the coming of the heavenly Redeemer figure from heaven, the mystic marriage of the initiate into truth, the conflict with the demonic powers, the descent into Hades—all of them part of the stock of Gnostic redemptive beliefs and aspirations.

Two hymns are included in the Acts: The Wedding of the Daughter of Light and the Hymn of the Pearl (which is produced with a few minor changes in the translation by A. J. F. Klijn, Acts of Thomas, Leiden, 1962). The single direct point of contact between this thoroughly Gnostic hymn and the New Testament is the Parable of the Pearl of Great Price in Mt. 13:45–46, although the point of the parable has been totally altered in order to make it serve the interests of Gnostic thought. The mingling of metaphors—treasure, robe, jewel, home, mirror—discloses that the hymn is an account of the journey of the soul, which has lost its true identity and has become entangled in a corrupt and alien world. When the heavenly message of redemption reaches the entrapped soul, the wanderer recalls his true origins, flees from his entanglements in this world, and returns to the splendid realms from which he came.

SECTIONS 108–113

(108) And whilst he was praying, all those who were in the prison saw that he was praying and begged of him to pray for them too. And when he had prayed and sat down, Judas began to chant this hymn.

The Hymn of Judas the Apostle in the Country of the Indians.
(1) When I was a little child,
and dwelling in my Kingdom, in my father's house,
(2) and was content with the wealth and the luxuries of my nourishers,
(3) from the East our home
my parents equipped me [and] sent me forth;
(4) and of the wealth of our treasury
they took abundantly [and] tied up for me a load

(5) large and [yet] light,
which I myself could carry—
(6) gold of Beth-'Ellaye
and silver of Gazak the great,
(7) and rubies of India,
and agates from Beth-Kashan;
(8) and they furnished me with adamant,
which can crush iron.
(9) And they took off from me the glittering robe,
which in their affection they had made for me,
(10) and the purple toga,
which was measured [and] woven to my stature.
(11) And they made a compact with me,
and wrote it in my heart, that it might not be forgotten:
(12) "If thou goest down into Egypt,
and bringest the one pearl,
(13) which is in the midst of the sea
around the loud-breathing serpent,
(14) thou shalt put on thy glittering robe
and thy toga, with [which] thou art contented,
(15) and with thy brother, who is next to us in authority,
thou shalt be heir in our kingdom."

(109:16) I quitted the East [and] went down,
there being with me two guardians,
(17) for the way was dangerous and difficult,
and I was very young to travel it.
(18) I passed through the borders of Maishan,
the meeting-place of the merchants of the East,
(19) and I reached the land of Babel,
and I entered the walls of Sarbug.
(20) I went down into Egypt,
and my companions parted from me.
(21) I went straight to the serpent.
I dwelt around his abode,
(22) [waiting] till he should slumber and sleep,
and I could take the pearl from him.
(23) And when I was single and was alone
[and] became strange to my family,
(24) one of my race, a free-born man,
an Oriental, I saw there,
(25) a youth fair and lovable,
the son of oil-sellers;
(26) and he came and attached himself to me,
and I made him my intimate friend,
(27) an associate with whom I shared my merchandise.
(28) I warned him against the Egyptians,
and against consorting with the unclean;
(29) and dressed in their dress,
that they might not hold me in abhorrence,
(30) because I was come abroad in order to take the pearl,

and arouse the serpent against me.
(31) But in some way or another
they found out that I was not their countryman,
(32) and they dealt with me treacherously,
and gave me their food to eat.
(33) I forgot that I was a song of kings,
and I served their king;
(4) and I forgot the pearl,
for which my parents had sent me,
(35) and because of the burden of their oppressions
I lay in a deep sleep.
(110:36) But all these things that befell me
my parents perceived, and were grieved for me;
(37) and a proclamation was made in our kingdom,
that every one should come to our gate,
(38) kings and princes of Parthia,
and all the nobles of the East.
(39) And they wrote a plan on my behalf,
that I might not be left in Egypt;
(40) and they wrote me a letter,
and every noble signed his name to it:
(41) "From thy Father, the king of kings,
and thy mother, the mistress of the East,
(42) and from thy brother, our second [in authority],
to thee our son, who art in Egypt, greeting!
(43) Up and arise from thy sleep,
and listen to the words of our letter!
(44) Call to mind that thou art a son of kings!
See the slavery, whom thou servest!
(45) Remember the pearl,
for which thou wast sent to Egypt!
(46) Think of thy robe,
and remember thy splendid toga,
(47) which thou shalt wear and [with which] thou shalt be adorned,
when thy name hath been read out in the list of the valiant,
(48) and with thy brother, our viceroy,
thou shalt be in our kingdom!"
(111:49) My letter is a letter,
which the king sealed with his own right hand,
(50) [to keep] it from the wicked ones, the children of Babel,
and from the savage demons of Sarbug.
(51) It flew in the likeness of an eagle,
the king of all birds;
(52) it flew and alighted beside me,
and became all speech.
(53) At its voice and the sound of its rustling,
I started and arose from my sleep.
(54) I took it up and kissed it,
and I began [and] read it;
(55) and according to what was traced on my heart
were the words of my letter written.

(56) I remembered that I was a son of royal parents,
and my noble birth asserted its nature.
(57) I remembered the pearl,
for which I had been sent to Egypt,
(58) and I began to charm him,
the terrible loud-breathing serpent.
(59) I hushed him to sleep and lulled him into slumber,
for my father's name I named over him,
(60) and the name of our second [in power],
and of my mother, the queen of the East;
(61) and I snatched away the pearl,
and turned to go back to my father's house.
(62) And their filthy and unclean dress I stripped off,
and left it in their country;
(63) and took my way straight to come
to the light of our home the East.
(64) And my letter, my awakener,
I found before me on the road;
(65) and as with his voice it had awakened me,
[so] too with its light it was leading me.
(66) It, that dwelt in the palace,
gave light before me with its form,
(67) and with its voice and with its guidance
it also encouraged me to speed,
(68) and with its love it drew me on.
(69) I went forth [and] passed by Sarbug;
I left Babel on my left hand;
(70) and I came to the great Maishan,
to the haven of merchants,
(71) which sits on the shore of the sea.
(72) And my bright robe, which I had stripped off,
and the toga that was wrapped with it,
(73) from the heights of Reken
my parents had sent thither
(74) by the hand of their treasurers,
who in their truth could be trusted therewith.
(112:75) And because I remembered not its fashion,—
and I too received all in it,
(76) on a sudden, when I received it,
the garment seemed to me to become like a mirror of myself.
(77) I saw it all in all,
and I too received all in it,
(78) for we were two in distinction
and yet again one in one likeness.
(79) And the treasurers too,
who brought it to me, I saw in like manner
(80) to be two [and yet] one likeness,
for one sign of the king was written on them [both],
(81) of the hands of him who restored to me through them
my trust and my wealth,
(82) my decorated robe, which

was adorned with glorious colours,
(83) with gold and beryls
and rubies and agates,
(84) and sardonyxes, varied in colour.
And was skilfully worked in its home on high,
(85) and with diamond clasps
were all its seams fastened;
(86) and the image of the king of kings
was embroidered and depicted in full all over it,
(87) and like the stone of the sapphire too
its hues were varied.
(113:88) And I saw also that all over it
the instincts of knowledge were working,
(89) and I saw too that it was preparing to speak.
(90) I heard the sound of its tones
which it uttered with its . . .
(91) "I am the active in deeds,
when they reared for him before my father;
(92) and I perceived myself,
that my stature grew according to his labours."
(93) And in its kingly movements
it poured itself entirely over me,
(94) and on the hands of its givers
it hastened that I might take it.
(95) And love urged me to run
to meet it and receive it;
(96) and I stretched forth and took it.
With the beauty of its colours I adorned myself,
(97) and I wrapped myself wholly in my toga
of brilliant hues.
(98) I clothed myself with it, and went up to the gate.
(99) I bowed my head and worshipped the majesty
of my father who sent me,
(100) for I had done his commandments,
and he too had done what he promised,
(101) and at the gate of his . . . ,
I mingled with his princes,
(102) for he rejoiced in me and received me,
and I was with him in his kingdom,
(103) and with the voice of . . .
all his servants praise him.
(104) And he promised that to the gate too
of the king of kings with him I should go,
(105) and with my offering and my pearl
with him should present myself to our king.

The hymn of Judas Thomas, the Apostle, which he spake in the prison, is ended.

Nonliterary Material from the Eastern Mediterranean

INSCRIPTIONS FROM THE EASTERN MEDITERRANEAN

Of the vast numbers of inscriptions in Greek and Latin that have been found in the eastern part of the Roman Empire (W. Dittenberger's *Sylloge Inscriptionarum Graecarum Orientalis* is the most convenient and complete collection for the east), three have been chosen for inclusion here, since they shed light on the New Testament from three different perspectives: the first furnishes the date for the term of service of a public official mentioned in Acts 16 as governor of Corinth at the time Paul was there; the second was originally placed on the balustrade that separated the Court of the Gentiles from the Court of Israel in the Temple at Jerusalem; the third illustrates the claims that were being made in behalf of the Roman emperors from the reign of the first to receive the title.

(1)   Tiberius Claudius Caesar Augustus[1] Germanicus Pontifex Maximus,[2] in the twelfth year of his tribunician power, acclaimed emperor for

---

[1]Claudius' reign began in A.D. 41, so that the "twelfth year" would be between January 25, A.D. 52 and January 24, A.D. 53.

[2]The emperor was also the chief priest of the state cult, the faithful and precisely accurate observation of which was believed by all Romans—even those inclined on

the twenty-sixth time,[3] father of his country,[4] consul for the fifth time, censor, sends greetings to the city of Delphi.[5] I have long been zealous for the city of Delphi and favorable to it from the beginning, and I have always observed the cult of the Pythian Apollo,[6] but with regard to the present stories, and those quarrels of the citizens of which a report has been made by Lucius Junio Gallio,[7] my friend and proconsul of Achaia[8] . . . will still hold the previous settlement.

(2)   Let no foreigner enter within the screen and enclosure surrounding the sanctuary. Whoever is apprehended so doing will be responsible for his own death, which shall take place immediately.[*]

---

philosophical grounds to be skeptical in matters religious—to be essential for the preservation of the state and for warding off baleful influences in the form of retribution wreaked on the state by offended divinities.

[3]The acclamation of the emperor could occur at any time the senate chose to do so, although it seems not to have been done more than three times in any single year. Acclamation usually followed on some military or political victory, or on the occasion of some act of divine favor in behalf of the state or its ruler.

[4]From the outset, the imperial system of Rome sought to foster a deep and reverent personal attitude on the part of citizens and subjects of Rome toward the emperor. This had its highest expression in relation to Octavian (or Augustus) in Vergil's *Eclogue* according to which the stability of the world and the universal peace that (for the moment) prevailed was directly traceable to the emperor, who guarded the welfare of the state like a father.

[5]Delphi, the famous city on the slopes of Mt. Parnassus, sacred to Apollo, god of the sun, and renowned for the oracle there, to which common people and statesmen alike turned for centuries in their quest for answers to perplexing problems of war, politics, and personal welfare.

[6]Pythian Apollo was associated particularly with the oracle located at Delphi. In an effort to demonstrate the continuity of Roman culture with that of Greece, while capitalizing on the esteem in which the shrines and oracles of Greece were still held, the emperors of Rome made a conscious effort to identify themselves with the Greek deities and to visit the sacred sites. Claudius is drawing attention to his own piety by means of the inscription erected in some public spot at Delphi. The immediate occasion was the dispute referred to, but Claudius well knew that the mention of his devotion to Apollo would not be lost on the thousands who annually visited the shrine or sought counsel from the Pythian Apollo.

[7]Gallio, brother of the even better known statesman-philosopher, Seneca, was consul in the year 52–53. Assuming Paul had been active for about two years before he came to the attention of the proconsul, it is virtually certain that Paul reached Corinth in A.D. 49 or 50. If this interpretation of the evidence is correct, then we have in this date one of the few fixed points for a chronology of Paul's career.

[8]Achaia was the name given by the Romans to the southern half of the Greek peninsula, including the area as far north as Mt. Olympus, the central region around Delphi, Athens, Corinth, and the Peleponnesus to the south. Paul refers to his first converts at Corinth as his "first-fruits in Achaia" (I Cor. 16:15).

[*]The temple precincts in Jerusalem were divided into a number of courts, of which the inner three were accessible to the following groups respectively: male Jews (the court of Israel); the priests (the Holy Place); and the High Priest (the Holy of Holies, or Holiest Place). Pompey horrified the Jews in 63 B.C. by entering the Holiest Place, but under the Roman policy, which permitted subject peoples full autonomy in their own religious affairs, the priests were at liberty to state publicly and enforce strictly the prohibition against Gentiles entering any part of the temple

(3)   The cities which are in Asia[1] and the districts and the peoples honor
Gaius Julius Caesar, son of Gaius, high priest and emperor,[2] and con-
sul for the second time; he is a manifest god,[3] sprung from Ares and
Aphrodite,[4] and universal[5] savior[6] of human life.

INSCRIPTION FROM THE THEODOTOS SYNAGOGUE[*]

Theodotos, son of Vettenos, priest and archisynagogos, son and grandson of archisynagoi, built the synagogue for the reading of the Law
and for the searching of the commandments; furthermore, the Hospice
and Chambers and the water installations for the lodging of needy
strangers . . .

---

other than the outer court, which was designated appropriately The Court of the
Gentiles. Several copies of this inscription were originally in position along the
balustrade that marked the limit beyond which only Jews could go.

[1]Asia was the Roman designation for the province that included most of eastern
Asia Minor, except for the regions bordering the Black Sea to the northeast and those
along the Taurus Mountains to the southeast. The coast from Troas to Cnidos and
the interior as far east as the Anatolian Plateau were included.

[2]Julius was, of course, the first to be so designated. And even though the venera-
tion of the emperor was viewed with deep suspicion as an oriental error, so that it
did not become widely accepted in Rome until well into the second century A.D.,
Caesar—and Augustus after him—were happy to promote the idea in the eastern
provinces, where it had a long tradition reaching back to Alexander and beyond,
and where it served an important function in giving the local populace an emotional
tie to the distant ruler in the West.

[3]The epithet here used of Caesar is the same as that applied by Antiochus IV,
the Seleucid ruler of Syria, to himself (see p. 11). Neither Greeks nor Romans had
any difficulty with the notion that a man who rose to power among men was in some
sense a participant in divine powers or specially favored of the gods, and so worthy
to be ranked among the divine beings.

[4]Various Roman leaders chose different Greek gods and goddesses with whom
they sought to identify themselves. Anthony claimed identity with Dionysius, Augustus with Apollo. Here Caesar asserts that he is the offspring of the god of war and
the goddess of love.

[5]The Romans, like the hellenistic rulers before them, stressed the unity of mankind. The greatness of the emperors lay in the fact that all mankind benefitted from
the peace and harmony which they established, or claimed to have established, so
that humanity was brought together under the blessings of the Roman authority.

[6]Savior is here used as the agent of peace and prosperity, not in a distinctively
religious or otherworldly sense. Terms like these were used in relation to the emperors in order to foster a kind of religious feeling, however, but in order to promote a
sense of contentment in the present life rather than to prepare men for another age
or a heavenly realm.

[*]From E. L. Sukenik, *The Ancient Synagogue of el-Hammeh*. Built in Jerusalem
before A.D. 70, this synagogue combined facilities for worship, study and lodgings.

*A group of Objects in Every-
day Use in Palestine.*

*The lamp here pictured is typ-
ical of those of the Herodian
period. A twisted bit of flax
served as wick, and the light
provided thereby was exceedingly feeble. The lamp imagery
is common throughout the New
Testament, from the gospels to
Revelation.*

Three quarters original size.

Three quarters original size.   One half original size.

*Perfumes and unguents were kept in jars of this type
with small opening and, in the case of the cylindrical
variety, cup-like mouths, so that a drop or two of the
precious contents could be poured out at any one time.
It is this type of unguentarium that would likely have
been used for preparing the body of a dead person, as
in the gospel narratives.*

PERSONAL LETTERS

Beginning in the later nineteenth century, scholars began to study and decipher the writings on bits of papyrus found in tombs and trash heaps of cities and villages, especially in Egypt, where the dry climate enabled the papyrus (writing material made from reeds) to survive. The documents are of unique importance, precisely because they are not literary productions in the sense of self-conscious writings set down to be read by a wider public or by posterity. They are the records of business transactions, official reports of little people to big government, and above all, private letters between individuals. As such they reveal, as no literary document could, how people actually lived; the fabric of basic human relationships is evident in the naive prose of these writings. The small group of letters reproduced here represents a range of human situations: letters home from soldiers, from absentee husbands, from estranged sons; a letter from a friend who has just returned from a journey. The stylized expressions used are often reminiscent of the language and mood of the New Testament, which lie closer to that of these informal documents than to the self-conscious diction of the true literature of the period.

Hilarion has gone to work in the big city—Alexandria, which he cannot spell properly—and has heard through a friend, Aphrodisias, that his pregnant wife has interpreted his failure to communicate with her as a sign that he is abandoning her and her unborn child. Hilarion has written to convey his love and to promise support for the child, so long as it is a male! The date is the equivalent of June 17, 1 B.C.

AN ABSENTEE HUSBAND WRITES HIS EXPECTANT WIFE

Hilarion to Alis his sister many greetings. Also to Berus my lady and Apollonarin. Know that we are still even now in Alexandrea [sic] Be not distressed if at the general coming in I remain at Alexandrea. I pray you and beseech you, take care of the little child. And as soon as we receive wages I will send thee up. If you . . . are delivered, if it was a male child, let it [live]; if it was female, cast it out. You said to Aphrodisias, "Do not forget me." How can I forget you? I urge you, therefore, do not be upset. In the year 29 of the Caesar, Pauni 23.

Endorsed: Hilarion to Alis.   Deliver.

A FAITHFUL SON GREETS HIS MOTHER AND PRODS HIS IRRESPONSIBLE BROTHER

The situation represented here is that Sempronius has left home to work abroad at great distance. Word has reached him that his next older brother has not assumed his proper role of *paterfamilias,* nor is he even looking out properly for the welfare of their revered mother. Noteworthy are the pious reference to Serapis, the divinity so widely venerated, and the divine epithets *(theos,* god; and *kurios,* lord) applied to the parents.

> Sempronius to Saturnila his mother and lady many greetings. Before all things may you fare well, together with my brothers also unbewitched. And further, I make intercession for you daily to our Lord Serapis. So many letters have I sent to you, and you have not written one back to me, though so many have sailed down. You are requested, my lady, to write me without delay concerning your welfare, that I also may live more free from cares. For this is my prayer continually. I greet Maximus and his life's partner and Saturnilus and Gemellus and Helena and those who are his household. Tell her that I have received from Sempronius a letter from Cappodocia. I greet by name Julius and those who are of his household, and Scythius and Thermuthis and her children. Gemellus greets you.

> May you fare well, my lady, continually.

> Sempronius to Maximus his brother many greetings. Before all things may you fare well, I pray. I heard that you are slothful in caring for the lady, our mother. You are requested, sweetest brother, do not grieve her in any way. If one of our brothers should be disobedient toward her, you should hit him with your fist. For you should now be designated as father. I know that you can please her without my writing to you [to do so], but do not be unhappy with me for writing you to offer advice. For we should worship the one who bore us as though she were a god, especially when she is good. I have written these things to you, brother, knowing the sweetness of our lords and parents. You will do me a favor if you write me concerning your welfare. May you fare well, brother.

> [On the reverse side:]
> Deliver to Maximus X from Sempronius X his brother

A TOURIST ON THE NILE REPORTS TO HIS FRIEND

Nearchus appears to have been a man of some means, enough obviously to be able to take an extended journey on the Nile solely for the pleasure of it. He went as far as the first cataract of the Nile at Syene (now Assuan), but journeyed also across the Libyan desert to the famous oracle of Ammon, which had helped catapult Alexander into international fame by giving divine sanction to his dreams of empire. Like untold numbers of tourists before and since, Nearchus carved a message on the ancient monuments he visited, but his aim was not to leave his name or initials, but to record his pious recollection of friends at the sacred spots.

Nearchus (to Heliodorus) . . . Greeting.

Since many [have become curious about the world] even to the point of taking a ship so that they may learn about the works accomplished by man's hand, I have done the same sort of thing and undertook a voyage up as far as Soene, at which point the Nile flows out, and to Libya, where Ammon sings oracles to all men, and I learned fine things, and I carved the names of my friends on the temples for a perpetual memory, the intercession . . .

> [End of the letter is missing]
> Endorsed
> To Heliodorus

A WELL-INTENTIONED BUT HEAVY-HANDED LETTER OF SYMPATHY

Irene seems eager to be genuinely supporting on hearing of the death of her friends' son, and has gone through the motions—presumably of votive offerings, priestly prayers, etc. But at the end she can only acknowledge that death must be accepted and cannot ever be explained or understood. Perhaps the fact of the letter rather than the inadequacy of its sentiments may have comforted the bereaved.

> Irene to Taonnophris and Philo good comfort.
> I am as sorry and weep over the departed one as I wept for Didymas. And I have done everything that was appropriate as have all of my [family], Epaphroditus and Thermuthion and Philion and Apollonius and Plantas. But even so, against such things there is nothing anyone can do. So comfort each other. May you be well.
> Endorsed:
> To Taonnophris and Philo.

A SLIGHTLY HOMESICK RECRUIT WRITES FROM HIS FIRST ASSIGNMENT

Apion is terribly pleased with himself for having survived the rough voyage to Italy, for gaining his first look at the sights of Italy in the vicinity of the Bay of Naples, for his pay in gold pieces, for his new name —much more imposing than the simple Apion—and for his assignment to a military unit with an equally imposing name, Centuria Athenonica, and for his chances of advancement. He is pleased to send greetings from his many friends in his unit to his friends and relatives back home in the Egyptian village. But he still would like to have a letter from his father.

> Apion to Epimachus his father and lord many greetings. Before all things I pray that you are in health, and that you prosper and fare well continually together with my sister and her daughter and my brother. I thank the lord Serapis that when I was in peril on the sea he saved me immediately. When I came to Miseni, I received as

viaticum [journey-money] from the Caesar three pieces of gold. And it is well with me but I urge you, my lord father, to write me a little letter: first, about your welfare; second, about my brother and sister; third, so that I may do obeisance to your hand, because you have taught me well and I have hopes therefore of advancing quickly, if the gods are willing. Greet Capito much and my brother and sister and Serenilla and my friends. By Euctemon I am sending you a little picture of myself. Furthermore, my name is [now] Antonis Maximus. Be well, I pray. Centuris Athenonica. The following send their greetings: Serenus the son of Agathus Daemon, and . . . the son of . . . and Turbo the son of Gallonius and . . . the son of . . .

[On the back]
To Philadelphis for Epimaxus from Apion his son.

Give this to the first cohort   of the Apamenians to [?]
                                         Julianus An . . .
the Liblarios, from Apion   so that he may convey it to
                                         Epimachus his father.

LETTER TO A WIDOW FROM HER RUNAWAY SON

This intensely human document was written by a young man who had apparently borrowed money that he was unable to repay and as a result ran away from his native village to another small town some distance away. His mother had gone searching for him, probably in Alexandria, but was unable to find him. A meddling fellow villager had chanced to meet Antonius and then reported to his distraught mother what his woeful plight was. Perhaps Antonius is suggesting that his mother pay off his debts, in which case he could return home without further disgrace. But most of all, he wants to confess his wrong and gain reconciliation with his concerned but estranged mother.

> Antonis Longus to Nilus his mother many greetings. And continually I pray that you may be in health. I make intercession for you day by day to the lord Serapis. I want you to understand that I had no hope that you would go to the metropolis, so that I did not come to the city. But I was ashamed to come to Caranis, because I walk about in rags. I am writing to you that I am naked. I plead with you, mother, be reconciled to me! Furthermore, I know what I have brought upon myself. I have been chastened in a way that is appropriate. I know that I have sinned. I have heard from Postumus, who met you in the country in the vicinity of Arsinoe and told you the whole story at an inopportune time. Don't you understand that I would rather be maimed than know that I still owe a man an obol? . . Come yourself . . . I have heard that . . . I beseech you . . . I almost . . . I beseech you . . . I will . . . not . . . do otherwise.
>   [The papyrus is frayed and breaks off at this point.]
>   [On the back]
>   . . . his mother, from Antonius Longus her son.

Bibliography

ANCIENT SOURCES IN TRANSLATION:

The Apocrypha and Pseudepigrapha of the Old Testament (2 vols.), ed. R. H. Charles, Oxford: The Claredon Press, 1913.

"The Apochrypha" in *The New English Bible*. New York: Oxford University Press, 1971; and in *The Revised Standard Version of the Bible*, published in various editions by permission of the National Council of Churches.

The Dead Sea Scrolls, tr. Millar Burrows. New York: The Viking Press, Inc., 1955.

The Dead Sea Scriptures, tr. T. H. Gaster. New York: Doubleday & Co., Inc., 1964.

"The Gospel of Thomas," in Jean Doresse, *The Secret Books of the Egyptian Gnostics*. New York: The Viking Press, Inc., 1960.

The Acts of Thomas, tr. A. F. J. Klijn. Leiden: E. J. Brill, 1962.

Corpus Hermeticum (Vol. I), text by A. D. Nock and translation (French) by A. -J. Festugière. Paris: Société d'Edition "les Belles Lettres", 1960.

Philo of Alexandria: Legatio ad Gaium, tr. E. M. Smallwood. Leiden: E. J. Brill.

Other classical and Jewish tests may be found in editions listed above under acknowledgments, pp. iv-vi.

STUDIES:

Bonsirven, J., *Palestinian Judaism in the Time of Jesus Christ*. New York: Holt, Rinehart & Winston, Inc., 1964.

266

Foerster, W., *From the Exile to Christ*. Philadelphia: Fortress Press, 1964.

Moore, G. F., *Judaism in the First Centuries of the Christian Era*. Cambridge, Mass.; Harvard University Press, 1932.

Pfeiffer, R. H. *History of New Testament Times*. New York: Harper & Row, Publishers, 1949.

Strack, H. L., *Introduction to Talmud and Midrash*. New York: Meridian, 1959.

Goodenough, E. R., *By Light, Light: The Mystic Gospel of Hellenistic Judaism*. New Haven: Yale University Press, 1935.

Goodenough, E. R., *Introduction to Philo Judaeus*. Oxford: Basil Blackwell & Mott Ltd., 1962.

Deissmann, A., *Light from the Ancient East*. Grand Rapids: Baker Book House. Contains letters and inscriptions illuminating the language and culture of the period of early Christianity.

Russell, D. S., *The Method and Message of Jewish Apocalyptic*. Philadelphia: The Westminster Press, 1964.

Grant, R. M., *Gnosticism and Early Christianity*. New York: Harper & Row, Publishers, 1959.

Jonas, Hans, *The Gnostic Religion*. Boston: Beacon Press, 1958.

Nock, A. D., *Conversion*. Oxford: Oxford University Press, 1961.

Cumont, Franz, *The Mysteries of Mithra*. New York: Dover Publications, Inc., n.d.

Index